THE LIBRARY

ST. M...

ST. M...   W9-BBB-202   20686

The Burden of Conscience

The Modern Jewish Experience

Paula Hyman and Deborah Dash Moore, *Editors*

THE BURDEN
OF CONSCIENCE

French Jewish Leadership
during the Holocaust

RICHARD I. COHEN

INDIANA UNIVERSITY PRESS
BLOOMINGTON AND INDIANAPOLIS

To my dear parents
Harry and Eva Cohen

The author wishes to thank *Jewish Social Studies* and *Yad Vashem Studies* for permission to reprint material that appeared in these publications. Material from *The Jews in Modern France*, edited by Frances Malino and Bernard Wasserstein, is reprinted by permission of University Press of New England. Copyright 1985 by Trustees of Brandeis University.

© 1987 by Richard I. Cohen

All rights reserved

No part of this book may be reproduced or utilized in any form or by any means, electronic or mechanical, including photocopying and recording, or by any information storage and retrieval system, without permission in writing from the publisher. The Association of American University Presses' Resolution on Permissions constitutes the only exception to this prohibition.

Manufactured in the United States of America

Library of Congress Cataloging–in–Publication Data

Cohen, Richard I.
The burden of conscience.
(The Modern Jewish experience)
Bibliography: p.
Includes index.
1. Jews—France—Persecutions. 2. Jews—France—
Politics and government. 3. Union générale des
israélites de France. 4. Holocaust, Jewish
(1939–1945)—France. 5. France—Ethnic relations.
I. Title. II. Series: Modern Jewish experience
(Bloomington, Ind.)
DS135.F8C635 1987 940.53'15'03924044 85–45991
ISBN 0–253–31263–9
1 2 3 4 5 91 90 89 88 87

CONTENTS

Illustrations follow Chapter IV.

INTRODUCTION

In September 1939, France declared war against Germany, joining the Allied forces to face German aggression. Buoyed by the surge of national unity, French Jewry mobilized its support for the war effort. Five years later, at the time of the liberation, as France was in a state of anarchy, with law and justice universally challenged, its Jewish community tried to assess the trauma of the previous years. That was the product of the havoc wreaked by the Vichy government's collaborationist policy during the war. The Holocaust of French Jewry was the worst consequence of that policy. By August 1944, close to 78,000 Jews either had been murdered in Auschwitz or had died in detention. The Nazi "Final Solution" to the "Jewish Question" had found in Vichy an amenable regime, eager to assist in its implementation.

But this book is not another work about the persecution of French Jews and their tragic fate. It is about the Jewish community and its leadership and how they interpreted their reality and responded. Clearly, the issues are intertwined. Germany's lightning victory over France in spring 1940 eroded the very basis of Jewish security in France. With the armistice agreement, the German army occupied northern France, leaving the French government sovereignty over only 40 percent of its former territory. The impact of occupation on the Jewish community was immediate. Some 350,000 Jews lived in France at the time, with at least 200,000 concentrated in Paris. A massive exodus to the south ensued, relocating the leadership and the large network of Jewish organizations to the unoccupied zone. Merely the image of a German occupation revolutionized the demographic distribution of the community.

But soon the community received a further jolt. The Vichy regime embarked on its own policy of active anti-Semitism, which hit hard at the economic and social bases of the Jews. Reeling from the shock of the discriminatory measures, the Jewish leadership had trouble bringing together its factionalized elements. As Vichy was a direct continuation of the turbulent 1930s, so the Jewish leadership inherited the tensions and countercharges that had dominated the community scene of the prewar period. A heterogeneous mixture of approximately one-third native Jews and two-thirds foreign Jews (the bulk of whom originated in Eastern Europe), French Jewry had developed insular communal patterns that belied integration. The lingering antagonism between native and immigrant Jews persisted even as they were lumped together in a commonfate, and it becomes a central concern of chapter two and the dominant theme of this study. The roots of that antagonism, the contrasting conceptions of Jewish existence, help to bring into focus the behavior of Jewish leaders during the war. But though that provides us with a certain explanation, it must not be carried too far, and it must be tempered by other considerations, particularly the fundamental geographic differences between the occupied and the unoccupied zones and the significant shifts in Nazi policy between 1940 and 1944. Jewish behavior during the war evolved both as a response to the objective conditions and as a natural outgrowth of the subjective perceptions of the community, which incorporated habits and patterns of thought of previous generations.

Too often, all that occurred during the war is seen from the perspective of Auschwitz. Jewish leaders, for example, have been vilified for collaborating with the Nazis and damned for aiding the destruction of their fellow Jews. Little attempt is made to place these leaders within their particular historical setting and to avoid positing a model of universal development. This work takes a different approach, hoping to place the leadership's decision-making process in an appropriate contextual framework. To be specific, "deportations to the East" did not always dominate Nazi policy. Annihilation of European Jewry became the Nazi solution to the "Jewish Question" in late autumn 1941 and soon after was translated into a full-blown bureaucratic process. But even before the Wannsee Conference of 20 January 1942, where the scope of the monstrous project was delineated, hundreds of thousands of Jews had been murdered in Poland and Serbia. From January 1942, however, all other temporary solutions—Madagascar, Nisko, emigration—were discarded, and the "Final Solution" was put into action. In each of the Nazi-occupied countries, France included, plans were then made to initiate it. Yet, from 1942 the supreme ideological goal of National Socialism—the "Final Solution"—constantly encountered obstacles that hindered its implementation. Inconsistencies with the Nazi goal appeared everywhere, an inevitable result of the considerations and complications that arose in fitting the destruction process into other Nazi programs. The situation was no different in France. Many periods reveal a lull in the mass arrests and deportations, implying a less monolithic German structure than is often portrayed. The ideological goal of annihilation remained, but it was often temporarily set aside, for a variety of reasons. These delays in the "Final Solution" have often been explained by an underlying, premeditated German tactic, with total disregard of other factors. Such is often the explanation offered with regard to the Jewish leadership. Seemingly, the German administration was completely unified and had throughout the war one overriding consideration—to deceive the Jewish leaders into assisting in the destruction process.

The obverse implies Jewish treachery and blindness in not facing the obvious consequences of Nazi policy.

Rather than follow this provocative and monistic approach, I have tried to show the real-life dilemmas of the Jewish leaders from their vantage point, shorn of the wisdom of hindsight. From 1940 to 1944, Jews were in need of welfare and assistance, in the internment camps, cities, and villages; how was the leadership to respond? Children needed foster homes after their parents were deported; how was the community to protect them? Individual releases from Drancy, the French assembly camp several miles northeast of Paris, were permitted in 1942 under strict regulations; could they be dispensed with? If eventually the Nazis were not going to stop at anything to deport Jews, then all aid was a mere placebo. But how were responsible Jewish leaders in the occupied and unoccupied zones to understand the starts and stops of Nazi policy, especially between 1940 and 1943, and to weigh them against their commitment to the community's needs? This, then, becomes a recurrent theme of the book: two missions, diametrically opposed, faced each other—one bent on destroying the Jewish community, and one resolved to sustain it under the harshest of conditions.

In focusing on the Jewish leadership of France, this study explores those community organizations that became, in the eyes of the Jews and the authorities, the representative bodies of French Jewry. German pressure to establish a compulsory roof organization in the occupied zone encountered many objections and unleashed mutual accusations between the native and immigrant Jews, but eventually it succeeded. An analysis of the Comité de Coordination's functioning in chapter two puts into perspective both the seething tensions within the community and the contrasting assessments of Nazi policy. But the Comité never satisfied the demands of the German authorities. A new apparatus was sought and after prolonged negotiations came into being. The Union Général des Israélites de France (UGIF), a German-Vichy creation patterned after Jewish councils in Germany and Eastern Europe, supplanted the Comité in the north and filled a vacuum in the free zone. Moral issues, self-perceptions, and political, religious, and cultural attachments all figured prominently in the internal Jewish debate on participation in UGIF. Here, too, we see the opposite of a shattered community. The Jewish leadership was troubled by the present but conscious of a historical responsibility, and it was no simple matter to decide one way or the other. Chapter three of the book tries to recapture the mood of the community leaders as they tensely walked a tightrope, uncertain where they were heading.

Once established, UGIF expanded into a middle-sized bureaucratic organization with separate, differently oriented councils in the north and south.

The extensive archival material available affords a detailed examination of the workings of both councils and their affiliated organizations. The documentation is revealing, discrediting any sweeping generalizations about the leaders' behavior.

The story of UGIF North, told in chapter four, inevitably offers only a partial view of what happened in the unoccupied zone but still unravels much of that historical process. Internal relations with its detractors among native and immigrant Jews, interactions with the French and German authorities, interventions on behalf of the community, and the program of social welfare all emerge from the source material. But the UGIF records also allow entry into the private deliberations of the council members, their moral imperatives, allegiances, expectations, and presence of mind. UGIF North, which assumed its function as German measures against the Jews of the occupied zone intensified, presents a model of legalistic behavior, rooted in a trust in France and fostered by generations of emancipation. Yet the model is at times marked by both acts of resistance and sheer cowardice, making it more intricate than is commonly supposed.

UGIF South always maintained a different stance. Tenaciously adhering to a federative structure, the council resisted the intervention of the French authorities into its affairs until late 1943. However, UGIF South and the Jews of the unoccupied zone could not escape German designs. Even before the Germans occupied the south in November 1942, thousands of foreign Jews were handed over to the German authorities by Vichy. But the south presented UGIF with other anomalies. Germany's ally, Fascist Italy, occupied eight regions of southern France in November 1942 but refused to yield to Nazi pressure on the "Jewish Question." For ten months the Italian zone opened its doors to fleeing Jews and opposed anti-Jewish legislation. UGIF South and its affiliated organizations had to adjust to and assimilate these new realities. Gradually, the latent ambivalences seem to have come to light. Official activity was carried on beside illegal work by important elements in the organization, and the pendulum swung as the attacks against the community and UGIF expanded. Chapter five investigates the drama and consequences involved in maintaining one form of activity or another.

The leaders of UGIF, all recognized figures in the community, assumed a common responsibility to alleviate its plight. However, the compelling problems of their particular regions led to different perspectives, as can be seen in chapter six. In tracing the interplay between the two councils, it becomes apparent that the northern council initiated a scheme to unify the councils and create a more uniform organization. Reorganization challenged UGIF South's very existence and could not but be rejected by it; however, the prolonged negotiations offer interesting insight into the nature of the organizations and their importance in the eyes of the French and German authorities. As in the case of reorganization, so it was with regard to the dismissal of the councils' immigrant employees. Here, too, a study of the affair reveals the different internal workings of the councils, their decision-making process, and their moral considerations. No room is left to portray the two councils in the same light.

When UGIF appeared, it met with the harshest criticism from the established representative of French Jewry, the Consistoire Central des Israélites de France. The Central Consistory had formulated Jewish attitudes towards French society since the Napoleonic regime and maintained a unique status in the community despite its transformation from a homogeneous society to a heterogeneous one. *Patrie* and religion had become the Consistory's trademark, but Vichy's anti-Semitic laws undermined that duality. Severance from France was incomprehensible to the Consistory, and in its continuous protests it never failed to hail the "true spirit of France." UGIF was a symbol of the new France. As such, the Consistory rejected it, but chapter seven attempts to show how the Consistory gradually moved from reconciliation with UGIF's existence to acknowledgment of its indispensability to the Jewish community. Yet even in this struggle for leadership among the native Jews, persecution and discriminatory measures were not sufficient to eliminate the moral and historical concerns of the Consistory.

In placing the history of UGIF and its antecedents at the center of this study, the role of the resistance organizations has inevitably become a secondary concern. Obviously that conflicts with the sensibilities of those who regard resistance activity as the supreme expression of Jewish honor during the war, but the history of Jewish resistance is clearly worthy of a separate study with different premises. My intention has been to evaluate the unique role of the central Jewish leadership, which was more acute and problematic than in previous generations of Jewish history, and to analyze the complexity of these leaders' human dilemmas. As such, this book belongs to the growing literature on the history of Jewish leadership during its period of exile and to the historiography of the much debated Jewish leadership during the Holocaust.

This book provides me the opportunity to thank those who helped me at various stages of the work. First and foremost, my teacher Shmuel Ettinger. From my very first days as a graduate student at the Hebrew University, he nurtured my interest in Jewish history by allowing me to benefit from both his profound understanding of and insight into Jewish history and his generosity of spirit. Over the years, as teacher, advisor, and colleague, he was always dedicated and giving, and I am forever indebted to him for his encouragement and intellectual stimulation. Otto Dov Kulka shared with me in countless conversations his sophisticated understanding and provocative historical conception of the Holocaust, which have certainly found their way into my work. I am especially grateful to Michael R. Marrus and Simon Schwarzfuchs, who read this work in manuscript form, saved me from several errors, and contributed valuable comments. Jacques Adler, Yehuda Bauer, Saul Friedländer, Michael Graetz, Paula Hyman, and Dina Porat offered insightful advice and criticism on various aspects of this study, and they deserve my thanks.

In the course of my research, I have been graciously helped by many institutions and their diligent staffs. I am grateful in particular to Mrs. Hadassah Modlinger and Mrs. Clara Gini of the Yad Vashem Remembrance Authority in Jerusalem, to Marek Web of the YIVO Institute for Jewish Research in New York, and to the late Zosa Szajkowski; to Ulrich Hessel and the staff of the Centre de Documentation Juive Contemporaine in Paris; to Mrs. Rose Klepfisz of the American Jewish Joint Distribution Committee and to Dr. Menahem Schmelzer of the Jewish Theological Seminary, both in New York; to Georges Weill and Mme Yvette Levyne of the Alliance Israélite Universelle in Paris; to Miss S. Couteau of the Central and Paris Consistories in Paris; and to the archivists of the American Friends Service Committee (Philadelphia), the World Jewish Congress (New York), and the Roosevelt Archives (Hyde Park, New York). The Memorial Foundation for Jewish Culture, the Lady Davis Fellowship Trust, and the Warburg Fellowship all provided generous support at various stages of the research for this book. The bulk of the book was written during my stay at the Institute for Advanced Studies at the Hebrew University in Jerusalem, in 1984–85. I owe particular thanks and gratitude to the former director of the institute, Professor Aryeh Dvoretzky, and his most helpful staff, who went far beyond mere performance of duty to make the institute a scholar's haven. I benefited especially from conversations and discussions with the colleagues of the institute's seminar on the Jews under National Socialism, headed by Professor Yehuda Bauer.

Ms. Terrye Pico and Ms. Rena Werber typed the different drafts of this study with professional skill and industry.

I owe my deepest gratitude to my wife, Shlomith, who has offered constant moral support, as well as intimate insight into the intricacies of moral responsibility.

The Burden of Conscience

I.

FRENCH JEWRY ON THE EVE OF WORLD WAR II

Background

For the Jews of France, the road to full legal and social emancipation was marked by interruptions. Forced during the French Revolution to struggle separately for their legal emancipation, which was not guaranteed within the Declaration of the Rights of Man, French Jews were later required to pay back "community debts" even though the community as a legal entity had been abolished. Nevertheless, the historic and unprecedented fact that a European country had granted Jews unconditional civic and political rights left its imprint on the Jewish community in France for generations, and on the course of emancipation of European Jewry.

The utopian vision of emancipation had anticipated a swift blending of Jews into French society and a rapid elimination of distinguishing Jewish characteristics. Faced with the staying power of Jewish particularism, Napoleon I tried to undercut its internal cohesiveness by setting up the Sanhedrin and pursuing it with the "Infamous Decree" of 1808. Integration of Jews into French life was highly regarded, and if not accomplished by voluntary acts, it had to be enforced by the ruling class. But there was a Jewish desire to mirror the majority population, and it found expression during Napoleon's regime. Following the example of French Protestants, who established a consistorial structure, Jewish leaders requested a parallel organization; here was an opportunity for Napoleon to determine a definite relationship between the state and the Jews, limiting the latter's authority. In 1808 he established a hierarchical consistorial administration, attached to the Ministry of Interior, and entrusted it with the supervision of ritual and religious affairs, the appointment of rabbis, and the preparation of Jews for loyal French citizenship.[1]

During the nineteenth century, various regional consistories, headed by the Central Consistory (Consistoire Central des Israélites de France), became channels to introduce the "French spirit" into the lives of the Jews. Emphasizing integration, the consistories strove to fulfill three primary goals: to ingratiate themselves with the regime in France, to blur the elements that differentiated the Jews from their neighbors, and to create a French Judaism in which the French component would be dominant. The consistories abided by their strictly religious definition and by and large refrained from interfering in political issues and problems relating to Jewish social acceptance. Although this stance occasionally aroused the opposition of small groups of Jews who criticized its lack of effectiveness in protecting Jewish interests, even these critics accepted the Consistory's "French" orientation.[2] For all its aloofness and aristocratic tendencies, the Central Consistory certainly reflected the consensus of the community. French Jewry blended remarkably well into every aspect of French life and culture and served as a model of successful integration for other Jewish communities in both the West and the East.

During the nineteenth century, Christian and socialist circles attempted gradually to nullify the principles of the French Revolution, and expressions of anti-Semitism were revived. Christian elements sought to restore the primacy of religion within French society, making blatant demands on the Jews to abandon their "Jewish" character and unique rituals. Maintaining that Jewish integration into France would be possible only when Jews recognized the obligatory nature of the external forms of a Christian state, they favored a reappraisal of Jewish rights. Moreover, through doctrinal opposition to the teachings of Judaism and presentation of the Christian outlook as the basis for national leadership, certain Christian thinkers hoped to save something of Christianity's waning status in nineteenth-century France. Their attempts to turn the clock back and undermine the achievements of the Revolution were premature, and they were forced to accept the bitter fact that "the enemy and handmaiden of Christianity" was living among them with equal rights. Nevertheless, for many years their traditional views of Judaism continued to be heard throughout France in various historiosophical and philosophical discourses. Clearly, their struggle for the soul of France, which continued throughout the nineteenth and twentieth centuries, was a recurrent background for the relations between French society and the Jews.[3]

Antagonism towards Jews and Judaism was not limited to the opponents of a republican society; it also found adherents among leading spokesmen in the socialist camp. Even prior to the Revolution of 1848, Jews were being accused of promoting capitalist methods, and the Rothschilds had already emerged as the symbol of the new decadent process. In the following decades, as competition for the masses of French workers intensified, French socialists tended to condone anti-Semitism, often seeing it as a preliminary stage in the workers' class consciousness. Having adopted many of their claims from the French *philosophes* of the eighteenth century, the socialists had created a strange breed of anti-Semitism, which combined "innate" Jewish traits with the particular capitalist twist. This tradition was not easily expunged, and long after the Dreyfus Affair, socialist thought in France continued to show vestiges of the writings of Proudhon and Fourrier.

But the significant manifestation of anti-Jewish sentiment in nineteenth-century France, with a long-lasting impact on French ideological currents, emanated from the political circles of General Georges Boulanger. Emerging on the political scene while Edward Drumont's notorious anti-Semitic work *La France Juive* (1886) was still sweeping through France, Boulanger himself tended towards a populist orientation, without particular interest in the "Jewish problem." The left-wing faction of his movement, most prominently the well-known journalist Henri Rochefort and the nationalist writer Maurice Barrès, disapproved of Boulanger's timid stance on the Jews and escalated the organization's anti-Jewish rhetoric. As Zeev Sternhell has shown, it was Barrès, more than any other French figure of his day, who recognized the political potential involved in anti-Semitism and was able fully to capitalize on it. Rejecting the purely racial anti-Semitism of Drumont, Barrès embarked on a populist crusade that called for a social and national upheaval aimed at freeing the Third Republic from its liberal chains. Jews were portrayed as high financiers who through speculation and parasitical means turned the poor workers into their slaves. Emphasizing the social ruin of France and upholding the virtue of its working class, Barrès identified anti-Semitism as the factor capable of bringing the conflicting factions together. Anti-Semitism could unite the masses, both the working class and the bourgeoisie, in a joint effort to reestablish a national ethos.

Barrès was not alone in this perspective. He was joined by a whole circle of gifted and less gifted French writers who in the fin de siècle struggle against the liberal democracy of the Third Republic made anti-Semitism into the common cause for those with social and nationalist aspirations. From the followers of Charles Maurras in the Action Française to the trade unionists who echoed the harangues of Robert Louzon and Georges Sorel against the Jews and the capitalists, the anti-Semitic proponents forged a union between social criticism and nationalism. By serving this function and repudiating the liberal and social democratic fabric of society, the anti-Semitic movement of the *Belle Epoque* bequeathed to the next generations a synthetic analysis of the "Jewish problem" easily applicable to the crises at hand.[4]

The Jews of France generally avoided entering into polemics with these antagonistic elements, preferring a passive response. Even the Alliance Israélite Universelle, established in 1860 in part as a response to anti-Semitism in Europe, saw as its main task the improvement of the civic status of Jews in North Africa and the Levant and refrained from countering anti-Semitism in France proper. Similarly, the Central Consistory hoped that the absence of a specifically Jewish response to anti-Semitism would serve the goal of French Jewry, namely, to be considered an integral part of France. Their behavior during the Dreyfus Affair is a case in point. Fearing the repercussions, the French Jewish leaders were hesitant to place their support behind Dreyfus. Dreyfus was viewed in the shadow of emancipation. An individual Jew was being tried for an act committed against the state; the community had no bearing on the outcome. Their outlook allowed the process to be seen as a purely political issue, relevant to the contemporary attack of clerical and antirepublican forces on the Third Republic. In minimizing the Dreyfus Affair's anti-Semitic connotations, Jewish leaders tended to accept the position upheld by leading Dreyfusards, novelist Émile Zola included. Moreover, the Affair reinforced their a priori adherence to a neutral political approach. Challenged by only a small minority, the image of the Consistory as the organization of "French citizens of the Mosaic persuasion" was preserved. The victory of the Dreyfusard forces provided French Jewry with overwhelming proof of the true nature of their homeland and the validity of their ideological perspective.[5]

Little more than a century after the French Revolution had granted the Jews equal rights, the small Jewish community of some 80,000 (excluding Alsace-Lorraine) could proudly claim to have made giant strides towards realizing the vision of the philosophers of emancipation—abandonment of Jewish particularism and integration into the life of France. Nor was the Affair followed by a cataclysmic period. The stormy debates on church-state relations that rocked France between 1901–1905 and ended with the separation of church and state threatened the Consistory's special status within the Jewish community but hardly roused its leaders from their political apathy. Once again, the Consistory refrained from discussing the Jewish implications of the legislation and taking a particularistic stand, allowing the political developments to determine their place in society.[6]

At the close of the century, French Jewry was still undergoing a major demographic transformation. The Jews of France, like those in communities in Central and Western Europe, gravitated to the focus of political, social, and cultural activity, to the capital. From a small and insignificant community at the time of the Revolution, Paris emerged as the new center of Jewish life, where more than two-thirds of French Jewry resided. The transfer of Jewish population from Alsace to Paris did not nullify the influence of the Alsatian Jews in the leadership of the community, but it did affect communal and religious life. Still a rather homogeneous body, French Jewry had just begun to absorb the first wave of immigrants from Eastern Europe, an immigration that was to change the nature of French Jewry in a revolutionary fashion. Initially, the numbers were small—about 8,000 immigrants prior to

1900—and presented no challenge to the image of the established Jewish population, yet even at that stage, the immigrants aroused negative reactions among the native Jews. As the number of immigrants grew and their cultural network expanded, the conflict with the native Jews intensified.[7]

Attracted primarily to Paris, the Eastern European Jews tended to concentrate in certain districts and maintained their own cultural, religious, and social lifestyle, which increasingly alienated them from established French Jewry. Often of minimal means, the immigrants found employment as artisans and unskilled laborers, but by and large they lived in poor, difficult conditions. The expanding working-class movements found in these quarters a warm reception. Specific Jewish workers' associations developed, displaying anarchistic and Bundist tendencies based upon ideologies imported from Czarist Russia by immigrants who had left Russia after the failure of the 1905 revolution. Those active in the workers' movement nurtured a Yiddish culture, sought to keep the workers from establishing ties with the Jewish bourgeoisie, and even encouraged strikes against Jewish employers. But immigrant activity was not present only in the area of workers' movements. By 1913, the Fédération des Sociétés Juives de France (Fédération—FSJF) had been founded, uniting more than twenty diverse immigrant societies and "assuming the defense of the interests of the immigrant Jewish population."[8] Immigrant Jews sought community life and had the required stamina to upgrade their status and protect their particular way of life. These ramified activities provoked the native Jewish population and were sharply criticized by the French-Jewish press, which followed their developments with concern. Coupled with the drastic demographic change taking place, native Jewry's apprehension became all the more predictable. Since the native Jewish population was almost static, and Eastern European Jews continued to flock to the capital, the homogeneity of the community was virtually lost. By World War I, 40 percent of French Jewry was of Eastern European origin, but the outbreak of war temporarily postponed the clash between these two communities.

All of French Jewry participated in the war effort with great fervor and saw the common front (*union sacrée*) with the French as paramount. The many expressions of brotherhood and friendship between Jews and non-Jews during the war years proved that, indeed, as in the words of Barrès, the Jews were one of the "spiritual families" constituting the French nation, enhancing its unity and internal strength. This feeling of solidarity between Jews and non-Jews also distinguished the relations between immigrant and native Jews during the war. The widespread participation of immigrant Jews in the war effort was positively viewed by native leaders and mitigated their former antagonism. Emerging from the war with a strengthened feeling of national pride, native leaders were now more willing to help draw the immigrants closer to France and into the ambience of native Jewish life.[9] But the following decade seriously hindered the process.

The Interwar Period

World War I and the civil war that followed the Russian Revolution increased the suffering of Eastern European Jewry, and the pressure to emigrate grew. However, the countries that had absorbed the bulk of the Eastern European migration in previous years—the United States and England—began to close their gates. By contrast, France, which had suffered huge losses during the war, encouraged the entry of immigrants in the hope of strengthening its severely depleted work force. During the 1920s, France became the promised land for millions of refugees and immigrants, among them tens of thousands of Jews from Russia, Poland, Lithuania, and Romania.

Like their predecessors, the new Jewish immigrants tried to duplicate their previous lifestyle, joining workers' unions and radical movements in large numbers. Merging class consciousness with Yiddish culture, the immigrants produced a vigorous Eastern European atmosphere, which intensified the aversion of the native Jews and French society. At the end of the 1920s and during the early 1930s, the native Jewish leaders became somewhat more open towards the immigrants and made serious efforts to ease their absorption into France. At the height of these overtures, attempts were made to attract new leadership forces from the immigrant community, but always from the vantage point of established Jewry's hegemony and patronage. The native leaders were sensitive to the "foreign culture" of the Eastern Europeans and feared its threat to the relations they had established within France. They tried to influence the immigrants to show loyalty to the state that had granted them refuge and to refrain from political statements that might impair relations between the Jews and the French. Acting out of their narrow view as French citizens of the Jewish religion, they were not able to make peace with or treat equally Jews who lived according to a different ethos. Consequently, little progress was achieved during this time of relative acceptance. In the Jewish community, most communal relations between well-established and immigrant Jews deteriorated during the excruciating prewar years, as did the relations between France and its Jews.[10]

From the early 1930s, economic and political problems intensified in France, seriously jeopardizing the resurgence the country had achieved during the previous decade. The internal tension led to additional problems. Traditional animosity towards foreigners and latent opposition to Jews combined with the drastic economic decline to prompt a barrage of accusations against immigrants and Jews. Encumbered by close to 3,000,000 aliens and approximately 1,000,000 unemployed French in 1933, a wide spectrum of society acutely felt the competition for employment and proposed ways to curb the influx of immigrants.[11] The economic malaise had other worrisome parallels. In response to the current vogue of pessimism and decadence, intellectuals sought new ways to revitalize the French spirit. Serious soul-searching brought back to the church such leading French thinkers as Georges Bernanos, François Mauriac and Étiene Gilson, improving its image among the intellectual community.[12] Others denounced Jews with an intensity unsurpassed by nineteenth-century French anti-Semitism. Robert Brasillach, Lucien Rebatet, Louis-Ferdinand Céline, and Jean Giraudoux were far from outcasts in their revolt against the oppressive intrusion of Jewish cultural modes into French society. Inveighing against Judaism as an alien and nefarious force, this literary circle began to see it as the cause of all the social problems. Jews had become their symbol of all that was wrong in France and the Third Republic.[13] Moreover, in the eyes of the French, it was these very Jews, along with Italian and Spanish refugees in France, who threatened to provoke France into an undesired conflagration with their particular enemies: Germany, Mussolini's Italy, and Franco's Spain. Nothing could have been more frightening and threatening to the French than war. Xenophobia had taken hold of France, and nationalist fever was high, but France wanted to avoid war at all costs.[14]

It took, nonetheless, several years before these views found concrete support in government circles. The French government had aired the problem of an overflow of immigrants in the early thirties but had enforced few restrictive measures, preserving the basic elements of a liberal immigration policy. Facing a potentially explosive sociopolitical situation, the government refused to yield to the xenophobic atmosphere, claiming that France could cope with both unemployment and the foreigners.[15] It was the Popular Front fiasco in the mid-thirties that changed the situation. Coming to power in 1936, Léon Blum boldly upheld an unrestrictive immigrant policy and expended huge sums of money to alleviate the plight of refugees in France. A true humanitarian, Blum went against public opinion and even in the face of the mass influx of Spanish republicans persisted in keeping France's doors open. But his fumbling foreign policy and untimely and counterproductive economic measures placed him and the Popular Front at odds with large sectors of the population.[16] Mythologized as the apotheosis of the Third Republic's tyranny of the French people, Blum and the Front aroused a frightening array of anti-immigrant and anti-Jewish sentiment, releasing traditional arguments. The recrudescence of anti-Semitism was based on the same themes that had dominated the revolt against Jews at the turn of the century: parliamentarism, liberal democracy, capitalism, and the decay of France were all part of the Jewish triumph over France, epitomized by

Blum's regime. Left, Right, and Center converged on a mutual enemy. According to Michael Marrus and Robert Paxton,

> Once it was accepted that Jews were a "problem," the way was open for other elements of the anti-Semitic world view to slip quietly into the consciousness of moderates. It is striking how widely fragments of the anti-Semitism position permeated moderate political vocabulary after the mid-1930s. Anti-Jewish expressions acquired new kinds of legitimacy.[17]

The Dreyfusard spirit was nowhere to be found. Those who dared to defend the onslaught against the Jews remained in the background, convinced that it was not the right moment to appear. Anti-Semitism had become commonplace in French society.

Blum's short-lived second term as prime minister (13 March-8 April 1938) was a last valiant attempt to stem the tide. The pitiful comeback finally enabled the internal agitation against immigrants and Jews to receive due treatment by governmental officials. Edouard Daladier, Blum's former minister of defense and chief nemesis on the immigrant issue, formed a new government based on wider conservative support and immediately went to the task expected of him. Within a month, Daladier was working on a new immigration policy. Extending the authority of border-control officials to refuse entry to refugees, the May regulations both restricted immigration and reduced the basic rights and freedom of movement of residing foreigners. Tragically, that was only the beginning. Having rejected Blum's policy of aiding the refugees, Daladier, the radical socialist, turned to more constraining methods—resettlement, internment, repatriation. Following the futile debates concerning refugees at the Evian conference in July 1938 and fearing a rise in refugees after *Kristallnacht*, Daladier became more restrictive with naturalized French citizens.[18] From 12 November 1938 they could be deprived of their citizenship if deemed "unworthy of the title of French citizen," designated "undesirable," and interned in special camps (*étrangers indésirables dans les centres spéciaux*). Euphemistically called "centers," "reception centers," or "supervised lodging centers," concentration camps were shortly thereafter established by the French to house a cross-section of their foreigners, but predominantly the hundreds of thousands of Spanish republican fugitives. Later in 1939, the Jews' turn would come. Although Daladier's decrees on residence rights and immigrants were not directed solely against Jews, and they were not specifically cited, as the months would show, Jews were clearly on the agenda.[19] The road to overturning the Third Republic's liberal principles had been considerably shortened.

Despite the cold public view of foreigners during the thirties, immigrants continued to reach France's cities and towns. We have no way of knowing for certain how many Jews were among those who arrived in France during this period and how many stayed on, but the approximations allow us to appreciate their impact on the community's make-up. It is estimated that about 120,000 Eastern European Jews settled in France between the wars, close to 70,000 in Paris alone, forming the majority within the Jewish community in the capital and in France.[20] Wary of this development and the evil winds in French society, native Jewry reverted to its pre-World War I approach. Native Jews were now a minority, and the leaders of French Jewry refused to grant reasonable representation to the immigrants in its institutions and became a closed oligarchy, completely isolated from the needs and thinking of the Eastern Europeans. Responding to the xenophobic atmosphere in French society, the leadership worked feverishly to limit the political and cultural activities of the immigrant groups and to hasten their integration into the life of France. Mutual antagonism and estrangement between the communities, however, made such overtures futile and volcanic.

The eruption came in May 1935 in a provocative address given by the president of the Paris Consistory, Baron Robert de Rothschild. In this well-known speech, Rothschild enunciated the growing antipathy of native Jews towards manifestations of Eastern European politics and culture. Professing to teach the immigrants a lesson in good citizenship, Rothschild attributed the increase in anti-Semitism to their political activity. He concluded sharply that if the immigrants did not learn to behave and continued their unbridled criticism of the French government, it would be best if they left France.[21] That was a representative statement of a leadership that had lost its influence over most of the Jewish population and the ability to forge a united community under its auspices. But it was also an appeal to the immigrants to be more conscious of the perils involved in irresponsible extremism.

The heads of French Jewry continued to believe that they exercised the responsible leadership in the community, and they did not abandon their goal to become an integral part of France and the French society. Preferring to view the anti-Semitic attacks as a temporary outgrowth of the volatile political context, native Jewry saw no benefit in a partisan defense of the Jews. Immigrant Jews thought otherwise and staked their future on the success of the Popular Front and other left-wing ideologies. Thus, owing to their contrasting conceptions of Judaism and perceptions of self-security in France, even the outside danger of growing anti-Semitism was unable to unite the two major elements of the community.[22] The thought that one day they might be forced to clash with France over their very existence was certainly beyond their imagination.

The implications of native Jewry's iconoclasm were felt by another wave of immigrants during the 1930s—German Jewry. With Hitler's rise to power in Germany, a new tide of refugees turned to France, fleeing the country they cherished. Fearing an invasion of Nazi agents and a serious threat to France's internal security, French officials took immediate precautions but did not impose restrictive measures. This immigration was of a different sort. The incoming Jews were seeking not a permanent refuge but only a temporary shelter until the Hitlerian euphoria passed. Indeed, of the thousands of Jews who made their way to France, often without residence permits, only some 10,000 were still residing there in 1938.[23] Thousands had returned to Germany during the first years of the Reich or had emigrated to the United States, England, or Palestine.

Yet, despite their smaller numbers and greater affinity to French Jewry in lifestyle and manners than the Eastern Europeans, German Jews were not warmly received by the established community. Native Jewish leadership, too mindful of its own interests, tended to favor the restrictionist position of right-wing elements in France, upholding a much firmer immigration policy.[24] Again, the heads of the Central Consistory opted to withdraw from the difficulties presented by the Jewish refugees, and for a time they opposed the establishment of a special organization to deal with their problems. Only in 1936, after a difficult struggle, did the Consistory lend its hand to the creation of the Comité d'assistance aux réfugiés d'Allemagne (CAR), headed by native Jews associated with the Consistory.[25] Practically oriented to treat the social and economic needs of the refugees, CAR gained the respect of French governmental institutions as well as the support of the American Joint Distribution Committee. Not a political entity, CAR stayed clear of any public campaign that demanded a reversal of France's immigration restrictions. German Jews, meanwhile, lived on the fringe of Jewish society in France with great trepidation as their attachment to Germany clashed with the patriotic ambience of France.[26]

Germany's aggressive domestic and foreign policy drove a new wave of refugees to France in 1938 and 1939. The Anschluss of Austria in March 1938, followed by the countrywide attacks on Jewish synagogues and premises on *Kristallnacht* and the invasion of Czechoslovakia in March 1939, all contributed to the increased emigration from Germany and the Greater Reich. Despite the French immigration policy, probably as many as 25,000 Jews reached France in frantic pursuit of shelter. They encountered a stricter French government, which sent thousands of them to the newly established internment camps.[27] CAR was put to a new test. Thousands of additional refugees requiring immediate relief turned to it for succor, fearing their peremptory deportation from France.

In the face of their deteriorating conditions and the impending dangers, voices within the Jewish community called on the French government to ease its restrictions on the refugees.[28] In the weekly *Samedi*, native and immigrant Jews lashed out at Jewish passivity to the Nazi threat, appealing for a more outspoken approach to the government's antiforeigner policy. According to David Weinberg, *Samedi* "was especially critical of the willingness of French Jews to forsake immigrants and refugees in order to save their own reputation."[29] Only one "establishment" Jew seems to have taken up this challenge, the editor of *L'Univers israélite* and CAR functionary Raymond-Raoul Lambert. In April 1939 Lambert demanded a cessation of the Daladier policy against the immigrants and a revocation of the 1938 immigration laws. He proposed a patriotic alternative: the immigrants should be released from the internment camps and permitted to serve the country, either militarily or in some other capacity.[30] However, these indications of a changing attitude came far too late and, more important, lacked political support. France was already saturated with refugees and well on the road to a more extreme policy. Appeals from Jewish figures in spring 1939 could hardly penetrate the heightened xenophobia. CAR could offer assistance, but the squalid conditions in which the refugees found themselves were not to be ameliorated.

On The Eve of War

As the months of 1939 passed, the French Jewish community of some 300,000 grew more and more fearful. The interwar years had created many urgent problems, none of which had been well attended to by the community. Paris, where two-thirds of the Jews were concentrated, was the microcosm of French Jewry's dilemmas. Native and immigrant Jews lived in separate arrondissements, affiliated with mutually exclusive societies, and showed little empathy for each other's cultural ethos. The native Jewish leadership leaned right of center, while the immigrants were often associated with leftist political organizations; politically at odds, they could not find a common approach to either of the community's burning issues, rampant anti-Semitism and the refugee problem. Each community went its own way, dismissing the other's perspective as counterproductive and disabling to the community's needs. Only the youth seem to have begun to find a workable synthesis, one that was critical of the "establishment" and the direction of French Jewry during the interwar period. The war years would catapult their synthesis into the center of the active Jewish struggle against Vichy and Nazi occupation.

The Nazi occupation and Vichy France were to present this thoroughly factionalized community with a predicament far beyond that which it had failed to deal with in the thirties. Pursuing the anti-Semitic orientation of the Daladier regime, Vichy was to knock down all those holy principles that native Jews believed in and to supplant them with the élan of the *ancien régime*. Furthermore, it was to offer more than a helping hand to the Nazis' diabolical plan to exterminate the Jews of Europe. One hundred and fifty years after the French Revolution, French Jewry was to be hurled into a whirlwind that would take the lives of almost 78,000 Jews. Stunned and often incapable of assimilating their past, glorious history with the current drama, Jewish leaders turned and twisted until they assumed the burden of leading the community. Their dilemmas and moral reasoning are at the heart of this analysis.

II.

THE FALL OF FRANCE
GERMAN OCCUPATION AND
FRENCH JEWRY, 1940–1942

French Jewry Enters the War

During the 1930s, the French government showed little interest in rekindling the historic struggle with Germany. Memories of World War I were still fresh in the French consciousness, and the ravages of the Great War continued to haunt large sectors of the population. This atmosphere was not conducive to a reappraisal of France's military capabilities; it encouraged a defensive strategy: the French wanted at all costs to avoid the devastation of their country and placed their security in the Maginot Line. France cringed as the war fever rose steadily during 1939, and only when all alternatives failed and war broke out did the Daladier government reluctantly declare war against Germany. The government's hesitancy was consistent with France's internal needs and followed the earnest attempts for reconstruction after the useless exploitation of World War.I.[1]

Declaration of war against Germany reawakened among French Jewry feelings of solidarity and sacrifice. Turbulent years and unnerving events had separated the community from the spirit of *union sacrée* of World War I, but the call to arms united its diverse elements to assert their duty to France. Impassioned voices urged the community to stand by France in its just cause against the enemy of mankind. Extreme protagonists, such as the Central Consistory and the Jewish Communists, now found themselves supporting mutual goals, relinquishing their former conflicts. The causes of war and its purpose were viewed differently by all, yet all realized the implications for French Jewry.

In the late thirties, representative figures of native Jewry vociferously denied any particular Jewish angle to France's relations with Nazi Germany. Speaking after the Munich agreement of 1938, the Chief Rabbi of Paris, Julien Weill, equated Jewish with French interests and emphasized that

French Jewry, while troubled by the fate of German Jews, would not in-
terfere with a possible rapprochement between the two countries.[2] While
stressing Judaism's vision of peace and unity of mankind, Weill and others
also declared Jewish willingness to fight for France if need be. Native Jewry's
restraint and neutral political stand disappeared as war became imminent;
pent-up patriotism and allegiance to France poured out, boundless and un-
inhibited. A special jubilee volume of *L'Univers israélite* was published in
September 1939 commemorating the one-hundred-and-fiftieth anniversary
of the French Revolution.[3] Article after article praised France for the generations of freedom and liberty it had granted the Jews and reveled in the
unique symbiosis between Judaism and France. Trying to gloss over the less
glorious pages of the past, Rabbi Maurice Liber appealed to the community
to join the French national community and disregard attacks against Jews.
The *union sacrée* must again become the supreme law. Other spokesmen
of the community drew parallels between allegiance to France and the lofty
ideals of classical culture, to which all lovers of justice and humanity strive.
Fighting Hitler and the forces of violence and barbarism that he epitomized
was thus an imperative for all allies of humanity.[4] France marched at the
head of these forces, and Jews must be prepared to join her ranks and sacrifice
"the last drop of their blood."[5] Inveighing against pacifism and neutrality,
Jewish leaders viewed America's noninvolvement as an act of appeasement
that endangered peace in the world.

Totally identified with France's stand against Germany, native Jewish
leaders became hypersensitive to the developments within the immigrant
community. Immigrant Jews were expected to show understanding of the
present situation and maintain a low profile, avoid loud discussions in foreign
languages, and refrain from voicing political opinions. Underlying the appeals
to the immigrants was the sentiment that nothing should be done to arouse
anti-Jewish feeling while irreversible ties were being solidified between
France and Judaism. Immigrant efforts on behalf of France were widely
publicized by *L'Univers israélite*, indicating the responsible path. France,
the haven of refugees, deserved their support.[6] For native Jewry, the war
effort was an opportunity to reestablish the historic symbiosis between
France and Judaism and to erase the memories of the turbulent thirties.
Encouraged by the immigrants' response to the war, native leaders hoped
it would mitigate the "source" of Jewry's tension with France.

France's Eastern European immigrant Jews constituted a volatile and heterogeneous community; politically and socially diversified, their wide variety
of affiliations and organizations were separate from those of the native Jews.
Nonetheless, their insecure predicament brought various leaders to express
in 1939 similar views on the wisdom of restraint and forbearance. Daladier's

legislation against refugees prompted certain individuals to be more careful in their political utterances. However, a government announcement in April 1939 allowing aliens to enlist in the French army prompted a wide-scale recruitment, which within a month encompassed several thousand Jews. Enlistment promised these Jews permanent residence in France while it offered an opportunity for them to vent their abhorrence of Nazism. The enthusiastic immigrant response somewhat baffled the French government, and attempts were made to curtail the patriotic fervor, to no avail.[7] Declaration of war and the German invasion of Poland intensified the dilemma for alien Jews. Intrinsically identified with the fate of their Polish brethren, they looked frantically for ways to support them. Thousands volunteered for service in the Polish army, but only a few were accepted. With the reopening of French and Jewish recruiting stations in September, more than 10,000 alien Jews assembled to register for the French army. But here too they faced a certain reluctance. Thousands were enlisted, but instead of being inducted into the regular military service, they were again herded off to the French Foreign Legion, where they would experience trying times.[8]

Eastern European Jews were encouraged to fight Nazism as part of a world struggle against the enemy of mankind. Emphasizing both the universalistic and the particularistic sides of the war, major immigrant leaders, such as Marc Jarblum, saw the bases of mankind and Judaism at stake: democracy, peace, France, humanist ideals, Jewish values, and the Jewish people were all being threatened by Hitler's hordes. No one had a right to evade the mission of saving the French Republic. These were not artificial appeals but profound expressions of the anticipated fears. Caught up in this atmosphere and the spirit of solidarity, the voice of the Fédération *Parizer Haint* warned the community against irresponsible acts. Almost reiterating the native Jews' appeals to the immigrants, *Parizer Haint* cautioned the fringe elements to abide by accepted behavior while it entreated immigrant Jews to do their service to save the Republic.[9]

On this issue there were no serious divisions among the immigrant organizations. Even the majority of Jewish Communists joined the anti-German campaign. Disregarding the Molotov-Ribbentrop agreement, which paralyzed many Communist parties across Europe, the Jewish Communists broke party consensus and actively favored participation in the war against Nazi Germany. Boldly opposing the hesitant position of their colleagues in the French Communist Party (PCF), the Jewish Communists tended to view the war with all its dangerous repercussions for the Jewish people. In the last issue of the Communist newspaper published before the war, Jews were solicited to defend France against the Hitlerian forces. The Jewish Communists were followed by other left-wing circles—Medem Farband, Bund,

Arbeiter Ring—which condemned the Russian-German alliance and declared their allegiance to the capitalist democracies' fight against fascism.
Neutrality was suicide for the progressive forces and the Jewish proletariat.[10]

Unequivocally aligned with France's war effort, the immigrant population
anticipated an eventual change in the government's refugee policy and a
certain rapprochement with the native establishment. France, however, was
caught up in xenophobia and reluctant to induct a large number of Jewish
volunteers into the army; only in December 1939 was the decision made to
allow them to join the French Foreign Legion. Moreover, several days after
the war began, some 15,000 German and Austrian Jewish refugees were
rounded up by the French police and sent off to internment camps in the
south of France; by December some 7,000 had been released, but that by
no means indicated a reappraisal of the French refugee policy. Nonetheless,
immigrant enthusiasm was not dispelled; all told, some 60,000 either volunteered or were enlisted to fight for the liberty of France. As for relations
with the native Jews, some progress was made, even though French Jewry
showed little concern about the internment of the Central European Jewish
refugees.[11] At Jarblum's initiative, and with the Joint's support, an emergency
committee was established, bringing together several organizations that as-
sisted refugees. It worked to improve the level of public canteens, and to
provide clothing and pharmaceuticals for the needy and relief for dislocated
intellectuals.[12] Although the extent and duration of its operations are unclear,
the committee seems to have contributed to a sense of mutual fate and
outlook, which Jarblum proudly alluded to on the eve of the German invasion
of France in May 1940.[13]

In the wake of Germany's successful blitzkriegs in Holland, Belgium, and
Luxembourg in spring 1940, French Jewry viewed its future with trepidation. The cataclysmic effect on the Jewish communities in the Low Countries,
in particular the waves of frightened refugees that reached France's borders
in spring 1940, drove home the point. Spread out on the southern coast of
France along the Spanish border, Belgian Jews wandered through small
French towns and villages in their quest for shelter. Thousands of these
refugees were arrested and sent to French internment camps in Saint-Cy-
prien, Gurs, Nexon, and Le Vernet. Treated with little compassion, some
even turned to the German Foreign Office to alleviate their plight; they
constituted only a third of the some 30,000 Belgian Jews, dislocated and
undesired. Soon they were to be joined by several hundred Dutch Jews who
had escaped Holland during the German invasion. All in all, on the eve of
the German move against France, French Jewry had been bolstered by close
to 40,000 Jewish refugees spread out in northern cities, southern townlets,
and French internment camps.[14] Their impact was felt in Jewish quarters.

Jacques Biélinky, the Russian-born journalist who moved freely in both immigrant and native circles, reviewed the war's potential outcome for French Jewry and the Jewish people: Hitler's pan-German vision, involving the subjugation of countries and peoples, made compromise with Germany unfeasible; to prevent a return to barbarism and the physical destruction of Jewry, total war with Hitler was imperative.[15] No other outlet was seen as possible; all of French Jewry's efforts and desires focused on victory and the defeat of fascism.[16] Completely geared to this result, French Jewry hardly prepared itself for another eventuality, the fall of France and German occupation.

The Fall of France, The *Statut des Juifs*, and French Jewry's Response

Patriotic allegiance and the complications of travel limited Jewish emigration from France in the winter and spring of 1940. Only a few wealthy Jews managed to escape the scene of battle. But when the collapse of France became a viable possibility, Jews joined the massive civilian exodus from the north. Following the advice and example of French governmental institutions, Jewish leaders and organizations evacuated Paris, stripping occupied France of experienced leadership; not a sole rabbinic figure remained. The disorientation and pandemonium of June 1940 encompassed all. At least 100,000 Jews, and some even double that estimate, took to the roads in those panic-stricken days. Part of an exodus that may have involved as many as 8,000,000 French residents, the Jews came from all walks of life and every ethnic background: demobilized Jews and recent refugees from the Low Countries, lay people and rabbis, rank-and-file community members, and leaders were all involved. The destinations of tens of thousands —Marseilles, Lyon, Toulouse, Nice—reflected the trend in modern Jewish history to move to the major cities, which became new centers of Jewish population. Many lower-middle-class Jews, however, fearing unemployment and possible anti-Semitic legislation, turned to less-populated places, farther from the hub of things. Their dispersal into hundreds of French towns and villages, where they came into contact with over 15,000 Jews who had fled Alsace-Lorraine with the outbreak of war in September 1939, was an unprecedented result of the exodus from occupied France and opened up important possibilities for the following years.[17]

Showing a keen awareness of the nation's morale, Marshal Philippe Pétain signed the armistice agreement with Germany on 22 June 1940, ending the hostilities and avoiding further German territorial gains. Almost three weeks later, in its new capital, the resort town of Vichy, the French National Assembly overwhelmingly voted to revise the constitution. The antirepublican and antiliberal values that had permeated French society in the late thirties now became the basis of Pétain's government. Pétain was granted extraordinary rights to rule over a country only 40 percent of which remained unoccupied. France had entered a new era of its history. Traditionalist values of *travail, famille, patrie*—Vichy's "New Order"—replaced the universalistic code of the French Revolution, and an authoritarian regime offered stability and order to a defeated and stunned people.

Instantaneously, the national humiliation gave birth to a form of patriotism in which citizens across France sought ways to revive the country.[18] And, indeed, in the ensuing weeks, life in the occupied zone began to return to normal. Recalling this period, the distinguished French-Jewish historian of Russian birth Léon Poliakov noted in his memoirs: "Life in Paris seemed normal. One was not even alarmed for the Jews. The Germans were 'correct'; there were no massacres and no pogroms."[19] Confronted with millions looking for security and employment in the unoccupied south and encouraged by reports of a liberal occupation, several million French and thousands of Jews began making their way back to Paris and to the occupied north. Aided and encouraged by German and Vichy authorities, the masses returned home to resume their lives. Prior to the restrictions enforced in late September 1940 by the demarcation line, as many as 30,000 Jews returned to live under the German occupation, raising the Jewish population in the Seine region to almost 150,000.[20]

What was natural for some was frightening for others; refusing to believe in a liberal Nazi occupation, thousands of Jews fled to the south as an escape route to Spain or Portugal. Their ultimate destination was the United States. In the summer months of turmoil and indecision, when new regulations were yet to be imposed, Jewish refugees were fortunate enough to receive the assistance of certain Portuguese and Spanish officials. Refused exit visas by the French government, they found a savior in the Portuguese consul-general of Bordeaux, Aristides de Sousa-Mendes. Mendes was moved by the Jewish plight and determined to show the true Catholic spirit: in defiance of his country's orders, he granted several thousand entry visas in a re-markably short period, before he was removed from office. Further efforts on his behalf in Bayonne and Henaye guaranteed the crossing of many more refugees. Spanish border officials along the Pyrenees cooperated with him by allowing refugees to cross over without any identification or on the basis of the Portuguese visa. These loopholes persisted until early September, when the Spanish, Portuguese, and French authorities clamped down on the various escape routes. But in the meanwhile, the partisan efforts of Mendes and Spanish border officers had granted safety to no fewer than 20,000 Jews.[21]

But not all Jewish migration was voluntary. In mid-July 1940, the German authorities began forcefully to expel the few thousand Jews who still remained in Alsace-Lorraine. Pushing to annex the region into the Reich and make it *judenrein*, the Germans drove these Jews into the unoccupied zone of France, where they were concentrated in three departments—Dordogne, Haute-Vienne, and Creuse. Having collectively fled and now having been expelled, the community of almost 30,000 Jews, including rabbis and lay leaders, quickly began to reorganize itself and avoid further hardships. Guided by the Chief Rabbi of Strasbourg, René Hirschler, the community relied on its own resources, receiving only limited help from governmental agencies and local relief committees. By October 1940, Alsace-Lorraine was *judenrein*; its Jewish community, resettled in southern France, had, however, shown much resilience and severely reduced the number of Jews requiring special assistance.[22]

Amid the general turmoil and tremendous dislocation, initial attempts were being made to reorganize the community, while contradictory assessments were voiced on the possibility of Jewish existence under Vichy. Unfortunately, contemporary source material on the ideological response of French Jewry to the fall of France is fragmentary. Nonetheless, from the little information available, certain tendencies can be reconstructed. The common experience Jews shared with the French during the war began to disappear as the armistice was signed and the Third Republic was dismantled. Pétain's installation as chief of state in July 1940 had a reassuring effect for most French people. As Richard Cobb stated, "His invitation to seek refuge in the bosom of the family and to sit it out at home would be to most middle-class people a more comforting programme than blood, sweat and tears."[23] For French Jewry, no similar overall statement could be made. Although some tried to find solace in the new principles of Vichy, the havoc of war and the end of free speech resulted in fear and indecision for most. Only a few days after Pétain formally became "Head of the French State" with extraordinary prerogatives, Raymond-Raoul Lambert echoed in his diary the troubled feeling of native Jews:

> Yesterday, following the military ceremony I went to the overflow service at the small synagogue. "France" replaced "Republic" in the prayer for the country. . . . French Judaism lives in particular anguish. It agrees to suffer like all but fears imposed discrimination, possibly by the enemy. This fear makes my future and my children's especially forbidding. But I still have confidence. France cannot accept everything and it is not for nothing that for more than a century my ancestors have mingled on its soil—that I fought two wars. I cannot imagine life for my wife, my children, and for myself under another climate, an uprooting which would be worse than amputation.[24]

This trust in France led native Jews to seek out the positive aspects of Vichy's policies. Convening in Lyon in early September 1940, the council of French rabbis drafted a declaration of allegiance to Pétain, wherein they emphasized the mutual tenets of Judaism—"to serve the motherland, to favor the family, and to honor work"—and the principles of Vichy's "New Order."[25] The rabbis further expressed their desire to cooperate in revitalizing the country. They were not alone. Members of the French-Jewish scout movement Eclaireurs Israélites de France (EIF), who in the thirties generated support for a restructuring of Jewish life, found Vichy ideals attuned to their teachings. In August-September 1940 they were buoyed by optimism. As Pétain called for a "return to the land," so EIF urged its followers to reorder their lives and adapt to the rural life—not out of simplistic assimilation to Vichy goals but as a way of reshaping the economic basis of the Jewish community. Contacts were established between EIF leaders and various French ministries, which both encouraged and subsidized the scouts' projects. Idealism was at its peak: the scouts tried to combine the traditions of French farmers with the development of Jewish life and preferred collective farms on untilled land "to augment in a precious way the productive French heritage." Underlying their motivation was the belief that agricultural groups of different religions could form a pluralistic association and further the joint cause. Meeting at their agricultural settlement in Moissac in August, the scouts proposed various ways to extend their farms and find a common synthesis with French society. Indeed, well into 1941 EIF received governmental support for several projects, including its agricultural training school at Lautrec. Herein merged Vichy's concept of a "national revolution" with EIF's attack on decaying Jewish urbanism and capitalism.[26]

This yearning for total involvement in the "national revolution" produced several advocates of a new discipline and authority for the Jewish community. Born in Palestine in 1892, Kadmi Cohen became a French citizen in 1914 after having volunteered for the French army. A Zionist with revisionist orientations, Cohen presented in his prewar writings an uncompromising stand on the Zionist vision: Zionist politics must be independent of international pressures and based solely upon the needs and eternal principles of the "Jewish race."

Exasperated by the inability of Jewish leaders to perceive the aimlessness of Jewish life, Cohen was driven to view National Socialism as the most important event in the modern history of the Jewish people. Following the collapse of France and the German occupation of the north, he wrote a fervent, unbridled critique of Jewish life entitled "The End of the Jewish Illusion." Of book length but never published, the work presented Hitlerism as the ultimate proof of the fallacious Jewish belief in emancipation. Nowhere, Cohen argued, could the Jew be an equal citizen, for he would always be seen as a Jew. Moreover, the contemporary developments made his predicament more acute. Both totalitarian socialism and totalitarian fascism undermined the liberal tenets of society, and the Jew would be forced to assume peripheral and parasitic functions under the new regimes. Stripped of his former way of life, the Jew must cease to believe in the countries he loves, put an end to futile struggles in favor of democracy and against anti-Semitism, and rally around the Jewish political demand for a Jewish territory.

For Kadmi Cohen, the "Jewish problem" was a direct result of the definition of a Jew as one who lacked a country: Jews must therefore politically unite, not on the basis of humanitarianism or progress but on the basis of power and aggressiveness. National regeneration of the Jews would follow when the Jews aggressively claimed their territory and returned to the land. But Kadmi Cohen recognized that only a people conscious of its peoplehood could proceed in such a fashion. Here is where the National Socialist victory loomed large in his construction. Renouncing all liberal platforms, National Socialism would convince the Jew that he could live as a Jew only in a Jewish state.[27] Unfettered by opposition, and rejected by leading French-Jewish personalities, Kadmi Cohen pushed forward his obscurantist proposal. Even after his abortive negotiations to publish a Hebrew and Yiddish edition of his *L'Etat Israel*, Cohen managed to recruit some support for his ideals, and his plans continued to surface until 1944.[28]

But most French Jews did not view National Socialism as a blessing in disguise and probably fell into the general category of silent supporters of Pétain's leadership. Trust in the reverent old man and the traditions of France kept native Jewry at an even keel. They reverted in the disarray of the summer to where they felt most comfortable, to a centrist position. Few saw de Gaulle as a viable alternative, and many were convinced that his was the act of a maverick. Like the French population, they too were part of the wait-and-see trend of *attentisme*, and they too were appeased by the Pétain mystique.[29] But then came the ignominious *Statut des Juifs* ("Statute on the Jews") of 3 October 1940.

Following the xenophobic trend of Daladier's regime, the "national revolution" increased the legislation against foreigners and Jews. Initiated by Vichy to curb Jewish activity in French public life and bring France back to the French, the *statut* defined a Jew as one who had two grandparents of Jewish race, and it eliminated Jews from a host of professions. Although exemptions were granted to certain Jews who had fought in the two world wars, no differentiation was made between native and immigrant Jews. Denial of equal civil status and isolation of the Jews, politically and nationally, became an integral part of the "national revolution."[30]

Native Jews responded with pain and anguish. As German Jews had reacted seven years before to the anti-Semitic laws in Germany, so now French Jews looked for explanations while raising their nationalist banner—patriotic French citizens of the Jewish religion. In Paris, Jewish merchants hung signs in their windows with the names of family members who had served France in previous wars and proudly but sadly showed their ancestral attachment to the country; others hung a yellow card as a sign of protest.[31] Convinced that German pressure was to blame for the statute, native Jews nevertheless felt betrayed by France's glorious tradition of liberalism. Ashamed for themselves and their country that it could stoop to the level of "a new revocation of the Edict of Nantes,"[32] French Jews passionately appealed to Pétain, the "Father of the Nation," as the Jews of Germany had addressed President Paul von Hindenburg in the early stages of the Third Reich. Singling out their unique contributions to France, native Jews affirmed their religious bond and strenuously denied any racial association. In countering the anti-Semitic accusations of Jewish responsibility for the country's downfall, they emphasized Jewish loyalty on the field of battle and in public service, and their special efforts in spreading French culture abroad. Moreover, their unswerving commitment to France made them pledge obedience even to those laws that limited their freedom.[33]

The Chief Rabbi of France, Isaïe Schwartz, surpassed all in trying to prove Judaism's eternal oneness with France. Invoking the memorable passage from *Les diverses familles spirituelles de la France* in which Barrès upheld Jewish rootedness in France, Schwartz equated the principles of Vichy's "New Order"—work, family, motherland—with the pillars of Judaism. Vichy was merely a continuation of the historic bond between France and Judaism:

> The French Jews ("israélites") have adopted a motto: Religion-Motherland. Constantly faithful to this ideal, we draw our courage and hope from the love of God and the Biblical lessons, the sources of the French people's spiritual life.[34]

French Jews adhered to the eternal fidelity that Schwartz espoused, refusing to admit the ephemeral nature of their cherished contact with France. Shaken by the *statut*, they protested tactfully to Pétain, showing their profound trust in his leadership. French Jews resigned themselves to suffer and wait.[35] For their immigrant brethren, the stakes were much higher.

On board the ship that brought him to America, the Russian-Jewish historian Elias Tcherikower entered in his diary a poignant conclusion to his life in France and Europe:

> And now something of history: how the ugly defeated and tormented France twists itself and enters the school of Hitlerism and Fascism and quickly learns the sin of official anti-Semitism. A most instructive fact.[36]

Written in mid-September 1940, Tcherikower's diary gave vent to a deep-seated pessimism, to the frightening thought that the exodus from Egypt would be relived in the "exodus from Europe," the "exodus from Poland, from France, etc." Tcherikower traced the evolution of a new period in

Europe in which the Jew would again be forced to assume his historical role as a nomad; the forces of fascism seemed invincible, and Tcherikower was convinced that the traditions of French culture were to vanish irretrievably. The occupation and the fascist threat that accompanied it were uppermost in his mind and overrode any minor considerations, such as the personality of Pétain or the revival of France. Other immigrant Jews of different political persuasion felt the same.

As in the case of French society, where "early Resistance in 1940 was the work of exceptional individuals, usually already outside the social fabric in some way,"[37] so it was in the Jewish community. Those elements who were politically antagonistic towards previous French governments and who denounced the Jewish leadership were the first to reject tacit consensus: first and foremost, the Jewish Communists. Having split with the PCF on the Molotov-Ribbentrop agreement, the Jewish Communists disregarded the closure of all Communist publications and began to publish, several days after the war commenced, an illegal journal, *Unzer Vort*. Although its content and frequency of publication are unknown, *Unzer Vort* already showed the Communist predisposition to oppose any kind of reconciliation with Nazi Germany.[38] Less than a month after the occupation of Paris, an issue of *Unzer Vort* was published clandestinely; it urged the Jewish community to join the French proletariat in its war against Germany and to struggle for the liberation of France. The Jewish Communists' categorical denunciation of Pétain and the armistice, while French Communists were still bandying the slogan "Ni Pétain, ni de Gaulle," ("Neither Pétain nor de Gaulle") placed them at the forefront of opposition in France. By summer 1940 the Jewish Communist youth had founded Solidarité and begun working in the heavily populated working areas of Paris. Several small groups of Communist activists combed these districts, warning Jews of the consequences of German occupation and urging them to participate in an organization to aid the needy, raise the morale of the community, and prepare for a war of liberation.[39] The call to an ideological struggle combined with social and moral concerns was unparalleled within the Jewish community in Paris, even among other immigrant social activists. Unoccupied France also saw opposition to Vichy sprouting from socialist and Communist affiliates, as well as a circle of Jewish youth, native and immigrant, who already in 1939 were vehemently attacking the French Jewish leadership.

Forteresse Juive was the name chosen by this group for their fledgling anti-Vichy committee. Launched in Toulouse in June 1940 by the former editor of *Affirmation*, David Knout, the "Jewish Fortress" tried to shape Jewish opinion in the direction of the erstwhile journal: the Jewish community must be assertive against Nazism and uplift itself by raising the classical Zionist idea of autoemancipation.[40] A poet of Russian birth, Knout

had been attracted to revisionist ideology in the thirties and now outlined
a course of action in a small pamphlet entitled "What Must Be Done?" Joining
Kadmi Cohen in concluding that the National Socialist victory had positive
implications, Knout maintained that Nazi anti-Semitism would hasten the
creation of a Jewish state. He too saw the war as a historic turning point for
the Jews to cease being objects of society and emerge as an organic community, fighting for the establishment of a Jewish state in Palestine. Knout's
call for armed Jewish resistance was premature and remained on paper only,
but it was symptomatic of his reasoning that force was the only way to change
the Jewish orientation and meet the Nazi threat. In the atmosphere of the
unoccupied zone in summer 1940, Knout could win the allegiance of only
a select few, who directed their energies to assisting Jews in the internment
camps.[41]

Most Eastern European Jews, however, seem to have been closer to
Tcherikower's perspective than to either the Communist or the ultra-
nationalist approach. Aware of their precarious status, they avoided fo-
menting conflict with the authorities and resigned themselves to the developments. Within this volatile situation, they too preferred the outlook of
attentisme and placed their hopes in observing the law, but to no avail. The
many anti-immigrant and anti-Semitic measures initiated by Vichy from late
August pushed the immigrant Jews into a most vulnerable predicament. Far
more than the *Statut des Juifs*, the "law concerning foreigners of the Jewish
race" of 4 October 1940 undermined their security. Published on 18 October
in the *Journal Officiel* on the same day as the *statut*, the law granted prefects
of the free zone the absolute right to intern foreign Jews in French internment camps or to place them under police supervision in assigned residences.
Nothing like the emotional soul-searching that characterized native Jewry's
response to the *statut* followed. Not surprisingly, direct protests were also
rare. The law of 4 October had far graver consequences for the immigrant
Jews than did the *statut* for native Jews. Stripped of their fundamental rights
and security, the immigrant Jews turned their attention elsewhere, especially
towards the upkeep of the community. Vichy had created a clear differentiation in the plight of two communities, and one that would leave its imprint
on the organizational responses to the fall of France.

Jewish Organizational Response to the German Occupation

As Paris was being overrun by the German army, a group of immigrant
leaders convened in June 1940 to discuss the social and political consequences of France's collapse. Various representatives of welfare and relief
societies associated with FSJF, together with members of more politically

orientated organizations (Arbeiter-Ring, Bund, Poalei-Zion) put aside pre-war antagonisms to extend their support to the immigrant community. Discussions revolved around ways to procure more substantial resources for relief activity, both from within the community and from international relief organizations, and around the need for some basic welfare functions—infirmaries, children's homes, public canteens, and relief centers. In deciding to form a special clandestine committee, known as Rue Amelot, the participants played down ideological differences in deference to social considerations. Colonie Scolaire, established in 1926 as an affiliate of FSJF to deal with immigrant children, became the legal framework through which Amelot operated, while FSJF agreed to put at the committee's disposal the limited resources it possessed prior to evacuating the northern zone.[42] A first step towards united action had been taken.

An examination of the committee's initial operations in the summer of 1940 shows that the community's needs were extensive and increasing rapidly. Forty-five thousand meals had been served by the various canteens during the summer months, and Amelot feared a further deterioration in the community's economic stability, while it saw itself falling into a serious financial crisis. Save for a subsidy from the foremost Jewish relief organization, the American Jewish Joint Distribution Committee (Joint), Amelot was cut off from international Jewish support and abandoned by the French-Jewish relief organizations.[43] With its back against the wall, Amelot initiated two courses of action. As the umbrella organization of several welfare agencies, it called upon wealthy Jews in the Seine region to coordinate a major appeal to save the relief centers. Rabbi Julien Weill, the Chief Rabbi of Paris, who returned to the city in August, supported the project, but the community showed general disinterest and contributed little.[44] Amelot looked for another way out of its financial predicament—it made overtures to the French-Jewish establishment to unify the community.

In September 1940 one of Amelot's founding fathers, David Rapoport, proposed to Rabbi Weill to overlook former conflicts and bring together the depleted leadership of both communities. Rapoport, who was FSJF's central figure in Paris at the time, was the first northern leader to recognize the indispensability of unification for meeting the social needs. Weill's focus remained on the immigrant issue, and he rejected the offer outright. Native Jews, he stressed, were hesitant to ally themselves with the immigrants.[45] Weill even withstood the pressure of the Joint officials. Pursuing Joint policy to unite relief organs in Europe, Weill was encouraged to establish a committee together with immigrant leaders to represent French Jewry and raise funds from the community. But Weill was adamant: ostensibly he feared that such a committee might provide the German authorities "an opportunity and a basis for levying fines against the Jewish community,"[46] but in reality native Jewry's disinterest in the fate of the immigrant Jews remained the obstacle. Faced with their obstinacy, Herbert Katzki of the Joint looked favorably at German attempts to establish a "Gemeinde"—maybe the German authorities would force the Jews to care for their own. In any event, Amelot's financial troubles persisted; the bulk of its budget for 1940 went to four public canteens, supported by Joint money (500,000 francs) and transferred by the American Friends Service Committee (the Quakers).[47] Only in September did native Jewry begin to help out: the bastion of philanthropic work, the Comité de bienfaisance israélite (CBI), established in 1809, reopened its doors to the public and was immediately swamped with requests for aid. However, never a forerunner of concern for the immigrant Jews, the CBI soon reverted to its traditional pattern.[48] Into this vacuum of communal cooperation entered SS-Hauptsturmführer Theodor Dannecker, appointed by Adolf Eichmann to head the Paris branch of the Gestapo's bureau IV B$_4$, specializing in Jewish affairs.

Together with numerous German agencies dealing with economic, military, political, and legal matters, a special police division was sent to Paris in the summer of 1940. Commonly known as the SD (Sicherheitsdient) or the "Gestapo," the Security Police in France were headed by SS-Obersturm-führer Helmut Knochen and were part of Reinhard Heydrich's massive Reich Security Division, the RSHA (Reichssicherheitshauptamt). A department within Knochen's RSHA Paris operation was devoted to Jewish issues (the Judenreferat), and Dannecker was its first head. This particular office was to initiate and expedite anti-Jewish actions and to struggle bitterly with the other German agencies for sovereignty over the "Jewish Question" and the right to impose Jewish policy. A young and brash officer, Dannecker brought with him the experience of three years of close cooperation with Eichmann in Abt. II-112 of the RSHA and in the expulsion of the Jews from Austria— good training for the job at hand.[49] In line with that training, Dannecker sought out responsible Jewish leaders. That coincided with the return of Julien Weill to Paris.

In September 1940 the Chief Rabbi, Rabbi Marcel Sachs, and the Judenreferat met for the first time. Dannecker was straightforward: the Paris Consistory must set up a central Jewish organization for Paris and the Seine region to deal with all political, social, and cultural problems relating to the Jewish population. The organization was to be obligatory for all Jews and was intended to isolate them from French citizens in a form of social ghettoization, to correspond with the measures taken against Jewish economic activity. Interested in establishing an authoritative body, Dannecker emphasized the importance the SD attached to the matter: by late October a German law would finalize the process, and if the Paris Consistory failed to come through, grave consequences would follow for the Jewish leadership and population. Moreover, Dannecker had already established a liaison with the French authorities in Jean François of the Paris prefecture of police and had directed him to prepare a set of regulations for the proposed organization. Whether it had already been submitted to the Consistory leaders or was submitted at a later date is unclear, but it drove home Dannecker's point.[50]

Representing the Paris Consistory's orientation, Weill and Sachs rejected Dannecker's demand on a legal basis. Basing their position on the separation of church and state in France (1905), they contended that Consistory members could lawfully engage in religious affairs alone but had no authority in other areas of activity. Consistorial authority was, moreover, limited to its 6,000 members, and neither it nor the rabbinical federation could coerce Jews to join a new organization. The Consistory's legalistic approach was upheld by François, who temporarily helped to block Dannecker's efforts. Seeing the Consistory's stubbornness, Dannecker tried to coax the prefecture of police into creating the organization by French law; but the prefecture refused. Later on, according to one report, François was won over by Dannecker and completely conformed to his demands on the "Jewish Question."[51] The Consistory had thus succeeded in withstanding Dannecker's first thrust.

Negotiations with Dannecker proceeded during autumn 1940, while in the background the anti-Jewish measures were being passed with no letup. Weill and Sachs remained firm. They received further encouragement from the Amelot committee, which overlooked Weill's opposition to their unity proposal, and established an informal forum with Amelot representatives (Rapoport, Leo Glaeser, and Yehuda Jakoubowicz). Dannecker, who was simultaneously vying with the other German agencies in Paris for sovereignty over the "Jewish Question," was determined to get the organization off the ground and show his efficiency. Without the legal support of Vichy and with the disinterest of the German military administration, he continued to pressure the Jews directly. They themselves would have to be maneuvered into setting up the organization. Interestingly enough, Dannecker ignored at this stage the existence of the immigrant operations. Amelot openly administered several highly populated canteens, but for some reason Dannecker neglected to negotiate with any of its constituent agencies.[52]

The standstill was counterproductive for Dannecker. Frustrated with the Consistory, he looked elsewhere; he apparently asked General André Boris, a highly respected native Jew outside the Consistory circle, to assume the leadership of the community. However, Boris was encouraged to refuse the nomination, since it could have implied that the Jews were constituting themselves as a national minority.[53] After reportedly negotiating with other Jewish personalities in Paris with similar results, Dannecker changed his tactics. Returning to the Consistory stronghold in November, he tried to cajole its members into reorganizing the community's philanthropic efforts to prepare for economic hardship. This time Dannecker maneuvered with a carrot in one hand and a stick in the other: he appointed Marcel Sachs as the head of French Jewry and gave him the authority to arrest any Jew who refused to provide assistance in creating the organization. Yet, he also authorized Sachs to appeal to the Jewish population to bolster the community's resources; as a ploy, Dannecker offered to deduct the contribution from an obligatory tax to be imposed shortly on the Jews.[54]

Dannecker had finally fallen upon the right approach: the needs of the community were being sorely felt by the Chief Rabbi and others. On 24 November 1940, an appeal censured and emendated by Dannecker's office was sent out to some 6,000 Jewish merchants according to a list provided by the Paris prefecture of police. The public appeal called for support of the relief activity while tempting the community with Dannecker's ruse on the tax deduction.[55] But Sachs was also ordered to call a meeting of Jewish leaders involved in relief work to discuss the necessity of a centralized Jewish body. Again, it was Dannecker who provided the names, which were obtained from the former head of the Union of Polish Jews, Dr. Reichman. Reichman's list consisted of the foremost immigrant personalities in Paris, who were all summoned to "hear the authorities' exposé of the modifications to be carried out in the organization of our Parisian community."[56]

The meeting took place in Dannecker's presence on 2 December 1940. Amelot representatives, who figured prominently on Reichman's list, boycotted the meeting, leaving the negotiations to the Paris Consistory and one immigrant spokesman, Jacques Rabinowicz. Dannecker set forth his basic proposition: if the relief agencies wished to continue their activities, they would have to do so within a united framework.[57] That was not a popular suggestion, and after the encounter, intensive communal discussions ensued. Rabbis, social workers, and representatives of the different agencies aired their hesitations and apprehensions but were also disturbed by their dwindling financial resources. Faced with the dismal results of the November appeal and Dannecker's underhanded exploitation of the funds, Amelot and the Paris Consistory reached a common perspective: refusal would destroy the fabric of Jewish relief work. Evidently the joint liaison between the immigrant and native leaders had mitigated their mutual distrust and opened up a sense of common fate.[58]

In this spirit, and at Dannecker's prodding, Sachs invited Jakoubowicz of Colonie Scolaire to align Amelot's affiliated societies with the Consistory's to improve the community's services.[59] Although promised an autonomous existence within the new arrangements, Amelot members reverted to their basic distrust of anything that hinted of German inspiration. Once again the traditional positions within Amelot reasserted themselves. The more politically oriented groups, Bund and Left Poalei-Zion, opposed merger, while the relief societies, OSE and Colonie Scolaire, rallied behind David Rapoport's outlook. The social fervor of this Russian Jew was boundless. Undogmatic and bearing no grudges, Rapoport spoke frankly. Invoking "Jewish solidarity" and confronting the vital community needs, he endorsed participation—native French Jewry must not be left alone with the entire responsibility.[60] Rapoport's position was accepted, and Glaeser and Jakoubowicz were appointed Amelot's delegates to the initial meeting of the organization on 30 January 1941. Brought together under the aegis of the Comité de Bienfaisance, the participants resolved to form the Comité de Coordination des Ouevres de Bienfaisance du Grand Paris (Comité) with an underlying principle: organizational coordination would by no means reduce the operational and financial autonomy of each participating body.[61] The Comité was born. Dannecker had finally brought about its creation; he had intimidated the Consistory into disavowing some of its legalistic considerations and assuming leadership of the organization. A "voluntary" Jewish body was formed, which preempted French or German legislation.

Modeled after the German Reichsvereinigung, the central Jewish organization of German Jews set up in 1939, the Comité allowed Dannecker to boast of a certain success—a cornerstone in the anti-Jewish edifice was laid. Only a few days before the Comité convened, Dannecker had already forecast its emergence: in a detailed report on the state of the "Jewish Question" in Paris in which he had deplored the lack of a "central Jewish office" operated by the French, he had pointed out the necessary conditions for evacuating the Jews from France and singled out the importance of a compulsory Jewish organization "already in formation." The Comité was to facilitate the solution of the "Jewish Question"—as it was currently perceived by the Nazis— Jewish emigration to an unknown territory.[62] An excellent student of Eichmann's, Dannecker wanted to duplicate the Austrian scenario and bring about a rapid and efficient deportation of Jews from France. His conception of the Comité stood in total contradiction to the way the Jewish leaders imagined its functioning.

Immigrant and native Jewish leaders overcame their opposition to Dannecker in order to improve their relief activity. OSE, Amelot, the Comité de Bienfaisance, and the Association Philanthropique de l'Asile de Nuit de Jour et de la Crêche viewed the Comité as a unique experiment in uniting the different community operations, although each had reservations about the German involvement. More legalistically oriented and hoping to avoid German intervention, the Consistory resolved to set up the Comité on the basis of a French law of 1901 pertaining to private associations, and thereby make it subject to French law and jurisdiction. But for the immigrant leadership the legal crutch was not sufficient support. Apprehensive throughout the negotiations, Amelot made the commitment with a heavy heart. The economic pressure on the immigrant community was too great for it not to accept a possible means of alleviation.[63] This same approach had prompted the Jewish Communists in Solidarité to seek admission to Amelot and, according to one report, to the Comité, as well. In both cases political and judicial antagonisms prevented Solidarité's inclusion, although its involvement in relief work (a public canteen in Paris) certainly qualified it for participation. Rejected by the Comité, Solidarité continued to function independently, combining social and political concerns, and could later claim to have avoided any official contact with the Germans.[64] The Comité and the SD were now left to struggle for the implementation of their mutually exclusive goals.

Focusing on the Comité's insufficient support from the community, the SD watched over the development in several key areas: the joint appeal, coordination of relief work, and preparation of a copy of the census of the Jewish population of the unoccupied zone ordered by the Germans on 27 September 1940. Furthermore, it showed particular interest in the publication of a communal weekly by the Comité and encouraged a joint budget for the participant organizations. The extent of SD involvement in these "technical matters" is evidence of the division's intention: to guarantee a self-sufficient, isolated Jewish community under the control and supervision of the Comité.[65] Originally an SD official was to be planted in the Comité offices to watch carefully over all its transactions, but the Comité's objection resulted in a different form of contact. An SD officer, Lieutenant Dobershütz, met occasionally with Marcel Sachs or Albert Weill to receive a periodic report on issues of German interest. The SD quickly realized that no dramatic changes in the community's unification or in the state of the relief works had resulted from the Comité's formation. Relief agencies remained in a dismal situation, and the Comité was in constant need of funds. Sachs tried to procure a release of the funds accumulated as a result of the appeal, but the German authorities clearly wanted something in return: a declaration by all Comité members of their complete obedience to Sachs's instructions. No such statement ensued. The Comité resumed its community appeal, now pressing the Jews of the unoccupied zone to contribute their share.[66]

Faced with the Comité's inertia, Dannecker showed his inventiveness. He appeared in mid-March with two Jews from Austria, Leo Israelowicz and Wilhelm Biberstein. Dannecker explained to Sachs the meaning of their presence: the Comité had failed to put the relief work into action and had shown general inefficiency. In short, he was unsatisfied and had decided to bring in two "technical advisors," who would serve as the liaison between the German authorities and the Jewish community. Their actions and orders were to have the authority of the occupying power; they would immediately be expected to publish a community journal. Their arrival was to shake the foundations of the Comité and disrupt the equilibrium between the native and immigrant leadership.

Biberstein and Israelowicz remain somewhat of a mystery. Having had no past involvement in the Viennese Jewish community or any other notable activity, they obviously came in contact with Dannecker during his Viennese post. Brought to Paris to instruct the community in the art of communal affairs, they immediately became the source of antagonism and renewed the discussion on participation in the Comité. Dannecker had made it clear— the German authorities in France were not bound to a legalistic framework, and, as in Germany, they could establish a committee to fit their needs.[67] Simultaneously, Dannecker was pressuring the French authorities to bring about the "central Jewish office." Having settled issues with competing German agencies, Dannecker received Admiral François Darlan's acceptance in principle at the beginning of March. On 29 March 1941, the Commissariat-General for Jewish Affairs (CGQJ) was established in Vichy, with jurisdiction over all of France, and Xavier Vallat was nominated as commissioner. Recently appointed secretary of the Légion Française des Combattants, a French veterans' league, Vallat was known to be both an arch French nationalist and anti-German, but his indisputable record of anti-Semitism made his selection acceptable to the Germans. Although consulted neither on the commissariat's statutes nor on the commissioner's appointment, Dannecker felt satisfied. On both fronts—the Jewish and the French—he got what he wanted, two arms to push forward Berlin's anti-Jewish decrees.[68] The stage was set.

The Comité de Coordination in Transition

The arrival of the Viennese Jews cast a serious doubt on Dannecker's promise of autonomous existence for the Comité. Meeting with them on 27 March, the Comité immediately recognized a new thrust: Israelowicz expressed reservations about Sachs's authority and the need for a more binding commitment between him and the Comité's members. A legalistic discussion revolving around the intent of the French laws of 1901 and 1905 on religious associations concealed the real issue: whether the Comité could conform to the new situation without disrupting the organization's autonomous existence. Rapoport and Glaeser skillfully attempted to avoid a direct confrontation. Ordered by Amelot to reject total subservience and a declaration of allegiance, they nonetheless looked for a loophole. Their apprehensions were shared by all. Word by word, the Comité members worked over a statement whose final formulation omitted the connotations of being German agents.

Sachs was formally elected president of the Comité, and all the members signed a declaration "by which they obliged to follow his instructions, conforming to the Authorities' directions."[69] Dannecker was to be given the meeting's minutes and the said declaration. But the German pressure did not end there. Previous demands to publish a community journal and formally establish the Comité with defined regulations were now pushed to the top of the agenda: Israelowicz and Biberstein were entrusted with the task.

The Comité had previously raised a host of technical issues, trying to gain time and avoid a formal establishment. Claiming, among other things, a lack of mandate from the community, the Comité refused to present a statement of purpose and the demanded regulations. These dilatory tactics were summarily discarded. Dannecker ordered the Comité to register with the prefecture of police or face the consequences. The Comité was taxed. To circumvent a German statute, it worked up its own, which was vague with regard to critical issues and avoided others: Parisian Jewry was not forced to participate; financial autonomy of the affiliated organizations was guaranteed, while the publication of a communal bulletin remained a Comité prerogative. No time was lost. At a meeting on 31 March, Sachs read off his proposal, and Israelowicz and Biberstein countered with theirs. Comité members still hoped to postpone the whole affair and reopened the debate, claiming that a German ordinance of August 1940 had made it illegal to establish new organizations. They even proposed a legal arbitration, but the decisions had been made. Sachs had already been summoned by Dannecker for the following day, and the Comité was forced to enter its final emenations.

On 1 April, the statute was presented to Dannecker together with an official declaration on the establishment of the Comité for the prefecture of police. To legalize the role of the Viennese, Dannecker demanded one revision, a regulation allowing the Comité to draft individuals unaffiliated with the relief works. He overlooked the fact that only four organizations were part of the founding committee, and he did not obligate them to coerce others into joining. Dannecker had reason to believe that that would be achieved by other methods.[70] Within two weeks, via Israelowicz and Biberstein, Dannecker turned the Comité into a formal institution (the Coordinating Committee of the Relief Works of Greater Paris) but also destroyed its unity. Having already split with Amelot over the declaration of allegiance, the leftist organizations became vitriolic in their criticism, pushing Amelot to the brink. The community publication, the next measure instigated by the two outcasts, intensified Amelot's dilemma even more.

Israelowicz and Biberstein were expected from the outset to put out a weekly for an estimated 65,000 Jewish families. Owing to the Comité's reluctance to publish a bulletin associated with the authorities, prior German attempts had gone awry. Unexpectedly, on 19 April 1941 "Informations Juives" appeared, prepared by the Viennese and containing an article by the Chief Rabbi of Paris. It called upon the community to identify with the Comité and contribute generously for the needy, but it conditioned support on affiliation.[71] Widely distributed, "Informations Juives" placed before the Comité a fait accompli, a bulletin slanted towards coaxing Jews into joining the Comité was being published in its name, apparently without prior consultation and discussion. Greeted with anger and disbelief within the community, the publication occasioned illegal leaflets condemning the Comité's collaboration with the Germans, and wagging an accusing finger at the two "Galician Jews" occupying the Consistory offices.[72] Even the native Jews felt a definite discomfort. Pierre Masse, the senator from Hérault and one of the few prominent Jews who had returned to Paris, censured the publication and concession to German demands. Though distant from community affairs, Masse was critical of Sachs's handling of the negotiations.[73] But most shaken by the publication was the Amelot leadership. Feeling guilty by association, Amelot members who had begrudgingly signed the pledge of allegiance now saw that as a foolhardy act. Glaeser and Rapoport joined Left Poalei-Zion and the Bund in advocating resignation. Their decision followed the respective interrogation of Rapoport and Jakoubowicz by Dannecker and Israelowicz for their opposition to the Comité's activity. Threatened with his life, Rapoport was also ordered to sign a personal pledge to Dannecker to refrain from further relief work. Nevertheless, Amelot procrastinated and only on 12 May submitted its resignation from the Comité.[74] The intervention of Rabbi Julien Weill succeeded momentarily in postponing its decision.

The native Jews on the Comité and Rabbi Weill had become more accepting of the immigrant leadership and sincerely wanted to prevent a rupture. They too were upset by the single-handed methods of Israelowicz and Biberstein, but they viewed them in a different context, within the French political sphere. Vallat's appointment as commissioner was a hopeful sign, Weill reasoned, and the Comité's resignation would only antagonize him. Aware of the accusations of anti-Semitism leveled against Vallat by Paris extremists (as in the rightist newspaper *Au Pilori*), but not blinded by his position on the "Jewish Question," native Jews proposed a period of grace before encumbering his position with the German authorities. Their argument was not totally dismissed by certain immigrant leaders, who also expected a change for the better.[75] But Israelowicz and Biberstein's persistent attempts to rally support for the Comité alienated the Amelot leaders and doomed the unification talks. Amelot did not completely sever relations with the Comité, but aside from Dr. Eugene Minkowski of OSE, who remained active,[76] the Comité was stripped of its major immigrant representation on the eve of the first massive internment of immigrant Jews.

On 13 May the Paris prefecture of police summoned some 5,000 immigrant Jews to report on the following day to designated police stations. Severe punishments were threatened to those who failed to appear. The German order was meticulously followed by the French police. On 14 May, 3,733 male Jews were assembled and sent off to French internment camps at Pithiviers and Beaune-la-Rolande in the Loiret area of the occupied zone. The community was stunned, no less by the mass internment itself than by the smooth collaboration between the French police and the German authorities. Whereas the immigrant organizations responded immediately with plans for helping the inmates, the Comité was rather lax, overly preoccupied with its own process of reorganization. Having had no prior information or involvement in the arrests, the Comité was at this juncture not condemned for its role. Dannecker, however, blamed the Jews themselves for the internment, attributing their arrests to their antagonistic attitude towards the Comité. He threatened them with more arrests if no change followed.[77]

The mass internment aggravated the already serious socioeconomic situation of the Jews in Paris. Since October 1940, French and German regulations had struck hard at the economic basis of the Jewish community. The toll was great, especially among the immigrant Jews, whose heavy concentration in the French textile industry provoked a sharp anti-Jewish response. Widespread dismissal of immigrant Jews forced hundreds to seek their daily meals at Jewish canteens, raising to over 2,500 those who availed themselves of these services. But Jewish business enterprises also were coming under fire. The process of the French takeover (Aryanization) of Jewish businesses was becoming a primary concern of French and German authorities, severely weakening the economic capacity of the more comfortable Jews. The mass internment created additional impoverishment. Hundreds of families were in immediate need of relief, while thousands of inmates lacked a basic diet in the camps. The excitement in the immigrant community reached an unprecedented height, alarmingly expressed by the journalist Jacques Biélinky.

> Enormous emotion among the Jewish population following the massive arrests. Thousands of women with children left without assistance are in danger of starving to death. Several of the inmates' wives went to the commissioners of police demanding to be fed.[78]

Israelowicz utilized this new predicament to reemphasize the importance of extending the Comité's public support. In a special meeting with Comité members and Jewish notables on 20 May, he announced that aid would be conditional upon a major campaign effort for the Comité. Realizing the Comité's failure among the immigrants, a Yiddish edition of "Informations

Juives" was suggested, as well as public appearances by the Viennese in Jewish circles.[79] Moreover, Israelowicz and Biberstein did not take Amelot's resignation lightly and together with Dannecker pressured the Comité for further immigrant representatives. Upon meeting Sachs's temporary replacement, Alphonse Weil, Dannecker let him know his expectations: an equal proportion of immigrant and native Jews on the Comité's staff and council, corresponding to the demographic division of Parisian Jewry.[80] (Dannecker was still relying on the German census of October 1940, which showed an equal proportion of French and immigrant Jews among the 148,024 Parisian Jews.) Weil was forced to look outside the Amelot affiliates. He found a Russian-born Jew active in the Fédération, Elie Krouker. A rather flamboyant character, Krouker brought to the Comité a well-assimilated immigrant Jew: with his past experience in relief work, with both native and immigrant societies, and his involvement in a veterans' association, he seemed fit for the task.[81] But beyond him Weil was unsuccessful. Nor was it easier finding prominent native Jews. Few remained in occupied Paris, and even fewer were willing to assume communal responsibility and give a boost to the Comité. One who did offer his services was Julien Weill's nephew, André Baur.

For André Baur the decision to join the Comité was one of commitment. Thirty-seven years old and the father of four, with no particular background in relief work, he was Weill's choice to improve the Comité's moral standing in the community. Baur could not hide his class or status. A wealthy Parisian banker and president of the Reform congregation on rue Copernic, he came from the Consistory circle. But it was the individual behind the aristocratic veneer that won Baur the respect of all. No one questioned his motives, and everyone regarded his entry into the difficult situation as an act of sacrifice. He was first presented to Dannecker on 21 May by Alphonse Weil, who claimed to have assumed Sachs's role on the condition that Baur be by his side.[82] In the background rumors circulated of a new statute on the Jews.[83]

However, even before Baur and Krouker were able to turn the Comité into a viable organ, they were faced with Weil's arrest in reprisal for failing to produce an enlarged committee. Furthermore, Minkowski and Jakoubowicz expressed their dissatisfaction with the Comité's new orientation, maintaining that individuals without prior qualifications were overrunning the Comité and were detrimental to its work.[84] They themselves were on the verge of cutting all ties, but Minkowski agreed to participate in further deliberations to revamp the Comité. These took place in the tense atmosphere of June 1941. Baur, who had become the central figure, set the tone:

> The situation is severe and whether we like it or not it is seen as a Jewish problem. The measures taken and those to be taken affect us all to different

degrees. We will have to make decisions which may bind the future of our
coreligionists.[85]

The discussions led to the creation of a new Comité, bringing together
some new personalities (Georges Edinger, Elie Danon, Fernand Musnik,
Alexandre Klein) drafted by Baur and Krouker. Following Amelot's lead,
Minkowksi wanted out. Their departure created a vacuum in the Comité,
as they were the lifeline to the immigrant community and the professional
community workers. Moreover, they resigned, casting aspersions on Krouker's integrity. Reported to have flaunted his new position as general secretary of the Comité, Krouker spoke favorably of the German occupation
and publicly advocated collaboration. He was soon seen by Baur as a liability
to the organization's revitalization and was dismissed in early July, amid
denunciations as a "Jewish Quisling."[86] His replacement was Marcel Stora,
a French-born translator, who had worked in the thirties as a journalist but
lacked experience in relief work. Referred to Baur by Juliette Stern, a WIZO
leader and future colleague, Stora was proficient in German and well acquainted with the different social and political tendencies in the community.
But above all he came to the Comité as a reputable individual. He accepted
the post only on the condition that if he was unable to avoid regrettable
incidents, he would be allowed to resign. His first test was to lessen the
influence of the Viennese by joining them in the editorship of "Informations
Juives."[87] With Stora's entry, the Comité adopted a new tactic. Rather than
continue Sachs's passive opposition and leave the front open to the "Viennese" influence, the Comité decided to push forward its own programs for
the community's benefit. But the immigrant community was still uncon-
vinced.

Parisian Jewry reverted to the friction of the thirties. After being momentarily united by German pressure, the community was again at odds as
a result of German maneuvering. Israelowicz and Biberstein were only symp-
toms; social and political perceptions coupled with natural tendencies of the
two communities were the real cause of the renewed antagonism. Yet a
major difference existed between the conflict of the thirties and that of 1941:
the native Jewish leaders in the Comité sincerely wanted cooperation for
the community's welfare and rejected the Consistory's patronizing attitude
of the thirties. But in 1941 the Comité was also opposed by a more militant
immigrant leadership. The Jewish Communists, who had gained grass-roots
support in the Parisian workers' districts, blamed the Comité for the lack of
concern about the mass internment in May 1941. In late July it organized
a large-scale demonstration against the Comité, clamoring for the release of
the inmates. For several consecutive days, scores of women crowded into
the Comité's offices, angrily blamed its officials for the arrests, and disrupted

its affairs. On one occasion, Stora prevented Israelowicz from calling in the police, but a few days later, the French police were brought in to remove the demonstrators.[88] Although nobody was arrested, this turn of events stigmatized the Comité among the immigrant Jews and further hampered Baur's attempt to strengthen it. Implicated by the authorities and condemned by Solidarité, the revamped Comité still felt driven to direct the community's affairs in a consolidated way. The recent legal measures and continued internments of immigrant Jews weighed heavily in their considerations.

The second Vichy *Statut des Juifs*, of 2 June 1941, had extended the definition of a Jew to include baptized Jews with three Jewish grandparents, which incurred the wrath of Christian circles and of many assimilated Jews. But the statute's immediate impact was in the economic sphere. By making it legal to oust Jews from the liberal professions, the statute hit hard at middle-class Jews and increased the community's impoverishment.[89] Following Vichy's active Aryanization and liquidation of Jewish public and private property, the statute impressed upon the Comité the need to alleviate the growing economic difficulties.

Renewing its call for support from Parisian Jewry ("Appeal to All Jews"), the Comité unveiled a new approach in early August: not only were the names of Israelowicz and Biberstein removed from the announcement, but the Comité's projects were emphasized.[90] Looking beyond support of the poor and the unfortunate, the Comité sought assistance for creating retraining centers, agricultural farms, and societies for the protection of youth. Parisian Jewry was compelled to find new sources of livelihood during these anti-Semitic times, and it was the community's responsibility to recognize this priority. The appeal embodied the Comité's direction since Baur had taken over. Turning to the German military authorities in late June, it had requested agricultural training schools for Jews.[91] Members of the Comité were convinced that if Jews were able to show the French population an ability to work the land, anti-Semitic arguments would be quashed and "the Jewish question would evolve in France in a totally different way."[92] They pursued the project further with officials of the Commissariat and Ministry of Labor and seem to have received enough encouragement that they tried to enlist the community's commitment.[93]

Hard-pressed to deal with the economic plight, the Comité leaders allowed themselves the naïve fantasy of a quick solution to the "Jewish problem," which would also be, or so they thought, of great service to French agriculture. Their appeal was full of enthusiasm; solidarity and concern for the future must replace individual egoism. Moreover, a voluntary contribution could avert an imposed German tax. The Comité's utopian intentions of restructuring the community's sources of employment needed wide-scale community support and backing from the authorities, but neither was forthcoming. The appeal neglected the burning issue for the immigrant Jews, the state of the interned in the Loiret camps, and at any rate could not expect significant assistance from that sector of the Jewish population;[94] and native Jews who had the means to back the Comité still did not accept its ideal that "the excess of some must assure the needs of the others."[95] Ultimately it was German policy that destroyed the Comité's project.

In response to the Comité's proposals for an agricultural solution to the "Jewish problem," Dannecker countered with the demand that the Comité must recruit thousands of Jews for agricultural work in the Ardennes. This proposal had already been made several weeks earlier but had been turned down by the Comité; now the Comité members were under direct pressure to comply. They were called together for an urgent meeting on 18 August. Jakoubowicz, representing Amelot, also participated. Stora presented Dannecker's plan for 6,000 males and females to be employed by a German firm, "Ostland"; their salaries would be forwarded to the Comité, which after covering its expenses would pay the workers; the fruits of their labor would be French profit and not transferred to Germany. But above all, on fulfillment of the request, Dannecker promised an end to arrests and a general liberation of those interned.[96] Stora also related Dannecker's stipulation that the participants must sign the meeting's protocol designating the number of recruits they could each assemble. Except for one, all present signed the protocol but refused to be responsible for the recruitment. Stora was openly opposed to the project and feared the implication of turning the Comité into a Gestapo agent. Subsequently, he prepared a statement, not included in the official protocol, in which he reiterated the Comité's support for professional retraining while categorically refusing to be responsible for the massive recruitment.[97] Well aware of the difference between the two orientations, Stora worked behind the scenes to dissuade Jews from registering. His efforts were commended by Amelot, which believed that "a great danger suspended over the heads of the active members of the Jewish relief works" was thereby avoided.[98] But the Comité's hopes of economic reorientation were overshadowed by a more serious German move.

The international imbroglio had a national impact. Germany's war with the Soviet Union prompted in mid-August a nationwide attack against Communists and fellow travelers. For Jews, who were seen as an integral part of the Jewish-Communist conspiracy, the consequences were far-reaching. On 20 August the heavily populated eleventh arrondissement of Paris was cordoned off, and more than 4,000 native and immigrant Jews were herded off to Drancy, the newly established makeshift camp northeast of Paris. Held there as "Communist suspects," they were soon joined by 50 Jewish lawyers and small groups of immigrant Jews arrested in three other Parisian arrondissements (nine, ten, and eighteen). The turmoil and terror of May 1941 returned to the community.[99] In this atmosphere, the Comité's ambitious propositions died for lack of support. All that it could do was to resist Dannecker's pressure for further recruitment for the Ardennes. Stora faced Dannecker's continuous threats respectably. On the one hand, he published the official notice demanded by the Germans, but on the other hand, he discouraged applicants. To the Germans, he explained the community's reluctance as an outgrowth of the internments.[100] All told, some 200 Jews (mostly immigrants and including Jews liberated from internment camps) volunteered for the Ardennes project, where they worked under extremely harsh conditions. Dannecker's proposal had at the time nothing to do with the "Final Solution," and it was opposed on the grounds that it aided the Germans, but the Ardennes eventually became a trap for the majority of the laborers. In December 1943 they were arrested and deported to Auschwitz.

Dannecker's basic plan for the Ardennes was thwarted, and his threats to hold the Comité's executive responsible were never carried out. He also failed to respond to the ousting of Israelowicz and Biberstein from their key positions in the Comité. By adding Stora to "Informations Juives" and establishing a presidency whose meetings brought together only bona fide relief workers and the executive, the "Viennese" influence was curtailed.[101] Dannecker had also shown disinterest in the merger of those organizations (including Colonie Scolaire and the Paris Consistory) that he had coerced into joining the Comité in July-August 1941. Possibly he was already looking forward to the new umbrella organization then under discussion. At any rate, he allowed the Comité freedom of activity until December 1941. In the absence of his intervention and frequent pressure, the Comité directed its efforts to the social realm, specifically to extension of the canteen service, development of youth activities, aid and welfare to families, and relief to internment camps. Yet, never well supported by the Parisian community, the Comité was unable to deal with the growing number of relief applicants. By January 1942 it had reached a high of 6,057 members, but only 4,096 of them actually paid regular dues.[102]

The Comité's major activity was the operation of the canteen service. Here it worked closely with Amelot, which had no alternative other than to function via the legal apparatus. The Comité valued this important contact with the immigrant societies and gave Amelot almost complete independence, often making decisions on the basis of Amelot proposals. For example, new canteens were set up in immigrant areas to meet the dwindling resources of the populace. Aided in this operation by the Secours National, the French relief society, the canteens were serving almost 50,000 meals monthly by December 1941.[103] Comité leaders had become convinced of the need for a coordinated Jewish relief society and looked favorably on the deliberations taking place with the French for such an organ. More authority could strengthen their position in the community.[104]

Months had passed since Dannecker had made his first attempt to establish a unified Jewish community. The tables had since turned. In autumn 1940, native Jewish leaders had rebuffed both his pressure and the immigrant leaders' overtures, preferring to continue as in the days of emancipation, when each sector safeguarded its own achievements in society. By autumn 1941 native Jewish leaders saw the Comité as beneficial to the entire community and earnestly sought immigrant involvement. However, the year's events were hard on the immigrant leaders, both morally and physically, and by autumn 1941 they had little interest in participating in the Comité's operation. Their fleeting cooperation had been a unique moment in the Parisian Jewish community. In resigning, Amelot left the native Jews alone to carry the burden vis-à-vis the authorities and the community at large. From then on, Amelot and the Jewish Communists began to present an alternative leadership for the immigrant Jews, returning to the communal scene of the thirties: a basic split in leadership, with the native Jews representing the community before the authorities, and the immigrant Jews standing in opposition, attacking the Comité's decision to work within the system. The Comité's attempts to purge the Israelowicz-Biberstein influence, obtain material resources for community projects, and grant Amelot control of the canteens were considered incidental issues beside "collaboration" with the Germans and the ingrained distrust of native Jews' motives.

Jewish Organizational Response to the Fall of France in the Unoccupied Zone

The massive migration of Jews to the south of France created a balance in the Jewish population between the two zones. According to the various censuses initiated by the German and Vichy authorities in 1940–1941, it would appear that towards autumn of 1940, close to 150,000 Jews had settled in the unoccupied zone. They included the majority of the community leaders, who set up their headquarters in Marseilles and Lyon. Soon after the government established residence in Vichy, representatives of Jewish organizations sought permission to reactivate their operations to grant assistance to the thousands of needy refugees. Aware of Vichy's refugee orientation, the Jewish leaders tried to absolve the government of responsibility while avoiding further deterioration of the refugees' status. They emphasized the role of Jewish organizations in alleviating the government's burden, and the large sums of money poured in by the Joint for the refugees' upkeep and integration into the country's economy.[105] Trying to ward off disaster, Herbert Katzki of the Joint assembled the different relief works to create one central Jewish organization, to facilitate contact with the Joint. His meetings with leaders of OSE, CAR, the Fédération, and the Rothschild operations in July 1940 hinted at the initial influences of the fall of France on Jewish organizations and at their hesitation to establish a voluntary umbrella organization.

Summer 1940 was a tense period in the unoccupied zone, especially for foreigners. Publicly blamed for France's defeat and the target of several legislative regulations limiting their freedom of movement, they were viewed suspiciously, along with Freemasons and Jews. Immigrant Jews were the focus of special treatment. Some 6,307 Jews were among those who lost their citizenship by virtue of a French law of 22 July 1940.[106] The pursuit of "undesirable elements" affected the Jewish community with similar intensity. As the French advocated France for the French, Jewish leaders called for a completely "French community." The conflict and lack of trust that had characterized immigrant-native relations in the thirties were revived in summer 1940, and the aggressive positions of native leaders were reechoed. Leaders of French relief organizations—CAR (Albert Lévy and Gaston Kahn) and the Rothschild representative (Georges Picard)—contended that in such a volatile time, when talk of imposing Nuremberg Laws on French Jewry was in the air, there was no room for a unified committee of native and immigrant Jews. Though not opposed to cooperating with Fédération (FSJF) leaders, they demanded ultimate responsibility for all decisions and the delegation of sole representation before the authorities to Jews "deliberating and thinking 'French.' "[107] Even religious practice was affected by the xenophobia. At the French rabbinical assembly in Lyon in early September, certain rabbis favored restricting the function of *mohellim* (circumcisers) to native Jews.[108]

The Parisian scenario was repeated in the south. Immigrant leaders in FSJF appealed for unity of the relief organizations, looking beyond the present established bodies. Neither CAR nor FSJF should be allowed to determine community policy; an independent organ responsive to the needs of all sectors of the community was needed.[109] Thus, immigrant leaders were the first to respond to Katzki's endeavor, and they formed the majority of an ad hoc committee. Such an arrangement was doomed to failure, however. Representatives of the different organizations wanted to guarantee a direct Joint allocation of funds, stripping the ad hoc committee of any substantial influence. Mutual suspicions abounded, and all were concerned primarily with their own projects. By September 1940 discussions revolved around a new committee to be headed by Rabbi Schwartz, as native Jewish leaders had resolved to reassume the reins of leadership and reorganize the community.[110]

After receiving authorization from Vichy in September 1940 to return to relief work, community leaders encouraged Joseph Schwartz of the Joint to come to the south to coordinate their efforts and arrange a revised budget. In the discussions with Schwartz, a proposal by the former rabbi of Strasbourg, Rabbi René Hirschler, was seriously reviewed. Concerned with the community's welfare, Hirschler proposed "that the assistance be methodically organized and suggested that the Chief Rabbi initiate the coordination of all the relief and aid organizations in the free zone."[111] Once again the immigrant leaders, Jarblum included, approved the proposal and showed interest. Yet, at this stage, neither Rabbi Schwartz nor his close associate Rabbi Maurice Liber was convinced of such a necessity; they maintained a traditional view of the rabbi's functions. Schwartz was preoccupied with his dual task as Chief Rabbi and interim president of the Consistory and was more concerned with representing native Jewry before the French authorities.[112] In the end he was prevailed upon by Joe Schwartz to accept the task, and in mid-October he invited the leaders of the major relief organizations to convene in Marseilles. The meeting was given a limited purpose, to discuss the means available to avoid economic deterioration of the Jews and duplication of relief functions. Administrative and financial centralization was ruled out from the beginning.[113] Two weeks later, on 30–31 October 1940, in the shadow of Vichy's *Statut des Juifs*, representatives of the relief organizations met in Marseilles.

The delegates at Marseilles presented a detailed description of their organizations' affairs since their transfer to the south, each emphasizing his group's precarious financial state and the need to find urgent solutions to the abnormal economic structure of French Jewry. Reacting to the implications of the statute, several prominent figures proposed ways to increase Jewish participation in agriculture and industrial fields. Several far-reaching suggestions were made to bring thousands of Jews from the internment camps to special training centers, still to be built; Jews were to be encouraged to turn to agricultural and technical pursuits.[114] Troubled by anti-Semitic claims that Jews were unproductive and lacked creative skills, these leaders wanted both to counter the propaganda and possibly to merge with Vichy's "New Order." Their deliberations pointed to French Jewry's urgent requirements but also to its ill-preparedness to respond to the growing dislocation. It was Hirschler who rose to the occasion, rebuking the French Jewish leadership for abandoning the refugees' needs in the thirties. Now the leaders were faced with a more complicated task, to "undertake an action tenfold as difficult in the most trying times possible." For Hirschler, the statute of 1940 ushered in an era of hardship for French Jewry that could be countered only by a united body bent on improving the organizations' efficiency and establishing a joint community fund. But well aware of the community's isolationist tendencies and disunity, Hirschler remained practical: "Centralization must not paralyse anyone . . . it is desirable to centralize, but every excess should be avoided in this pursuit."[115] His candid presentation reflected the current of opinion; CCOJA (the Commission Centrale des Organisations Juives d'Assistance) was the outcome of the various compromises.

Bringing together the major Jewish relief works, CCOJA was to guarantee contacts with governmental and public authorities, to establish a communal fund, and to coordinate the various bodies within the community. Special committees were set up to deal with the pressing areas—internment camps, children's welfare, general assistance, emigration—and CCOJA saw as its main goal to direct French Jewry through the difficult period.[116] But the commission did not attempt to achieve real unification of the activities; it succumbed to the predominant current among the organizations. Continuing to object to CCOJA's control of their affairs, the organizations feared mostly indirect funding. Relying on the Joint for more than 70 percent of their budgets, both CAR and FSJF were reluctant to have their money divided among other projects. CCOJA was mostly decorative, but it served the purpose of showing the Joint French Jewry's serious attempts to unite and raise money locally. In effect, the agencies preferred the status quo and continued to vie for a larger portion of the Joint's support, preferring to reduce CCOJA's influence to a minimum.[117]

The Joint representatives correctly attributed CCOJA's formation to their prodding and astutely recognized the problems inherent in indirect funding; bitter discussions would weaken CCOJA before it got off the ground. Resigned to this stalemate, the Joint tried to further cooperation between CAR and FSJF while supporting them separately. But the Joint workers had no way of assessing the lingering conflict between the immigrant and native Jewish leadership.

CCOJA: Between Community and Individualism

Throughout the nineteenth and twentieth centuries, Jewish communities in Western and Central Europe bowed to emancipation and its temptations, often lauding the individual's success in society at the expense of the community's needs. The Hitler years placed this legacy of emancipation in a different light. Jewish leaders began to question the price of individualism and personal achievements and to value the community as the supreme entity that needed the individual input. So German Jewish leaders in 1933, in forming the Reichsvertretung der Juden in Deutschland, the union of Jewish communities and political and national organizations, pleaded for the community's cooperation and the rejection of particularistic goals and interests. Seven years later, CCOJA would be formed in a similar thrust. This time it was René Hirschler who renewed the call to put the community first and to suppress the individual Jew's egoistic traits bestowed by emancipation. Like the Reichsvertretung, CCOJA would be forced to combat particularism to succeed.

CCOJA inherited the tense community relations of the thirties and proclaimed their improvement as one of its goals. It also inherited the different conceptions of social welfare adhered to by its representatives. Native Jews, who were more prominent in CCOJA than immigrants, tended to have some association with the Central Consistory and regarded it as the only authoritative body to represent French Jewry. Exasperated by consistorial attitudes in the past, Marc Jarblum looked to CCOJA for a new form of leadership. In December 1940, in accordance with his social philosophy, Jarblum demanded an extension of CCOJA's mandate and activity to include a permanent lobby at the regional and local prefect level to guarantee an equal treatment of Jewish refugees.[118] Several months before, Jarblum had applauded French refugee policy,[119] but he was now appalled at the deteriorating economic status of the refugees in the southern cities and the hostile attitude of the authorities. Already CCOJA was caught in native-immigrant crossfire. The organization failed to move on the proposal, continuing to see "political" intervention as part of the Consistory's jurisdiction. The animosity of the thirties reasserted itself, as Herbert Katzki astutely reported to Schwartz:

> The foreign Jews, despite the good will expressed by the French, do not think that they can rely 100% upon the assurances they give them. In consequence, they will continue taking whatever steps they deem proper through their representations to protect themselves.[120]

The conflict over CCOJA's direction continued for several months, with the tension increasing between the two polar approaches. Consistory representatives on the commission looked askance at FSJF's political interventions and wanted them to cease. In their image, CCOJA was set up as a mediating relief organ without political attachments. But Jarblum was not to be won over easily. He attributed the deteriorating status of foreigners to French Jewry's timid dealings with the authorities and threatened to represent immigrant interests unilaterally if no change followed in native Jewry's attitude. The Consistory was not overlooked in this regard and was blamed for its failure to adequately represent the immigrants. Though aware of the Consistory's iconoclasm, Jarblum felt that the time was not right to boycott the leadership. Turning to the president of the Consistory, Jacques Helbronner, he demanded an unofficial FSJF representative in Consistory deliberations to plead the case of tens of thousands of immigrant Jews. Again he threatened the ultimatum of separate FSJF activity.[121] Jarblum was not alone. Joseph Fischer, the Jewish National Fund representative in France, advocated a CCOJA independent of the Consistory's influence and prepared to initiate "political interventions for Judaism's benefit."[122] Trying to muster up support for their approach, they involved the World Jewish Congress and the Joint, but with little success. Katzki was present at a heated CCOJA session in June 1941, but his efforts to unite the factions, even for economic reasons, were futile. A Consistory representative guaranteed Jarblum a permanent position in the central committee; however, there is no indication that it materialized during the war years.[123] Moreover, CCOJA members refused to change the orientation of the organization, upholding the native leaders' attitude.

The economic demands on CCOJA were no less pressing than the political ones. At its June session, the state of the some 150,000 Jews in the south was presented in all its complications. More than 30,000 Jews were still interned in the French internment camps, and CCOJA members, active in the interdenominational Nîmes Coordination Committee, were involved in alleviating their condition. Interventions with French officials had been under way for some months via the Nîmes channel to release Jews from the camps to departments in the south, but that was a slow process requiring extensive negotiations with local and Vichy officials, and it was necessary until such time to work in the camps to supplement the meager supplies and diet offered by the French commission on camps. Within six months, more than 20,000 Jews were released, and their resorption into the French economy engaged CCOJA's special "commission on camps," as well as the services of CAR, FSJF, OSE, and HICEM.[124] The latter two organizations were convinced that emigration was the best solution for the interned Jews, and they made extensive efforts to coordinate their passage. But endless bureaucratic procedures hampered the process, and it is difficult to determine how many Jews they succeeded in bringing from the camps to the transatlantic ships. All told, HICEM, the European Jewish emigration agency (department 6 of UGIF), seems to have actively helped close to 6,500 Jews reach America until summer 1942, while OSE's project to bring parentless children to the United States faced huge obstacles and had to limit itself to no more than 350 children.[125] Financing was a problem for all the organizations and all the projects, and in the "liberal atmosphere" of the unoccupied zone, the economic rationale could determine the success or failure of a project. CCOJA remained without resources, and its affiliated organizations continued to rely almost exclusively on Joint funds.

The progressive proletarianization of the Jewish masses worried CCOJA leaders. Although no instant solution was at hand, René Hirschler was one who saw beyond the particular interests of the immigrant and native communities and called for a revolutionary development in the CCOJA's social structure. Attacking again the leadership's failure in the thirties to prepare for different developments, Hirschler advocated an extensive professional retraining program to solve the problem of the unemployed and the rapidly disappearing Jewish middle class. He expressed alarm at the growing civilian antagonism towards Jewish unemployment and feared widescale economic exploitation of the Jews. By creating trade centers and rural apprenticeships, CCOJA could help affect the trend.[126] Hirschler's analysis revealed how French Jewry understood its predicament. In the summer of 1941, Jews in the unoccupied zone saw the major threat emanating from an anti-Semitic French backlash to the economic distress, resulting in Jewish unemployment and widespread reliance on relief agencies and French societies. It was to the economic whirlwind that William Oualid of ORT (the Organization for Rehabilitation and Training of Jews) referred when he proclaimed: "We are on a raft. We must try to save everyone and not only these or those individuals."[127] The fear had penetrated CCOJA that no sector of Jewish society was immune to the proletarianization. Within this context, the German presence in France seems to have remained a remote phenomenon.

Between the diagnosis and the implementation of a treatment fell the shadow. A decision was made to set up a joint fund that *would* distribute money to native and immigrant agencies, in contradiction to the decision of October 1940. Although meant to show the Joint that French Jewry was doing its share and to guarantee continued Joint support, the declaration went beyond mere propaganda. As Hirschler stated dramatically, French Jewry was facing a period of suffering unsurpassed in Jewish history, either during the time of the destruction of the Temple or during the expulsions from France or Spain. Hirschler, the driving force behind the joint fund, condemned French Jewish egoism, the product of generations of emancipation, which now threatened the future of the community. Only by sensing a common fate, only by bringing all elements of the community together, could the upcoming crisis be surmounted.[128]

However few Jews were willing at this stage to heed the call. Five months after Hirschler's July appeal, the Jews of the free zone had contributed only 600,000 francs ($7,500) to CCOJA, a fraction of the Joint's annual subsidy to the French relief organizations.[129] Unprepared to accept the motto of the proclamation that "tomorrow everyone may be a refugee," the community had shown its allegiance to emancipation's attractive legacy: the comfortable were far from willing to feel one with the unfortunate Jews, many of whom were "foreigners." Rejected by the community, CCOJA remained powerless to activate Hirschler's scheme and left the field of philanthropy open to the individual organizations. In July 1941, Hirschler was aware of the movement under way in the French bureaucracy to establish a "Solidarity Fund" that would apportion funds to Jewish relief organizations from expropriated Jewish property, and he expressed his desire that the community would prevent such a disgraceful fund by initiating its own. French Jewry did not rise to Hirschler's challenge and was faced with Vichy's "Solidarity Fund," established by law on 22 July 1941. But that same law, with its significant Aryanization clauses, proved to be the impetus for wholesale Aryanization of Jewish public and private property.

CCOJA was disbanded in March 1942 after a rather undistinguished career. Neither the political direction demanded by Jarblum and Fischer nor the socioeconomic upheaval proposed by Hirschler received due attention.[130] CCOJA was relegated to a forum for airing problems but was not taken seriously enough, either by its leaders or by the community. Thus, the Consistory guarded its unique position in the native community, and masses of French Jewry remained tied to traditional patterns of philanthropy, unprepared for the cataclysmic years ahead. Leadership did not emanate from CCOJA, and the ideology of emancipation preserved its cherished place in the hearts of the leaders and constituents.

III.

THE ESTABLISHMENT
OF UGIF

With the German invasion of Poland in September 1939, the plight of European Jewry worsened. With the rapid progress of the German army came
the Nazi specialists on the "Jewish Question" to pursue their goals. Poland
was to be the first conquered country where they would implement specific
Jewish measures culled from their experience with the Jewish communities
in the Reich. The creation of Jewish councils was one such policy. On 21
September, Heydrich ordered their establishment with the stipulation that
they include respectable Jewish leaders responsible for the Jewish community and capable of representing it before the Nazi authorities. Rabbis,
lay leaders, and communal functionaries found themselves coopted into such
councils in the ghettos of Eastern Europe and in Nazi-occupied Europe, in
accordance with Heydrich's original order. Denigrated and discredited by
contemporaries and historians, and often blamed for contributing to the huge
number of Jewish victims, the Jewish councils aroused more controversy
and sweeping generalizations than any other problem in the history of the
Holocaust. The French case, with its unique variations, has often been included in such discussions.

The formation of a compulsory umbrella organization for French Jewry in
autumn 1941 was a direct outgrowth of the SD's strategy in the Nazi-occupied
territories. However, in attempting to apply that strategy to France, the SD
authorities found themselves in a complicated situation. First, within the
German administrative offices in Paris, the SD's policy met with opposition,
mainly from the foreign ministry and military officials. Close to a year of
internal negotiations and infighting was necessary before the SD was able
to dominate Jewish affairs. Second, the French, who retained sovereignty
over the south of France, were reluctant to grant the SD control over the
"Jewish Question," being most sensitive to any infringement of their sovereign rights. Finally, the Jewish leadership had more than a passive role
in the negotiations. And here, the division of France into an occupied zone

and a free zone determined the atmosphere of the negotiations with the various Jewish leaders. Eventually, after almost six months of deliberations, UGIF (the Union Générale des Israélites de France) came into being, long after the German authorities had originally designated.

The establishment of UGIF was unprecedented in the formation of analagous organizations under German occupation. It revealed the internal workings of the German administration in France and their sources of conflict with French officials but also, above all, the existential drama of the Jewish leadership. No other event during the entire war period elicited such extensive soul-searching among the community's leaders, and no other event illuminated so poignantly their trials and tribulations. These moments of decision are at the heart of this chapter, and no generalizations will bring us closer to understanding the predicament of these leaders.

The Initiative

It was logical that when the German authorities in Paris ultimately decided to establish a Jewish council, they turned, through the offices of the Commissariat, to the Jewish organization they had fabricated early in 1941, the Comité de Coordination. We have seen the SD's failure during the first half of that year to turn the Comité into an organization with widespread authority over the Jewish community in occupied France, and also the pressure exerted, especially by the indefatigable Dannecker, on other German authorities to set up such an organization. The Military Command in France (MBF) withstood Dannecker's constant demand by claiming that such a law would upset the French, since it was beyond the terms of the armistice agreement. This line of argument fitted well with the "collaborationist" mentality that characterized the German ambassador to Paris, Otto Abetz. Abetz had been central in promoting German interests in France during the thirties and was not about to jeopardize his position to satisfy the extremism of Dannecker. Dannecker also faced the opposition of Vallat, who had his own idea of how to conduct the anti-Jewish campaign and preferred as little German interference as possible.

By August 1941, Dannecker had managed to obtain authority over the "Jewish Question" from the MBF and was instrumental in organizing the mass arrest of Jews in the heavily populated eleventh quarter of Paris. It was not the first mass arrest of foreign Jews instigated by the German authorities, but it provoked opposition, to which the French interior minister Pierre Pucheu and the German authorities responded by further clamping down on the activity of various "fifth columns," Jews in particular.[1] In the wake of the arrests and the repressive measures, Dannecker was able to secure the support of Abetz to push ahead on the Jewish council. The result of their cooperation was a directive sent by Dr. Schmidt, an official of the MBF, to Vallat on 29 August 1941 instructing him to begin plans to establish a Jewish organization to include all "the Jews residing in the occupied territory."[2]

Schmidt clearly spelled out the German expectations from the Jewish organization and the French authorities. Ostensibly such an organization was needed to help meet the heavy responsibilities incumbent upon the Jewish welfare societies, resulting from the growing number of Jewish internees and the legal restrictions imposed on Jewish employment. However, Schmidt stipulated that the real reason was the lack of authority in the existent Comité de Coordination, "since it encompasses organizations that have only voluntarily participated." He further stated that the entire Jewish community would belong to the future organization and that it would have complete authority over social problems, would be the sole representative of the community before the German authorities, and would have the prerogative to impose taxes on its membership. The organization would replace all existing organizations (except those of a purely religious character) and would be under the supervision of the Commissariat. Schmidt warned Vallat that if the organization was not established, the German authorities eventually would be forced to create it by decree. A basic outline of the proposed organization was expected by 25 September 1941.[3]

The German design was specific: it would be the responsibility of the Commissariat to set up the organization under close German supervision. The arrangement was not at all to Vallat's liking. He was certainly no lover of the Jews, but he ardently hated the Germans and despised their interference in his affairs, in French business. The French were capable of dealing with their Jews without German prodding. The French law of 22 July 1941 had already anticipated the suffering of thousands of Jews and had made provisions for them by establishing the "Solidarity Fund." Moreover, the prefect of the Seine region had been instructed to prepare special funds for the Jewish families. Vallat intimated in his response to Schmidt that these French initiatives had nullified the importance of a new umbrella organization, although he added that the German proposal would be brought before the French government together with the stipulation that if the law was not prepared by 25 September, it would be enacted by the Germans themselves.[4] For all his bravado, Vallat took the German authorities seriously. Thus, between 6 and 25 September, negotiations over the proposed law continued, with both the German and the French authorities preparing possible drafts, and with German officials constantly reminding Vallat of their intention to publish the law if the French did not come through on time. In order to convince the French that they meant business, the Germans handed a draft to Vallat on 17 September.[5]

The German draft went along the lines of Schmidt's letter to Vallat but specified that the Jewish leadership would be appointed by the Germans.[6] This new condition angered Vallat, who immediately sensed the curtailment of French sovereignty and replied with renewed French vigor. The Commissariat alone would be in charge of the organization, and the members of the Jewish council would be held solely responsible for their actions and not as "preferred hostages" (*otages préferentiels*) for the entire Jewish community. Moreover, in trying to outsmart the Germans and stamp the Jewish organization with a French certification, Vallat resolved to include the Jews of the nonoccupied zone in the organization.[7] This French initiative went beyond Schmidt's letter and the proposed German law and clearly related to the sovereignty issue. As with French law, a law concerning the Jews could not be valid for only part of the country. Vichy anti-Jewish laws would have equal bearing on the Jews in the north and the south. The proposal was in accord with Vallat's general scheme of bringing about "harmonization between the two areas" on the "Jewish Question" and minimization of German jurisdiction,[8] but whether it was his initiative or the French government's is unclear, since the latter's response to these German maneuvers is still hidden in the classified Vichy archives. Nevertheless, the French did not wait for German approval, and on 23 September Raymond-Raoul Lambert of CAR-Marseilles was summoned to Vichy.[9]

The Germans responded calmly to Vallat's maneuvering. They returned to the Commissariat direct responsibility for the Jewish organization, reserving German intervention for cases of Jewish defiance.[10] The German authorities, possibly seeing the extension of the organization to the south as an unexpected gift, lessened the pressure on the French for immediate action; they withdrew and let Vallat take over. During the following months, the negotiations between Vallat and the Jewish leaders proceeded almost endlessly, with German officials waiting by to see the outcome of Vallat's tactics. Dr. Werner Best of the MBF received the detailed French proposal in mid-October and affirmed it with no particular comments several weeks later.[11] It seems that only Dannecker of the SD was bitter over the extensive delay, and he and Vallat held a mutually accusatory session in early November,[12] a preview of their well-known February 1942 meeting, which signaled the end of Vallat's career in the Commissariat. But notwithstanding Dannecker's position, the responsibility was left to Vallat and the Jews to work out a French law that would satisfy the German demands.

Vallat Meets the Jewish Leaders

On receiving the German clarifications, Vallat began his discussions with Jewish leaders in the north and south. In the occupied zone, where the presence of the German occupation was a predominant factor, Vallat had less trouble in reaching an agreement with the Jewish leaders. André Baur, the president of the Comité, and Lucienne Scheid-Haas, a respected lawyer who Vallat knew from the *cour*, were his counterparts.

Born in Strasbourg in 1911, Scheid-Haas was a descendant of the distinguished Alsatian Scheid family and a relatively well-known figure in the thirties, when she served as the first secretary of the French bar association. While most Jewish lawyers were removed from office by the Vichy laws of October 1940, Scheid-Haas was "overlooked" and remained active throughout most of 1941. Although her prior commitment to and involvement in the Jewish community had been minimal, her contacts with the French administration and her unique professional status provided her with important qualifications in these difficult moments. Scheid-Haas was introduced to Baur and became convinced of the need to aid her fellow Jews. Her rekindled consciousness of community was fleeting. Years later she would explain her decision to become involved with the Jewish council as a Bergsonian act of commitment, and like Henri Bergson she allowed herself to listen to her inner calling only after the war. In 1947 Scheid-Haas converted to Christianity.[13]

Vallat presented these Jewish leaders with the German draft of the law, and according to him and Scheid-Haas, the three worked together cooperatively to limit German authority.[14] For Vallat that was proof of his desire to alleviate the suffering of the French Jews. The law would not be discarded, but efforts could be made to make it more tenable for the community. That was the premise from which they worked. What were the major issues that troubled the Jewish leaders? First, the organization had to be directly linked to the Commissariat, its leaders responsible for its own actions, and to refrain from involvement in the education of the community. The leaders feared that taking on the area of education would carry the isolation of the Jews from the rest of society one step further. Second, and according to Vallat, the council members had to be French citizens. This proposal was apparently intended to oust the two "lackeys," Israelowicz and Biberstein, that Dannecker had brought from Vienna in March. The Jewish leaders trusted Vallat and believed that his intentions were decent, though not pure. They saw him as the lesser of two evils, a Frenchman who wanted to relieve their plight, at least somewhat, and they concluded that outright opposition would bring them no advantage.[15] Vallat needed little coaxing, and it appears that until the publication of the UGIF law in late November, he had only occasional meetings with Baur and Scheid-Haas. Such, however, was not the case in the south, where he met with strong opposition.

Vallat's first meeting in the south was with Raymond-Raoul Lambert. By choosing Lambert, Vallat indicated his preference for someone involved in the welfare organizations. Lambert was proud of his achievements in communal work and convinced that his record of activity had brought him to Vichy. "It is for personal and professional reasons (it is ten years that I am known in the ministries) that Vallat summoned me as an official liaison, as a technical expert."[16] Lambert's meeting with Vallat was the turning point in his career; it was to catapult him into one of the influential positions in Jewish life in unoccupied France.

Born in 1894 in a small suburb of Paris, Montmorency, Raymond-Raoul Lambert was a descendant of a French-Jewish family from Metz. Following the trend of nineteenth-century French Jewry, his family settled in Paris and quickly blended into French society.[17] Lambert grew up while the French educational system was still reeling from its traumatic Prussian defeat, and the traditional animosity between France and Germany was exacerbated. Nevertheless, he became deeply attracted to German culture, developing through the years a perfect mastery of the language and an intimate acquaintance with its literature. During the premiership of Aristide Briand (1909–1911), Lambert, like many of his fellow students, was a proponent of détente between France and Germany and called for a rapprochement between the two nations.[18] Only a few years later, however, the two countries were again on opposing sides in World War I, and Lambert found himself following the path of his family, going to war for the first European country that had granted emancipation to the Jews. He remained extremely proud of his army service; he was decorated with the Chevalier de la légion d'Honneur after World War I and was promoted during World War II to the rank of captain.

World War I left a marked impression on Lambert. He encountered the havoc and cruelty of war and saw its terrible consequences for hundreds of thousands of homeless, among them his fellow Jews. Undoubtedly this trauma caused Lambert to spend the next years of his life trying to solve some of the Jewish and non-Jewish refugee problems. He attempted to remodel Jewish charitable organizations in France along the lines of those German-Jewish organizations that had so impressed him at the end of the war.[19] It was to this task that he brought a most interesting personality: a man of action, he was also an intellectual who wrote novels and short stories;[20] even though he was more involved in French tradition than in Jewish culture, from 1934 he was the editor of the French-Jewish weekly *L'Univers israélite*, the publication reflecting the views of the Central Consistory. As editor, and as the secretary-general of CAR from its founding in 1936, Lambert was one of the leading figures of French Jewry during the interwar years. During this turbulent period, his trust in France and his commitment to Judaism remained solid. On the eve of World War II, his writings echoed the spirit of *union sacrée* of 1914: France and Jerusalem must unite against the forces of immorality and barbarism.[21] Late in 1939 he returned to the army full of devotion to his country and its principles.

The swift victory of the German armed forces was a devastating blow for France:

> No one who lived through the French debacle of May-June 1940 ever quite got over the shock. For Frenchmen, confident of a special role in the world, the six weeks' defeat by German armies was a shattering trauma. . . . The moral and psychic wounds were even more tender than the material ones in France in the summer of 1940. . . . The stunning shock of defeat, which turned a proud and skeptical people briefly into self-flagellants craving the healing hand of suffering and discipline, passed as quickly as the daze of an automobile accident victim.[22]

For Lambert, however, the "stunning shock" did not pass. His wartime diary begins characteristically with the comment that the recent developments were "the most tragic of our history [France's] and for me the most terrible agonies which I have ever known."[23] Typical of his fellow Frenchmen during this period, he also pondered the moral activity that should be carried out among the soldiers before their demobilization.[24] It was Lambert's assessment that the defeat was in part due to the lack of enthusiasm and moral stamina of the French soldiers, and unless they underwent a spiritual reformation, the country could not be revived. He proposed holding seminars with the soldiers on themes of French history to illustrate how the defeat could rejuvenate France.[25] Lambert's moralistic perspective and positive view of defeat were not unique, yet he was far removed from the common attitude, which saw the collapse of the Third Republic as a fortunate outcome.[26] Lambert was too enamored of the Republic's libertarian principles to castigate it, in no small measure because of his awareness that the cataclysmic events portended uncertain times for French Judaism. He again affirmed, as in the 1930s, that his loyal devotion and his family's could not have been in vain, and he could not imagine life on different soil. The laws enacted by Vichy from October 1940 struck deeply at the synthesis that Lambert had created. His response was direct.

Though he saw these anti-Semitic laws as the direct result of German pressure upon Vichy, Lambert did not absolve Vichy itself. For the first of many times, he was ashamed that France had betrayed its glorious tradition of free thought and had stooped to the level of anti-Semitic propaganda and racist legislation.[27] He continued to wrestle with the causes of the discriminatory laws and gave them more attention than their actual consequences in his daily life deserved. Several months after the anti-Semitic legislation, he again inquired into the causes that had brought France to break with its humanitarian tradition, dwelling on the reasons for France's defeat. German propaganda, he concluded, had penetrated the writings of French journalists and authors and, together with the anti-Semitic activity of the Action fran-çaise, gradually had eroded French ideals. Undoubtedly, Jewish influence in politics, the arts, finance, and the press lent credence to racist arguments, but it was the unsolved immigration issue that most influenced public opinion. Here Lambert's criticism was directed more against the Jewish leadership, whose blindness towards the need for a clear position on immigration led to a source of major tension,[28] than against the immigrants themselves. Lambert was unable to reach a definitive conclusion about the source of the anti-Semitic legislation, and as the months passed and the laws intensified, he placed even more responsibility on France, seriously questioning whether it could ever return to its previous ways. Although Lambert continued to recognize German inspiration in many of the new clauses (such as the legislation of 22 July 1941), his disappointment with France for breaking all of its commitments (including its "imperial missions") was great, and he feared "that there will be bloody confrontations here."[29] France's total rejection of its historical path in enacting laws condemned twenty years earlier was only a symptom of the general loss of freedom throughout Europe, which held no hope for the Jewish people.[30]

In his analysis of France's defeat, Lambert pointed to the military, political, and moral issues. Militarily, France was simply no match for the well-trained (and better-armed) German forces. The French general staff was inadequate, and on the battlefield, there were few commanders willing to sacrifice, as evidenced by the large number of prisoners.[31] Politically, Lambert felt that war had been declared without desire and without a conception of German force by unqualified leaders of the second rank, some of whom were even contemplating defeat during the actual hostilities. Overall, there had been a moral collapse, in which both the leaders and the populace had lost sight of the goal —individual liberty—and were prepared to accept defeat above total occupation.[32] This lack of moral stamina had caused Pétain to sign the armistice and to uphold in May 1941 the politics of collaboration, to which Lambert responded: "What infamy! . . . Poor people of France whose lethargy is so deep that they do not deny this affront to their entire past and to our generation of the Great War."[33] Lambert was still aware of the sympathetic attitudes of some churches and individuals to the plight of French Jewry, but they were overshadowed amid the general apathy of French society.

The events from October 1940 to the summer of 1941 raised many questions for Lambert concerning his security in France. During these months, his pain was obvious. To the October laws he replied with stubborn determination to remain French and not deny his Judaism. His French identity was so much a part of him that even as he condemned France he recognized that nothing in the world was closer to him. He resigned himself to endure.[34] Lambert envisioned a bleak future for French Judaism, a return to medieval days of bowing one's head and submitting. Although he had fleeting thoughts of revolt, they were quickly discarded as he thought of his family responsibilities. His internal deliberations were similar to those that had faced German Jews in 1933—and he pondered the same alternatives. He considered suicide but rejected the idea, though he mentioned several times his preference for an honorable death on the battlefield to the life of a pariah.[35] Yet he feared that the intensification of anti-Semitism would bring more Jews to that end. Lambert was critical of the leaders and of the wealthy members of the Jewish community who had fled France right after the debacle, leaving the community without leadership, yet, in May 1941 he, too, toyed with the idea of leaving France, and overtures were made on his behalf.[36] This decision was made with deep personal turmoil:

> I have put out feelers to find a temporary shelter in New York. It makes me ill, but must I not save the future of my children? I will remain a Frenchman until my death, but if the French nation legally rejects me from its midst, do I have the right to decide that my children must be pariahs?[37]

Whether Lambert remained in France because of difficulties in receiving a visa or because of his own reluctance to leave is not clear, but whatever, his fate was to remain in Vichy France, to endure and to suffer.

While Lambert was grappling with his new status in France, he was called to Vichy. In the background, ominous events were taking place: the successful German drive into Russia; the establishment of a new Pétainist government bent on dictatorship, with further curtailment of the freedom of speech and a clear-cut policy of collaboration. All of these things were in Lambert's thoughts when he and Vallat met on Saturday, 27 September 1941.

The purpose of their meeting was for Vallat to collect information on the state of the welfare organizations and to delineate his scheme to create a compulsory Jewish organization with two separate sections. Lambert emphasized the technical nature of his position and suggested that Vallat meet with other Jewish leaders, especially the president of the Consistory, Jacques Helbronner. Lambert's observations about their discussion were those of a strong personality, responsible and proud, certain in his path as a Jew and a Frenchman: "I agreed because he is the legal authority but I also hope to be better placed to preside one day over the liquidation of this Commissariat for Jewish Affairs which will last no longer than a long ministry as in former times." As for his impressions of Vallat: "He seems to express resentment to the Germans for their excessive persecutions by being sympathetic to us."[38] After the meeting, Lambert sent Vallat a list of six representatives from the major Jewish organizations in the south, including his own name, not, as he claimed, to promote himself but "in order to facilitate the contact and then to disappear, if you deem it preferable, when the time comes."[39] Furthermore, he requested that their conversation remain secret. What prompted Lambert to ask for Vallat's discretion is unclear, and his doing so is perplexing in light of the fact that Vallat, in all of his postwar writings aimed at absolving himself, never mentioned his cordial relationship with Lambert. Their contact would not be renewed until early November, but from then on they maintained a frequent association, which became a source of tension and controversy within the Jewish community.

In the interim, Vallat seemingly met with only one other Jewish leader of the free zone, Jacques Helbronner. Helbronner, a man with a very different outlook from that of Lambert and twenty years his senior, discussed with Vallat the proposed law and succeeded in removing the Consistory from its jurisdiction. Vallat also recognized the Consistory as the supreme moral and religious authority of the Jews of France. These concessions appeased Helbronner but were not sufficient to prevent the Consistory from strongly opposing enactment of the UGIF law.[40]

Deliberations in the Community

The Central Consistory had responded to the Vichy anti-Semitic laws in disbelief and pain, but with pride in its traditional allegiances. It continued to trust the ultimate goodness of France and its bond with the Jewish religion. Helbronner's meeting with Vallat opened up a new period in the Consistory's history, for it now faced French legislation of a racial character that challenged the very framework of the Consistory's existence.

How did the aristocracy of the French Jewish community accept this further retreat from French liberal principles? The extensive discussions that began in mid-October indicated the Consistory's belief in its power to bring about a reversal of the French designs. Helbronner brought the proposed law to the attention of his colleagues two weeks after his encounter with Vallat. He informed the Consistory of his unsuccessful attempts at silent diplomacy, including his private interventions with Pétain, and suggested more radical means. Pétain had not lost his attraction for these leaders; however, they assumed that it was not wholly within his authority to reverse these measures.[41] For the Consistory the law had enormous significance, as it posited the creation of a compulsory organization with a racial definition, in contrast to the traditional conception of the community based on voluntary religious identification. Even though the first two years of the war had trampled basic concepts of human rights, the moral issues raised by the law were significant and could not be easily dismissed. The Consistory leaders struggled with such moral questions as whether Jews could rightfully use the spoils of seized Jewish property, participate in an organization that could become the instrument for further anti-Jewish legislation, tax fellow Jews, and altogether participate in a racially constituted organization. In these preliminary discussions and in consultations with members of CCOJA, the Consistory resolved to protest the law strongly, stressing that the true spirit of France lay in the tenets of the French Revolution. Thus, any attempt to return the Jews to the ghetto was in contradiction to "French public order."[42]

Resorting to its traditional form of protest, the Consistory addressed a detailed report to Vallat, renewing its claim to being "completely and undivisibly" part of France. However, this report went a step further, echoing the internal tensions of the Jews in France during the thirties. The Consistory rejected the French attempt to lump the native French Jews together with the immigrant Jews, which would thereby discriminate them from their fellow Frenchmen.[43] The native Jews were deeply insulted. It was beyond their comprehension that the French could see them only as Jews, no different from Jews who had little or no roots in French soil. The Consistory failed at that moment to represent the heterogeneous nature of the Jewish community, opting to emphasize its unique ideological position, which saw Jewish life in France as based on the same agreement that existed between the state and the dominant religions. Judaism was presented as a religious belief alone. As in the thirties, despite the condemnations of the immigrant Jews, the Consistory again presented a monolithic view of the Jewish community, a parody of the actual state of affairs.[44]

Finally, in rejecting Vallat's law, the Consistory proposed in its place a voluntary, federative organization to include the various welfare societies with autonomous status, and they would be the electors of the council, responsible to the Commissariat. In effect, the Consistory suggested maintaining the status quo.

Almost a week after the Consistory convened, leaders of the major welfare organizations grouped in CCOJA met to discuss the law, resenting Helbronner's procrastination in bringing it to their notice. This forum consisted of those individuals with the major responsibility for the welfare societies. The continuation of the multifaceted community welfare program was thus their primary concern. Rabbi René Hirschler put the situation of French Jewry into historical focus. He compared it with the predicament of the Sanhedrin during Napoleonic times. In 1806, Napoleon had brought together leading Jewish authorities under his rule to answer a series of questions relating to the nature of Jewish existence within the modern state. He had wanted to verify the extent to which Jews were willing to cast off their particular religious way of life and accept state law as ultimate and obligatory, or, as Hirschler put it, whether the Jews were ready to leave the ghetto. Now, Hirschler contended, the Jewish leaders were being asked how to return to the ghetto: "But just as the Sanhedrin deliberations still weigh upon us after one hundred and thirty years, for the good and the bad, so in these grave hours the decisions the leaders of French Judaism must take will weigh upon us, our children and our grandchildren, regardless of the future."[45] He stressed that the leaders would be forced to decide on a course of action and must do everything to save the welfare work.

Hirschler's call echoed the speech he had delivered a year before on the necessity of creating CCOJA, but his choice of historical paradigm is instructive. Hirschler and many other French Jews viewed the historical events in France from the perspective of French history, and French history alone. His existential identification with the crisis of his forefathers during Napoleonic times, and not with that of his brethren in other Nazi-occupied countries, indicates how Vichy policy was being perceived in terms of the historical relationship between France and the Jews. The frightening times that befell European Jewry seemed to be of a different nature. In the catastrophic days of the Holocaust the self-image of the community and its attachment to the fatherland were nurtured as much by the particular French historical experience as by a collective Jewish historical memory.

Hirschler's presentation reflected the opinion of other members of CCOJA, who opted for a moderate approach. Cooperation with the Commissariat was at the basis of their position to avoid a further decline in the status of the community and its welfare organizations. Various individuals, representing native and immigrant societies, sensed the need to present technical propositions to the Commissariat while openly protesting the intended law. However, there were spokesmen, most notably Marc Jarblum, who condemned any contact with the French government in propagating a racial law. Jewish tradition and solidarity with Parisian Jews were invoked in claiming that participation in the infamous law was treacherous.[46] The honor of French Jewry was at stake for most of the discussants, but one influential immigrant leader, Israel Jefroykin, voiced a wholly different view of the matter. The spiritual leader of FSJF saw a positive side to the law: from a nationalistic point of view, the compulsory organization could eventually lead to the spiritual rejuvenation of French Jewish society. Jefroykin may have been continuing his romantic fantasies, which began with the "return to the ghetto" movement during the late thirties,[47] but he reflected a phenomenon of the Nazi era. Similarly, in the early thirties, individual Jews in Germany viewed the separation of Jewry from German society as a positive act that could contribute to a renascence of Jewish life. A decade of Jewish suffering had not brought an end to a national-territorialistic outlook on Jewish life, and even after UGIF was established, Jefroykin remained steadfast in his optimism.

Community opinion did not agree with Jefroykin's visions, and the discussions led to the adoption of a resolution condemning the establishment of the proposed organization. But the welfare leaders relied upon negotiations with the French and were determined to avoid the disintegration of the existing structure. Their perspective was in general more realistic than the Consistory's, which fact became apparent in the joint meeting of the two bodies on 26 October 1941.

In this session, the Consistory remained adamant about submitting an alternate proposal that would preserve the voluntary nature of the community and its religious character. The community would be reorganized, with the Chief Rabbi of France maintaining the dominant position.[48] The Consistory members, sensitive to their pride as Frenchmen, showed their vulnerability to the law while being overly concerned with how history would judge them. As one member stated: "It is preferable to denounce the faults rather than attempt to correct them and thereby be exposed to the criticisms of having collaborated."[49] The attitudes and suggestions of Consistory leaders were evidence of the shadow that fell between the desires of French Jewry and the government's intentions, and they brought home to certain welfare leaders (and Lambert above all) the questionable nature of the Consistory's ability to lead French Jewry in its hour of crisis.[50]

On 4 November, Lambert received another invitation to meet with Vallat. Three days later, after consulting with Albert Lévy, the president of CAR, Lambert went to Vichy.[51] This time the meeting went in a different direction. Vallat wanted to push things forward. He wanted names of individuals capable of leading the organization and expected greater cooperation from the Jewish leadership. While criticizing the leaders' negative response to the project, Vallat tried to assure them of his good intentions. He had incorporated Helbronner's reservations regarding the independent nature of the Consistory and guaranteed the free flow of Jewish money from abroad to the French community.[52] Lambert in turn rejected Vallat's proposition to become the general-secretary of the organization, maintaining that he was simply a "functionary" with no authority to act without his superiors. They, in turn, would do nothing without the approval of the Consistory and "our colleagues in Paris." Lambert left the meeting with the impression that the law would be enacted regardless of the Jewish opposition, since Vallat was under heavy pressure from the German authorities.[53] Lambert had come to the conclusion reached earlier by the foreign-born leader of OSE (the Oeuvre de Secours aux Enfants), Joseph Millner, who was astonished that the French were even consulting with the Jewish organizations.[54] Their "realism" would bring them closer in the following weeks and drive a wedge between them and other figures in the Jewish establishment.

Lambert reported to CCOJA the following week. That session dealt with a detailed report on the welfare structure to be submitted to the Commissariat, preferably by the Consistory.[55] The following day the permanent section of the Consistory met and redeclared itself as the sole representative of the Jewish community, conditioning private intervention with government officials on prior agreement of the Chief Rabbi and the Consistory. The Consistory granted CCOJA the right to distribute copies of the report to various ministries only after Helbronner presented it at Vichy. In the same spirit, the members of the Consistory restricted Lambert's private talks with Vallat: "It is inconceivable that this individual [R.R.L.] acts as if he were the Chief Rabbi of France, the President of the Central Consistory, and the Vice President of the Welfare Organizations all in one."[56] The Consistory's actions and statements were an attempt to reassert its hold over the Jewish community, which, even among the native Jews, was not as solid as it liked to believe.

In spite of Vallat's advice to Lambert to cease protesting, CCOJA leaders sent him a detailed report on the welfare structure of the community. They wished to impress upon him that the diversity of the community made centralization of the institutions unfeasible and necessitated their autonomous activity. The report dealt with three major topics: a general description of Jewish aid, reservations about the proposed law and its dangers for the Jewish needy, and a comprehensive list of the various organizations and their specific functions. According to the report, thousands of families (close to 23,000 persons) were in need of aid for basic maintenance, and this number was on the rise. The wide scope of social activity—medical aid, social and spiritual welfare assistance, occupational retraining—exemplified the complex demographic character of French Jewry and the hardships it was enduring.

In its criticism of the law, the report upheld the principles of the French Revolution but rejected turning the Jewish community into a minority group separated from the rest of society with limited rights and under public control. From another angle, it emphasized how the community had rejected mixing politics with welfare, only to be faced now with a law that confused this principal distinction. Moreover, articles of the law contradicted its pronounced aims and were counterproductive: the goal of reducing the number of organizations and increasing their efficiency had already been achieved by the creation of CCOJA; the organizations were always open to public criticism and were recognized by the authorities; the financial resources to be made available were insufficient, as foreign aid would probably not be forthcoming in the future setup. In conclusion, the report claimed that in view of the energies expended to establish these societies, it was unfeasible for the state suddenly to assume the care of thousands of needy people: "Possibly after many long trials the new services would be able to accomplish this heavy task. However we cannot reckon on what material and technical basis, especially from abroad, it can rely. Although the government maintains a serious and legitimate interest in emigration, it will be slowed down remarkably. As the means will diminish and expenses rise, the government will have created a new and difficult problem."[57] The report was positive in spirit and assumed that France had not lost its concern for the suffering of the Jewish community. The Jewish leaders were still hoping for a positive response from the French officials, but in fact the memorandum was received with indifference and had no effect on the draft law.[58]

The report was presented to Vallat while he was working on the final form of the law. After Best's approval of the earlier draft, the law was examined by the French Justice Department and the Ministry of Interior, who focused on the form of taxing the Jewish community.[59] Eventually the law contained eight articles defining the scope and contours of the new association. The organization was to deal particularly with social welfare and occupational retraining but not with general education; as a public, autonomous organization, its employees would be state-employed. All Jewish citizens of France and all Jews residing in the country would be members, while the existent organizations (save purely religious ones) would be dissolved and their functions turned over to the new organization.[60] The taxation issue was left open, to be determined by the Commissariat and the councils. On 22 November, Best granted his consent in the name of the German authorities in Paris. However, Vallat had yet to receive a commitment from the Jewish leadership. Towards this goal, he called Lambert to Vichy once again.

Lambert's third meeting with Vallat was set for 21 November. On his way Lambert met with the Chief Rabbi of France, Isaïe Schwartz, and Helbronner, at the latter's request. This stormy session increased the tension in the community to a critical point. Schwartz and Helbronner pleaded with Lambert to cancel his trip to Vichy, criticizing him for his partisan activity. They maintained that the Consistory was highly respected by Pétain's office, and all interventions should be directed there. Lambert withstood their pressure. He denied having initiated anything and suggested that Helbronner go in his place. Helbronner refused, and Lambert went on, with no qualms about having compromised his principles. "But I continue my path with a clear conscience and a lucid desire to remain an excellent Jew and an excellent Frenchman. I reread Maurice Barrès and Henri Franck."[61]

Placing before Lambert the final draft, Vallat promised extensive autonomy (although under Commissariat control) for the organization and continued relations with Jewish organizations abroad if recognized Jewish leaders would participate. But Vallat was out of patience with negotiations that resembled Third Republic politics. His point was clear: "The government had committed itself to putting an end to parliamentary debates, and it was those individuals useful to the country who must count."[62] When Lambert described his meeting with Vallat to the leaders of CCOJA, he was not censured, nor did they prohibit any further contacts.[63] Apparently they too were leaning towards a more realistic attitude by trying to determine their terms for participation in the inevitable council. They laid down four conditions: 1) Jewish representation would deal solely with areas of welfare, retraining, and assistance; 2) the religious basis of the community could not be eliminated or supplanted by an ethnic-racial definition; 3) the organization must refrain from utilizing funds derived from the seizure of Jewish property; and 4) the welfare societies could be dissolved only if they were replaced by an organization with wide-ranging autonomy.

So stood the community on the eve of the creation of the Union Générale des Israélites de France (UGIF) on 29 November 1941. The law was published in the *Journal Officiel* on 2 December.[64] The community leaders were split between those who advocated continued negotiations to improve the decree or to dispense with it altogether, and those who recognized the inevitable and resigned themselves to the new organization. For the former, two dominant tendencies merged. The Jews were dealing with the French, and even if they occasionally sensed the German presence in the background, that was a secondary thought. They were neither intimidated nor frightened as were their colleagues in the north, who also negotiated with the French but were facing the German occupation daily. Second, these leaders could hardly come to grips with the rupture in French-Jewish history being perpetrated by the French. That was especially true for the Consistory leaders, the autocratic leaders of French Jewry, who never relinquished their dominant position in the community. They were witnessing a division between Jews and Frenchmen while the "technicians" of philanthropy were usurping their role in the community.[65] The Consistory members felt that their birthright was being challenged, but they struggled tenaciously to retain it.

UGIF, Vallat, and the Jewish Leaders

On 30 November, Vallat informed Lambert of the impending law and invited him to come to Vichy. Lambert's request to be accompanied by other leaders was refused, but in a gesture of good will Vallat promised to delay publicizing the names of the nominees to the council, which he revealed to Lambert. The list included five individuals who had appeared in Lambert's letter of late September. Lambert trusted Vallat and was convinced of the need to find a way to accept the new measure, as harsh as it was. He was already looking beyond the law, towards creating a welfare institution par excellence, fearing that it otherwise would fall into the hands of incapable and irresponsible persons. From the beginning of December, Lambert became more certain of his role. He rejected the resentment of community leaders about his activity and debated the wisdom of their political foresight. Not that Lambert himself was an astute analyst. He tended to waver between flashes of stark realism, when he sensed the predominance of German designs, and prolonged periods of deception, when he would wallow in the particular French-Jewish fantasy so characteristic of the Consistory leaders. He too had reservations about UGIF and voiced them, but he opted to struggle to overcome them in his activity.[66]

On the basis of Vallat's information, Lambert and five other nominees (Jarblum, Lévy, Kahn, William Oualid, and David Olmer), all respected welfare figures, met to discuss the consequences of UGIF. They agreed in principle, provided that Vallat accept the conditions laid down by CCOJA.[67] At the request of Olmer and Oualid, the decision was brought before a wider forum of CCOJA, which affirmed the initial approach. However, for the first time this organ came down heavily on Lambert and tried to prevent his going again to Vallat.[68] Lambert defied them. He had committed himself to Vallat and would go in a private capacity. And so he did.[69] This time he came away with what he thought were significant assurances of Vallat's good will. For one thing, Vallat agreed to meet with a larger delegation from the welfare organizations and handed Lambert a *note-verbale* delineating the UGIF mandate. Specifically, the UGIF could utilize the "Solidarity Fund," receive gifts and wills, and temporarily postpone taxing the community.[70]

Lambert's expectation that his interventions would now receive their due credit was quickly dashed by an extraordinary meeting of the Consistory, held in Lyon on 7 December. The indefinite character and responsibilities of UGIF continued to trouble this body, and the *note-verbale* was seen as mere tokenism. It hardly weakened the impact of a law that threatened to bring about a spiritual and material ghettoization of the community and was the first step towards creating a "Reichsvertretung" according to German demands.[71] That was Helbronner's pessimistic assessment, a definite accentuation of his analysis of the situation. But beyond that, the Consistory's thrust was to reassume its central role in community affairs. As Chief Rabbi Schwartz stated: "The Central Consistory must reclaim its responsibility at this tragic moment."

In this spirit, Schwartz led the campaign against Lambert, disparaging his interventions with Vallat as the unauthorized acts of a layman.[72] This tone was continued in the decisions made by the Council of French Rabbis on the same day, which condemned the law for its attempt to separate the religious and social fields. Judaism is a religion, and as such its representatives must be religiously inclined and its welfare carried out by religious functionaries.[73] Yet the council's negative appraisal of the law was moderate, leaving open the possibility of having a rabbi represent the spiritual needs of the community in the council. In all cases, the Council of French Rabbis, CCOJA, and the Consistory did not at this stage totally reject participation; but they conditioned it on receiving a clearer specification of UGIF's fields of activity and responsibility. That was the directive given to the representatives who went to meet Vallat on 12 December.

The continual discussions and resolutions were indicative of the damage that the UGIF law had done to the self-perception of these French Jews. The changes that the Consistory had successfully resisted within the community between the two wars were now taking place. In response, the establishment turned to the sacred principles of the past. For these leaders, these issues were not abstract concepts but the true inner substance of their lives. Oualid, Millner, Lambert, and André Weill met Vallat with these considerations in mind. They wanted to reach a common solution to satisfy both history and the present. Oualid presented the objections of the welfare groups, focusing specifically on UGIF's responsibilities.[74] He failed, however, to receive the commitment desired to limit the council to dealing only in welfare, although Vallat specified that it would not be called upon to undertake police duty. The forum agreed that Vallat would send out individual invitations to nine leaders nominated to the council, and they would each respond affirmatively, while expressing the common objections.[75]

The substance of this meeting was repeated two days later at a marathon meeting of the Central Consistory, in which various welfare leaders participated.[76] The pendulum had swung. Vallat's verbal promises seemed to have done the job, and the participants turned down proposals to reject the law. However, the moral dilemma, both private and public, continued to concern Consistory members. A clear-cut decision, either way, was impossible. Helbronner, who was himself in despair over his unsuccessful efforts, was also torn between an immoral decision and a moral one that could leave the welfare organization bankrupt. The only solution he saw was to have several Consistory members participate in the council, thus insuring continuation of Consistory principles. But as Helbronner himself sensed, even this solution was problematic: "There is an absolute incompatibility between being a member of the Consistory and a member of the Secretariat of the Union."[77] With these thoughts in mind, the Consistory adopted a resolution drafted by André Weill. Upholding participation in the union on the basis of Vallat's formal promises of 12 December, the resolution was to be submitted to Vallat by the nine nominees. With that decided, the French Jewish leadership had seemingly reached a united position on UGIF.

However, on receipt of Vallat's invitation to join the council, the consensus was again disrupted. On 18 December, several of the nominees met and decided to alter Weill's resolution, putting stronger emphasis on Vallat's commitment. Helbronner sanctioned the revision, and eight of the nominees met four days later to finalize the text. The conflicting opinions created two clear camps: one that opposed participation (Jarblum, René Mayer, Oualid, Olmer) and one that approved (Lambert, Robert Gamzon, Lévy, Millner). The latter group submitted to the former, and together they agreed to send identical negative replies to Vallat emphasizing that his inability to change the law and define precisely the scope of their responsibility had proved insurmountable.[78]

What determined this sudden turnabout? Neither the news of the dramatic events taking place in Paris (mass arrests, forced labor, and strict price control, etc.) nor the reports Jarblum received from FSJF in Paris, which strongly objected to participation, seem to have been the cause.[79] Rather, the moral dilemmas and legalistic hairsplitting that had dominated these discussions since October again came to the fore. Jarblum noted retrospectively that on receiving Vallat's official offer, he was utterly disturbed: "This idea aroused in me such a feeling of disgust and indignation that I immediately began to contest the project."[80]

Vallat was no longer in a position to receive vague responses. He immediately turned to Lambert for help in working out his predicament. Joseph Millner joined Lambert for another remarkable meeting with Vallat on 30 December 1941. They met an impatient commissioner. Vallat meant business. He had to be in Paris on 5 January 1942, and if he did not have an agreed list, he would appoint eight "margoulins" (unscrupulous individuals) unidentified with the relief organizations to the council. Vallat further expressed his disappointment at not being able to bring André Baur to the south to convince the leaders of the dangers involved in procrastinating. Lambert shared Vallat's disappointment and encouraged him to delay his decision and in the meantime to send separate telegrams to the appointed eight, reiterating Vallat's "promises" on the nature of UGIF jurisdiction. Vallat agreed. In turn, Lambert drafted the telegram himself, which was to be the verbatim text sent by Vallat. Millner then proposed that the telegram be postponed until 2 January, closer to the date of Vallat's departure for Paris, and thus exert further pressure on his colleagues. Lambert and Millner intended to elicit individual responses and to force the replacement of those who continued to deliberate. They kept the knowledge of the impending telegrams secret, expecting them to have a uniformly positive response.[81]

After receiving their telegrams, the nominees met for a heated six hours of deliberations, in which the two camps persisted. Jarblum stressed the events in the north as reason for his demand to include the northern council in Vallat's "promises." In the end, Oualid and Olmer joined him in wiring Vallat of their acceptance conditional upon this new consideration. Lambert, Lévy, Gamzon, and Millner wired their acceptance.[82] Vallat rejected the conditional acceptances, but instead of implementing his threat to appoint "margoulins," he let Lambert propose replacements. Lambert immediately suggested three more individuals, all associated with Jewish relief work.[83] On 8 January Vallat gave Lambert and Millner his consent to the southern council, and the next day, the lists of the two councils were officially published in the *Journal Officiel*.[84] Albert Lévy was appointed president and André Baur vice-president, while Lambert and Stora were to serve as the general administrators in the north and south respectively. Here was further indication that the French had waited for the Jewish leaders to come up with their own council but were now being pressed by the Germans for results.

With this official act, the formation of the southern UGIF council terminated, but in no way was that the end of the bitter arguments in the Jewish community of the free zone. The Consistory and the Fédération continued to oppose UGIF and its leaders for a long time. The UGIF leaders, however, especially Lambert and Lévy, were not to be shaken. They remained convinced of their decision, which in their minds had sacrificed nothing while it salvaged the relief works from dispersion and manipulation by unqualified persons. In guiding this course to its end Lambert had participated consciously with the Commissariat, and he and Millner had acted single-handedly, duping their fellow colleagues. They sincerely believed that it was in the best interests of the community to do everything possible to help Vallat obtain the best conditions. Lambert had been the instrumental figure, sensing the need for perspicacity, "reading the moment" as one of crisis for French Jewry, where action was the order of the day. In his diary he summarized his observations:

> I know that in Paris Germany demands and Vallat can do nothing. He [Oualid] does not understand and debates law just as in the nineteenth century. . . . These poor old people reason as if before the war and forget that a minister, in an authoritarian regime, demands of them a telegraphic response. . . . One passes by those who revel in discussion and do not want to understand that in the unoccupied zone one has to play on the sincerity of Vallat—but in the occupied zone, neither he nor us can do absolutely anything. The Union will be established without them and Judaism can only gain from it.[85]

Parisian Jewry and UGIF

The public announcement of the establishment of UGIF on 2 December signaled the beginning of a month of extreme hardship for the Jews of Paris. German and French officials vied with each other to expand the tough anti-Jewish legislation of 1940–1941. The Paris prefect of police placed Jews under periodic surveillance and prohibited them from leaving the Seine area. Foreign Jews were sent abroad to labor battalions at the initiative of the French, while more than 7,000 Jews were still interned in various French camps in the occupied zone. The German authorities escalated the anti-Jewish measures when in mid-December they arrested some 1,000 Jews, more native than foreign, interning them at Compiègne. The Germans, furthermore, refused at this stage to allow the International Red Cross to visit the camps.[86] The leaders of the Comité de Coordination were extremely troubled by the oppressive nature of these events and the worsening plight of the Jewish community.

But that was only the beginning. On 15 December, the same day that 95 hostages (including 53 Jews) were killed by the German authorities in retaliation for measures against German soldiers, Dannecker informed André Baur of the German intention to impose a milliard franc fine on the French Jewish community.[87] The fine was to be paid through the offices of UGIF, which had yet to begin operations. Dannecker added his usual cynical proviso—immediate payment would prevent more mass arrests. For Baur and his fellow coworkers in the Comité that was a formidable task, which put an end to any thoughts they had entertained of postponing the UGIF. For all intents and purposes, UGIF North now came into being, and support from the community was essential to avoid disaster. Baur saw these measures as irrevocable and sought the unity of the community. Thus, Vallat's intention to bring Baur to the south to impress upon the leadership the crucial nature of their decision was not merely a good tactical move on his part but also an expression of Baur's desire and dilemma. It was, then, the milliard franc fine that dispelled Baur's hesitations and those of other Comité members. They continued their previous functions in the same capacity until the public announcement of 9 January 1942 turned them officially into the northern council of UGIF. Conscious of the new role imposed on them, they sent a letter of protest to Pétain on 20 January, rejecting the idea behind UGIF, the separation of French Jewry from the rest of French society. These French Jewish leaders reiterated their unswerving commitment to the principles of their forefathers. Their adherence to Judaism was in no way contradictory to their attachment to the French national community, and so they promised to persist in this duality, regardless of the anti-Semitic laws. In this spirit they vowed to fulfill their welfare responsibilities to all of their brethren, foreign and native, even though they were not elected representatives of the community but were appointed by Pétain.[88]

The UGIF was finally established several months after the German initiative. During these months the Jewish leadership in the south struggled unsuccessfully to improve its status and to discourage attempts to isolate it from French society. The leadership saw its goal in preserving the dual existence of Jews in France—religious and national—notwithstanding the Vichy laws of 1940. Within the community, the breach became inevitable between those welfare leaders, especially Lambert, who were willing to take on a new role, and those who felt bound to the conscription of the Consistory. In the north, the leaders of the Comité accepted their new status, committed to serving the community and deriving some optimism from Vallat's positive attitude towards them. Vallat had truly gained the trust of the Jewish councils, and despite his vigorous propagation of anti-Semitic legislation on many other fronts, particularly the economic one, his consideration of the French Jewish leadership seemed to be thwarting this German measure. Vallat promised his support for the preservation of the welfare organizations and allowed the community to find its own representatives. In dealing with Vallat in the unoccupied zone, the Jews tended to lose sight of the German presence in Paris and thus prolonged their discussions, while in the north, the occupation forced a rather quick transformation of the Comité into the UGIF. The community, however, remained divided even after UGIF was formed, and the divisions went much deeper than the apparent split between immigrant and native Jews. These important pockets of dissension will be further explored in the following chapters dealing with the activity of UGIF North and South.

IV.

UGIF NORTH UNDER THE
ANVIL OF GERMAN
OCCUPATION, 1942–1944

As the members of UGIF North (UGIF-N) filed their impassioned protest to Pétain, Nazi officials gathered at Wannsee to work out the technical outlines of the "Final Solution."[1] The juxtaposition of these two events, which occurred on 20 January 1942, is instructive. The Jewish leaders were placing their trust in the spirit of French law and the glorious tradition of 1789 while the Nazi bureaucrats were deciding how to erase all egalitarian laws and annihilate those protected by them, the Jews. For the Jewish leaders, the ideal was to aid the community by granting welfare and social assistance; for the Nazis, the goal was to destroy European Jewry (including some 850,000 Jews of France, as was erroneously estimated).[2] Both parties would take up their missions with zeal, but only one would suffer from its vision. For in the shadow of the mass arrests and deportations, UGIF-N carried out its social functions and performed its daily chores, but the Nazi "mission" seldom dominated the consciousness of its existence.

The First Months

UGIF-N was the direct successor of the Comité de Coordination, inheriting its staff, areas of activity, and points of conflict. One problem that had deeply troubled its leaders was the lack of community support for the Comité. The leaders of the immigrant societies had succeeded during 1941 in diverting the assistance of its constituents away from the Comité and had severely weakened its hold over the community. With the creation of UGIF, the old suspicions were aggravated, and though Rue Amelot was promised complete autonomy, the leaders remained far apart. These immigrant leaders had little trust in the good will of their French counterparts and in their concern for the immigrant community, and they were reluctant to cooperate with the authorities responsible for anti-Semitic legislation. More extreme was the Communist leadership, which had a large following in the Eastern European community and viewed participation in UGIF as treacherous. Many native leaders were nonetheless convinced that in these troubled days only they could responsibly and effectively represent the entire community. But the leaders of UGIF-N opted for conciliation and broader involvement in the organization. Encouraged by what they perceived as a reversal in Vallat's attitude towards the "Jewish Question," UGIF-N hoped to convince the immigrant leaders of the positive side to the Vichy bureaucracy. Thus, as one of its first acts, the council invited several leaders of the major immigrant organizations to discuss the role of UGIF-N. This unique encounter took place on 28 January 1942 and served as a forum for airing out the vices and virtues of the Comité's activity, as well as the legitimacy of future cooperation.[3]

André Baur opened the session with a clear statement of purpose: UGIF-N wanted to continue the welfare projects and needed the assistance of the immigrant leaders. Baur viewed their former conflict as past history and believed that the most important task was to rise above the differences that separated them to reach a common understanding. As he stated, "In the meanwhile, the foreign Jews regard us with suspicion. If there are nationalists among the French Jews they are not among our colleagues and we are distraught by this distrust."

Following Baur's outline of intentions, the participants engaged in an illuminating discussion on three sources of contention: 1) whether the Comité constituted collaboration with the Germans; 2) the feasibility of the welfare organizations' participation in UGIF; and 3) the nature of UGIF's strategy. The fundamental question was whether joining UGIF was tantamount to collaboration with the Germans. Consequently, both sides defended their courses of action in the Comité. Leaders of UGIF, especially Marcel Stora, contended that if all the people with integrity had left the Comité, the Germans would easily have reached their goals. Stora showed how the manipulations of certain members within the Comité enabled nonparticipating organizations, even those that withdrew, to continue their activity without undue interference from the Germans. He cited two examples: first, he allowed David Rapoport and Yehuda Jakoubowicz of Amelot to submit fabricated welfare lists to the Germans, and second, although forced to publicly recruit volunteers for the Ardennes, the Comité worked behind the scenes to discredit the project. Stora considered it to the Comité's credit that only 200 Jews enlisted for the project, nowhere near the 6,000 workers demanded by the Germans. But the issue for the immigrant leaders was different. The question was one of collaboration with the union and thereby with the Germans, and Rapoport agreed with Baur that it had no relevance to the immigrant-native tension. In this context, both he and Eugene Minkowski saw participation in an already existing organization as being beyond their moral commitment: "But we are presently before a *fait accompli* and cannot accept the smallest portion of responsibility for what will be done." Disregarding the entreaties of Baur and others to join UGIF and strengthen it with their professional advice and expertise, the immigrant leaders preferred to remain outside UGIF and thereby preserve their contacts with other welfare organizations.

In a sense, the tactical and moral issues were intertwined: each side had a positive view of the way it maintained the welfare projects, and each judged its former road as being both "moral" and judicious. This free interchange, at the UGIF's infant stages, poignantly elucidates its moral and existential challenges. Both UGIF members and their detractors squarely faced the implications of collaboration but reached mutually exclusive responses. Although distrust of and conflict with UGIF persisted, a limited working relationship was established, which promised joint consultations and UGIF's financial backing for certain immigrant organizations outside its purview.[4]

UGIF's commitment to these projects was not simple. The Comité's budget was in a sorry state. The Comité had existed on the basis of contributions and a taxation of the community, but with the establishment of UGIF all the contributions were suspended, and its leaders preferred to postpone taxation for as long as possible. In the absence of other means, UGIF turned to the French authorities to receive an advance on the "Solidarity Fund." The "Solidarity Fund" raised moral issues, for both UGIF and the immigrant leaders, but the necessity to meet the needs of more than 3,000 families supported by the Comité was uppermost in their minds.[5] Thus, from the outset, UGIF-N had to dispense with what was regarded as a moral absolute and succumb to a moral reality that was much more relative.

Beyond the communal differences with the immigrant leadership and the weight of responsibility to support the thousands of needy, UGIF-N faced from its outset the radical turn in German policy in France. The month of December had witnessed an upswing in anti-Jewish activity, including the heavy fine imposed on the Jewish community. Dannecker's ultimatum to the Comité to pay the fine within thirty days was taken seriously by the Jewish leaders. Fearing a further intensification of German measures, the Comité involved the French government in its predicament. The request did not go unheeded. The French Ministry of Finance was eager to avoid having Jewish property fall into the hands of the Germans and consented to loan 250,000,000 francs to UGIF using the blocked Jewish accounts in the Caisse des Dépots et Consignations as collateral. In accordance with this position, a Vichy law was published on 16 January 1942 that sanctioned the loan and limited the taxation to Jews in the occupied zone.[6] This speedy procedure allowed UGIF to begin fulfilling its commitment to the Germans, set a pattern for further payments, and prevented the loss of Jewish property to the Germans that the French government itself intended to expropriate. The transaction proved to the Comité leaders that it was necessary for them to assume the duties connected with the newly established UGIF. However, their compliance with the German demand further alienated elements within the immigrant community, as expressed by Marc Jarblum: "On the billion [fine], the Brith [UGIF] has already advanced a portion; it contracted a loan from the banks, but already it draws on Jewish wealth everywhere to pay the interest and amortization on the loan; it ruins all the Jews."[7]

Dannecker's pressure on the Jewish leaders continued immediately after the list of UGIF council members was announced in the *Journal Officiel*. His first demand was that Israelowicz be appointed as a special liaison with the German authorities, responsible for relaying Jewish requests to the Germans. Since all individual requests would be rejected, Dannecker emphasized that this position would help to turn UGIF into a representative Jewish organization. Along the the same lines, he ordered the continuation of the Comité's bulletin under a new heading to constitute the UGIF's only publication.[8] Consistent with Dannecker's line of operation in Paris since 1940, the bulletin would lack any independent spirit, being in effect a means of publicizing German directives to the Jewish community. But Dannecker's intervention did not stop there. The council was further obligated to submit weekly reports on the state of its economic, administrative, and social situation, continuing the pattern set during the Comité's days.[9]

Along with this show of strength, Dannecker also tried to utilize the services of the new Jewish organization by obligating it to report on any meeting with Vallat or his associates.[10] Dannecker was then building up his case against Vallat, whom he regarded as soft on the "Jewish Question" and responsible for the long delay in setting up UGIF. Vallat's recent opposition to the milliard fine and to German attempts to seize more Jewish property further antagonized Dannecker, although it gave UGIF-N leaders reason to believe that opposition to collaboration with Germany was growing in French circles.[11] However, UGIF leaders were unable to capitalize on Vallat's conflict with the Germans. After his heated meeting with Dannecker on 17 February 1942, Vallat became persona non grata in the occupied zone, and his days as commissioner were numbered.[12] Undaunted, and opting for the lesser of two evils, UGIF-N leaders made a final attempt to prevent Vallat's dismissal. In early March, Marcel Stora was sent secretly to Vichy to meet with Pétain and to impress upon him the importance of retaining Vallat. The meeting, arranged by the head of Vallat's cabinet, Chomel de Jarnieu, had little success. Pétain promised nothing and could do nothing against the German demand to replace him.[13] Soon after, in a direct confrontation between the French and the Germans, which involved UGIF, the council realized who had the upper hand. The German authorities eliminated French opposition even before it materialized.

In mid-March, Dannecker ordered UGIF to supply the Germans with large quantities of shoes, blankets, food products, etc.[14] The demand, the first of its kind, came as the German preparations for the first deportation of Jews from France to Auschwitz were finally completed. The delivery of the goods was to coincide with the deportation, set for 27 March 1942. There were to be 1,112 Jews included in the deportation, half of whom were interned at Compiègne since their arrest in December 1941.[15] This demand was not divulged to the UGIF-N council, and no discussion of it can be found in the minutes of the council's intervening weekly meetings. But on 26 March, in a strong letter of protest to Vallat, Baur criticized the German demand for supplies as a violation of UGIF's charter. In support of his argument, Baur mentioned that even de Jarnieu believed that it violated a French-German agreement. Before acting, he wanted the commissioner's authorization.[16] However, Vallat's demoted status left the protest unanswered. Within a month, UGIF-N had sent some six tons of supplies to Auschwitz, fulfilling the German request.[17] A new dimension was added to UGIF's activity, one that would continue throughout most of the war period.

UGIF's interaction with the authorities in this affair exemplified its legalistic approach to the new reality. It relied upon French law and officials when that same law had created UGIF on racial grounds. Moreover, it pitted law against Dannecker's grotesque designs. But when the law failed to support the council, it withdrew its protest, fulfilling the demands completely. For the Germans, the eventual success in this venture prompted them to turn it into a major and efficient avenue of contact with UGIF.

UGIF and the Deportations of Summer 1942

Following the first deportation of Jews from France, various Nazi departments began to work out a more detailed plan for the occupied territory. Some 130,000 Jews continued to reside in Paris and the occupied zone, and gradually the number of Jews planned for deportation in the first major sweep soared to 100,000. That was to become the ignominious figure bandied about by Himmler's representatives in Paris and their French counterparts. Between March and June, at the height of these negotiations, no deportations had taken place, but in June, four train loads brought 4,038 Jews from Drancy to Auschwitz. UGIF was not involved in these operations, although during this period Dannecker occasionally turned to the council to prepare a reserve stock of clothing and food products to be delivered to imprisoned Jews. Dannecker's first concern during this period was to procure the trains needed for deportation, and as these were not forthcoming, his pressure on UGIF was minimal; UGIF responded with similar deliberateness, setting up a special service (Section 4—Supplies) in early May, long after Dannecker's first request.[18] But once Dannecker was assured by the Wehrmacht that trains would be put at his disposal for the deportation process, he pushed UGIF into establishing an emergency stock.[19] This time, the council acted swiftly and activated Section 4 immediately, probably believing that the supplies were needed for Drancy or other internment camps in or outside of France. A week after Dannecker's demand, Baur wrote the president of the French Red Cross on the possibility of receiving information on the Jews deported to Auschwitz in order to grant them "moral and material sustenance."[20]

Dannecker's efforts to activate UGIF now found better reception in the newly revamped Commissariat. Darquier de Pellepoix, an avowed anti-Semite who had been involved in various anti-Semitic frays in the thirties, was called upon to replace Vallat in early May 1942. Darquier, who knew little of government and proper bureaucratic ways, brought with him personal acquaintances and individuals eager to pursue the anti-Semitic orientation.[21] One of these was Joseph Galien, the owner of a tire plant, who had helped to disseminate anti-Semitic literature in the thirties and had financially supported Darquier at certain junctures. Galien became the head of Darquier's cabinet and immediately went to work to meet the SD's requirements, in effectiveness and in ideology. During his short stay in the Commissariat, terminated in November 1942 after a private feud with Darquier,[22] Galien saw UGIF as a way to vent his anti-Semitism. First, he tried to arrange UGIF's shipments of supplies for the Germans in a more organized fashion. That was no easy feat in the war years, when production had been severely debilitated, but Galien was determined to establish special relations with private factories and to reach an agreement with various ministries, whereby high priority would be given to UGIF's orders. Galien, who had been a Gestapo agent for several years, was convinced that by so doing he was making an important contribution to the improvement in Franco-German relations. Consequently, the UGIF council began to correspond with various French companies in order to purchase the necessary goods, while repeatedly calling upon the Jewish community to join in the endeavor.[23] There was a moralistic tone to these appeals—the community was called upon to show its solidarity with the suffering individuals and their families.

The new leadership of the Commissariat was threatening for French Jewry in general, and for UGIF-N in particular. While Vallat's circle had tried to preserve some semblance of French sovereignty and had objected to total German domination of the "Jewish problem," Darquier's group brought a new élan to the Commissariat, extending the SD spirit in new directions. Galien made a second move to coordinate UGIF, emulating Dannecker's strategy. In late May he informed the council of the Commissariat's refusal to receive requests from individual Jews unless they were filed by UGIF, and he forced the council to establish a special liaison with the Commissariat.[24] Galien was determined to turn the organization into the supreme authority of the Jewish community, and that was to be one of the means. Another was by making it conform to a recognized "public institution," diligently recording checks and balances and submitting annual budgetary and professional plans.[25] But as he showed Prime Minister Laval's office, Galien was more ambitious. He intended to create a close relationship between UGIF's two councils, convinced that without sufficient support from the south and a sense of commitment to the needs of the north, the northern council would soon collapse. Galien saw it as the duty of the French authorities to intervene in such a case and compel the south to act in the spirit of the law.[26] The particular problem that Galien raised was a new German demand for a supply of products for some 7,000 Jews, which without the assistance of the south could not be filled. This huge order, obviously connected with the impending deportations of mid-July, was brought to UGIF's attention only on 1 July 1942, two weeks before the mass arrests in Paris. In turning to Baur, Galien stressed the "urgent need" to prepare blankets and clothing for 7,000 Jews and envisaged that the efforts of the entire Jewish community would be required to meet the German demand.[27] Galien further placed his offices in the service of UGIF to expedite the matter.

Galien's request of UGIF-N was a new point in German-Commissariat relations. For the first time, the French were allowed to handle the affair directly, which indicated that they had a definite trust in their agent. For UGIF, the request had a significant meaning. The council allowed itself to discuss freely with the Commissariat the impact of the order, feeling that common ground existed with the French authorities; it also brought UGIF into the planning stages of the deportations and raises the question of its involvement in the summer roundups.

The first indication of the council's response came in the form of André Baur's reply to Galien's letter. Written a week later, on 8 July 1942, Baur's letter continued the line of thought that UGIF had assumed from its inception. Baur understood that another, large deportation was imminent and that the Commissariat was making him privy to the plans, but he was wary of the direction to take. The Jewish community, he claimed, would not supply products without wanting to know their ultimate destination. Moreover, UGIF refused to disseminate information on further deportations and create panic in the community. Baur went on to say that such an act was a grave responsibility, which "we are not willing to assume unless you authorize us to do so in writing and with the agreement of the occupying powers."[28] Thus, the council decided to hold Galien's letter in strict secrecy. UGIF's chimerical sense of legalism and obsequiousness appears here almost as a parody. But that was not the end. Baur also contended that the massive demand was contrary to a French law of 4 October 1940 which allowed such large appeals to be undertaken solely by the Secours National (the state-run charity), and regardless of the legal problem, the indigenous Jewish community was unable to meet the demands.

Baur's emphasis on the fine legal points, as in his letter to Vallat in March 1942, can be comprehended only within the French context: to Frenchmen, his countrymen, he felt the need and the duty to write in this spirit. Yet, it does not seem that he expected that to have any effect, for he concluded that Section 4 of UGIF, and not the Jewish community, would purchase the goods with the help of the Commissariat and would perform the task with "the same competence and the same diligence which they have shown to this day."[29] Baur and the council were too caught up in legalism, the product of generations of emancipation in France. The alternative, to disseminate the horrible news, was not within their psychical powers. They preferred to forestall panic and financial distress while withholding information from the community on the impending disaster. The extent of UGIF's knowledge of and involvement in the deportations is crucial and needs further examination.

The extensive documentation on the mass deportations from Paris in mid-July 1942, culled from German and French sources, leaves little doubt as to the specific role the authorities designated for UGIF-N. In the discussions between the German authorities (especially the SD) and their French counterparts (officials of the French national police, the Commissariat, the prefect of the Seine, and, above all, Laval himself), UGIF was assigned a minor role in the huge operation. That is apparent from an important operational meeting that took place on 8 July 1942. In the presence of such central figures in the "Jewish Question" as Dannecker and SS-Unterscharführer Ernst Heinrichsohn from the German side and Darquier, Galien, and Jacques Schweblin from the French side, the issue of Jewish children was again discussed.[30] By then, Laval had already given his approval to the deportation of children under sixteen, but the confirmation still had to come from Germany. While the decision was pending, the authorities agreed to place the children of the deported in UGIF's homes. On that same day, the Commissariat inquired into the state of those homes; UGIF responded that 300 places were available and another 1,250 children could be accommodated if the French and German authorities were willing to evacuate seized Jewish offices.[31] Subsequently, Dannecker informed Adolf Eichmann on 10 July that he had room for only 1,400 children, about 10 percent of the number expected, according to his plan;[32] he wanted Eichmann's permission to deport the remaining children in the tenth convoy. Eichmann's affirmative reply came ten days later; Dannecker would no longer be in France, but his successor, SS-Obersturmführer Heinz Röthke, would carry out the deportation of the children who were not in UGIF's homes but were temporarily interned in Pithiviers and Beaune-la-Rolande.

On 11 July the "technical commission" again convened to complete certain outstanding arrangements for the operation. This time it was decided to utilize UGIF services to supply the washbasins for the trains, following the pattern set by Dannecker in March 1942.[33] Again UGIF was given a very short time to come through, and possibly for this reason Baur was called to the Commissariat to meet Galien on 11 July for an "important and urgent" briefing.[34] Unfortunately, no report of this meeting exists, and we have no way of knowing whether Galien gave Baur further information on the impending events or whether he merely delineated the functions UGIF was to carry out. In any event, it was not until 15 July, the day before the mass arrests began, that the Commissariat again addressed UGIF on the upcoming operation. This address came in the form of a cynical letter sent by Galien, ostensibly in response to Baur's reply a week earlier. Obviously wanting to leave behind an unblemished record, Galien denied ever mentioning that a large deportation was in store and urged Baur to do all he could to reassure the community and deny the false rumors. But at the same time he reminded Baur that the goods for 7,000 people were still required as a safety measure, and in turning to the community for support, Baur should merely avoid mentioning the quantity needed.[35] Putting aside Galien's dubious tactics, the evidence shows that UGIF was aware of the impending deportations. Two days after Baur's meeting with Galien, he and Stora relayed the information to David Rapoport and offered protective passes for Amelot's employees.[36] Furthermore, two UGIF workers attested to activity in the UGIF offices on the eve of the roundups: one claimed to have overheard a discussion on 14 July on the expected event, while another mentioned her involvement, together with other women, in preparing tags for the deportees.[37] These bits and pieces provide us with an indication of UGIF's anticipation of the German-Vichy designs.

On 16 July the French police and their supplementary forces began to round up as many Jews as possible. On the first day close to 10,000 Jews were taken, the majority of whom were herded into the Vélodrome d'Hiver sports arena in Paris; the following day another 3,000 were arrested and sent off either to Drancy or to the Vel d'Hiv.[38] All told, 12,884 Jews were seized in the operation. Anxiety within the Jewish community was at its peak, especially among immigrant Jews, the victims of this attack. UGIF was on hand to provide medical help for those packed into the Vel d'Hiv, although Röthke and Galien limited them to two doctors per shift. Members of the UGIF council appeared at the arena and were attacked by the detainees, and Baur even accompanied Röthke on one occasion, hoping to obtain an increase in the medical staff.[39] Röthke, of course, could not be budged on this point, and all that was left for UGIF to do was to comply and work on those terms and in the other area assigned to them—the care of children. The council organized some 70 Jewish youth to help coordinate the reception of several hundred children in the UGIF homes and to offer moral support to children interned in Pithiviers and Beaune-la-Rolande, designated for Drancy. UGIF also gave these children medical treatment after the trying days of the roundup and the trauma of the Vel d'Hiv but was not called upon to select children for Drancy, as almost all of them were indiscriminately sent to Drancy on their road to Auschwitz. For the UGIF council there was a feeling of satisfaction at having done the utmost to relieve the suffering.[40]

The only protest filed by the council came a few days after the roundup. It was not an absolute protest but a selective one addressed to the French authorities and relating to only two categories. The council demanded the release of descendants or family members of war veterans—a traditional call to French patriotism—and of French children arrested with their "foreign" parents.[41] UGIF held to its belief that the French authorities would show sympathy to these native cases, and in fact, in early August some native French Jews were freed as a result of the intervention of a French official. This unique development moved Baur to thank Laval personally for his efforts on their behalf and to renew a request to Pétain to free innocent French Jews, many of whom were war veterans and had been arrested in August and December 1941.[42] Was that a sign of UGIF's betrayal of the foreign Jews and protection of the native-born? According to the documentation, UGIF's official response attests more to opportunism than to outward callousness towards the immigrant community. In those issues with regard to which its members believed they were legally or patriotically justified, they asserted their position, but when fate seemed sealed they conceded defeat.

During the preparations for the deportations, UGIF exhibited little foresight and ingenuity. The council members received official and unofficial information almost two weeks before the roundups began and reacted passively; maybe, as has been claimed by some council members, some of the information was leaked to the community, but only in a partisan and disorganized fashion.[43] The truth remains that the council acknowledged the serious connotations of Galien's letter of 1 July but felt chained to silence—

tacitly watching the arrest of almost 13,000 Jews. UGIF did make itself available in those spheres of social and medical assistance permitted by the authorities and worked effectively and with concern, but its aid was limited by the Germans. UGIF-N was not called upon to perform police measures of any sort, owing to the high level of collaboration reached by the French and German authorities. However, it continued to be a source of supplies for their actions. UGIF-N passed through the horrible days of July without protesting the deportations and without reshaping its structure. Larger sections of the community, immigrant and native, found themselves alienated by the central organization but often still tied to its financial support.

UGIF and the Authorities: The Economic Perspective (1942–1943)

The summer events marked a turning point for many elements in French society, awakening protest and motivating resistance against the German-Vichy collaboration. Within the Jewish community a definite split was being established between those groups and organizations that saw illegal activity as the only possible response, and UGIF, which continued to function openly, employing the same types of tactics and policy as before the deportations.

Amelot and Solidarité emerged from the deportations as the real representatives of the immigrant community. They had shown a clearer understanding of the dangers facing the Jews and had made serious efforts to warn the community of the anticipated arrests. Hundreds of Jews had these organizations to thank for their not being at home when the police came to arrest them, and many of them now turned to Amelot and Solidarité for future guidance. But Amelot and Solidarité pursued different approaches. In the autumn of 1942, as Solidarité turned more forcefully to armed resistance against the German occupation, Amelot devised illegal methods to maintain immigrant Jews living covertly. But both organizations were determined to expose the murderous policy of Nazi Germany and to show UGIF's complicity. UGIF did not change its course.[44]

Soon after the Vel d'Hiv, the German-Vichy police raids decreased considerably. UGIF returned to its daily obligations, including the German demands for supplies and the Commissariat's requests in economic affairs, ranging from the milliard fine to taxation of the community. UGIF again resolved to find a path of concessions. In the following months, the Commissariat tried to increase control over UGIF in the spirit of Galien's programmatic letter of June 1942. That was especially true in the area of supplies: UGIF was expected to maintain a constant supply for 1,500 people and to clear every order and delivery to the camps with the Commissariat.[45] Baur informed Galien on 13 August that UGIF was doing its best to comply, but the speed with which it was asked to act created difficulties and necessitated acting without prior notification.[46]

This situation was unacceptable to Galien, whose desire to please the German authorities knew no bounds. Pushing ahead with his plan to create "Jewish solidarity," he forced UGIF to make weekly announcements in its bulletin that every Jewish family should participate in the welfare project by providing a complete set of goods.[47] Galien could produce reams of letters to government offices and private factories to attest to his diligence in trying to obtain the necessary products, prior to the deportation of Jews from Drancy to Auschwitz. Röthke was still unimpressed and critical. Galien, not wanting to let down his German associates, wrote Baur in early September a stinging letter demanding a daily courier with a copy of every letter sent from UGIF offices.[48] He was to assert his authority in the one definite area in which he had control over UGIF—the economic one—and he sent a duplicate to Röthke to assure him of his intentions. Clearly Galien's drive was also an expression of futility that distressed the hierarchy of the Commissariat through much of Darquier's regime. Countless suggestions to Vichy on how to turn UGIF into an effective organ and in turn to grant the Commissariat more power were seldom treated seriously by Vichy officials. Galien was therefore not going to let UGIF slip out of his reach. Baur, somewhat stunned by this brazen Frenchman, asked a week later for an audience with Darquier to improve the contacts between UGIF and the Commissariat.[49]

As a public institution, subordinate to the Commissariat, UGIF could not escape the watchful eyes of its officials, in particular in the economic context. All aspects of the UGIF charter dealing with its budget tied it to the Commissariat—each one pulling in a different direction. UGIF faced the growing impoverishment of the community and dwindling funds, while the Commissariat endeavored to see the community completely dependent on UGIF, but without utilizing all the blocked Jewish properties intended for French expropriation. It was in these areas, not insignificant to the economic welfare of the community, that UGIF showed versatility in avoiding the Commissariat's designs. Thus, from the summer deportations until the summer of 1943, economic issues governed the relations and contacts between UGIF and the authorities, notably the Commissariat: one such issue was the repayment and redistribution of the milliard fine.

The fine was to be paid to the Germans in currency, as opposed to property, through loans granted to UGIF by the consortium of French banks. After making its initial payment of 250,000,000 francs in January, UGIF made three more equal payments by the end of March; later on it repaid the banks after having expropriated approximately 300,000,000 francs from blocked Jewish accounts in the Caisse des Dépôts et Consignations. This form of repayment to the French was far from egalitarian (as well as much more than the sum loaned UGIF), and on 1 August 1942 Galien demanded that UGIF begin to organize the repayment by dividing the remaining sum among the Jewish community in the occupied zone.[50] Galien proposed that the organization utilize the directory of Jews available at the regional prefect offices, with the payment to be divided among the heads of families in the area. The members of UGIF's finance committee immediately assessed the situation pessimistically, not seeing how the redistribution could in effect be made: for one thing, they envisaged a long process before a complete list of Jews would be available, and, more important, it seemed that not more than 4,000 Jews would be able to meet the Commissariat's criteria, obligating each of them to pay as much as 250,000 francs, beyond the capacity of most Jews.[51]

Later on in the month, Baur presented the gist of these arguments to Galien in the context of a general description of the economic state of the Jews in the occupied zone.[52] His message was unequivocal: redistribution would be a long and arduous project, and UGIF would not shorten it by drawing money from the "Solidarity Fund," the lifeline to its welfare activities. Baur did not report to the Commissariat on the results of UGIF's preliminary preparations, and during the following months he showed little enterprise and initiative. On 28 January 1943, Darquier, feeling rather exasperated with Baur's efforts, again required UGIF to submit a biweekly report on the progress of the preparations;[53] this intervention did not change the situation to any great extent, and UGIF continued to work on the lists with little vigor, seldom submitting the reports demanded. In fact, Auguste Duquesnel, a Commissariat official, was still trying to satisfactorily arrange the redistribution in November 1943, when the community was severely depleted.[54] But even this final attempt failed miserably, so that by the time of liberation and dissolution of UGIF, repayment had not been made.

It appears, then, that the initial 300,000,000 francs from the blocked Jewish accounts was the only sum ever repaid to the French banks. Redistribution was not carried out, largely because of the role played by UGIF.[55] UGIF realized that Commissariat threats carried little weight and therefore never put itself at the disposal of this project. The council clearly saw the bureaucratic problems involved in redistribution and the Commissariat's inefficiency in putting it into effect. Once again, the Commissariat's tenuous position within the Vichy bureaucracy worked against it. The inability to enforce the repayment was a product of its lack of authority, which it constantly decried. Such was also to be the case in the effort to base UGIF's monthly budget on contributions from the Jewish community.

In early August 1942, Galien changed direction in his goal to organize UGIF's financial status: to verification and redirection of the council's revenue.[56] UGIF was officially allowed to maintain welfare activity by utilizing three sources: the "Solidarity Fund," the property of dissolved Jewish organizations, and taxation of the community. Opposed to the notion of taxation, UGIF turned for money to private sources, namely, the Central Consistory and the Joint. The Commissariat was interested in preventing the "Solidarity Fund" from becoming the only official source and tried to base the organization's budget on voluntary community contributions. This tendency was legally formulated on 28 August 1942 by Darquier in total disregard of appropriate legal procedure. The law, like the two previous ones relating to UGIF, dealt exclusively with economic issues. Here it was explicitly established that UGIF must voluntarily collect 6,000,000 francs monthly from Jews in both regions to cover its monthly expenses.[57] However, a proviso was added that if the money was not forthcoming, a per capita levy would be imposed after consultations between UGIF and the Commissariat. The enormous sum reflected UGIF's heavy expenses since the summer deportations and the Commissariat's desire to maintain UGIF's continued existence.

In placing the onus on both regions, the Commissariat showed its understanding of the superior economic standing of the Jews in the south, but at the same time it caused numerous problems between the two councils. In fact, prior to the promulgation of the law, Darquier met with Lambert and another council member and heard their objections to it.[58] The UGIF-S leaders contended that the UGIF budget for 1943 was already prepared and the anticipated expenses accounted for, making the law irrelevant. Darquier pretended to accept their argument and promised to withhold the law, provided that UGIF-S would find the means to forward the north "a massive monthly contribution and thereby satisfy the interests of the occupying authorities."[59] The next day the UGIF leaders were led to believe that the law would be tabled; as usual, when the law was published on 5 September 1942 in the *Journal Officiel*, they were told that German pressure had prevailed. Their intervention had basically failed, except for the addition of the voluntary nature of the contributions. When funds were later solicited from UGIF-S, Lambert would deny ever making such a commitment. His denial and the disagreement over the size of the contribution were to aggravate the relations between the councils in the following months.

In passing the law, the Commissariat was trying another approach to establishing voluntary cooperation between the Jewish community and UGIF and to strengthening the latter's hold.[60] UGIF-N saw the law in a completely different way. Sensitive to the growing criticism in the Jewish population, it feared that the present law would drive away whatever support UGIF still possessed.[61] Opposition took various forms, expressing both moral and social concerns. Prior to committing themselves, the council members wanted to confer with their southern colleagues and discuss the nature of communal responsibility implicit in the law. Practically speaking, UGIF-N feared the repercussions for the south were it to object to the law, noting that a parallel blocking of accounts in the south could ruin the community, which was already incapable of raising the monthly sum required. UGIF proposed a mediating step: a minimum levy and the reopening of the blocked accounts. The latter was the key to UGIF—if the owners of these accounts were granted permission to draw money freely, they would make substantial contributions to UGIF. The leaders of UGIF, although interested in showing mass community support, never deceived themselves that such was the case, nor did they anticipate an equal distribution of the financial burden. They looked to those accounts of the established native Jews to save them from taxing the community and to eliminate the absurd situation that wealthy Jews, deprived of their accounts, turned to UGIF for welfare. On the basis of these guidelines, Baur presented a programmatic rebuttal of the law's goals, two weeks after it was known.[62]

Baur dismissed outrightly the possibility of raising 6,000,000 francs from an increasingly impoverished community while the French and German laws on Jewish property and accounts remained in effect. Taxation required the same bureaucratic process as the repayment of the milliard fine and would likewise necessitate months of preparation. His proposals were far below the Commissariat's expectations but congruent with the community's financial status: the levy would be limited to 120 francs per annum per capita, while 5 percent would be automatically deducted from Jewish accounts—if those proved insufficient, UGIF would seek a loan from the French government. Baur's strategy was designed to continue the moral rejection of taxation, upheld since the German demand in 1941, and to achieve three results: 1) to postpone the implementation of the tax for as long as possible—UGIF-N did not think that taxation could be avoided but believed that by using delaying tactics the enforcement would be postponed;[63] 2) to eliminate the Commissariat's objection to opening the blocked accounts; and 3) to use the economic pressure to force a meeting with UGIF-S and possibly obtain further financial support, both official and unofficial.[64] UGIF-N showed a certain perspicacity in dealing with the Commissariat in regard to this economic issue, as well; by mounting practical difficulties, it was able to delay taxation for another nine months and avoid further friction with the Jewish population. Baur's other goals were less easily achieved—another half-year would elapse before the Commissariat allowed a meeting between the two councils, while the opposition to the blocked accounts persisted for a long time.

The Jewish community in the north was in growing need of UGIF's welfare after the summer deportations, but the organization lacked the means to meet the new situation. In early January 1942, UGIF had submitted a monthly budget of 1,500,000 francs, and by August the Commissariat's law related to a monthly expenditure of 6,000,000 francs; by the end of the year UGIF's expenses ranged from 4,500,000 to 7,000,000 francs a month, and often they were above UGIF's credit line;[65] 15 percent of the budget was devoted to the purchase of goods for the German authorities. Thus, UGIF could not remain a small organization with limited scope, as its detractors had demanded in their meeting in January, without cutting the support of an increasing number of Jews who requested aid. UGIF's budget is indicative of the welfare obligations it had assumed. For example, the budget proposal for 1943 grew to 100,000,000 francs, averaging 8,300,000 francs monthly, most of which (26 percent) was to be allocated for direct assistance to the needy.[66] UGIF formulated this proposal on the basis of the average expenses for the last four months of 1942 (approximately 7,000,000 francs monthly), together with the anticipated increase in cost of living and welfare cases. The Commissariat, which had to ratify the budget, raised several objections: it cut 6,000,000 francs off the intended expenses, considerably reduced the budgetary items to avoid possible manipulation by UGIF, and warned UGIF against oversized allocations.[67] In the following months, as the number of needy grew to some 7,500 families, the Commissariat often censured UGIF's overly generous policy and demanded stricter criteria in allocating funds.

All of these things considered, the council was pressed to increase the incoming funds, especially in light of its decisions not to withdraw money from the assets of the Jewish organizations and to reduce the sums drawn from the "Solidarity Fund." The council was apparently aware that a move was under way in the Commissariat in spring 1942 to establish a separate Jewish school system and to force UGIF to assume the care of the internees in Drancy. Both of these moves would require a huge hike in UGIF's expenses, and it saw the need to preserve funds for the actuality. (Aryanization of the French educational system was proposed by Darquier's circle and discussed several times with the German authorities, but was never carried out.[68] UGIF was obliged, however, to maintain the internees in Drancy from the summer of 1943.) Consequently, UGIF-N needed new sources of support for the welfare projects; thus, it saw the joint proposal of Darquier and Lambert from late August 1942 to grant the north a monthly subsidy of 1,000,000 francs as falling far below the obligation UGIF-S ought to assume.[69] Through different channels, UGIF-N and some of the affiliated sections were receiving a minimal stipend from the Joint, but it had no way of knowing whether that would continue or whether the authorities would discover it. The Central Consistory had been supporting UGIF from early 1942 with certain unrecorded funds, which grew to around 200,000 francs in early 1943.[70] These minor allocations were not nearly enough to avert the disaster

UGIF expected, and in early March 1943 Baur expressed this concern to his uncle, Albert Manuel, the secretary of the Central Consistory in Lyon: "I would prefer that the monthly 200 frs. [probably 200,000] be sent to me rapidly since the needs are multiplying in the suburbs [the immigrant areas of Paris.] An augmentation would be welcome."[71] Yet none of the above produced a major change in UGIF's budget, and it was left to negotiate with the Commissariat to open up the blocked accounts or at least procure a certain allocation from them.[72]

The Commissariat, as we have seen, was reluctant to open up these accounts for UGIF's purposes owing to its own organization's desires, and thus delayed the decision for several months. The interpretation of the law of 28 August 1942 was unyielding, and the Jews were expected to come through and show their solidarity. Moreover, as in the area of assistance to the needy, the Commissariat was distrustful of UGIF and did not take its financial grievances seriously. Early in December 1942, Darquier informed Baur that the commissioner on Aryanization, Lucien Boué, was prepared to have certain Jews contribute to UGIF from the blocked accounts in order to guarantee the execution of the law.[73] Opening the blocked accounts was UGIF's guarantee to receiving a monthly stipend not dependent on changes in the economic situation, but those Jews had to be promised repayment in some way. This stipulation was totally unacceptable to Boué, who saw it as an underhanded method for UGIF to secure additional funds for itself and for private Jews.

Boué was of the opinion that these Jews could well afford their voluntary contributions without receiving any kind of reimbursement.[74] His directives to Darquier were thus straightforward—money would be released from the accounts for that sum specified as a contribution, but under no circumstances would individuals be reimbursed by UGIF. The Commissariat was adhering to its policy that a contribution to UGIF constituted an act of "Jewish solidarity" and was by no means tantamount to opening up the blocked accounts.[75] Although the council realized that the Commissariat did not want it to be the intermediary between the accounts and the Jewish population, the conditions that Boué attached to the contributions did not diminish UGIF's satisfaction.[76] In February 1943, Baur announced at a joint session with UGIF-S that the Commissariat intended to siphon off money from the Caisse des Dépots for UGIF.[77] Little did he know that at about the same time, the management of the Caisse was coming out strongly against opening the accounts, save for those of a few individuals, and had succeeded in enlisting the Commissariat's agreement. Behind the scenes, financial interests within the French government were at work to block the step, fearing that the support of the Germans for the move indicated their desire to obtain the funds for themselves.[78] This setback came as the commitment of UGIF-S to contribute 5,000,000 francs every two months failed to eventualize.[79] Once again UGIF-N was thrown back into a precarious situation; in spring 1943 it had almost no resources at all.

With all of the channels closed, UGIF-N had to reassess the moral position it had chosen with respect to the assets of the Jewish organizations. UGIF's moral code was not lost in the atmosphere of arrests and deportations, and the organization struggled with these issues as in more tranquil days. If in the end that was another instance when the organization relinquished an absolute moral stand for a relative one, it came after long and hard thinking. Thus, only after consulting with the president of the Consistory, Jacques Helbronner, and receiving his consent did UGIF-N proceed. Helbronner supported the move from both a legal and a moral standpoint, claiming that if no other way existed to maintain the organization, it was morally obliged "to convert part of the patrimony of the organization."[80] As UGIF was proceeding to subsist on the basis of these funds, it faced another Commissariat-inspired law, which also conflicted with its moral precepts.

The law of 11 May 1943 ended months of continued discussions between the commission on Aryanization, the Finance Ministry, the Commissariat, and UGIF about the necessary conditions to insure UGIF's continued existence. Based on five previous laws dealing with French Jewry and UGIF, the law began by allowing Jews to contribute to the council from their blocked accounts.[81] Since the money to be collected was now deemed insufficient, every male and female over the age of eighteen in the Jewish community was to be taxed: 120 francs (occupied zone) and 360 francs ("unoccupied zone"). Furthermore, and in accordance with Baur's memorandum to the Commissariat in September 1942, a 5 percent levy was imposed on all private financial transactions.[82] UGIF had constantly objected to taxation and, now that it came in the form of a law, viewed it as a deviation from the previous laws upon which it was based. The council again asserted its legalistic mentality: in June 1943 it sought legal advice to determine whether there were grounds to file a complaint to the Commissariat.[83] The advice received a month later discouraged any thoughts of protesting.[84] The consequences of the law were not considered damaging to the Jewish community or a serious deviation from the basic orientation in UGIF's charter and the law of 28 August 1942. UGIF-N, hoping to keep the conflict to a minimum, resolved not to object, securing a verbal promise from the Commissariat that if it was able to receive sufficient voluntary funds, the specific aspects of the law would not be enforced.[85]

As things turned out, the law was imposed but with insignificant results, far below the budgetary needs of UGIF. By the end of the year, close to 4,000,000 francs had been accumulated from the taxation paid by over 25,000 Jews in the north, and 1,300,000 from the levy; the significance of the poor collection was clearly understood by the Commissariat.[86] In a report he submitted to Darquier on 11 November 1943, Duquesnel blamed the general disregard of the tax on the lack of enthusiasm in the political campaign against the Jews, characterized by the aversion of the French press to disseminating Commissariat notices on the Jews' obligations; moreover, the Jews themselves preferred a nomadic behavior for security reasons, avoiding registering for the tax as a possible first stage before their arrest and deportation. The attempt to begin taxing a disintegrating and dispersed Jewish community proved to be far beyond the capacity of both the Commissariat and UGIF.

The failure of the May law to solve UGIF's economic needs became apparent soon after it was promulgated, and UGIF's leaders were hard-pressed to finance their welfare projects. Immediate concern centered around the threats of the *nourrices* (Gentile women who illegally cared for Jewish children) to return the children if they were not paid their normal subsidy.[87] After continued discussion, the UGIF's finance committee decided to sell bonds of the disbanded Jewish organizations and turned to the Commissariat for a 25,000,000 franc loan, offering the blocked Jewish property as collateral.[88] The Commissariat again rejected the proposals,[89] but at the end of July or in early August it suddenly approved a massive grant to UGIF from the "Solidarity Fund," enabling the organization to continue to function.[90] This change of heart, which reversed the stand taken in May 1943 (disallowing further withdrawal of money from the "Solidarity Fund" until UGIF-S abided by its commitment), was overshadowed by a more serious development—the direct intervention of the German authorities in the workings of UGIF. The organization could not be allowed to collapse. Thus, the irony of history turned against UGIF: it was saved from extinction, but for the most diabolical reasons. A new era in UGIF's history was about to unfold.

Radicalization of German Policy: Summer 1943

Vel d'Hiv had no sequel in the occupied zone. The mass roundup of July 1942 was not repeated in the following year, and the some 70,000 Jews in the region became accustomed to longer periods of reduced tension. Like their brethren in major ghettos of Poland, thousands of immigrant Jews continued to find salvation in working in "protected" industries supplying foods to the Nazis. Others placed their faith in the disintegration of the German machine, heartened by the precarious German situation in the Soviet Union. Yet periodically they faced a localized German raid that rudely shook their temporary quiescence. For the German authorities, these were insignificant achievements. They had succeeded by the summer of 1943 in deporting from all of France 55,000 Jews, far below their quota. The "Final

Solution" was proceeding too slowly for their liking, and measures had to be found to hasten its development.

Greatly disturbed by the lull in deportations, Röthke had laid out a plan in March 1943 to transport up to 10,000 Jews weekly to Auschwitz,[91] but he faced several obstacles. Jews in greater numbers were successfully avoiding German and French hunts, either by escaping into the Italian occupied zone of France or by dispersing into hundreds and even thousands of small villages and townlets in the north and south of France. They were supported by UGIF, Amelot, Solidarité, and other Jewish organizations and by the French civilian population, which provided them an outlet for existence. Moreover, Röthke faced a recalcitrant French government that had begun to retreat from its open-ended participation in collaboration. By June 1943 it was clear to the SD that Röthke's plan had failed; it had netted only 6,000 Jews and had incurred the wrath of Berlin. After examining the situation, the SD again stepped up its drive to arrest and deport more and more Jews. First the SD urged the French government to strip citizenship from all Jews naturalized since 1927.[92] The SD planned to utilize the new law for a mass deportation of the denaturalized Jews in July 1943. Vichy failed to budge on this measure, and the operation was repeatedly postponed. In the meantime, another measure was broached. SS-Hauptsturmführer Alois Brunner, one of Eichmann's experienced administrators, was dispatched to France. Brunner came from Salonika, where he had been active in deporting Greek Jewry to Auschwitz, and he arrived in France with a unique entourage of twenty-five men, authorized to function autonomously, outside the German chain of command in Paris; Brunner was to receive orders directly from Berlin.[93] He immediately focused on Drancy, where he would leave his sadistic mark.

For more than a year, the German authorities in Paris had virtually given the Commissariat a free hand in overseeing UGIF's affairs, rarely making their presence felt. That changed radically with Brunner's arrival in France. His immediate move was to push aside the French authorities, including the Commissariat, and deal directly with UGIF. Initially, Brunner ordered the removal of the French police from Drancy, to be replaced by parallel German units. At the same time, he instructed UGIF to assume the administrative upkeep of the camp, which the council had feared for many months. These swift measures, taken on 30 June 1943, preceded Brunner's administration of Drancy, which began in early July. On that same day, without notifying the Commissariat, Brunner summoned Baur and Israelowicz to an introductory meeting with him and SS-Hauptscharführer Bruckler.[94] There were two purposes to this encounter: first to inform UGIF of the new responsibilities it was to assume in Drancy—daily supplies to the camp, improvement of parcel service, supplies for the deportees to the "East," medical care, and the setting up of cutting and shoemaking apprenticeships. UGIF was expected to turn the ineffective camp into a self-subsisting unit. Seemingly related to this task was the second purpose of the meeting—Brunner's diabolical "missionary plan" to allow families the opportunity to voluntarily join their interned relatives in Drancy. Brunner added a bonus to his offer—every family that complied could bring its personal belongings to the camp. UGIF was to be entrusted with this scheme and was expected to encourage the community to enlist. But Brunner's cynicism went further. Several days after his arrival in Drancy, he set up a special "missionary bureau," which dispatched interned Jews to the city to seek out their families or relatives; Brunner's eventual goal was family deportations. At least 150 "volunteers" fell into this trap and joined their families.[95]

The UGIF council had operated since 1942 within a French framework. It had faced many trying moments and had accepted several dubious functions within that system. However, Brunner's demand was beyond anything it had ever been expected to carry out. Baur's response was mixed: on the one hand, he saw the possibility of coming to the aid of the internees in Drancy by undertaking their care; but on the other hand, he rejected the "missionary" role outright. In his response he correctly assessed the role of UGIF. The Jewish community, he contended, did not maintain the level of discipline and sense of solidarity required to carry out the "missionary" project, nor did UGIF possess sufficient influence within the community to bring it to that level of solidarity.[96] For Baur, UGIF had purely a social role, and he had no intention of extending it into the shady areas proposed by Brunner. Several days later, the UGIF-N council unanimously upheld Baur's position and expressed what Baur had failed to say directly to Brunner. "The council claims unanimously that it is not within its role to intervene in measures of a police nature"[97] (*un caractère policier*). The council understood the import of Brunner's remarks on 30 June, when he also spoke of the need to stem the tide of Jews fleeing to Spain and the Italian zone and to widen the distribution of UGIF's bulletin. It was clear to them that by sidestepping both Röthke and the Commissariat, Brunner was trying to strengthen UGIF to utilize it as a police arm of the SD. But the council had no intention of resigning and began to involve itself with the administration of Drancy.

Baur informed the Commissariat of the meeting with Brunner but discussed openly only UGIF's new financial obligations. These necessitated the Commissariat's guarantees that UGIF would have sufficient funds to meet the German demands for supplies. Baur feared that if the German authorities failed to meet their building deadlines in Drancy because of UGIF's lack of funds, the Jews would suffer severe repercussions. He insisted that if the Commissariat could not come through, UGIF must inform the authorities of its inability to perform the new functions.[98]

Baur's strong letter to the Commissariat triggered two responses: first, the Commissariat was now convinced of UGIF's poor financial situation; it intervened with the prefect of the Seine to continue to provide money for the camp and, as we have seen, decided several weeks later to grant UGIF a major subsidy from the "Solidarity Fund." Second, the letter seems to have contributed to Baur's arrest and that of other leading figures in UGIF who dealt with supplies to the camp and were in liaison positions with the German authorities. His letter was probably brought to Brunner's attention, who could have seen it as a continuation of Baur's refusal to cooperate with the "missionary project." Moreover, at the same time and with the full support of his council, Baur took a rare step. Via the Commissariat, he turned for the first time in the history of UGIF-N to France's political arm, requesting a meeting with Prime Minister Laval. Baur explained that the "present conditions and our fear for the national interest make it our duty to solicit . . . a private audience."[99] Baur was clearly disturbed by Brunner's tactics and sensed that the regular channels were not sufficient during these times. He forcefully presented his request to Joseph Antignac, a virulent anti-Semite who had risen through the Commissariat's ranks to be Darquier's right-hand man in 1943,[100] angrily protesting Brunner's torturous procedures in Drancy and vicious policy towards the Jews of Paris.[101] Baur's request was never answered.[102] But less than ten days later he was arrested, ostensibly in reprisal for the escape of two internees from Drancy, one of whom was his cousin.

Brunner's explanation for Baur's arrest was accepted completely by the UGIF council and Baur's family.[103] Brunner fallaciously promised Baur's release if the escapees' were returned, prompting the council to make extensive inquiries into the whereabouts of the two, both in France and abroad.[104] On the basis of its efforts, it implored Brunner to free Baur. Brunner, who knew of the interventions, was unrelenting. Baur himself asked the head of the French prisons, via Darquier, to endeavor to have the two extradited from Switzerland. He further emphasized the urgency of the matter since he headed a public institution.[105] Apparently the desire for Baur's release was so great that the council could not come to grips with the more plausible explanation for his arrest.

From 30 June 1943, Baur showed signs of opposition to the new German measures instigated by Brunner. His request to see Laval, his meeting with Antignac, and his correspondence with Duquesnel were adequate reasons for Brunner to dismiss Baur if UGIF was to become a totally servile organization.[106] Yet, it is not unlikely that Brunner cynically used the German doctrine of "family responsibility" to cap off the arrest, especially because Baur objected to it. Baur's arrest, moreover, was analogous to developments in other Nazi-occupied countries, where original leaders of the imposed

Jewish organizations were often arrested after a year in office at a point when the German authorities sensed the slightest opposition or required more subservient individuals.[107] In Baur's case, the escape of his cousin was a diversion. Brunner wanted yes men. His arrest signaled a new attitude on the part of the German authorities towards UGIF-direct intervention in order to achieve maximum obedience. In the following days, weeks, and months, Brunner continued this pattern by making several arrests of UGIF leaders, and by demanding the end of special treatment for individual cases. All of these things were meant not to bring UGIF to an end but to bring it to its knees. A week after Baur's arrest came the turn of Israelowicz, Armand Katz, and Marcel Lévy, all prominent figures in the organization. Brought to Drancy for investigation, the three were interrogated on the functioning of the liaison service (14) with the German authorities, headed by Israelowicz, and on the supply service to Drancy, under Lévy's directorship. But Brunner was still not satisfied. The following day he arrested UGIF workers in their office on Rue Bienfaisance, where several social welfare services were centered. These services, and especially the homeless children service (42), had been mentioned in a secret memorandum that Antignac had sent to Röthke in May 1943 as evidence of illegal UGIF activity. Brunner obviously suspected these services, for he turned to their central headquarters and not to UGIF's head office on rue Téhéran.[108] As in the previous cases, the arrests took even the Commissariat by surprise, although it had suspected that Brunner was trying to suppress UGIF.[109]

On 30 July, Georges Edinger and Stora were called to Drancy for a special meeting with Brunner. He emphasized the importance of the functions imposed on UGIF, particularly in the areas of supplies to the camp and inmates, and expressed his wish that they act in an efficient and disciplined manner. Brunner also stressed the need to carry out the German demands for provisions, even by pressuring the French administration to do its utmost to comply with the requests.[110] He promised his help in this regard and to liberate several key UGIF officials interned in Drancy. Although he did liberate a few UGIF workers, his intervention frightened the remaining council members, who decided to increase the obedience of their workers and to demand a strict application of the organization's regulations.

UGIF's leaders were convinced that regardless of the difficulties involved, they must continue their enterprise. As Stora stated, "[It] is not only UGIF which is at stake, but the fate of the whole Jewish population in the northern zone."[111] UGIF's workers were called upon to show exemplary behavior in order to guarantee the purpose of the organization—the welfare projects. "It is the problem of safeguarding French Judaism which is being questioned and must be resolved favorably," they were told. They were also given exact instructions on how to act in the case of further German raids.[112] Furthermore, Edinger and Stora asked the finance committee to grant them unlimited authority to facilitate the personnel changes. Rejecting the complaints that his move was motivated by personal ambition, Edinger stressed its temporary nature until Baur's return.[113] He believed that only by closing ranks and avoiding unnecessary leaks could the Jewish community return to normal. Again, the leaders adopted an optimistic outlook; perhaps the moderates, Röthke and the French, could overcome Brunner's extremist tactics. Thus, as more and more Jewish organizations were intensifying their illegal operations, the council decided to persist and assist the community officially.[114]

Brunner's pressure on UGIF did not decrease. On 2 September 1943 another transport of Jews, including several UGIF section heads, was deported to Auschwitz.[115] The following day, accompanied by Armand Katz and Israelowicz, Brunner raided UGIF's main office and demanded a list from Stora. Stora refused and aggressively answered Brunner; the Nazi officer summarily arrested all of those present (Stora, Edinger, Maurice Brener, and Musnik) and sent them to Drancy.[116] Stora, who refused to hand over either a list of children's homes or addresses of welfare cases, was the only one to be retained, indicating the consequences of opposition to Brunner. The release of the other three, two council members and Lambert's personal secretary, who was involved in illegal work, indicated conversely that Brunner was not quite ready to terminate UGIF's existence.

Edinger returned to Paris and again called on UGIF workers to stay at their posts. Speaking before the organization's section heads on 9 September 1943, he glossed over the recent events while emphasizing the moral obligation of "soldiers" who pursue their cause to the end: the children, poor, and aged "all count on us. . . . It is imperative that everyone at all levels remains dignified and courageous."[117] Since he regarded responsibility to the community as a supreme commandment, Edinger pledged his commitment to continue the services. Calling on the staff to follow his example, he warned against frivolous behavior: "Talking is dangerous but UGIF gossip is criminal, since we are responsible and we risk spreading panic."[118] UGIF workers apparently were not abiding by the strict discipline he had demanded, and he held them responsible for any negative repercussions. Brunner had shaken UGIF's sense of security, and the council began to rearrange the staff and work procedures to reduce visits to the UGIF offices. A minor admission was made to the new era.[119]

Brunner's intensive activity against UGIF-N was only one facet of his overall attack on Parisian Jewry. In July he deported hundreds of Jews from Beaune-la-Rolande and the Rothschild hospital in Paris to Drancy for their eventual deportation to Auschwitz, while deporting 300 Jews to labor camps in the west (IODT). All of these actions were undertaken by Brunner's special units (including French fascist groups), without the participation of the French police. In response to these provocations and encouraged by underground movements, Parisian Jewry looked for alternative ways of existence. Yet, since close to 60,000 Jews remained in and around Paris and thousands of them continued to live openly, UGIF's assistance was still relied upon. The council was determined to support them and refused to ignore the plight of the Jews in Drancy or the children in UGIF homes. From the summer of 1943 to the liberation, UGIF waged a harrowing struggle with the German authorities in these two areas. It saw the care and protection of the children as its principal concern and during 1943 was successful in this regard. But during 1943 the clash between UGIF and the German authorities over the children became a tragic drama, emphasizing the council's failure to rise above the moment.

UGIF Services (1942–1944)

The Nazi occupation of northern France during 1940–1942 had severely undermined the economic basis of the Jewish community's existence and contributed to its isolation. Aided by Vichy's anti-Semitic legislation, the German authorities portrayed the Jew as an enemy of the Reich who had to be controlled. UGIF was one of the means that the Nazis utilized for this purpose. By the time the organization was formed, the Nazis had, however, gone beyond isolation and begun their plans for the "Final Solution."

UGIF came into existence at the crossroads of Nazi tendencies, but its leadership was concerned only with a social purpose—to counter the Vichy-German efforts to debilitate the community. Towards that goal, UGIF-N waged an endless struggle with the Commissariat on economic issues and developed an extensive system of services, ranging from vocational centers to old-age homes. Many of these activities were in operation prior to World War II and were associated with the Comité, but others were added as a result of the special circumstances of the war, and some merged into UGIF after the enforced dissolution of all Jewish organizations. Canteens, clothing centers, children's homes, parcel services for internees, and liaisons with authorities were some of the general categories included in UGIF's eighty-four services, spread over Paris and the northern zone. To meet the needs of the community, UGIF retained a staff of more than 750 employees, of French and immigrant origin, far below the number employed by comparable communities and Jewish councils in Eastern Europe. A bureaucracy nonetheless, with a centralist orientation, UGIF prepared to preserve a kind of self-sufficient Jewish existence, caring for the daily needs of a dislocated community. But the organization could not continue within its limited framework, and as the Nazi designs became more radical, it opened up new services, seemingly for the community's welfare but fitting neatly into the Nazis' system. As a result, the horrible consequences of some of UGIF's services made a mockery of its original motivation.

UGIF's Children's Homes

Vel d'Hiv exposed a traumatic problem—the fate of Jewish children whose parents were deported to Drancy. Preceding the mass arrests, German-Vichy deliberations had specified a definite role for UGIF in caring for such children, but Laval's surprise consent to deport children under sixteen severely reduced their number. Nonetheless, several hundred children, either abandoned by their parents or sent to the organization by regional prefects, fell under UGIF's responsibility. A week after the Vel d'Hiv, it's bulletin began publishing call for all "stray children" to register with the organization. Possibly Nazi-inspired, the notice was designed to facilitate centralization and supervision of all isolated children. Three months later, UGIF was operating eleven homes with approximately 2,000 children, tended by social workers, doctors, and related personnel.[120]

Approval by the authorities was at the basis of UGIF's services in and around Paris. Two restrictions guided the authorities. First, transfer of children to Aryan families was strictly forbidden; thus, contact between Aryans and Jews was diminished, and these children's care and supervision were left entirely to the Jewish community. Second, removal from UGIF centers to Jewish relatives or families was absolutely prohibited. Underlying the German rationale was the ultimate destination of these children—Auschwitz—and their centralization and close control in UGIF institutions meant to serve that purpose.[121] Considered "blocked" by the German authorities, the children in UGIF homes or Jewish families were meticulously listed by the Gestapo and forbidden to leave their area of residence without German permission.[122] Within this framework and under the strict condition that the children be held in UGIF institutions, the SD experts on the "Jewish Question" released children from Drancy to UGIF. Liberation from these horrendous conditions was viewed by the UGIF personnel as a vital concession to their demands and a ray of hope for the children, and so they did everything possible to avoid giving the Germans a reason to retract their policy. Fearing that the German authorities would not grant any more liberations from Drancy, UGIF guarded against any interference with the "blocked" children. In this spirit, André Baur rejected an OSE activist's request to transfer children out of the northern zone: "In view of the fact that these children were released from a camp, they are blocked in our home and cannot be delivered to you."[123] Baur's refusal from 28 June 1943 pointed to the mixed blessing inherent in UGIF's status as guardian of Jewish children. Nonetheless, through spring 1943, the organization could be proud of the course it had chosen: children's homes remained untouched by the Nazis, and liberations from Drancy continued.

Regardless of the council's suspicions and concern about jeopardizing releases from Drancy, certain UGIF workers reached a different conclusion. Viewing the official homes as potential German targets, they favored dispersing the children. Taking great care to avoid the attention of the council and the authorities, they began in winter 1942 to remove children and hide them. A rather simple system was devised, which required much coordination and supervision. Small groups of children were brought by social workers to UGIF's dispensaries, ostensibly for medical treatment, and from there they were taken to secure residences by Christian foster nurses (*nourrices*). In turn, the children were dispersed among public and private Christian organizations, and among private homes, which were supported by UGIF funds. These included both "blocked" and "free" children, entrusted to UGIF by families who had difficulty going into hiding with their children. Responsible for these efforts were former OSE workers, now realigned within the UGIF system, who acted with the express direction of Dr. Minkowski. Several hundred children were removed from UGIF's custody by this procedure which received an added boost when Jewish Communists from Solidarité raided UGIF's homes in February 1943 and snatched some 163 children. Rue Amelot, which also maintained a legal orientation within UGIF, worked along the same lines as OSE, dispersing hundreds of children through the assistance of nourrices. Amelot workers often tried to convince UGIF to disband the homes, but to no avail. Later on, towards summer, EIF, through its newly formed activist wing La Sixième, began organizing convoys of children from their center at rue Claude Bernard, across the demarcation line. The concerted efforts of these various agencies drastically reduced the number of children in official UGIF homes, and by the summer of 1943, some 650 remained in their care. More than 1,600 had found shelter in France or abroad.[124]

Confronted by the Communist raids in February and urged by participant agencies to disband the official homes, UGIF's council was well aware of the developments in its homes. The support given to the underground methods by two council members, Fernand Musnik and Juliette Stern, was directly linked to their participation in the council. Musnik, a member of EIF and an important figure in La Sixième, had maintained consistently good working relations with the immigrant agencies, especially with Rue Amelot, and often secured for them false papers. His involvement in transferring children across the border was a further example of this cooperation. As for Stern, who directed the UGIF's social service, the problem is more complicated. French reports submitted to Röthke in spring 1943 specified her central role in the placement of Jewish children with nourrices and her responsibility for Section 42, directed by Madame Getting, which was intrinsically associated with the subterfuge policy. Stern was in charge of delivering false identity papers to the children and creating contacts with Amelot and Christian institutions. Yet, she was castigated at UGIF's postwar community trials for having determined the organization's policy to keep public the official homes and was suspected of being a Gestapo agent. Undoubtedly, the fact that she was suspected of illegal activity but never was arrested contributed to Jewish distrust of her, but Nazi policy was never implemented unswervingly or one-dimensionally. Nonetheless, she was charged with responsibility for the tragic events of 1944.[125]

UGIF's sense of security was jolted with Brunner's arrival in summer 1943. The atmosphere changed dramatically. In Paris itself, some 700 children were in hiding as a result of the efforts of OSE, Amelot, and the Communists, and some 650 were "blocked" in UGIF homes. As will be recalled, Brunner pounced on Section 42 in September 1943, arresting several workers in an attempt to put an end to the concealment of children. UGIF realized that Brunner meant business and the threat of impending disaster hung over their homes. Thus, even though Brunner put an end to liberations from Drancy, UGIF remained cautious in removing the children. Things remained at a standstill until early 1944, when indications of a new policy appeared, associated with Juliette Stern. She seems to have been working on two fronts simultaneously. According to the testimony of an EIF activist, Albert Akerberg, Stern began coordinating a methodical dispersal of the children in collaboration with La Sixième; while in January 1944, according to other testimony, she established a clandestine service for the rescue of adult Jews together with other WIZO women. Stern established contact with Joseph Fischer of Keren Kayemet and traveled incognito to Lyon to receive financial support for these projects.[126] Seemingly, some 200 children were hidden by these efforts. But Stern's work was countered by the legalistic approach of other UGIF officials. For example, Israelowicz's replacement as liaison with the German authorities, Kurt Schendel, turned to Röthke for permission to regroup the "isolated children" in Paris. That was in late April 1944. Cynical as always, Röthke granted permission, provided the children be interned in one home in Seine-et-Oise, and promised their immunity.[127]

Warned and condemned by resistance elements in the community and faced with Röthke's demand for centralization, the council wavered. Stern announced on 11 July 1944 that her service was involved in "a total revision of the files," probably referring to a plan to slowly erase all evidence of the children's whereabouts, and alternatives were submitted to alert the homes in case of emergency.[128] But the council refused a scheme proposed by a joint committee of resistance organizations to disperse the children.[129] Approximately 500 children were still in UGIF's care and they were to stay put. On 21 July Brunner's troops encircled six UGIF children's homes; almost a year after his last direct raid on UGIF offices, he seized close to 300 children and personnel. For four days his forces acted swiftly, arresting and interning the "blocked" children and staff. They were rushed to Drancy to join the last major convoy from France to Auschwitz—the seventy-seventh—containing 1,300 Jews, 300 of whom were under eighteen. Only 209 adults and children from that trainload survived the war.[130]

Brunner was the man responsible for the operation. In detailed testimony presented a month after the deportation, Schendel described his meeting of 20 July with Brunner. Furious about a leaflet concerning Jewish resistance fighters who boasted of killing Germans, Brunner announced his decision to arrest the youth and children, "the terrorists of the future." Schendel's refusal to provide him a list of institutions had no significance. On the following day, Brunner began to carry out his plan. UGIF's cautiousness had backfired; on 25 July the council decided to close all but two of its clinics and to reduce personnel drastically. Pushed on by inertia, it also resolved to pursue "the council's mission" for the estimated 30,000 Jews still living openly in Paris.[131]

UGIF's failure to protect these children was not a mere oversight. More than 3,000 had passed through its homes since 1942, and most of those were safely tucked away in the north or south, often with tacit UGIF cooperation. Less than 700 children remained in its homes in September 1943, when the council was relentlessly urged to find alternate ways to maintain them. Fearing the watchful German eyes, UGIF opted for a deliberate procedure that reduced the number of children. But when push came to shove in spring 1944, it upheld its policy. Juliette Stern, then the dominant figure in the council, seemingly prevailed in her decision to continue the gradual dissolution. Was that an act of criminal collaboration with the Nazis, as elements in the resistance movement implied, or a simple lack of courage and foresight to upset the status quo?

Drancy and UGIF (1942–1944)

For more than 70,000 Jews, Drancy was their last view of France before arriving at Auschwitz. Established by the German authorities in August 1941, the camp was under the authority of three central figures involved in the "Final Solution" in France—Dannecker, Röthke, and Brunner—and each left a definite mark during his reign of terror.

Life in Drancy and the other northern internment camps (Compiègne,

Beaune-la-Rolande, Pithiviers) necessitated menial functions. Rather than allow the inmates to live under wretched conditions, UGIF saw it as its responsibility to improve their lot. Realizing the Red Cross's reluctance to guarantee its presence in Drancy, Baur turned to Dannecker a month after UGIF began to operate: "It is indispensable that we replace its services as soon as possible in Drancy and the other camps, especially Compiègne."[132] Baur saw a moral virtue in granting assistance to the inmates, and from then on UGIF expended a healthy portion of its budget to improve the sanitary conditions and morale of the internees. A special service was entrusted with forwarding parcels to internees, relieving somewhat their poor physical conditions. Until Brunner's administration, Jews were permitted a weekly parcel, and although UGIF served only as the liaison with the families, it occasionally provided a special allowance for the parcel service. During the mass deportations of 1942, when as many as 5,000 Jews were crowded into Drancy, UGIF was sending almost 3,000 parcels weekly, reaching a total of twenty-seven tons of produce. Jews who resided in Drancy for extended periods of time, between autumn 1942 and summer 1943, benefited most from this constant addition to their diet. UGIF also assumed the contact between Drancy and the outside world, creating a daily courier service between the internees and their families. By virtue of this function, the organization was able to liberate children from the camp, artificially prove non-Jewish descendancy, and negotiate sporadic releases.[133] Periodically, it dealt with the inmates' clothing. Limited laundry resources existed in the camp, and in order to avoid spreading diseases, a special service was set up to bring clean clothing to the camp. All in all, UGIF's functions in the camp remained basically constant until Brunner's arrival in July 1943, except for one service that went beyond strict welfare—Service 14, the liaison with the Gestapo, administered by Leo Israelowicz.

Brought by Dannecker to Paris in March 1941, Israelowicz was stigmatized for the duration of his activity in the Comité and UGIF. Indeed, his original association with the SS officer remains part of his historical image.[134] Myth and reality are intertwined in this individual, a result of the unique power invested in his hands: Israelowicz was the ultimate authority in deciding whether a special request on behalf of a Jew, often an individual request for liberation from Drancy, was to be filed with the Germans. Undoubtedly, his was a position of extreme power in a powerless society.

Israelowicz's annual report for 1942 and his periodic requests from the German authorities remain the significant documents for evaluating Section 14's activity during 1942. Claiming to have released 817 Jews from Drancy and Pithiviers, Israelowicz bragged about the small number of German refusals—83. On the basis of the thousands of requests his office received, it is clear that a sifting process was at work. Herein lies the delicate issue.

There are no known sources that describe the criteria for submitting dispensations; only examples of German refusals and acceptances exists. They reveal something but conceal more. Widows, the sick, orphans, and the aged were released, either to old-age homes, the Rothschild hospital, or UGIF orphanages. Concentration under UGIF institutions was the only precondition for liberation. Similarly, requests of widows, the sick, orphans, and the aged and special situations were turned down. For 1943, no statistics exist, but it is clear that the number of releases declined considerably and came to a standstill by the summer.[135]

Understandably, UGIF was pleased with even this limited success: liberating Jews from the squalid conditions of Drancy was the ultimate fulfillment of its welfare motivation. The council expressed its confidence in Israelowicz's activity and seemingly ceased to regard him as an undesirable element.[136] Was that part of an Israelowicz-German fraud? Were the releases part of a deceitful, prearranged tactic by the two to dupe UGIF? The Germans' liberations of some Jews are often attributed to a certain logic: by granting UGIF a sense of importance, conciliatory behavior was evoked.[137] UGIF indeed graciously accepted the German concession and demanded compliance to internal regulations to continue the liberations, but its behavior does not necessarily prove such German motivations. Releases from Drancy in 1942 and 1943 may have resulted from common bureaucratic negotiations and interventions that persisted until summer 1943 without necessarily being part of a precise, intentional plan to entrap UGIF. The demonic German mind with a clear conception of how to dupe UGIF is one of the mythical characteristics attributed to the Nazis; however, the council was up against German functionaries who in 1942–43, for one reason or another, granted certain releases. Its impact on UGIF is clear: UGIF was not living with the consciousness of a "Final Solution," and the status quo offered some rewards. Seemingly, Israelowicz was included in that thinking; he negotiated with his German counterparts for those requests that appeared "feasible" to him without being privy to the German designs. Neither Israelowicz nor the UGIF could foresee in 1942 that some of their institutions housing liberated Jews would eventually be shut down by the Nazis. The road of least resistance, the road of *shtadlanim*, appeared more effective.

Brunner took charge of Drancy in July 1943: the French administration was removed, and UGIF was ordered to take over.[138] On the one hand, Brunner put an end to UGIF's relief work and requests for liberation, while on the other hand, he presented a list of demands for the internal upkeep of the camp. UGIF viewed the new role positively. If the organization could no longer supply special relief assistance, through administration of the camp it would be able to provide more substantial relief and moral support. From summer 1943, Drancy became UGIF's central concern, and Edinger, who replaced Baur in early September, saw the daily upkeep of Drancy as the major moral and economic priority.[139] Judging from various accounts, UGIF's council went all out to supply the camp with large amounts of clothing, food, maintenance equipment, and office supplies: according to some reports, UGIF smuggled into the camp far larger quantities of food than prescribed by the German authorities and significantly improved the conditions there.[140]

Pressed by the increase in deportations from September and the large turnover of inmates, the council entered into another prolonged negotiation with the Commissariat to increase its budget. Supported by Duquesnel, UGIF eventually received a special grant of 15,000,000 francs from the French treasury and brought about a French law in March 1944 that permitted it to draw larger sums from the "Solidarity Fund."[141] Thus, in 1944 almost 4,000,000 francs monthly (close to 40 percent of the organization's budget) went to Drancy to alleviate the inmates' internment.

In the last months of the German occupation, thousands of Jews passed through Drancy and were tended to by UGIF personnel, who continued to perform welfare chores—liaisons with families, parcel services, etc. UGIF remained associated with Drancy until after the liberation. In mid-August 1944, 1,500 Jews were still interned in the camp, destitute and barren; Edinger, under strong attack from resistance forces, opposed a Red Cross proposal to leave Drancy as a temporary residence for those Jews without accommodations and proposed instead their relocation to UGIF centers in Paris. His position was seemingly accepted, and 600 Jews were moved under UGIF's aegis to Paris.[142] A few days later, Edinger himself was arrested by a resistance unit, *milices patriotiques juives*, and brought to Drancy, ending ignominiously two-and-a-half years of UGIF's involvement in the German camp.[143]

For three long years Drancy haunted the Jewish community of France. Immigrant and native Jews reached the camp after being arrested in their *patrie* or newly found homeland by France's historical enemy. Although it passed through several types of administration, Drancy had from March 1942 only one constant purpose—it was the gateway to Auschwitz. Facing an internment camp only three miles northeast of Paris and constant deportations to the "East," UGIF countered with its own welfare objectives. Placing its facilities in the service of the inmates, the organization developed patterns of assistance in an attempt to improve basic conditions, and when the time came even assumed administration of the camp. Operating then clearly within the German system, the council did not relinquish its sense of responsibility to the inmates and constantly looked for ways to increase the budget for further support. Yet its struggle for the preservation of human dignity also had tragic effects—German expenses and personnel were reduced to a minimum, and the deportations proceeded without interference.

UGIF's Welfare Activity (1942–1944)

Divided among numerous Jewish societies, the community's welfare network touched on all aspects of daily life. Merged into UGIF's operation, the
services took on an increasing responsibility as the economic situation of the
community worsened. The financial problems were acutely felt in the area
of family welfare and public canteens, and UGIF was determined to meet
the needs of the impoverished, both the immigrant and the native community.

Prior to UGIF-N, the public kitchens in and around Paris were operated
by several organizations, half of which were affiliated with Rue Amelot. Most
of the canteens' organizations had a leftist orientation, a reflection of the
political spectrum of the Eastern European immigrants. Ideologically opposed to UGIF, these organizations originally refused to collaborate with it,
but lacking funds to support their canteens, some eventually agreed to receive the council's financial backing.[144] Consistent with its goal to convince
the immigrant organizations of its sincere intentions and impressed with
these kitchens' necessity, UGIF appropriated 15 percent of its budget in
January 1942 to the canteens. Nothing was demanded in return.

Amelot, the least dogmatic in its opposition to UGIF, agreed to receive
support so long as the council refrained from intervening in its internal affairs.
A year later Amelot was able to report that UGIF was supplying 25 percent
of the canteens' budgets without demanding a written report from the institutions or an account of Amelot's other sources of income.[145] UGIF and
Amelot reached a practical compromise: Amelot continued to oppose the
UGIF's existence and functioned in contrary ways but still relied on its
support. This basic cooperation lasted even after Rapoport's arrest on 1 June
1943. Several canteens were closed, but to Amelot's complete satisfaction
those that remained open continued to enjoy an almost independent existence, though they were almost exclusively funded by UGIF. Apparently,
six canteens continued to function until the end of June 1944, serving almost
31,000 meals monthly; although that was 5,000 meals fewer than the monthly
average in 1943, the continual high rate of attendance attested to the pressing
needs of thousands of Jews who overcame their fears of association with these
UGIF institutions.[146] (None of the canteens were ever raided by the German
police.) The case of the canteens reflects the relationship established between UGIF and Amelot in other welfare areas (dispensaries, clothing, family
welfare, children's homes): UGIF overcame its opposition and agreed to
support Amelot, and in this sense it abided by its commitment to the immigrant leaders from 28 January 1942.

Direct welfare to the families was another major task that UGIF inherited
from the Comité. Here, too, it was not alone; the various immigrant orga-

nizations that remained outside of UGIF involved themselves in this area, as well. However, UGIF had more resources to deal with the community's needs, having availed itself of a share of the "Solidarity Fund" from early 1942. Needs of individual families varied, and there is no indication that UGIF looked disparagingly upon the needs of the immigrant Jews. Two types of direct welfare were instituted: some families received a monthly stipend, based on the number of members in the household, while other families required special assistance for particular items—parcels for inmates, medical services, legal aid, etc.—covering the whole range of life's requirements. UGIF's basic orientation towards assisting the community to sustain itself appears here, and judging from the high number of applications, it fulfilled a purpose. Whereas some 2,500 Jews turned to UGIF for assistance in January 1942, by August 1942 almost four times that number were wanting some form of aid. To what extent the sums extended were significant for the families is impossible to assess, but the steady flow of applications spoke for itself.[147]

Under the watchful eyes of the Commissariat, UGIF was often censured for distributing sums of welfare beyond what was deemed necessary. The council ignored the criticism and continued to allocate close to 4,000,000 francs (about $30,000) monthly for welfare purposes to more than 7,000 Jewish families.[148] Moreover, certain UGIF services continued to support families in hiding, disregarding the Commissariat's warnings. Complicity of this kind in illegal activities clearly disturbed the French authorities, and they conferred with their German counterparts about initiating joint efforts to stop it. Antignac saw this activity as a flagrant violation on UGIF's part and an act of resistance, but nothing was done until Brunner's arrival.[149] Guided by Juliette Stern, who from rue Bienfaisance watched over this activity, the services assisted some 400 families clandestinely. Registered with UGIF under fictitious names and addresses, these families received their relief either at UGIF offices or via social workers who knew their correct addresses. It would seem that in the summer of 1944, UGIF was caring for almost a third of the 30,000 Jews living openly in Paris, and consequently it refused, time and again, to terminate its services.[150]

UGIF's determination to help Jews subsist was vehemently condemned by the various resistance alignments in Paris. As the war drew to a close in France, they emphasized their position by occasionally raiding and attacking UGIF offices. The council withstood all and claimed its indispensability to the Jews of Paris. But painful historical questions relative to UGIF's assistance remain to be posed—i.e., to what extent did UGIF's aid boomerang? Were the recipients of this aid easy targets for the German police? Did the Germans utilize UGIF lists in their last raids in Paris in spring 1944? UGIF possessed two detailed lists: one contained the names of its needy, and the other consisted of names from the various prefects for paying off the milliard fine. As far as we know, the German police never seized these lists from UGIF offices, although they may have easily obtained them by other means.[151] In any event, the German authorities had various lists of Jews from different sources, but their spring raids netted only a small number of Jews. More significant issues stood in the way of another Vel d'Hiv, minimizing the importance of the UGIF lists. However, even if UGIF's lists were not directly used for German arrests, its aid may have had a more subtle influence by increasing the community's reliance on an open existence: UGIF leaders did not publicly encourage the population to go into hiding, and its publication, *Bulletin de l'Union Générale des Israélites en France*, essentially reiterated German regulations. In this sense UGIF clearly differed from some immigrant organizations that actively proposed a route of escape from open life in the cities. And tragically, it appears that on a few occasions, Jews were arrested in the process of receiving their welfare.

United by a feeling of responsibility to the Jewish community, and motivated to serve the needy in the orphanages, camps, and cities, members of the council rejected resignation. Only towards the end of June 1944 were the names of several members (Dr. Benjamin Weill-Hallé, Dr. Alfred Morali, Albert Weill, and Lucienne Scheid-Haas) deleted from the council's minutes. Their persistence overcame the constant criticism from different corners of the community and found expression in their confidential consultations of 12–13 July 1944.[152] Refusing to accept the claim that their aid only endangered the community, they emphasized the catastrophe that would befall the community if their services were terminated. Liberation appeared to be at hand, but nothing was yet certain, neither the allied landing nor the reconquest of Paris: weeks or months could still pass. In this turbulent moment, the council restated its credo: closure was contrary to "the indispensable nature of the north's activity, recognized by all."[153] In this same spirit, it called upon the southern council not to close its doors.

UGIF North: An Appraisal

UGIF-N came into being in the shadow of an intensification of German policy and was disbanded with the liberation of northern France; it had been criticized from the outset by immigrant organizations, and its functions were terminated by UGIF amid clamors of condemnation by the same elements. One consistent source of contention was the "Solidarity Fund." Viewed with particular venom as a definite act of collaboration, the "Solidarity Fund" was judged symptomatic of UGIF:

> They covered their treachery with the cloak of relief that the UGIF gave to the Jewish poor with the millions that were robbed from the Jews themselves and that were put at the disposal of the organization by the Germans. This organization is the greatest disgrace of the Jews in Paris.[154]

In this issue, as in many others, the UGIF council upheld a different moral ethic and understood reality and commitment in a totally different way.

UGIF's primary purpose was to serve the needy, and all its efforts went in that direction. As Jews were being arrested and deported to Drancy-Auschwitz, UGIF was waging a long and arduous bureaucratic battle with the Commissariat to safeguard the economic basis of the organization and relief services. The long economic negotiations resulted in some significant gains for the Jewish community (postponement of taxation, deferral of repayment of the milliard fine) but failed to provide the council a substantial budget, which would have dramatically supplemented the meager support it was able to supply. In dealing with the Commissariat, UGIF faced a bureaucratic complex with contrasting tendencies and personalities but with two overriding considerations: UGIF's existence had to be guaranteed in order to avoid French responsibility for indigent Jews; and UGIF must be refused access to blocked Jewish money and property so that the French could carry out their extensive plans for Aryanization. But in its overall attempt to turn UGIF-N into a totally subservient organ, the Commissariat failed, owing in no small measure to its own lack of authority within the Vichy bureaucracy. As Baur rightly contended in July 1943, UGIF had little influence over the community's actions, and the Commissariat could do absolutely nothing about it.

Within the German scheme, UGIF-N was perceived differently. Legends and myths aside, the northern council began to "serve" the Germans by supplying materials for the inmates to be deported to Auschwitz. That remained a significant aspect of UGIF's functions, as in the mass deportations of summer 1942. A bureaucratic relationship was also established between the two enemies: the Jewish experts pressed for compliance with anti-Semitic regulations, ordered UGIF to publish a "community" paper, created a liaison service (14) to centralize Jewish requests, and demanded Jews for forced labor; UGIF carried out these orders in order to guarantee its own vision: thousands of Jews, immigrants and natives, needed some form of assistance and protection. Under this German-Vichy patronage, UGIF brought together a comprehensive welfare program that covered all aspects of the community's needs and was occasionally granted German concessions. Fearing German reprisals and struggling to insure the continuation of relief, UGIF conveyed to its personnel and probably to its constituents the need for restraint and order. To keep things at an even keel, it acted at times vigorously, at times flexibly. Until summer 1943, UGIF limited itself to social relief and was not called upon to change its orientation. And when confronted with Brunner's demand to turn UGIF into an arm of the Gestapo, the leadership unanimously stood firm and upheld its moral posture. For Baur, Stora, and Musnik, that meant deportation to Auschwitz, but UGIF continued to function as a relief organization supporting thousands of Jews.

UGIF's existence and functions took on a different meaning for its critics in the resistance organizations. By participating in the legalistic framework offered by the Nazis and Vichy, UGIF became in their eyes an accessory to German measures: it collaborated in sending children to their deaths, offered lists for German raids, negotiated with the Germans for its own safety, and endangered the community by leaving its premises vulnerable to a German roundup. UGIF *was* unable to restructure its framework as the moment called for, but the outcome of events is not necessarily indicative of the underlying forces, tendencies, and orientations. Although a centralistic organization, UGIF-N was not totally monolithic, and conflicting patterns of leadership found their expression within the general operation. Legalistically oriented, as was so blatantly the case during the days before Vel d'Hiv, UGIF leaders often encouraged Jews to abide by the anti-Semitic legislation. Georges Edinger insisted that Jews wear the yellow star and wrote to a UGIF official in 1943, urging him to

> demand from our coreligionists to scrupulously conform to all the regulations in force, however tedious they may be for daily life. It is absolutely necessary that all bearers of a protective pass strictly obey to the present regulations.[155]

But legalism was not all-encompassing. As Edinger was insisting on obedience, Juliette Stern and Fernand Musnik were already involved in promoting clandestine activity through UGIF's services. Concerned with the overall position of the council, they worked on a modest scale to avoid German retaliation and internal squabbles. Moreover, individual UGIF services operated independently of UGIF's directives, providing assistance to Jews in hiding, and helping to rescue children. Yet the diverse elements of UGIF-N were united by a common denominator: acceptance of the legal framework to provide the community with social relief. Thus, as the council rejected Brunner's policelike demands, it agreed to administer Drancy to alleviate the inmates' plight, fully aware of the assistance it provided thereby to the German policy of oppression. The council supported certain of Amelot's relief projects, disregarding its constant criticism of UGIF's legalism and with the clear knowledge of Amelot's illegal efforts. Each of these organizations was drawn to the other for its own reasons: Amelot needed financial backing, and UGIF had a social function to perform. Amelot's economic reliance on UGIF had many parallels within the community at large, wherein thousands of Jews found the organization's meager aid helpful to enable them to live through the traumatic occupation years. Undoubtedly, UGIF turned that reliance into an obligation, which bound it to the community until the liberation.

UGIF-N was not a resistance organization; it did not transform its social functions into rescue operations or fighting units, or into centers of German opposition. UGIF never sought to influence the community and seldom forewarned it of impending events, nor did it encourage dispersion. Even when rescue activity and dispersal were coordinated by UGIF personalities, official institutions remained open. UGIF-N clung to its social conception of 20 January 1942 "to improve the fate of our coreligionists, fellow-countrymen and foreigners, living in France" and remained an organization of relief. As such, its orientation had direct tragic consequences for hundreds, indirect repercussions for an unknown number, and relief for thousands.

V.

UGIF IN SOUTHERN FRANCE, 1942–1944

The German measures that forced UGIF-N into action left little imprint on the south. Under the impression of the mild atmosphere of the south and unhampered by the German occupation, the UGIF-S council expected a gradual dissolution of the welfare organizations and their smooth incorporation into UGIF. Its eventual recognition that such was not to be the case was the first of many instances in which the freedom of the unoccupied zone proved to be illusory. During the ensuing months, this predicament recurred constantly; UGIF-S was torn between an optimistic appraisal of its freedom and a pessimistic assessment of the reality and was often forced to compromise in its decisions and courses of action. For UGIF-S the almost exclusive contact with the French authorities during 1942 concealed the real threat, the German authorities. The German presence during 1942 was not constant, but when it appeared it dispelled any fallacious sense of safety. Thus, the history of UGIF-S recounts the ways in which its leadership tried to decipher the contrasting tendencies of the authorities and create a workable solution to protect and aid the community of some 180,000 Jews.

UGIF-S officially came into existence when the names of its council members were published in the *Journal Officiel* on 9 January 1942, four months before the council's inaugural meeting in early May. During this period, two events occurred with long-lasting importance for UGIF's activity: first, the German decision to oust Vallat as commissioner of the Commissariat, and second, the reorganization of the welfare services and their incorporation into UGIF. In a sense, the two events were related. Vallat had led Lambert to believe that the German authorities were not as concerned with UGIF-S as with the north, and it was within his jurisdiction to decide when to activate the southern organization.[1] But he underestimated the German pressure and overestimated his own power. It was after SS Sturmbannführer Kurt Lischka's accusatory letter of February 1942 that Vallat understood that the German authorities had no intention of dragging on the affair indefinitely.[2]

Vichy broadsheet and postcard. Pétain calling on the French people to follow him. "Frenchmen! You are neither sold out nor betrayed nor abandoned."

Vichy broadsheet and postcard. On the left side a tottering house of France, disrupted by the corrupt influence of Jews and Freemasons. On the right side a sturdy house of France, bright and clear, firmly upheld by the pillars of the National Revolution: Work, Family, Motherland.

Scenes from the roundup of Jews in Paris in late August
1941. (Courtesy of Süddeutscher Verlag, Munich.)

German and French police rounding up Jews in Marseilles in late January 1943. (Courtesy of Süddeutscher Verlag, Munich.)

These children were cared for by OSE social workers in southern France and were deported in April 1944 to Auschwitz by order of Klaus Barbie. Photograph taken in 1943.

Leading figures in UGIF South. From
left to right are Gaston Kahn, Albert
Lévy, Raymond-Raoul Lambert. Photograph from autumn 1941. (Courtesy
of Lambert family, Paris.)

André Baur, vice-president of
UGIF and head of UGIF
North. (Courtesy of Centre de
Documentation Juive Contem-
poraine, Paris.)

Raymond-Raoul Lambert in autumn
1941. (Courtesy of Lambert family,
Paris.)

His subsequent meeting with Dannecker dashed any hopes of German in-difference and any possibility of his remaining in office.

Lambert was privy to the attempts to dismiss Vallat and was encouraged by him to present his structure for UGIF-S as quickly as possible.[3] Lambert trusted Vallat and immediately came up with a plan whereby UGIF-S would consist of seven departments and a general administration:[4] the former were to include all the main welfare societies and were designed to continue their previous activity with minimum intervention by the general administration.[5] Lambert's federative plan, which promised each society independence of action and spirit, was accepted by Vallat with no objections. Vallat was also sympathetic to Lambert's request to stay the dissolution of the societies for several weeks but found himself unable to combat the German demands.[6] When his efforts were unsuccessful, Vallat turned to Lambert to dissolve the Jewish welfare societies.[7] Two days later, on 9 March 1942, the *Journal Officiel* published the first list of disbanded organizations. Although the process of dissolving the Jewish organizations was to last more than two years, the initial lists included the major southern societies.[8] For Lambert, that was truly a failure. He had promised and cajoled, hoping to postpone the dissolution of the leading societies (OSE, HICEM, Alliance, etc.), but all of them were dissolved in March.[9] The swiftness of the move intensified the community controversy about the orientation of UGIF.[10]

The Dissolution of the Welfare Societies

The Fédération, spearheaded by Marc Jarblum, was the organization most vociferously opposed to UGIF. Jarblum took special pride in his efforts to influence native and immigrant Jews not to join UGIF and called upon his supporters to persist in their opposition.[11] A month after UGIF's inception, when the leaders of the Fédération met in Marseilles to discuss the recent developments, Jarblum elaborated on his ideological critique.[12] He upheld the Fédération's unique perspective of social welfare and Jewish nationalism and emphasized its unique message for immigrant Jews. Moreover, accord-ing to Jarblum, the Fédération was the only body capable of preserving a Jewish outlook, and it alone was the custodian of Jewish honor. Jarblum also condemned the elitist attitude of the French Jewish leadership, which had disavowed its commitment to the entire community. All of these considera-tions strengthened his opinion that the Fédération must continue its work among the immigrant community and outside of UGIF.[13] However, Jar-blum's position was challenged. Among those who supported his rejection of UGIF were proponents of a more moderate view, which upheld participation in UGIF for as long as the traditional methods of the Fédération could be maintained. Underlying this point of view was a financial consideration: if the Fédération refused to join the legal framework, its financial resources would soon disappear. They, like Jarblum, were concerned with the Fédération's honor but feared that if it became bankrupt, it would lose its constituents to CAR and be vulnerable to future criticism.[14] They concluded that since UGIF existed, the Fédération should take it into consideration and negotiate with it.

Israel Jefroykin, the venerated leader of the Fédération for many years, took a more extreme position, opposing Jarblum once again; their former differences of opinion reechoed in this discussion.[15] Jefroykin saw the issue as an institutional one rather than a personal one. Since he did not think it was possible to survive illegally, he believed that opposition to UGIF would signal the end of the Fédération. This attitude was consistent with Jefroykin's position in the debates of 1941, when he had demanded a separate department for the Fédération to be run autonomously by its personnel. Jefroykin rejected the approach that mixed Jewish honor and morality with the welfare problem: the Fédération was obligated to deal with the plight of the immigrant Jews and to work from within to guarantee an equitable division of funds, but to refrain from political involvement. Opposition to UGIF should be the last alternative, only after a serious attempt to cooperate proved unfeasible. Jefroykin's son, Jules (Dyka), was willing to accept this approach if certain conditions were fulfilled—namely, if UGIF became an authentic representative of the entire Jewish community, fulfilling the historic Jewish goal for an organized community (Kehillah). Jules was well aware of the complexity of such a decision: "When one agrees to collaborate one is exposed to criticism but conscious of having at least fulfilled a duty by ameliorating the fate of French Jewry."[16] Jefroykin's argument is noteworthy. It follows the line of several young native French Jews (Gamzon, Brener, and members of the scout movement) who agreed to participate with UGIF out of a more "realistic" appraisal of the Jewish tragedy.

These practical considerations prevailed and overcame Jarblum's opposition. The Fédération decided to enter into negotiations with UGIF to set up a special section under its supervision. However, Israel Jefroykin left France shortly thereafter, leaving the organization's leadership completely under Jarblum's influence. Jarblum proceeded to block the merger of the Fédération with UGIF and to withhold the transfer of its assets. He succeeded in doing so for several months, disregarding the dissolution law. Finally, in late June 1942, Vichy intervened and officially disbanded the organization.[17] Jarblum was not ready to succumb, and on the same day he presented his credo to Fédération leaders: "Even if we submit ourselves to the obligation of merging and even if we offer our experts, we will not stop talking against UGIF. . . . The essential aspect of our task is to influence other societies in a negative way."[18] Thus, Jarblum's belief that the Fédération should appear to be working within UGIF but should simultaneously be undermining the organization and its leaders, was clearly formulated prior to the summer deportations. In this regard, his actions mirrored the behavior of the northern immigrant societies.

Other leaders of the major welfare societies expressed their suspicions of merger with UGIF, but none shared Jarblum's total denunciation. But like him, in weighing the pros and cons of UGIF they were influenced by their evaluation of its personnel. Dr. Aron Syngalowski of ORT encouraged the council to include someone acquainted with ORT's work. Syngalowski reasoned that American ORT would be placated by such a move and would continue to provide aid to the organization's projects in France.[19] The fear of losing American financial support was common among the welfare leaders. Wladimir Schah, a prominent figure in HICEM France and a recently appointed member of the UGIF-S council, even called upon Jewish interest groups in America to intervene in Washington to maintain an autonomous role for HICEM, possibly outside UGIF.[20] In contrast, organizations such as the Alliance, OSE, and CAR, which were aware of Lambert's past experience, refrained from criticism and called upon their offices to grant UGIF a period of grace.[21] In the end, all of these major societies were doomed to accept the law and resigned themselves to finding a workable compromise with UGIF. By summer 1942 the French laws had dissolved the organizations, though not their goal to remain in an autonomous framework carrying out their particular social mission.

Beyond the reluctance of individual leaders to join UGIF, a common pattern of Jewish community life in the last generations emerges here: the struggle of different bodies to preserve their particular characteristics and avoid entering into an umbrella organization. Opposition to a centralistic organization was prevalent in French Jewish society in the twenties and thirties and had parallels in other European Jewish communities of the period. This individualistic approach was one of the deep-seated legacies of emancipation, and any attempt to create an all-encompassing Jewish organization was seen as undermining that legacy. In this case, the welfare societies feared that merger meant an end to their unique character and approach, not only because UGIF was an imposed organization. Lambert, who in the thirties had gone against the individualistic trend and called for unity in the community, was aware of the sensitivities of the various societies and their opposition to centralistic tendencies. He attempted through his structure for UGIF-S to overcome these hurdles, granting maximum independence to the societies and minimal interference to the general administration. In so doing he greatly limited the role of the council. The council could have authority in internal organizational issues, in relations with other Jewish and Gentile organizations in France and abroad, and in negotiations with the authorities. However, it was to represent the Jewish community solely in the technical areas of welfare and assistance. These guidelines were drawn up to stress UGIF's disinterest in usurping the functions of the other organizations and in becoming a powerful centralistic organ. UGIF-S was caught up in Lambert's spirit of optimism that the Jews in unoccupied France could continue their lives as before the debacle. These were sacred principles for the southern council, and their observance guided it in its operations during the following months.

The UGIF South Council: Character, Orientations, and Patterns of Activity (1942–1944)

Deportations: Summer 1942

In April 1942, Pierre Laval returned to the prime minister's office in Vichy. In choosing Laval, Pétain gave further indication of his plan to court Nazi Germany at all costs. France was seeking a prominent role in Hitler's new Europe, and Laval was the man to bring it about. Laval echoed that sentiment, declaring publicly France's desire for a Nazi victory to curb Bolshevik world domination. Although Hitler and the Nazi leadership paid little attention to these proclamations, the Vichy government proceeded, hoping to strengthen its bond with Germany. As part of this new drive, Laval sent more French laborers to Germany and intensified anti-Jewish legislation in the north.

The policy of *relève* (exchange) was fully under way when UGIF-S began its operations in spring 1942. However, the council, like large segments of the Jewish population of the unoccupied zone, was not overwhelmed by these events and was heartened by the increasing signs of opposition to Vichy among the French population, which culminated in the massive demonstration in the south on Bastille Day. This demonstration, the first of its kind, was adequate proof that not all of France blindly followed Laval and that the unoccupied zone allowed Frenchmen to express their true feelings. This impression was reinforced by the discrepancy between anti-Semitic legislation in the north and south. For example, the yellow star imposed on the Jews in the north on 7 June 1942 was never enforced in the south. These visible indications reinforced the belief that the south was indeed not under German influence.[22]

When the UGIF-S council convened in early May, it was more concerned about the dismissal of Vallat than about Laval's new direction. Pierre Seligman, a distinguished member of the Conseil d'État, who was called upon to replace the foreign-born Millner at the last minute, expressed the feeling exactly: "I could have accepted a nomination by Mr. XV but it makes me ill to be appointed by a note signed by his successor. With the latter, all collaboration is, I believe, impossible."[23] Lambert was still optimistic, believing that the important work UGIF would accomplish would turn its detractors into advocates.[24] However, before UGIF was able to establish credibility within the community, it was faced with the grave events of the summer.

The deportation of foreign Jews from the unoccupied zone had been agreed upon by the Vichy government in early July. No serious obstacles seemed to present themselves, as the French internment camps in the south were to supply the Jews to the German authorities. However, when Dannecker inspected these camps in July, he found the number of Jews to be far below the 40,000 anticipated. (In fact, no more than 13,000 Jews were still interned.) The German authorities pressured French officials to augment the numbers and in general received their fullest cooperation. The Commissariat and the French police discussed the details with the SD and promised assistance, urging local prefects to prepare for the upcoming operation.[25] UGIF-S was never mentioned in the planning stages, but it is reasonable to believe that it was expected to fulfill social functions similar to those carried out by UGIF-N during the July deportations.

UGIF-S was unaware of the impending tragedy until late July, when two members of the council heard about the rumors circulating in Vichy.[26] Lambert and Raphaël Spanien, a leading figure in HICEM and a UGIF-S council member, were suddenly face to face with the Vichy collaborators. They acted swiftly in several directions. They tried to arrange a joint delegation with the Central Consistory to Laval, encouraged the Joint to utilize its contacts with the American government, and alerted representatives of the Nîmes Committee. Their efforts met with a mixed response. The Consistory refused to cooperate, dismissing the information as preposterous, but Joe Schwartz of the Joint went to work with his usual gusto. On 31 July 1942 he went to see the American chargé d'affaires, H. Pinkney Tuck, and relayed to him the unsettling information. Tuck, who was to loom as a beacon of humaneness in this sordid month, was pessimistic. He interpreted the French submission as part of Laval's attempt to appease Germany, and he saw no hope in opposing the move. Members of the Nîmes Committee received from their own channels corroborating evidence of the intended deportations and hastily met to coordinate efforts.[27] For its part, UGIF presented a protest to Laval's secretary, avoiding an encounter with Laval on the grounds that it was unauthorized to represent the Jewish community in issues unrelated to welfare.[28] By adhering to a strict definition of its role, UGIF-S refrained from meeting Vichy leaders throughout the month of August, and no joint démarche with the Consistory was undertaken. This development is all the more striking in light of the persistent interventions initiated by representatives of the Nîmes Committee.

On 5 and 6 August 1942, Pétain and Laval were approached by international delegations who had come to plead the cause of France and the Jews. Prominent Quaker leaders (Lindsay Noble and Roswell D. McClelland) and leading figures of the Nîmes Committee and the YMCA (Donald Lowrie, Tracy Strong, and Père Arnou) impressed upon the French leaders that their actions were causing irreparable damage to France's image in the world. They further demanded that Jews holding valid American visas and children be detained until all possibilities of their emigration were checked.[29] Their strategy is worthy of note. Their goal was to bring about a cessation of French collaboration, but when that seemed unlikely, they reverted to specific demands to save at least particular groups of Jews.[30]

Saving the children became their crusade. Here they hoped to find a certain sensitivity on the part of both the French and American governments. The Quaker representatives urged their headquarters in Philadelphia to do all in its power to obtain 7,000 visas for children. Whether this course was actually pursued is unclear, but the tone of a telegram to Secretary of State Cordell Hull on 14 August lacked urgency. The Quakers described the terrifying atmosphere in the south and the fear that "Jews and other refugees including children" would be deported. Hull was not implored to open the gates to these Jews but was asked to intervene with the French government, for "American influence [is] still effective." The State Department responded laconically a week later that several hundred Jews in line for deportation might be saved by their transfer to a free country.[31] No offer was forthcoming from the U.S. government until a month later; for the time being there was only a cold bureaucratic reply, indicative of the massive emotional gap that separated officials in the free world from the events in Europe. The pressing call to save the children was shelved with similar requests, including, perhaps, such fantastic schemes as one proposed by Wladimir Schah of UGIF-S. Panic-stricken by the events, Schah rushed a proposal to HICEM offices in New York, whereby the American government would agree to receive 30,000 refugees, mostly children, and concentrate them in internment camps until they were cleared by security. Schah, like the other welfare workers, stood by helpless while the deportations were taking place before his eyes.

The first bits of information that reached UGIF and the international relief organizations spoke of 10,000 deportees, of whom 3,600 were to be taken from the internment camps: Gurs, Noé, Récébédou, Les Milles, Le Vernet, Rivesaltes. UGIF proceeded to set up welfare teams for the respective camps, bringing together various experts from its participating organizations.

Together with representatives of the Jewish Chaplaincy, these teams worked alongside the international relief organizations and French Christian societies.[32] Their functions were similar in each camp. In conjunction with the regional prefects and the camp supervisors, they were obliged to prepare the lists of interned Jews destined for deportation. The procedure followed a common pattern. According to the prefects' lists, those Jews who were to be deported were separated from the rest of the camp. The prefects, however, were permitted to juggle their lists and were open to the requests of interested parties.[33] This situation was fully utilized by both the Jewish teams and the international organizations. They pleaded for the protection of children and holders of foreign visas, but when the opportunity presented itself, they did not fail to widen the circle of special cases. Moral considerations mixed with partisan concerns. UGIF, for example, demanded that children between two and fifteen be put under its supervision, although its leaders shuddered at the horrible dilemma that that presented to the parents. Faced also with the possibility of preparing complete counter lists to those of the prefect, the UGIF with the support of Rabbi Hirschler rejected the French suggestion.[34] Again, a relative moral code asserted itself in the midst of the deportations. Intervention on behalf of special cases had certain justification. As Schah stated: "We intervened without enthusiasm knowing that a determined number of persons had to be deported. This means that in case of success our protegees would have been replaced by other refugees who had no chance to emigrate."[35] But no justification existed for determining who was to be deported.

These painful decisions were made in mid-August, when the deportations began to encompass the immigrant community in the heart of the south. The fears increased that France was to offer another 15,000 Jews and to suspend all special categories. This tense atmosphere produced renewed efforts on the part of UGIF to obtain certain restrictions. Lambert and Lévy addressed the French government in late August and this time urged special consideration for four categories of Jews. 1) UGIF employees, 2) holders of foreign visas, 3) immigrant war veterans, and 4) children between two and fifteen. The council leaders' approach to dispensations expressed their faith that France continued to hold high certain principles.[36] Similar appeals were forwarded by Hirschler in the name of the chaplaincy and by the Central Consistory.[37] The deportations had forced them all to be more selective, with practical considerations figuring side by side with a moral outlook. For these organizations, as for the international relief organizations, there was no question what the moral imperative commanded if the deportations could not be stopped: to try and protect whomever one could.

Within this process of selection, general standards of human conduct were applied: the weaker (women, infants, the aged) and those with better chances of dispensation (visa holders or war veterans) should be protected. Yet none denied his own particular interest group, and each tried to save either his staff or those ideologically akin to him. That explains the readiness to participate in the "sifting committees" in the internment camps and also the outright moral opposition to drawing up counter lists to the prefects' lists. In this sense no difference existed between the pastor who "made special efforts to save the Christians, both Protestant and Catholic"[38] and the Jewish welfare worker who sought protection for his personnel. But all the organizations found that in the roundups in late August, little attention was paid to their requests.[39] Lambert and Lévy wired Vichy frantically in early September. Convoys of Jewish refugees were being deported to Drancy in total disregard of the special categories. They again invoked the "French tradition" to assert itself to save the infants, women, sick, and war veterans, and to maintain France's reputation "among the neutral and Christian countries,"[40] but their efforts were useless. The French government remained impervious to their pleas. All told, 10,522 Jews (most of whom were refugees who had fled the Reich to France after 1936) were deported from the unoccupied zone to Drancy during August and early September.[41] UGIF and the relief societies had failed to make much of an impact on the German machine.

UGIF's interventions were doomed to failure. Pitting a moral ethos against the designs of calculated murderers was counterproductive when no political or military force stood behind it. The council was left to fulfill welfare functions in the internment camps along with the other relief societies. Stationed in Gurs, Récébédou, Les Milles, etc. prior to the deportations, UGIF workers provided basic sanitation for the freight cars and supplied the deportees with food and beverages. In numerous cases they were asked to safeguard belongings or to pass on messages to families. But the most demanding task was taking responsibility for children between the ages of two and fifteen whose parents decided to leave them behind. Here the intervention of the various societies had been successful, and UGIF was entrusted with the safekeeping of these children. OSE homes (department 3 of UGIF) were to feed and shelter them. But the OSE and scout workers were not content with this arrangement and had little confidence in the authorities' guarantees. Subsequently, they were involved in rerouting many of the children from the internment camps to hiding places in the unoccupied zone.[42] Cooperation with the general relief societies was essential for this purpose, for it was through their contacts that hundreds of children were concealed in private homes, convents, religious schools, and institutions. This illegal network worked effectively from late August and was of great concern to the French and German authorities, who were facing the adamant solidarity of Jews and Christians, Protestant and Catholic.[43]

The rescue of children from the deportations of August was engineered by OSE and EIF workers, who had recently merged into UGIF departments 3 and 4 respectively. Through the official channels provided by UGIF, they gained access to the camps and developed instrumental relations with the other relief societies. In undertaking the illegal rescue of children, these organizations fully utilized their autonomous nature, but the question remains whether their activity can be identified with "UGIF." The answer lies in the functioning of UGIF-S during the deportations.

The UGIF-S leadership, that is, the council, was spread over southern France and never met during the entire period of the deportations. Only two of its members, Lambert and Lévy, were Marseilles residents, and they, together with their veteran companions Gaston Kahn and Raphaël Spanien, directed UGIF's interventions. The other council members were not consulted on these decisions and learned of them only at the council's October session. These members were removed from the central decision-making process and involved themselves with the daily running of the welfare societies with which they had been associated prior to UGIF's establishment.

UGIF policy was thus formulated by a small circle, and frequently by Lambert and another member. During the entire month of August, Lambert was the central figure of the council, and his personality very much shaped its policy. However, the nature of this leadership allowed the participating organizations a wide range of freedom without a set orientation or a compulsory norm of behavior. Organizations such as OSE and the scouts were only loosely associated with the council and in effect could follow their own policy with little intervention. Thus, during the summer deportations they were able to pursue either a legal or an illegal course according to their unique philosophies, using UGIF's official stance to conceal their activity. For instance, Robert Gamzon asked the head of the Protestant youth movement to obtain hiding places for 600 immigrant Jewish scouts. Gamzon acted as the head of EIF and not in his capacity as a UGIF council member. That was indicative of the heterogenous style of leadership. The council per se followed a traditional legalistic direction, because of both its educational training and the efficacy of that course of action. But the actions taken by participant organizations within an illegal framework were neither sanctioned nor condemned by the council. Thus, from the summer of 1942 UGIF-S fulfilled contrasting functions: while the council toed the legalistic line and presented its demands through the regular bureaucratic channels, its constituent societies often initiated illegal operations to continue their welfare work.

Facing the extensive deportations shortly after it had begun to operate, UGIF-S responded with determination. It regarded the protection of the Jewish refugees as one of its essential functions and persistently intervened with certain levels of French authorities.[44] Both its leaders and members of the societies were present at the internment camps and offered their as-sistance to the deportees. The UGIF workers felt morally obligated to involve themselves in these humane tasks. UGIF was not attacked for this activity, but if in the following months criticism of the council grew, that had more to do with the increasing suspicions that were attached to legal work.

An Attempt to Rescue Children

In early August 1942, the Vichy government became more restrictive about the emigration of Jews from France. A constant fear of the Jewish organizations was coming true, threatening to block the only means of sal-vation from Nazi Europe. The decision coincided with the first indications of the deportations from the unoccupied zone and produced immediate pres-sure on the French government. The international relief societies that in-tervened on behalf of the Jews demanded that Laval withhold the implementation of this regulation for children until the possibility of their possible emigration to North and South America was fully explored. But Vichy's evasive attitude convinced these agencies to press forward with their plans through alternate routes. In mid-August they convened in Geneva to discuss the future of over 7,000 children stranded in unoccupied France and the ways to accommodate them. Their strategy was clear. They must first persuade the American government to guarantee visas for the children and then present the case anew before the Vichy officials.

For several weeks after their deliberations, the organizations placed per-sistent pressure on the U.S. State Department, aided in no small measure by Tuck's efforts. Eventually Hull conceded and agreed in late September to grant 1,000 visas, with the possibility of increasing the number to 6,000. Hull, of course, stipulated that first the French government must remove all obstacles to the children's departure. At that point Lambert and Lowrie went to Vichy to solidify the agreement. Vichy remained adamant in its refusal to release the children. Tuck, however, would not take no for an answer, and he continued to negotiate. He met Laval in mid-October and managed to elicit a French promise to go along with the American proposal. Laval, who had kept the Germans informed of the negotiations, decided to hand the affair over to René Bousquet, the secretary general of the National Police, in full knowledge that Bousquet would bargain a hard line with his American counterparts. And so he did. On 16 October, Bousquet met with Lowrie, Tuck, and Quaker representatives. His attitude was downright hos-tile. The French were suspicious that the affair would be utilized for anti-French propaganda but were willing to test the sincerity of American in-tentions. Bousquet agreed to grant 500 visas for Jewish orphans, fulfilling Laval's promise to the German authorities, and added that if the first group was sent off without any anti-French backlash, further children could be included in the arrangement. He blamed the religious organizations in the unoccupied zone for French reluctance to cooperate. By illegally hiding Jewish children, they were complicating the government's position and giving the impression that the government, by permitting wide-scale emigration, was condoning such activity. Beyond this ruse was France's indifference to American pressure, as shown by Laval's delay in carrying out the agreement. Tuck was again forced to intervene with Laval a week later to procure a definite commitment.

While these negotiations proceeded, plans for the evacuation of the children via Lisbon continued. The major responsibility for these arrangements fell to the Quakers, who together with UGIF-S prepared the lists of children. These lists were to be assembled from children in hiding, in OSE homes, and in the internment camps. HICEM was entrusted with preparing the passageway from Marseilles to Lisbon, while the Joint was to bear the cost of transport to the United States. In order to eliminate further delays, the relief societies agreed to postpone all of Laval's other demands until the first group was released. They also refrained from protesting against a new French regulation making UGIF the only body responsible for the Jews and the sole organ allowed to intervene with the French authorities. In the end their caution was unnecessary; the Allied forces reached North Africa on 9 November, America severed diplomatic relations with France, and Germany invaded most of the unoccupied zone. These international events put an end to one of the most intensive efforts to rescue Jewish children during the Holocaust.[45]

Laval opted to placate the Germans rather than the Americans. His concerns at this juncture necessitated harmony with the country that demanded French forced labor and not humanitarian considerations with the power that stood in the way of a New Europe.[46] Vichy's image was tainted. The impact of its outright procrastination to heed the call of humanity was not lost on the relief societies. They now recognized Vichy's complicity and responsibility. For UGIF's departments, the failure of this legal endeavor strengthened the trend towards illegal work, and even members of the council (Spanien, Schah, and Gamzon) began to advocate illegal activity in the areas of emigration and protecting children.[47] Nonetheless, neither they nor others professed a clear break with the official-legal posture.

Facing German Occupation and the Italian Buffer Zone

The rather peaceful occupation of the unoccupied zone by the German and Italian forces in early November 1942 put an end to the euphemistic "free zone." Though German manpower remained limited in the south, the authority of the German police representatives grew extensively. Strategically placing SS officials in French prefectures, the SD increased its close supervision over the "Jewish Question" and demanded further French measures against the Jews. The French would soon follow suit. Rather than being tempted to adopt a more liberal policy as initiated by the Italians in their sector, the French leadership, and Laval most prominently, demanded German intervention to end the independent Italian policy. The Italians remained firm. In the eight departments occupied east of the Rhône, they refused to yield to French or German pressure on the "Jewish Question," continuing Italian fascism's lack of interest in anti-Semitism. A new haven opened up for the Jewish community in southern France. For the 20,000 Jews dispersed throughout the area, although they were concentrated in Nice (Alpes-Maritimes), the Italian zone offered an escape from anti-Semitic legislation and complete protection from the French and German police. Encouraged by this island of humanity and searching for refuge, more than 10,000 Jews slipped into the area during the following months.

The tens of thousands (as many as 140,000) who remained in the newly occupied German zone were less fortunate. They encountered an invigorated Vichy administration driven to pursue its anti-Jewish policy with greater fervor and repressiveness. Individual prefects often joined in energetically, trying to reap some of the benefits of a restrictive anti-Jewish administration. Once again, proposals to isolate Jewish children from the educational system, to impose the yellow star, and to revoke citizenship of Jews naturalized since 1927 were discussed. None of these measures was enforced, but on 9 November a French law forbade immigrant Jews to leave their area of residence without special permission, and a month later, on 11 December, all Jews were obliged to stamp their identification cards with the epithet *Juif*. These orders were expressly designed to isolate the Jews and prohibit their contact with the French population. Coming as they did in the wake of the prefects' attempts to withhold subsidies from Jewish refugees in their departments, thus forcing UGIF to assume their upkeep, they signified the new atmosphere in the south.[48]

The UGIF leadership countered the prefects' partisan activity by rejecting their legal right to stop the subsidies prior to a governmental decision. Lambert presented UGIF's case dramatically. The council did not have the means to undertake an immediate increase in welfare, nor was it expected by law to be the sole provider for these individuals. Its role was merely supportive, and it could not replace the governmental agencies that dealt with the "refugee problem." At stake was a serious infringement on UGIF's activity and a further retreat in French responsibility for its immigrant population. The UGIF council decided on 22 December to oppose the rulings on legal grounds, claiming the same rights for Jewish refugees as for others.

In the balance was the plight of a large number of Jewish refugees from Alsace-Lorraine who had escaped to the south in autumn 1939 and summer 1940 and relied on governmental help for their daily existence. Having received the support of the director of refugees, UGIF successfully intervened with the Commissariat to postpone the decision.[49] Although in some cases the issue resurfaced and the regular subsidy was refused the Jewish refugees, in most instances UGIF's persistent intervention settled the issue. For hundreds of Jewish families from Alsace-Lorraine, UGIF's success prevented complete financial distress.[50] But not all of its interventions were as successful.[51]

In early December, Antignac notified Lambert of the Commissariat's intention to dismiss UGIF's foreign employees* and disband its youth societies (department 4).[52] His pretext was that department's illegal activity. Darquier had been given incriminating evidence about the scout movement's methods of hiding children and transporting them over the border, and he was determined to put an end to them. Subsequently, on 4 January 1943 he ordered the dissolution of the movement. On the following day Darquier outlawed the headquarters of department 4 in Moissac and opposed its reconstitution.[53] Lambert was again forced to challenge the Commissariat's actions, viewing them as a violation of UGIF's charter. Although he contemplated resigning in protest, he proceeded to Vichy with his personal secretary, Maurice Brener. Lambert and Brener impressed upon Antignac the illegal aspects of Darquier's move and pleaded for a reconsideration. UGIF's stand was upheld by the president of the French Scout Movement General Lafont and by the distinguished French-Jewish poet Edmond Fleg, but the Commissariat would grant only a limited concession: two sections of the department were to remain, but the scout movement was forced to disband.[54] The organization that had guided Jewish youth for a generation, teaching French traditional values and Jewish ethics, would use the crisis as the point of departure for a new, glorious chapter of its history. Gamzon publicly called upon the scouts to abide by the government legislation, but at the same time the way was being prepared for their secret realignment in the form of the "Sixth" section (La Sixième) of department 4.[55] In that capacity the scouts continued their apparent contact with UGIF.

The Commissariat's decrees were painful and disturbing, but French Jews in the south were on the threshold of a more trying period. They knew nothing of Hitler's explicit order to arrest and deport all of the Jews from France or of the future major deportations from the highly populated cities of Lyon and Marseilles. Marseilles was the first to be hit. Ostensibly in reprisal for underground activity against German soldiers in the city at the

---

* See below, chapter 6.

beginning of 1943, Himmler issued a directive on 18 January to his representative in Paris, Karl Oberg. One hundred thousand persons were to be deported to concentration camps in Germany, and entire areas of the city were to be razed. French cooperation would be needed to supplement the insignificant number of German troops on hand. The French authorities succeeded in reducing the German demand to 20,000, who were in fact dislocated from the area of the Old Port to other parts of the city.

Jews were also among the victims of the "cleansing" process.[56] More than 2,000 were included in the first major roundup since the summer. The German pressure to fill the convoys destined for Auschwitz overcame the previous inhibitions of the French police. This time native French Jews and UGIF workers figured prominently in the wave of arrests that began on 22 January. The local Jewish organizations had no prior information and were taken completely by surprise. Lambert immediately coordinated the efforts and activities of UGIF in cooperation with chief rabbis Salzer and Hirschler and Professor Olmer. They appealed to all the French authorities in Marseilles who had a part in the operation, hoping to receive their support for the release of the Jews deported to the Compiègne camp in the north or of those still interned in the Fréjus camp in the south. Frantic telegrams were sent to Pétain, Laval, and the Commissariat demanding an immediate halt to the deportations.[57] Hard-pressed and with no other recourse, they turned to the French government for help, deluding themselves that it had the power to free the Jews and actually wished to do so. Their appeals were in vain, and the Jews who had been deported to Compiègne never returned. After a week of constant fear, Marseilles settled down to recuperate from the German penetration and take stock of its ruins. UGIF-S had little time to recover, however. Within a fortnight it faced a German raid in Lyon.

On 9 February 1943, the Gestapo descended upon UGIF offices of department 5, where they discovered false identification papers and arrested all present, including the UGIF staff.[58] Apparently the incriminating material was found in the FSJF offices (Section 2, department 5), which were subsequently closed and forbidden to distribute welfare. The number of arrests was small, but the fact that a public organization was not secure against German *Aktionen* contributed to further uneasiness in the UGIF council. Yet its bleak appraisal that the raid implied a threat to the organization's existence was somewhat allayed when Lambert and Robert Kahn intervened with the regional German authorities. Most of the UGIF offices were reopened, and assistance was again administered, but no German guarantee was forthcoming regarding the security of UGIF employees.

All of these developments left their mark on UGIF-S. The council convened in Italian-occupied Nice on 15 February and proceeded in some new directions. Albert Lévy's resignation was officially presented to the council.

Several weeks before, he had fled to Switzerland, and in his resignation speech, probably authored by Lambert, he proposed that the council members extend further assistance to Lambert. The time was no longer right for single-handed running of the council. Five regional representatives were then appointed to represent UGIF before parallel French and German authorities; the representatives were also entrusted with the supervision of the local UGIF services. The general director remained responsible for the Marseilles region. Moreover, Lambert's proposal to appoint Jules Jefroykin and Maurice Brener as "social inspectors" of UGIF services was approved by the council. This ordinary administrative appointment may have had underlying significance. Jefroykin and Brener were both Joint representatives and by this time were actively involved in shifting Joint finances to illegal activity, undertaken in large part by constituent UGIF organizations. The purpose of their new association was to receive UGIF immunity to provide them easier passage throughout France. Whether Lambert's initiative contained this same thrust is uncertain, but it is not unlikely that by so doing he helped those organizations that were involved in some form of illegal work. Yet even if this was his concern, Lambert was not yet ready to devote himself entirely to illegal work: the raids of January and February certainly shook his equilibrium, but not to the point of abandoning the legal framework.[59]

In the following months, the Jews in the south underwent another series of arrests and deportations and further encroachments on UGIF's freedom. In March, the UGIF's foreign employees were dismissed, and in mid-April the Gestapo carried out extensive raids on the Jewish communities in Marseilles and neighboring cities (Carpentras, Avignon, Aix, Ciotat, Nîmes). Prior to that onslaught, Schah pleaded with Lambert to reconsider his stand: "Having been informed of the recent measures taken against the Jews in Marseilles, I am alarmed and return again to the issue. Don't you think it is time to forewarn all the Jews of Marseilles to evacuate this city and to tell them that they cannot expect any protection? And your services, are they not also in danger?"[60] Lambert was not to be moved. Marseilles continued to harbor several thousand Jews.

A few days later, on 19 April, the German squads moved into Provence and Languedoc. Driven to please their superiors and increase the number of Jewish deportees, Gestapo troops rounded up immigrant and native Jews and rushed off small convoys to Drancy. That was not the end. On 1 May, the French Resistance injured two SS men and provoked immediate retaliatory actions. Jews were accosted and arrested in various public places. On 5 May Lambert was ordered to report to Eichmann's representative in Marseilles, SS Bauer. Bauer offered him a painful alternative: either present a list of two hundred Jewish notables in Marseilles or surrender with 10 percent of his staff. Lambert rejected the ultimatum. His refusal was quickly attended to. The following day, the Gestapo raided the UGIF offices in Marseilles, arresting some sixty indigent Jews and UGIF workers.[61] Bauer informed Lambert that those arrested served as the nucleus for the notables, and any further act of resistance would immediately result in serious repercussions for the Jews.

With his back against the wall, Lambert protested the German action as a violation of the armistice agreement between France and Germany and submitted a list of demands from the German authorities—including the demand that he be forewarned of any future action against UGIF offices. Lambert's legalistic argument was supported by the French regional inten- dant of police, Robert Andrieu, who passed on Lambert's protest to Vichy and energetically intervened with the German authorities. Surprisingly, the interventions had a positive effect: several special cases were liberated, while the blanket threat of mass arrests in Marseilles was not implemented. In the following days, Jews continued to be publicly arrested, though in very small numbers.[62] A few days later, Marseilles returned to normal. Another storm had blown over. For the UGIF-S council run by Lambert, the results did not confirm Schah's call to abandon Marseilles, but they did affirm the Lambert strategy: proud and bold representation of the Jewish cause could provide certain protection for the community and even compel the German authorities to curtail their far-reaching plans. This posture did not necessarily conflict with the apparent change of emphasis Lambert had begun in Feb- ruary 1943, but the new wave of arrests increased Jewish reliance on UGIF's minimal aid and official presence, disallowing any major reorientation.[63]

Lambert's Arrest

The Commissariat added to UGIF's worries with a show of strength in mid-year. It repeatedly questioned UGIF on aspects of the welfare program and criticized the nature of its organization. But the council stood firm, repudiating the authoritarian role envisaged by the Commissariat. It re- mained a coordinator of the various activities, allowing the societies to pre- serve their autonomy.[64] In this spirit of independence, the council faced the Commissariat-initiated tax of 11 May. Although it decided to postpone its reaction until UGIF-N had reached its position, the council resolutely adopted a critical perspective. The new law undermined UGIF's authority to exempt Jews from the tax or to set equitable scales for the taxation, while it made the council wholly accountable for any complications in the imple- mentation. Legalistic issues with policelike implications were not easily dis- pensed with, and they drove Pierre Seligman to submit his resignation in early July. Seligman was a central figure in the council and a respected jurist, and his unyielding move pushed the council to appeal the tax on legal grounds, disregarding the agreement with UGIF-S.[65] The council's unexpected decision came only a few days before Lambert asked to meet Laval, and it possibly was related to this dramatic step.

The UGIF council had reached a crossroads and wanted to speak out openly against the current of events. Brunner's brutal actions in the north, further arrests in the south (in Aix, for example), and now a law that would turn UGIF into a watchdog over the community were too much for the council to accept. UGIF's status as a public institution constituted to serve the Jewish community was in jeopardy. Like the northern council a few weeks earlier, the southern council saw Laval as its last hope. It too had held steadfastly to its definition as a relief organization, but now the time had come to turn to the political authorities in the name of the community. Lambert wanted to strengthen his case by appearing together with the Central Consistory, but it declined his offer. Left alone with the responsibility, Lambert went to Vichy on 14 August, where he met Laval and Jacques Guérard, Laval's general secretary, and protested sharply against the recent developments. Several minutes later Röthke entered Laval's office, and upon hearing the content of the previous conversation, he ordered Lambert's arrest. No resistance of any kind could be tolerated. A week later, on 21 August, the man who had guided UGIF-S since its inception was deported to Drancy along with his family of four children.[66] In the meantime, Antignac sardonically rejected UGIF's appeal of the 11 May law and pressed the council to quickly come up with solutions for its objections.[67]

Lambert's arrest brought to an end the first period of UGIF-S's history. UGIF-S was Lambert's creation in style and format, and it was his leadership that determined the activities in which UGIF became involved. Not surprisingly, the southern council often seemed to be a one-man show, with the other members far removed from center stage. Their dispersion could have been avoided, but Lambert never saw the need to have them all concentrated in Marseilles. He seemed to have no fear, either to stand alone against his colleagues or to protest at the highest levels: he maintained his sense of self-worth at all times. Yet Lambert, the decisive individual that he was, could not determine whether to lead UGIF-S into outright resistance activity or simply to maintain a legal structure. He wavered and opted for a middle road. From February 1943 until his arrest, Lambert gave indications of a new course for UGIF policy, collaboration with the clandestine forces of the community: as we will see, he supported vicariously the efforts of Brener, Jefroykin, Gamzon, and others; struggled to preserve the autonomous nature of the organizations under UGIF's control; began to reorganize the welfare distribution; established contacts in the Italian zone for possible relocation of the children; and took part in the establishment of the Centre de Documentation.[68] On the other hand, he also continued the legal facade, continued to stand on principles and legal issues, and continued to negotiate while maintaining open offices in Marseilles and other cities. He shared this dual existence with many coworkers in the south and with several organizations associated with UGIF. They too pursued this solution until autumn 1943, when German pressure forced more and more of them into totally illegal activity.

Lambert's arrest left the UGIF-S council without a strong personality. It came at an inopportune moment: the German "Jewish experts" were doing their utmost to arrest more Jews, while the security of more than 30,000 Jews in the Italian zone was rapidly disappearing. Some three weeks later, the area became part of the German occupation, opening up a new arena for deportations to Drancy. UGIF found itself completely incapable of dealing with this rapid development, which overshadowed all previous arrests of native French Jews.

UGIF's Strategy (1943–1944)

During the first half of 1943, the SD officials responsible for carrying out the "Final Solution" actively worked together with Darquier to extend the operations against the Jews, especially by denaturalizing those who had acquired citizenship since 1927. These officials were troubled by the reports that close to 200,000 Jews remained in the "unoccupied" zone, and they greatly needed Laval's assistance to make them accessible for deportation. However, Röthke's meeting with the French prime minister on 14 August 1943 dashed any hopes he may have entertained for further French legislation.[69] Laval's refusal made the occupation of the Italian zone all the more central to the German plan as laid out in the SD's plan of action of 4 September: "The complete evacuation of the Jews in the former Italian occupation zone is not only necessary in the interests of the final solution of the Jewish Question in France, but is also an urgent security need for the German troops." Thousands of Jews had made their way into that area since November 1942, encouraged and often supported by various Jewish organizations. UGIF-S was also involved in this trend. Lambert had met the influential Italian Jew Angelo Donati several times during the spring and summer of 1943, apparently to arrange a transfer of children to the secure zone. However, nothing came of the meetings because of the changing political climate.

The collapse of Mussolini's regime in July 1943 determined the course of events. Planning to retreat to the area east of the Tinea-Var line and sign an armistice with the Allies, the new Badoglio government ordered a pullout of all Italian troops except from Nice and the surrounding region. The evacuation plan became public knowledge, and some 2,000 Jews from "assigned residences" were brought to Nice by the clandestine Jewish committee of Boulevard Dubouchage, under the presumption that the city of almost 20,000 Jewish refugees would remain outside the withdrawal area. The committee's miscalculation proved disastrous. On 8 September, United States General Dwight D. Eisenhower prematurely announced Italy's decision to join the Allies, triggering a rapid abandonment of Nice by the Italian troops. A coordinated plan to evacuate the Jews to Italy was thus thwarted, and Nice was left open for a German invasion. Like most of the Italian zone, Nice turned into a trap for the Jews, who were hunted down by German or French fascist bands driven to fulfill Röthke's master plan.[70] Some Jews escaped to Italy and found clandestine residences in the south of France, but from October to April 1944 more than 10,000 were deported to Auschwitz from the former Italian zone. In the background of these endless raids and arrests and following Lambert's deportation, UGIF-S tried to reorganize.[71]

Prior to the Italian evacuation, the UGIF-S council was encouraged to persist by its colleagues in the north and the Central Consistory. But more important, elements involved in illegal activity emphasized UGIF's necessity. Gamzon and Brener, for example, appeared at the council's initial meeting after Lambert's arrest and upheld this view. They saw UGIF's official posture as relevant to their unofficial work, and they secured Gaston Kahn's approval to apply for their entry permits to the north. Nonetheless, UGIF was in disarray. Only four of the original council members—Gamzon, Schah, André Lazard, and Laure Weill—were still somewhat active, and Weill resigned in early October.[72] In this state of disorganization, Kahn replaced Lambert, and Brener became his right-hand man, continuing the unofficial position he had held alongside Lambert. However, the constant arrests in the south debilitated UGIF-S and prevented it from becoming a unified council. An attempt to realign and strengthen its position by uniting it with the Central Consistory also met with complications, for the Consistory was not yet prepared to dismiss all its objections to UGIF.[73] UGIF's council remained disordered and vulnerable.

UGIF's official existence was further shaken by a traumatic affair that occurred in mid-October. Agents of the Gestapo in hot pursuit of Jewish enclaves appeared at UGIF's head office in Marseilles. They ordered its leaders to prepare for the deportation of the La Verdière children's home in La Rose, near Marseilles. The operation was scheduled for the following day, and the Gestapo threatened Kahn that if the children were not available, Marseilles's Jewry would undergo a massive raid. The situation was almost identical to that in May 1943, but this time UGIF-S acted differently. Wishing to avoid a greater disaster, Kahn overruled Brener's proposition to allow a resistance unit to disperse the children and rescue them from the Gestapo.

On 20 October the children of the home and their devoted directress, Alice Salomon, were assembled by the Gestapo and transferred to Drancy.[74] A few weeks later they were deported to Auschwitz.

The affair stunned the UGIF leadership and further divided the council; Gamzon and Brener were extremely critical of Kahn's behavior and distanced themselves from official UGIF work. From Drancy, Lambert deplored Kahn's approach, urging a more firm response: "Alice reported to us the consultation which preceded the voyage. If what she told me is true, I am of your [Brener's] opinion and hope that if such a crisis erupts anew, one will act more daringly and will conform to the instructions of Dr. Sabord [to scuttle]. These concessions to the sickness will not postpone the entrance to the clinic [Drancy] of the fearful, and of the more fearful."[75] Lambert's suggestion came as constituent UGIF societies were making their ultimate break with the legal framework. OSE, for one, realized that the La Verdière precedent demanded the dissolution of its official homes as soon as possible.[76] Branches of the UGIF followed a similar course, while the council itself failed to convene during the ensuing weeks, except for special sessions in the north. La Verdière haunted UGIF, but no directive was issued; further UGIF centers in Nice and Sisteron were raided in October and November by Gestapo troops, but UGIF still pushed on.

At the beginning of December, the council faced renewed attacks against the organization's headquarters. For three consecutive days, Jews were arrested in the CAR offices in Marseilles. At this stage Gaston Kahn, who had been ineffective in dealing with the general turmoil, interceded with the German authorities in Marseilles to bring an end to the new series of arrests. However, Kahn was tipped off that at that very moment German troops were on their way to arrest him. He and several workers immediately escaped, not to be heard from until after the war. His act of desperation took its toll. Infuriated by his absence, the German officer in charge, SS Bauer, retaliated by returning to La Verdière, where thirty-five Jews, mostly elderly, were still residing. They were all deported.[77]

The intermediate post-Lambert era had come to an end. The remnants of the council traveled a few days later to Paris to negotiate with Röthke and the northern council about the implementation of reorganization. The independence of UGIF-S now belonged to the past.

As 1943 drew to a close, UGIF-S entered its third period. The new director general, Raymond Geissmann, was appointed by Röthke in mid-December. Thirty years of age and a lawyer from Mulhouse, Geissmann was an energetic figure who had been responsible for UGIF's section dealing with refugees from Alsace-Lorraine. He gradually rose through the UGIF ranks, accepting special duties, the most prominent of which was as the liaison with the Consistory from early 1943. Geissmann's perfect fluency in German had served UGIF well several times. He had successfully intervened with the German authorities for the release of Rabbi Schoenberg, who was arrested in Lyon in May 1943, and had represented UGIF in its efforts to reopen certain welfare offices in February 1943.[78] Now he faced a more difficult task—he became the captain of a sinking ship. The council, like the Jews in the south, was living in the shadow of deportations but was motivated to continue to aid those who still relied on them. Professor Fernand Carcassonne, who was drafted into the southern council in September 1943, expressed the dilemma well in February 1944. Carcassonne notified the president of UGIF that he possessed information regarding the German intention to expel the Jews from the Mediterranean coast and anticipated further casualties to UGIF. But his decision was firm: "As for me, I remain loyal to my post in Marseilles until such time as a new order is dispatched."[79] Likewise Schah argued that so long as Jews depended on UGIF, the leadership was obligated to remain and provide the necessary welfare.[80] However, Carcassonne's information was accurate.

Even before Brunner and Knochen signed a last-minute far-reaching plan (14 April 1944) to comb the south for more Jews, UGIF offices in Vichy, Brive, Limoges, and Périgueux were raided and their personnel arrested.[81] From one of the offices that was invaded, Geissmann was asked to intervene with the German authorities to release the UGIF staff. And again, as in former days, he was instructed to emphasize that UGIF could not continue its existence unless its workers were secure. Geissmann in turn pressed Edinger to do all in his power to protect the UGIF services. But Geissmann was not blind to the events and their import. The arrests were designed to terminate UGIF's social welfare, and only a radical move could prevent that. He proposed closing most of the UGIF offices in the south and concentrating the welfare in the hands of the regional directors. Geissmann was motivated to salvage the welfare program without falling victim to the German bands. "I therefore think that it is advisable to close the large majority of our existing local offices while preserving the regional departments or even by disbanding these as well; the entire professional work will be carried out from Lyon, partly by correspondence and partly by means of itinerant agents responsible for inquiries, visits and urgent aid who will provide the Director-General with either general or specific reports, which ever necessary to facilitate his social work."[82]

It was on 7 April 1944, a week before the German plan was issued, that Geissmann addressed Edinger; the time had come to disband UGIF's structure and to maintain a low profile to be engineered by Geissmann himself. Geissmann's sweeping suggestion was modified by Edinger, and instead, several of the organizations' branches were merged. Although Geissmann was convinced that the security of the institution was better served by his plan, he lacked the authority to implement it.[83] Herein lay the crucial aspect of the south's subservience to the north. But at this stage the initiative was wholly in the hands of the German authorities and their lackeys. The renewed German drive against the Jews of the south was under way, and nobody was capable of providing security to the UGIF workers and the needy. The French militia pounced on the UGIF offices in Limoges, and on 22 May the German troops raided the Toulouse office, which previously had served the regional director of the organization. In both cases arrests were made, and deportations to Drancy ensued.

Geissmann's prognosis proved to be accurate. In response, he decided to forgo Edinger's express permission and proceeded to put into operation his original plan. On the local levels he appointed representatives for each of the regional departments. They were to be the sole intermediaries between the UGIF headquarters in Lyon and the general authorities, and between the Jews and their welfare agencies. Subsequently, on 26 May 1944 he ordered the closing of all UGIF offices except the Lyon headquarters and the office in Montpellier, which was relocated to Lozère.[84] At this point Geissmann expanded the scheme whereby aid was essentially distributed by post. His decisions were made after consultations with members of the Central Consistory and his northern colleagues; the southern council was for all intents and purposes nonexistent and during these harrowing months failed to convene even once. Geissmann had centralized almost all of UGIF's social activity and policy making in his own hands; that was not of his own choosing. Time worked against him, and even when he tried to convene the council in August, he was unsuccessful. Jérémie Hémardinquer, one of the council's late draftees, advised Geissmann to coordinate the council's opinion to the matters at hand by mail.[85] Thus, Geissmann was left alone to face the community's growing criticism of UGIF's activity. In mid-July, elements within the resistance movement raided the UGIF offices in Lyon and began a community trial of the council's affairs.

UGIF South On Trial

UGIF's community trial began as the German retreat from France and liberation seemed imminent. Mutual accusations were vehemently traded in the French public between supporters of "resistance" and "collaboration," and they were soon to take center stage in the famed postwar trials. UGIF's trial was part of the same passionate atmosphere and revolved around very similar issues. Even though most of the UGIF-S offices had been closed in May and June, the final closure remained. In these last hours of the occupation, that decision became a burning moral dilemma: whether the community should voluntarily terminate UGIF's activity or wait until it was liquidated by the provisional government.

The community debate about the collaborative nature of UGIF's activity began with preliminary discussions on the establishment of the organization in late 1941. A central argument that had been presented then—that co-operation with any anti-Semitic government is ipso facto an act of treason to the community—recurred throughout the war and during the deliberations of July-August 1944. But representatives of the resistance organization Comité Général de Défence des Juifs were now able to sustain their a priori condemnation with the cold facts of UGIF's history. Indeed, two of UGIF's foremost critics, the FSJF and the Communists, pointed to several sensitive issues: Jews were arrested in UGIF's offices and rounded up according to lists the Gestapo seized from its premises, and children were deported from its homes. Moreover, UGIF had failed to prevent arrests and deportations, had failed to forewarn the community, and had failed to release prisoners, while it provided a false sense of security with its official existence. In short, UGIF had decreased the possibility of resistance activity and had aided the Nazis in controlling the community. Its leaders were not castigated for ideological collaboration, and their good intentions were cited, but overall the scales tipped heavily to the guilty side.[86]

Geissmann's apologia placed UGIF in a totally different light. Rejecting the claim that the organization had become an agent of the German authorities, Geissmann emphatically stressed its dual role in legal welfare work and underground activity: UGIF was responsible for the tens of thousands of Jews who had opted to maintain an official existence, while it provided a front for those organizations involved in illegal work. UGIF, he claimed, was nothing more than an association of the traditional welfare societies, which received its backing to further their goals in an official capacity. As for the more telling arguments against UGIF, even they seemed unwarranted to Geissmann. The Gestapo did not utilize lists found in the organization's offices for their roundups and had seized no more than 150 Jews on its premises. The image of an all-powerful body with the capability of preventing deportations could hardly describe Germany's powerful enemies, let alone a relief organization stripped of all means of retribution. And, according to Geissmann, UGIF was essentially preoccupied with maintaining the welfare services of its constituent agencies and preserving a minimal standard of living for the thousands of Jews who were economically incapacitated. In his opinion, UGIF's wide-scale welfare program was the basis upon which the organization should be judged.[87]

Geissmann's presentation well reflected UGIF-S's credo from the beginning. UGIF saw itself as a patron of the welfare societies, and the task of its council was to develop good working relations with the authorities, as well as with the international relief organizations. The trust established between Vallat and the UGIF council, particularly Lambert, stemmed from the French anti-Semite's intention to enable UGIF to work effectively, not out of love for the Jews but out of his hatred for the German occupation. During his term as commissioner, Vallat had led the UGIF leaders to believe that France would struggle to preserve its laws and reject German dictates. His dismissal and replacement by Darquier greatly troubled the council. It had little trust in the new commissioner and never felt compatible with him. But that did not lead UGIF to relinquish its reliance upon France. Notwithstanding the anti-Semitic legislation passed by France, the council regarded the legal framework as binding and intervened when it was breached. Often, as Geissmann hinted, UGIF was able to lessen the consequences of a certain measure and considered that important.

For more than a year after the deportations of 1942 and 1943, official interventions continued; and even as some council members became involved in illegal activity, they continued to uphold the legal structure. Lambert was in fact deported as a result of such a legal intervention. After his arrest, UGIF-S floundered, unable to find a definite direction. Official interventions decreased, and the dependence on French authorities diminished considerably. Moreover, UGIF became a target for German raids, causing several constituent societies to renounce their official association. The council resolved to maintain some semblance of existence. That was not an easy decision. Geissmann was torn between closing down UGIF and continuing the aid for the needy. On 7 April he opted for the latter. He was aware of the increasing illegal activity in UGIF's departments but did nothing to limit it. In this sense, Geissmann continued the council's attitude of nonintervention in the departments' affairs, and like his predecessors he did nothing to help the authorities to curtail the illegal activity. The division of labor between the council and the welfare societies remained constant, and Geissmann, like Lambert, refused to turn the council into an arm of the authorities. UGIF-S never sought influence per se and never attempted to bring the community under its control; thus, it played an insignificant role in the German deportations and in the French process of economic Aryanization, but also in determining the community's direction.

Geissmann's apologia could not, however, conceal the lack of political insight that distinguished the council. The leadership was never blessed with acute perceptiveness or foresight; essentially it reacted and responded to what was happening. Thus, it is difficult to accept Geissmann's assessment that UGIF-S consciously became a facade—publicly an official organization, but in reality the instrument for illegal activity. This situation evolved slowly within the organizations associated with UGIF but was by no means occasioned by a council directive. The character and orientation of the council belied such a development. Dispersed, factionalized, and legalistic, the council rarely formulated policy for the entire organization. It was under the constant influence of the dominant figures—first Lambert and then Geissmann—and both of them refrained from establishing a set course. Thus, the council's heterogeneity allowed for a Gamzon, involved in resistance work, to sit alongside a Seligman, immersed in the legal process. And consequently, when resistance work was advocated by the welfare societies, the council followed course and gave its approval ex silentio. UGIF-S was, then, a mixture of these contrasting currents and the diverse activities of the participant societies.

Relief and Welfare Activity of UGIF South, 1942–1944

In his design for UGIF-S, Lambert took special notice of the diverse tendencies within French Jewry. In establishing seven departments with subsections for particular organizations, he tried to do justice to the prevailing currents in the community and allow a wide range of welfare activity. Between the two world wars, these organizations had often been at odds with each other, vying for financial support from both French and international Jewish sources. Now, coerced to unite, they were not prepared to accept an overall ideological and economic policy.

Prior to UGIF's establishment, the major relief organizations, CAR, FSJF, EFI (Entraide Française Israélite), and OSE, had assumed the burden of supporting the needy. EFI (department 1, the Family) was the only one to subsist completely on local funds, which included the Consistory's "Chief Rabbi's Fund." CAR (Section 1, department 5) was supported until 1939 by matching funds from the Joint and French Jewry, but after the outbreak of the war, this arrangement came to an end; by 1940 French Jews were providing as little as 25 percent of the budget. FSJF (Section 2, department 5) had various sources abroad owing to Jarblum's wide network of political and cultural contacts, including the Joint, the World Jewish Congress, Relico, and some minimal local support. OSE (department 3) was supported by the international OSE and the Joint. As these and other organizations legally merged into UGIF by mid-1942 and were faced with the council's principle decision to refrain from utilizing the "Solidarity Fund,"[88] the conflict over Joint money and local funds became hostile. Until UGIF was created, the Joint had supported the organizations separately, providing CAR with the largest subsidy, but now it feared UGIF's control over the funds. Those fears were premature; Joint money continued to be distributed independently of UGIF.

Local funds were collected through an arrangement between the Joint and the Jewish National Fund (JNF) in France. JNF put at the Joint's disposal money it collected but could not transfer to Palestine; the Joint, through its agents in France (Brener and Jefroykin), divided this money among its supported organizations and repaid the JNF in Palestine. In order to insure a constant flow of cash, the Joint promised the individual contributors repayment after the war. Brener and Jefroykin were in charge of dividing the funds. The UGIF-S council was not always aware of the amounts received by the departments, and in its fabricated financial reports to the Commissariat, it consistently neglected to specify the sources of income. The Commissariat remained in a quandary, and repeated attempts to reveal UGIF's financial backing were thwarted by the council. The secrecy surrounding the funds proved to be a major asset in implementing Lambert's federative system.[89]

CAR, OSE, FSJF, and EFI constituted the three central departments of UGIF, and together they utilized 75 percent of the budgets UGIF submitted to the Commissariat, somewhat reflecting the Joint allocations. Their operations provided the bulk of UGIF assistance. (It remains unclear what funds the council possessed and how they were distributed.) Three other departments—Labor (2), Emigration (6), and the Alliance Israélite Universelle (7)—were much less prominent and in some cases were almost inactive between 1942 and 1944. The Youth department (4) was dissolved in January 1943, but two sections of the scout movement continued their activity within other UGIF frameworks. The breadth of the assistance extended by these societies to the Jewish community was, in effect, UGIF's raison d'être.

The "Family" Department

The "Family" department was formed through the merger of local aid societies in Lyon and Marseilles with general relief works operating in the south. Since the former committees, personnel, and needy were of native French origin, the department preserved a definitively French character. EFI was its dominant section, established in 1939 with regional branches in the major southern cities. EFI, like the other relief organizations, viewed the future of France's Jews as dependent on their ability to generate a self-sufficient community and thus placed special emphasis on its role as intermediary for new sources of employment. Other goals, such as providing legal advice and an information service for families, grew out of the particular plight of the Jewish population. EFI also sought to continue those projects that it had assumed while in CCOJA.[90] For example, in response to the vast migration of refugees to the south in 1940 and the ensuing employment

problem, EFI expended a great deal of effort to establish agricultural settlements. However, these attempts met with little positive response on the
part of the community and local inhabitants. But the constant flow of refugees
to the major cities in the free zone did not subside, and during 1941 and
1942, EFI bureaus were swamped with requests for food and lodging. The
regional branches in Lyon, Marseilles, and Toulouse again raised the possibility of agricultural settlements in the summer of 1942 while encouraging
the refugees to find their permanent residence in townlets and villages. EFI
failed in this regard, as well. It lacked the means to redirect the internal
migration and was faced with the mounting problem of French employers
who dismissed Jewish employees, fearing negative repercussions from the
authorities. In this stalemate EFI found it increasingly difficult to plan an
organized welfare program.[91]

EFI was in constant financial trouble. It often was in conflict with CAR,
which had bureaus in the same cities and received approximately 75 percent
of the budget allocated to families. EFI's recurrent complaints about its status
as the "poor parent" fell upon deaf ears, and during 1943 the deteriorating
financial situation began to take its toll.[92] Internal migration, especially from
the coastal region (including Marseilles), to the south's center in Toulouse,
Périgueux, and Ales and from the cities to the towns required constant
adjustments on the part of EFI and heroic efforts to find employment for
the needy. The threats by regional prefects to curtail the aid to Jewish
refugees could mean total catastrophe for EFI's refugees from Alsace-Lorraine, and it pushed the UGIF council to act immediately on the issue. But
the growing impoverishment of the Jews in the south necessitated a change
in EFI's emphasis. Regional bureaus opened up departments to provide
clothes, food, and pharmaceuticals for the ill; some even took on the upkeep
of children in special homes or in the custody of Christian women. These
functions had broken down almost completely by summer 1943. EFI, under
Geissmann's direction, had been receiving small contributions from local
French Jews and minor sums from the "Chief Rabbi's Fund" and the Joint,
but nothing substantial to meet the growing needs. Constant appeals to
wealthy Jews in France failed to produce a significant result. As a report
from the Lyon bureau dejectedly concluded in October 1943,

> It is sad to often see that the holders of large fortunes have no understanding
> of the level of extreme poverty to which some of their coreligionists have
> reached while they continue to amass wealth instead of aiding the desti-
> tute . . . and we unfortunately often recognize that like the other grievances
> which are levelled against the Jews, the reproach that we "support each other"
> is also false.[93]

EFI lacked more than 7,000,000 francs in early October 1943 to meet its commitments to the almost 5,000 Jews it supported with a minimal monthly subsidy.[94]

EFI remained aligned with UGIF's official course until the war's end. In spring 1944 it merged with department 5 and continued its functions in that official capacity. Throughout, it was motivated to deal judiciously and effectively with the disabled Jews, and from the monthly reports it appears that even the small support helped hundreds to maintain a basic existence. EFI pursued traditional patterns of welfare but lacked the means to treat the extensive problems that the anti-Semitic measures produced: it tried to redirect Jewish migration but failed, as it did in devising a special emergency plan. In that area, department 3 of UGIF excelled.

The Health Department (OSE)

In 1912 a group of Jewish doctors established the Society for the Health of the Jewish Population (Oeuvre de Secours aux Enfants-OSE) in St. Petersburg. During the following decades, OSE opened branches in various countries, continuing the original purpose of maintaining the standard of Jewish welfare by creating vocational training courses, agricultural settlements, children's homes, etc. After the Russian Revolution, it established its headquarters in Berlin, and it relocated to Paris in 1933. In the next six years, OSE was to preoccupy itself with the large influx of immigrants from Central Europe and expanded its program accordingly. With the fall of France, the department's headquarters were transferred to Montpellier in the south, leaving the reduced Paris offices under the responsibility of Dr. Minkowski. The southern operation became extensive and assumed a wide range of activities: development of urban medical centers and children's homes, social assistance at the internment camps, and cooperation in facilitating the emigration of children to the United States. The Joint and international OSE supported these projects, which included the treatment of approximately 1,400 children and the medical care of a few thousand families under the supervision of Dr. Joseph Weill. OSE's constituents included immigrant Jews from Central and Eastern Europe and a much smaller number of French Jews from Alsace-Lorraine and northern France.[95]

OSE's merger into UGIF as department 3, headed by Joseph Millner, was as smooth as could be expected. The UGIF leadership accepted OSE's internal set-up and enabled its leaders to carry on their work in the same spirit and using the same methods as before. The first significant divergence between the council and OSE occurred during the August deportations of 1942, when representatives of OSE, led by Georges Garel, illegally removed children from the Vénissieux children's home near Lyon. The children were dispersed among Christian institutions and homes, under the guardianship of the Amitiés Chrétiennes. However, at the same time, in its official capacity, OSE became responsible for some 730 children who were released to UGIF from the internment camps. Thus, by autumn 1942, OSE had already begun to lead a dual existence: supervision of children in OSE homes and institutions alongside a plan to disperse children among French families.[96] Yet even at this early stage of its dual existence, it received the support of the Joint. Joseph Schwartz explained his rationale in a report to the Joint office on 26 October 1942:

> Many thousand including women and children are being hidden in churches, monasteries, convents and forests, as well as private homes. Cost of support those hidden who now have no food cards enormous and constitute tremendous burden all our committees. Have been compelled make special one time grant 2,500,000 Francs for persons in hiding.[97]

Not all of the $20,000 went to OSE, but the portion that did substantially strengthened its entry into the underground activity. Moreover, the mere knowledge that the Joint would assist an illegal operation provided OSE with an added incentive to continue in that direction.

In the first year of their collaboration, OSE was not hampered by its association with UGIF. OSE's activities increased, and UGIF officials viewed the development positively. Fourteen homes housed close to 1,200 children, while double that number received some kind of treatment from the official OSE bureaus in the southern zone. The council was kept abreast of the extensive work by the monthly OSE reports; however, the 1,600 or so children concealed by Garel were never officially mentioned. Geissmann's contention to the contrary, it would seem that the council had only an inkling of this operation, but surely not of its scope. The policy of subterfuge was aided by the strategic positions occupied by two important figures of the Garel operation, Julien Samuel and Alain Mossé. Samuel, who headed the OSE health center in Marseilles and later the "sector Limoges" within the Garel circuit, was UGIF's liaison with the French authorities in the Limoges region; Mossé, the director of OSE's bureau in Chambéry and a member of the steering committee of Garel's operation, served as the UGIF liaison with the German authorities for the third department. Both Mossé and Samuel utilized their dual roles and the council's trust to further OSE's illegal orientation without abandoning other UGIF interests. But the council could not have remained totally unaware of their activity, for it was often apprehended by the authorities for their specific work. Thus, the precarious duality within UGIF continued through mid-1943, with OSE playing a significant role in concealing children and transporting them over the border while maintaining the official institutions. This situation would be seriously challenged by the brutality of German policy and the occupation of the Italian zone in late summer 1943.[98]

OSE's assessment of the situation was gloomy, and its leaders saw few signs of hope. That did not free them from their dilemma. OSE preferred to disperse its children among Jewish and Christian families and dissociate from official work; however, that was a complicated logistic arrangement that necessitated finding more and more families willing to endanger their own security. Autumn 1943 was a tense time. Fear of German reprisals increased, and the populace was increasingly wary. OSE realized that by involving itself totally with illegal work prior to total dispersal, its official homes could be jeopardized. Also, the upkeep of the hidden children was no simple matter, for the homes and institutions that housed them demanded remuneration. This problem was solved by a special Joint grant, a result of Donald Lowrie's desperate communication to Katzki of 8 September 1943. Lowrie reported the Nazis' plan to exterminate all of French Jewry, specifying their search for children concealed in French villages, and urged special support for the OSE activists. Saly Mayer, the Joint's controversial representative in Geneva, was informed of Lowrie's request and was deeply moved. Mayer had profound trust in OSE's ventures and especially valued its work in France. He obtained another $300,000 from the Joint, providing OSE with sufficient means to maintain the children in their foster homes. The Joint's grant further enabled OSE to expand its dispersal activity, but in itself that could not resolve the complex issue at hand.[99]

During September and October 1943, the German pressure on UGIF to close ranks was intense. To finalize matters, a joint meeting between the leaders of the north and south was held in Paris in late October in Brunner's presence. Alain Mossé in his UGIF capacity was also present. Mossé's stark account of the encounter with the German officials dispelled all faith in the legal framework. The German police pushed for closer control of all UGIF activities and demanded

> a detailed and complete list of all children's homes of all employees and lastly of all children with indications concerning the former and actual addresses of their parents.[100]

Mossé also reported an interaction he had had with Brunner, in which the Nazi officer had chided him:

> So you continue to hide from us your children, do you? That's all right, we'll have opportunity to speak about it later.[101]

Coming soon after the seizure of the La Rose children's home, Mossé's chilling report jolted OSE leaders and helped to solidify a decision to disperse. There were 1,250 children remaining in official homes, but within a month 850 were dispersed and several OSE homes were appropriated by the French authorities to expedite the dispersal. OSE had ideologically lost its trust in a legal operation and in UGIF, and all that was left was to find a temporary shelter for the remaining 450 children. That was accomplished at the beginning of 1944.[102]

After the decision to abandon legal work, OSE and UGIF went separate ways. OSE continued to focus on the treatment and care of the thousands of its children dispersed throughout twenty-two regions of southern France and on further attempts to arrange the crossing of children to Spain and Switzerland. It maintained, through the Joint's assistance, close to five thousand children and managed to prevent their deportation.[103] But in 1944 it suffered two painful setbacks. In February its Chambéry offices were raided by the German police, and Mossé and several of his collaborators were arrested. At that point, Mossé ordered the closing of the remaining OSE institutions. But OSE's misfortune did not end with Mossé's arrest. Two months later, on 6 April, the Gestapo chief in Lyon, Klaus Barbie, issued an order to seize a children's home in Izieu (Ain region); forty-one children, who had been evacuated from an OSE home at Palavas-les-Flots in Hérault at the end of 1942, were arrested and deported together with ten adults. Even the most successful underground rescue operation could not totally escape the German raids.[104]

Throughout the last months of the war, OSE workers participated in the organized crossings of children into Spain and Switzerland. Here OSE worked in collaboration with various Jewish organizations and French resistance movements, making it difficult to determine its exact responsibility. However, leading OSE personalities, such as Mossé, Andrée Salomon, and Georges Loinger, figured prominently in the operations.[105]

OSE's pioneering spirit was manifested in the breadth of its operations, and even after it became an official organ of UGIF, it carried on independently. OSE chose to remain a part of UGIF until November 1943. It utilized that organization's official status to establish contacts with French, Italian, and German authorities but was not hampered in its efforts to develop the alternate routes that it operated. Herein lay the essence of their association. OSE's eventual success in dispersing and providing for thousands of children was a result of the official contact it maintained within UGIF for a year and a half. UGIF's umbrella gave it the freedom it needed for its rescue attempt, and it is difficult to imagine that its operations would have reached the scope that they did, undisclosed and untarnished, without that protection. The split between the two organizations was a slow process, which reached its turning point when the offices of OSE became a direct target of the German oppression. Only then did its leaders strongly criticize UGIF for maintaining an official presence that endangered the welfare of French Jewry. Joseph Millner, who had been Lambert's confidant in the negotiations of 1941–1942, reached this categorical position in April 1944:

As you see, all our efforts to continue legal work must result in failure and the arrest of both our fellow workers and needy. Unfortunately, people understand too late our insistence that they change the conditions of work; and the leaders of UGIF who continue to stay there have not been persuaded. The recent raids have begun to influence them. As for us and our colleagues, we have completely withdrawn from the official circuit.[106]

CAR and FSJF: Two Contrasting Tactics

In the closing months of 1941, when Lambert strongly advocated CAR's participation in UGIF, he was particularly concerned about future aid to thousands of destitute Jews. CAR was then allocating monthly subsidies to more than 10,000 Jews of every origin and had assumed the major responsibility for all the relief organizations. Headed by Lévy and Lambert, CAR naturally became a central organ of UGIF, merging smoothly into department 5. Such was not the case, as we have seen, with FSJF. Jarblum was determined to support the Fédération's needy outside of UGIF's framework and influence. Close to 6,000 Jews were being partially maintained by FSJF, through Joint and other funds, and Jarblum hoped to continue along this line.[107] Nevertheless, FSJF also became part of department 5. Another section dealt with internees in the internment camps and Jews in forced labor camps, continuing the work performed by the commission of camps in CCOJA.

CAR's social work was extensive. Bureaus and agencies were spread throughout the south in some twenty-five cities, dispensing from 3,000,000 to 6,000,000 francs monthly ($10,000–$20,000). CAR proceeded along traditional lines of welfare during most of the war period, reflecting the spirit of the UGIF council. Until the summer of 1943, it remained the major recipient of Joint funds, allowing it to support almost 16,000 Jews with a monthly subsidy often exceeding the level of assistance provided by other UGIF bureaus.[108] Even the arrest of CAR workers in Lyon in February did not seriously hamper the continuous existence provided by the organization, but difficulties began to arise in late spring 1943. First, CAR was no longer favored by the Joint. The other societies conducting illegal work received a continually larger share of Joint help, seriously cutting into CAR's budget. CAR officials reported on the deteriorating financial status of their constituents and their inability to meet the new demands of other Jews. Within half a year, the organization was supporting only 8,000 Jews.[109] Undoubtedly, the deportations and the decrease in Joint assistance had taken their toll. But from the summer of 1943 CAR was faced with another problem. It became the major target of Commissariat attacks against UGIF. Antignac accused CAR of excessive family allowances and prohibitive administrative expenses and called upon the council to intervene and establish a uniform

system. These accusations placed CAR in a sensitive position and also reduced the organization's flexibility.[110]

CAR bureaus continued to operate officially until December 1943; some
dispensed aid from their premises, while others mailed it out to avoid congregation at CAR offices. But the arrest of CAR officials in Marseilles and
Kahn's disappearance marked a turning point. The autonomous existence
came to an end, and UGIF's general administration assumed CAR's responsibilities. More than a dozen CAR offices remained open to the public,
but they could hardly provide the regular support their needy had become
accustomed to. Many Jews who opted to maintain an official existence apparently sought assistance from other societies, especially FSJF, while the
open offices were gradually closed during spring 1944 as Geissmann allocated
the assistance through his offices.[111] Unable to adapt to the new situation
and unprepared to redirect its efforts into other channels, CAR adhered to
the council's temperament and lost much prestige within the community.

FSJF's beginnings were wholly different. Geared to deal with Eastern
European immigrants, the Fédération keenly sensed the impact of anti-
Semitic legislation. It went beyond the traditional monetary type of welfare,
providing clothing, food, and medication and organizing a systematic operation for forwarding parcels to internees. The parcel service expanded
tremendously between 1942 and 1943 and involved several thousand Jews.
But FSJF did not limit itself to social welfare. The political perspective that
Jarblum incorporated into his communal work was forever present. FSJF
documented the status of Jews in both zones, surveyed closely public opinion
on the "Jewish Question," and disseminated anti-German and anti-Vichy
leaflets.[112] In this particular venture, it created difficulties for UGIF. Lambert, in an unprecedented move, tried in July 1942 to halt these activities
before they became known to the authorities. He, of course, feared the
consequences for UGIF's social work, but in so doing he contradicted his
promise of complete autonomy.[113] His caution and suspicions were not unfounded. The French authorities interrogated Jarblum several times about
clandestine political work and forced him to seek asylum in Switzerland.[114]
Nevertheless, FSJF remained politically oriented and strongly opposed to
UGIF's tactics.

FSJF adhered to the spirit of Jarblum's declaration on the day of its official
dissolution and constantly opposed UGIF. The deportations of August 1942
solidified this outlook, for from then on the Fédération took up the cause
of concealed Jews. Although it was forced to maintain an official presence
in UGIF, its unofficial activity became its major focus. When the Italian
zone offered protection to Jews, FSJF encouraged immigrant Jews to evacuate the German-occupied territory. This activity prompted the Fédération
to set up a wide support system in the Italian area, creating a buffer zone

for Jewish life. UGIF-S was censured by the German authorities for allowing this migratory move to continue but neglected to impose its authority, actually condoning the migration. Nevertheless, UGIF and FSJF were to be forced apart in early 1943. The Gestapo raid in Lyon proved to be a decisive factor. FSJF was hit harder than CAR by the seizure. Workers were arrested, archival material was taken, and the Gestapo temporarily closed down the organization's Lyon headquarters, hindering contact with the regional bureaus. A month later, FSJF immigrant employees were dismissed by a Commissariat order, an act that totally disrupted the organization run almost exclusively by immigrants.[115] These developments, together with Jarblum's escape to Switzerland in March 1943, put an end to any real contact between FSJF and UGIF. Jarblum's departure left FSJF without a formidable leader, but upon his arrival in Switzerland he began to lobby for an increase in funds from the international Jewish organizations to guarantee FSJF's existence outside of UGIF. He maintained close contact with his coworkers in France and relayed to the Jewish organizations an up-to-date report on the developments there. He especially pressured Saly Mayer. These two vastly different individuals cared little for each other. Mayer accused Jarblum of acting irresponsibly with Joint money and disapproved of his political contacts, notably with the World Jewish Congress, while Jarblum was antagonized by Mayer's seemingly bureaucratic methods of assistance. In spite of their personal animosity, FSJF received substantial support from Mayer, which enabled it to maintain several thousand Jews in the Italian sector.[116]

While in Geneva, Jarblum endeavored to find money for FSJF to use in the illegal crossing of Jews to Spain. Chaim Barlas, the Jewish Agency's representative in Istanbul, was the first to offer aid. From June 1943 Barlas forwarded a monthly subsidy of some $8,000 via the agency's representative in Geneva. Barlas provided FSJF with an outlet to carry on this activity for several months, until it was able to obtain funds from other sources.[117] The Joint remained opposed to supporting Jarblum in this project, but Jarblum was adamant. All assistance granted to UGIF, he demanded, should be redirected to this goal, since "Raoul's business [UGIF] . . . should be liquidated and replaced."[118] Eventually, the Joint contributed close to $100,000 for FSJF's involvement in the evacuation to Spain. As we have seen, some 600 children and youth were brought to safety in Spain as a result of the cooperative efforts of several relief societies in the south.[119]

FSJF's rescue activity vindicated Jarblum's uncompromising condemnation of UGIF from early 1942. The historical development revealed that whereas in September 1942 he was appreciative of every contribution made to FSJF, a year later he felt secure enough to censure any support of the legal organizations. FSJF's status had gone through a radical transformation, and Israel Jefroykin's fears had proved unfounded. FSJF's underground work did not result in bankruptcy or abdication to CAR but rather secured for the Fédération a larger share of the allocated funds and a more central role within the Jewish community. Moreover, in the critical period of rescue, between September 1943 and May 1944, FSJF received four times the amount of support granted to CAR by the Joint. That occurred while CAR remained attached to UGIF and FSJF had broken all ties with the legal framework.

Emigration Initiatives

The problems of emigrating legally from Nazi-dominated Europe multiplied as the war proceeded. From mid-1941 the only opportunity for emigration from France existed in the unoccupied south, but within a year that hope too was dispelled by the summer deportations. Vichy ceased granting exit permits for Jews from Central European countries and canceled those already distributed. HICEM, which had recently formed UGIF's sixth department, tried to fight this decision. Interventions by officials with various levels of the Vichy bureaucracy produced limited results, and no more than 500 Jews left France legally between the deportations and the German occupation of the south.[120] But as HICEM was struggling to keep the legal channels open, another tendency was developing, which affected a large percentage of the Jewish community.

While the August deportations proceeded, Jews began bravely to make their way to the Swiss and Spanish borders. Those who fled to Switzerland escaped with no valid identification, relying upon the Swiss tradition of neutrality and humanism, and took advantage of the easy terrain and rather lax border control. These group crossings were in large part a spontaneous reaction by a frightened Jewish population and were not initiated by any Jewish organization. The Jews arrived in Switzerland without any means of support and quickly became a burden to the host society. On 13 August 1942, the director of the Swiss Federal Police, Dr. Heinrich Rothmund, ordered the border sealed to all but political refugees. This category did not include Jews. Rothmund's stern, antihumanitarian declaration produced a wave of protests in Switzerland and an immediate turn of events: in September, the Jews who reached Switzerland were permitted to cross a virtually open border. Although this situation did not continue and several thousand Jews were turned back (*refoulés*) from the Swiss border and handed over to the Vichy and German police, it appears that close to 8,000 Jews from France were allowed to remain in Switzerland between August and the German occupation.[121] The Swiss set up relatively humane camps to intern the refugees with the intention of housing them until after the war, when they would preferably find a permanent residence abroad, especially in the United States.[122] At this juncture of the war, even the fear of *refoule-ment* did not dissuade Jews from preferring Switzerland over Spain.

The illegal route to Spain was complicated by the difficult mountainous terrain and the uncertainty of the Spanish reception. Thus, this escape route was limited to a few who possessed some official documentation and the means to pay the exorbitant fee of the professional guides who smuggled them across the border. Although some Jews received the support of Christian institutions and individuals, such as Father Pierre Marie Benoît, no more than a few hundred Jews migrated to Spain in the autumn of 1942. Indeed, the Barcelona police cracked down in October 1942 on the illegal movement and interned the Jews in squalid conditions, far below the standard of living in the Swiss camps.[123]

How did HICEM deal with this growing illegal movement? Fearing negative repercussions for legal emigration and lacking sufficient funds, the organization refused to finance the covert activity.[124] Schah, who headed HICEM-France, seems to have favored the illegal route to Spain, but he sought assurances as to its wisdom. He feared that an irrational response would lead Jews to accept a relative or illusive security before exhausting all possibilities within France.[125] Spanien, who had left France and the UGIF council to resume his role in HICEM-Lisbon, encouraged the courageous flight to Spain. In order to influence HICEM-France in this direction, he sent Schah optimistic descriptions of the Spanish scene.[126] But not everyone believed that any alternative was preferable to remaining in France, and some offered cautious appraisals "in order to prevent refugees from taking steps which might have been harmful to them, as they were not aware of the situation outside France."[127] These contrasting approaches expressed HICEM's reluctance to take a firm stand one way or another. The organization vacillated between two predicaments: the dangers involved in crossing to Spain and residing there illegally, and the insecurity in France. Thus, it would be difficult to attribute to its initiative the small number of immigrants to Spain at the end of 1942.

From November 1942, all legal emigration from France was prohibited. From that point, HICEM, together with several other Jewish and Christian societies, involved itself in illegal emigration to Spain and Switzerland, facing difficult odds. First and foremost they encountered the repressive measures enforced by the German police and the French milice, who sent back the captured escapees to forced-labor camps and to Drancy. Emigration decreased but was not terminated. The authorities also threatened UGIF-S several times for encouraging the operation, but with no effect. UGIF-S had no influence over the grass-roots migration and refused to intervene in HICEM's participation in the process.[128] HICEM's share was limited; it allocated 1,300,000 francs ($10,740) to the Spanish efforts in 1943. However, neither it nor any other Jewish organization was able to bring the various efforts together, and none was able to provide a definite direction.[129] All told, some 25,000 Jews reached Switzerland and Spain illegally from France during 1942–1944, but only a small percentage of those emigrations were the result of organized Jewish activity. The pressure on the individual Jew was the incentive, and he independently preferred to risk capture by the German police or the milice, rather than to live clandestinely in southern France.

Switzerland and Spain offered new solutions, temporary rescue, which prior to 1942 had not been considered by the relief workers. HICEM had counted on more secure countries, across the ocean, distant from the battlefield. The secure countries did not come through, and the Jewish organizations did not turn to France's neighboring countries until thousands of Jews had taken this route on their own. Once the various societies, including HICEM, became involved in the illegal activity, internal and external issues kept them from greater success. The significant historical fact remains that under duress and facing total occupation of the south, more Jews were able to escape France on their own between 1942 and 1943 than emigrated legally with the help of "organized Jewry" during 1940–1942.[130]

La Sixième

As Vichy propagandists called for a "return to the land" in the summer of 1940, members of the Eclaireurs Israélites de France (EIF), the French Jewish scout movement, evoked similar themes. Motivated for years to revitalize Jewish youth, EIF internalized the French doctrine and embellished it with a unique Jewish twist. Leaders of EIF sensed a common élan with Vichy for a time, but as Vichy anti-Semitism increased, the enthusiasm for Vichy dwindled, and the gap between their orientations widened. Nevertheless, EIF forged ahead, expanding its agricultural farms, setting up in the internment camps professional retraining camps, nurseries, scout groups, etc., and organizing summer camps for children from the camps and cities. Functioning in accordance with a clear prognosis of French Jewry's ailments, EIF faced UGIF's establishment with stark realism. Robert Gamzon, EIF's guiding figure, voluntarily offered his service to the UGIF council in order to protect EIF's institutions and social relief. Trust in France had not been totally lost, and Gamzon relied on Vallat to guarantee the continuation of EIF's program and its ties with French scouts. In this spirit, EIF joined UGIF, and the council placed department 4 (Youth) under Gamzon's responsibility, emphasizing the continuity of EIF's orientation within UGIF.[131]

EIF accepted its new identity as UGIF's department 4 with little difficulty until the summer of 1942. Various services were set up along the lines of

EIF's previous interests, and they functioned smoothly. However, the mass arrests in Paris jolted the movement, triggering an immediate response. EIF leaders created a special social relief section for youth and established its "Service Social des Jeunes," bringing together EIF members and activists of the Mouvement de la Jeunesse Sioniste (MJS). La Sixième, as EIF's sixth division was popularly known, began to operate during the mass arrests from the south in the three major internment camps—Gurs, Les Milles, and Rivesaltes—illegally releasing children from the deportations. One act led to another. In order to guarantee the children's safety, EIF activists soon transferred some forty children to Switzerland and began searching the south of France for hiding places. Under the inspired leadership of Denise Lévy, Ninon Weyl-Hait, and Henri Wahl, La Sixième also ventured into the fabrication of identification papers, enabling the youth and their protectors to obtain the basic necessities of everyday life. Other EIF services voiced their concern for the future of these youth and continued their professional training clandestinely so that the youth would be able to contribute their share to the development of the movement's farms. Only in December 1942 did La Sixième arrange its first transfer of children through the Pyrenees to Spain.

By the time of the German occupation, EIF had lost total trust in France and had taken a large step outside of UGIF's purview. It energetically encouraged the illegal hiding of children and youth, began the dangerous crossings of France's borders, and continued the educational orientation of the movement by providing both religious and professional instruction. Various EIF services conducted such educational work, legally and illegally; it was EIF's bridge between its traditional areas of emphasis and the bold new enterprise.

Unfortunately, EIF's illegal work, carried out under UGIF's umbrella, was not hidden from the authorities, and in January 1943 Darquier ordered the dissolution of the movement. Following the council's intervention, two of the department's six services were allowed to continue under different arrangements: the section that dealt with agricultural, educational, and social work was moved to department 2, while La Sixième was attached to department 3 (OSE). Whether the UGIF leaders were aware of La Sixième's illegal ventures and protested accordingly is unclear, but the significance of the reorganization was to increase cooperation between La Sixième and OSE. The new attachment to OSE enabled EIF to coordinate the monthly assistance of some 2,000 welfare cases and to grant special aid to individuals and families. EIF's network grew by leaps and bounds. On 3 March 1943 the leadership convened in Montauban to appraise the movement's development. Tending to several hundred youth had become impossible and dangerous for the central body; it resolved to divide the organization into seven regions, each with a department head and a dozen social workers, responsible for contact with the various French authorities and the daily upkeep of the children. Moreover, as the EIF network spread out and contacts were established with EIF's representative in UGIF-N, Fernand Musnik, La Sixième established in spring 1943 a center in Paris to bring children from the north to the Italian section. On Gamzon's official UGIF mission to Paris in May 1943, further lines of operation were coordinated: official homes were to be emptied and the children dispersed throughout the EIF's seven regions. But much of this planning depended upon the Italian presence; the children's evacuation brought a new crisis to the scout movement.

EIF's leaders viewed the German occupation of the Italian zone as a direct threat to the Jewish population, and after the arrest of several prominent EIF figures in Nice in September, they argued for a gradual dissolution of the organization's remaining official establishments. The movement showed great flexibility in this harrowing hour. Casting aside a parochial organizational perspective, it united with diverse Jewish organizations to further its particular interests. With OSE, La Sixième cooperated in dispersing the children in official homes while maintaining in its own right some 853 youth in hiding. From September 1943, EIF encouraged members to participate with the Armée Juive (AJ) in arranging border crossings to Spain, while it continued to work with OSE and MJS in the escape route to Switzerland. Within both of these frameworks, EIF could legitimately claim to have contributed to the successful transfer of almost 200 young Jews across the borders. But the department went further. Early in 1944 it reached an agreement with the AJ, recorded only on 1 June 1944, in which EIF put its maquis units under the AJ's authority, and about a hundred members of the movement participated in military operations against the German occupation. Despite their heroic efforts, EIF leaders and rank and file were themselves victims of German and French reprisals. Some 150 members were either deported or shot.[132]

These diverse underground operations were all undertaken outside the UGIF framework, but interestingly enough, certain EIF leaders, such as Marc Hagenau and Gamzon, preferred to utilize UGIF premises to further their illegal work and did not completely dissolve EIF's official homes in Lautrec, Taluyers, and Moissac until late spring 1944. Undaunted in their resistance activity, the EIF leaders were nonetheless reluctant to disturb the sense of security felt by the inhabitants of the farms. Once again, it took the Gestapo raids to jar them out of their tranquility.

EIF's gradual metamorphosis from an organization that publicly applauded Vichy's ideological outlook, to a voluntary participant in UGIF, to a participant in armed resistance does not reflect the French Jewish community during the war. This transformation occurred gradually as the plight of French Jewry further deteriorated. Alongside this process, the movement intensified its ideological goal of revitalizing Jewish youth and persisted with its special retraining projects until spring 1944; the dissolution of official contact also was gradual, reaching its peak when all Jewish institutions were German targets for raids and deportations.

UGIF-S: Conclusion

Unlike UGIF-N, which was German-inspired, UGIF-S came into being as a result of Vallat's initiative to unify the anti-Jewish laws in both zones and to promote French sovereignty throughout France. UGIF-S was thus established in a unique way, wholly unlike the Eastern European model of a "Judenrat," and was given the rare opportunity to develop its own bureaucratic structure. The complicated plan that was devised was designed to protect the Jewish community from further impoverishment, to offset the disastrous effects of anti-Semitic legislation, and to maintain the community morally and spiritually during wartime. By creating a federative structure, with various sources of authority, Lambert hoped to preserve the specific goals and spirit of the former relief societies and their autonomous existence. But that was in the optimistic days of the "free zone." During the next two years, French Jewry underwent a cataclysm, and UGIF was rocked and shaken; its structure was put to many tests and confrontations. How the organization adapted to the new reality and whether it maintained a limited scope of operation, avoiding German designs, remain basic problems of the historical inquiry.

UGIF-S was established as Vichy ruled the south independently; within several months it had its first encounter with the collaboration between German "Jewish experts" and Vichy bureaucrats to implement the Nazi "Final Solution." Shortly thereafter, it faced a German and an Italian occupation, each presenting a different predicament to the Jewish community. Then followed the German occupation of the entire region, leaving the council without energy and direction. Throughout, UGIF-S never appeared as the monolithic organization that contemporary hindsight has stereotypically portrayed it to be. The southern council remained a federation of the departments and their sections, in which the decentralized nature of French Jewry prevailed. Itself a heterogenous entity, whose members preferred a loose association with UGIF and a nonauthoritarian council, the UGIF-S council lacked any real authority and influence over the departments and the Jewish community. It thus was never exploited by the Nazis to carry out arrests, deportations, or selections, nor did it attempt as a council to direct the community into a particular course of action.

Although the official, legalistic spirit set the council's tone, the council members, who remained active in those areas of welfare that had distinguished them prior to UGIF, often advocated and implemented contrasting programs. Their only major point of consensus until early 1944 was the need for UGIF to exist. Moreover, UGIF's federative structure limited the council and the general administration to only a few areas of activity—relations with the authorities and relief societies, and technical and budgetary items. Yet, in the latter respect, the council was also stripped of any significant influence. Since UGIF-S remained throughout the war morally opposed to drawing money from the "Solidarity Fund," it had limited independent finances and consequently minimal influence over the departments' budget. Financially independent of the council and free of its interventions, the departments maintained an almost autonomous existence, engineering their services in the spirit they desired. This division, whereby the societies carried out the relief and assistance while the council represented them before the authorities, was in keeping with UGIF's charter, only the UGIF leadership deepened it and sanctified it. Thus, from the deportations of 1942 on, UGIF worked on various levels, guided by different perspectives and understandings of reality.

Cooperation between the council and the departments was peaceful so long as they all saw an advantage to UGIF's official existence. The Italian evacuation of the southern zone marked a turning point for some departments, and they gradually turned their backs on the official UGIF framework. The ensuing clash was bitter and unrelenting, creating in effect two different entities: those departments that eschewed the legal course and adopted radical methods to rescue what was left of French Jewry, and the council and certain departments that kept to the official framework and maintained traditional methods of welfare. At that juncture, Lambert's federative structure loomed as an insurmountable edifice: the legalists had neither the means nor the desire to impose their principles on the other societies, which utilized their autonomous status to the utmost. UGIF was functioning as a polyarchy, unable to serve the German designs even if it so desired. Having come into existence to safeguard the community by protecting the relief societies, UGIF-S was in the end overrun by them.

VI.

CONFLICTING STRATEGIES
UGIF NORTH AND SOUTH,
1942–1944

Reorganization

The Jewish leaders in France constantly had to make painful decisions in their endeavor to serve the suffering community. Inclined to view the world optimistically, they slowly became aware of the oppressive nature of their enemy and tried to protect French Jewry from any further hardship. But in each zone, the leaders developed a unique consciousness, which had much to do with the reality of their particular area. Seldom did they view the drama in its entirety, and they responded accordingly. In the previous chapters we have followed the leaders through their complex dealings with the German, Vichy, and Italian authorities and surveyed their acts of compromise, courage, and deliberation. However, the strategies of these leaders were carried out within a community with diverse tendencies. In the following chapters, we will examine how Jewish leaders incorporated the general French Jewish calamity into their policies, assimilated political and social differences, and coordinated their efforts. Keeping in mind the important regional variations and the changing historical development, our attention will focus on the relations within the leadership. Our interest lies in understanding the perceptions and moral imperatives of these leaders while concentrating on the way in which they dealt with their moral and religious principles in the face of daily cruelty. In this chapter we will investigate the interrelations of UGIF North and South as they were reflected through two problems: one long-term, the issue of centralizing UGIF, and one short-term, the case of the organizations' immigrant employees. These episodes elucidate both the intricate nature of UGIF and the conflicting strategies of the two councils.

Although UGIF was designed as one body, the workings of the two councils and their administrative apparatus proceeded in different directions. This situation was built into the charter of UGIF, which allowed for two separate councils and did not specify the nature of their contacts. Consequently, UGIF-N centered its welfare activity in Paris under one central administrative directorship, while UGIF-S functioned as a federative structure, allowing its participant organizations an almost autonomous existence. Remarkably, both the French and the German authorities allowed this divergence to continue until mid-1943, when initial attempts were made to consolidate the organization. At times the Commissariat had expressed its dismay at UGIF's lack of influence, but its periodic efforts to change the nature of the councils' activity and to expand their control over the Jewish community were inconsequential. On the other hand, the German officials in France left the handling of UGIF to the Commissariat and rarely intervened in their interplay.

However, it was not only the authorities but also UGIF-S that showed little interest in establishing a tightly knit organization. The southern council isolated itself from the northerners' predicament and constantly rejected their overtures for cooperation. The northern council tried to create contact with its counterparts in the south from the early days of UGIF's existence and enlisted Vallat's support for a joint meeting, but Vallat could not obtain the approval of the German authorities.[1] Yet several months later, in March 1942, when Vallat's position as commissioner was in jeopardy, he helped to arrange Stora's clandestine passage to the south to meet with Pétain. Stora utilized this opportunity to meet for the first time with representatives of UGIF-S and to present the northerners' case. For Stora and the north, the paramount concerns were strong leadership, support, and solidarity—none of which they thought were being provided by the south. On the contrary, Stora sharply criticized the representatives of UGIF-S for their failure to resist the French designs and for capitulating meekly to Vallat. Stora further accused Lévy of being Lambert's puppet, while Lambert was censured for his subversive activity and general acts of treachery to the Jewish community.[2] Stora's stern appraisal of UGIF-S and his call for the dismissal of its leaders antagonized those leaders and created a rift between them, which would not be easily overcome. Lambert, for one, saw Stora's specific claim that he was pressing Vallat to activate UGIF "as the same story. In life it is those who do not understand the root of things who talk . . . and accuse."[3] After this abortive meeting, the southern council rejected several proposals for a joint session, standing firmly on the principle that such a meeting could take place only in the south.

The northern council's tenuous economic situation proved to be a constant factor in its insistence on contact with the south. The various demands imposed on the council by the German authorities severely debilitated its financial resources, to which the Commissariat officials were attentive. In June 1942 Galien proposed a joint session of the councils, contending that the Jews of the unoccupied zone must, in the spirit of "Jewish solidarity," regard themselves as equally responsible for the plight of the north. Despite a German veto of this proposal, Galien and Baur again raised the issue after the French law of 28 August 1942. This time Röthke replied affirmatively, provided the meeting be held in the occupied zone, a stipulation that was unacceptable to UGIF-S. The southern council had no intention of meeting under the watchful eyes of the occupying powers and of risking their intervention in its affairs. Thus, the divergent situations of the occupied and unoccupied zones brought the two councils to an impasse: the north urgently sought the resources to cover its welfare projects and the German demands, while the southerners, even after the occupation in November 1942, adamantly rejected Baur's proposals and pleas for help, held steadfastly to their independent stature, and insisted on a meeting in the south with limited scope. These negotiations persisted during the second half of 1942, and throughout, the southern council refrained from allocating funds to the north, without any repercussions from the authorities.[4] That might have continued had it not been for Baur's renewed pressure in early 1943.

Baur's Plan for Reorganization

After months of futile attempts to coordinate a meeting between the councils, Baur and his secretary, Armand Katz, traveled to the south in mid-February 1943 to consult with various Jewish leaders. Their mission, seemingly initiated by Baur himself, finally received the approval of both the Commissariat and Röthke. During their two-week stay in the centers of Jewish life in the south, they met frequently with UGIF officials, with the leaders of the Central Consistory, and with SS officials in charge of the "Jewish Question" in the area. However, only on Baur's return to Paris did the purpose of his visit become clear. In a memorandum forwarded to the Commissariat, Baur presented his plan for the reorganization of UGIF, which he claimed "was agreed upon in a spirit of complete harmony with my colleagues of the southern zone."[5] The central element of this proposal was the creation of one council, centered in Paris, with representatives from both existing councils, but with a clear majority from the north. Accordingly, a general administration would be established in the south, in Lyon, responsible to that council and in charge of centralizing and supervising the work of the regional representatives; the administration would be in constant contact with the authorities and would communicate the directives from Paris. A combined budget was envisaged to collect money from both regions, in the hope that larger donations could be obtained from the Jewish population, thus solving UGIF's financial problems. In essence, Baur's plan for disbanding the councils and replacing them with one centralized authority had as its basic goal the establishment of "perfect harmony in the work of both zones,"[6] and greater solidarity within the community. However, it is hard to believe that it in fact emerged "in the spirit of complete harmony" with his colleagues from the south. Indeed, Lambert's response even challenged the original notion that the south had granted its consent to the reorganization plan.

Baur's scheme was surely unacceptable to Lambert. It stood in direct contradiction to the principles of UGIF-S, and its implementation would have brought an end to the form of technical assistance carried out by the south. Lambert stormily emphasized that the normal functioning of UGIF-S depended upon preserving the tradition of autonomous welfare organizations, and any deviation would be tantamount to disbanding the council's original structure. On the basis of conversations he held with Vichy officials, Lambert was confident that the southern zone continued to be different from the north; that allowed a certain freedom of activity, which would be eliminated by Baur's plan.[7] But on another level, the personal one, Lambert could not be satisfied with reorganization. The proposition that he become director-general of the south, subservient to a northern council, a mere messenger boy with no real authority, was unthinkable for a man who saw himself as a leader accustomed to making decisions and to handing out orders. Yet, in order not to reject the dialogue outright and to try and clear the air, he suggested that the north send a further mission to the south.[8] But in the meanwhile, it was not only Lambert who opposed the realignment but also the Commissariat.

The Commissariat failed to see the advantage of a more centralized organization and feared its consequences. Duquesnel reviewed Baur's presentation and found it wanting on every account:[9] there would be no benefit from reducing the number of council members, or from granting them free passage across the demarcation line; the southern leaders, he surmised, would be wary about leaving their homes and families and would prefer not to participate, leaving the decision-making process to a small minority. Duquesnel presumed that before long the south would become wholly dependent upon the north and would demand an end to the unification. Furthermore, the Commissariat showed little enthusiasm about the possibility of Baur's appointment as the new president of UGIF. This issue surfaced at the same time as Baur's mission to the south, when Albert Lévy's resignation was officially tendered at the joint council meeting and Lambert's nomination was proposed.[10] Nevertheless, at the UGIF-N's council meeting a week later, Baur's nomination was suggested. That was in tune with Baur's memorandum to the Commissariat in which he agreed to become president if he could exercise "rigorous control over all of UGIF in both zones."[11] But Antignac quashed this move, preferring a candidate from the south. Subsequently, in early March, Lambert was appointed interim president.[12]

The Commissariat had openly rejected Baur's scheme, opting to leave things as they were. Its reasons are difficult to understand: the Commissariat was being offered by the Jewish leaders an opportunity to establish a cohesive Jewish community that would toe the line with respect to its concerns, but refused it. There are two possible explanations—one, that in fact, as Duquesnel had pointed out, the Commissariat was suspicious of Baur's motives and wished to avoid intensifying the conflict between the north and south; and second, that Baur's project was German-inspired. Neither presumption adequately explains the Commissariat's puzzling decision. It is similarly difficult to comprehend Baur's desire for "complete harmony" in and "rigorous control" of UGIF. Was Baur pressed to act merely out of economic reasons, or was there German involvement? What advantages did he foresee from rigorous control of UGIF? Did he fear that the south's autonomy would lead to German retaliation against the north? Finally, was Baur so naive as to believe that a cohesive structure would better serve the Jewish community and prevent its falling into the hands of its enemies? A categorical answer is unavailable to any of these questions, but the ensuing months showed that Baur was not going to abandon his plan. He accepted Lambert's offer and sent three leading council members (Stora, Musnik, and Weill-Hallé) to the south for further discussions.

The second delegation from the north negotiated two central aspects of reorganization: the presidency and unification of the councils. At a joint session held in Grenoble on 29 March 1943, the members of the councils brought up the names of various distinguished French Jews (e.g., Edmond Fleg, Léonce Bernheim, and Pierre Seligman), but the choice for president seemingly fell on Baur himself. Even Lambert surprisingly supported the nomination, though he may have done so for tactical reasons, presuming that Antignac would veto the candidacy. The apparent agreement on this issue did not extend to the more significant topic of unification. Stora maintained that Baur's memorandum was "only a proposal" and was based upon a conversation he and Katz had had with Lambert in Lyon. Lambert denied that, claiming that his consent was for the establishment of a network of regional representatives to represent UGIF before the Germans, which had already been set up in February.[13] Supporting Lambert, the southern council upheld his objection to any revision that undermined the autonomous nature of the welfare societies in the south. Nonetheless, this encounter was more

positive than the previous one; the council leaders recognized their differences of opinion but were united in their desire to maintain a certain contact.
In this spirit, it was decided to send a southern delegation to the northern
council to study its organizational structure before any changes were made.[14]
By so doing, Lambert hoped, among other things, to postpone a decision
on unification with the north.

The northerners returned to Paris more sober and realistic. In their assessment of the controversy with the south, as presented to their council on
13 April 1943, the north was striving for contact, while the south preferred
to hold on to its independent status for as long as possible.[15] At this session,
the wide range of issues that separated the councils was fully discussed,
including the controversial issues that had surrounded UGIF from its inception: the limits of its representation, the autonomy of the welfare societies, and the "Solidarity Fund." In all of these areas, the south had
maintained an unblemished record—it did not represent the community in
political or religious affairs, it had preserved the autonomous structure of
the welfare organizations, and it had refused to utilize the "Solidarity Fund."
However, the situation of the north was different: the north had been forced
to be the sole representative of the community in all areas of life, had preserved a certain independence of the welfare societies but with much greater
centralization, and had drawn on the funds of the expropriated Jewish property. The northern council was at an impasse and did not see any way to
further promote its design for reorganization.

The Commissariat, the third point of this triangle, preferred to remain
at a distance from the negotiations, waiting for a joint proposal by the
councils. Yet on those issues that divided them, it gave special attention
to the autonomous behavior of the southern organizations. The Commissariat was critical of UGIF-S for not doing more to eliminate those issues
and for allowing a wide range of political orientations within the community, in contradiction to UGIF's mandate. Furthermore, it warned the
south that if it did not provide the north with the monthly subsidy promised in February, the Commissariat would "be obliged" to undertake
measures of reorganization with important repercussions for the activity
of the southern zone.[16] These criticisms and their accompanying threat
came in late April and reflected the ambivalence and/or confusion within
the Commissariat. On the one hand, the Commissariat rejected Baur's
plan, which was precisely intended to eliminate the south's behavior,
while on the other hand, it seemed to be in favor of "Jewish solidarity"
and southern responsibility for the north. What special interest the Commissariat had invested in this situation is also unclear when considering
its neutral position on the south's decision not to use the "Solidarity

Fund."[17] In the face of this indecisive policy, UGIF continued its recip-
rocal delegations, ostensibly to further cooperation.

Attempts at Conciliation

At the beginning of May, the first mission from the south traveled to the
north. It consisted of three people—Gamzon, Brener, and Dika Jefroykin,
only the first of them a member of the south's council; Brener and Jefroykin
had been given the fictitious titles of "social inspector" of the UGIF's services
in mid-February 1943, and they were instrumental figures in Jewish resistance activity in the south. This delegation was not, then, the most representative of UGIF-S; Lambert's absence and the emphasis on people
associated with resistance work are indicative of the true nature of the journey, the solidification of ties with resistance groups in the north.[18] Lambert
was in close contact with each of the three, and his decision to have them
represent UGIF is further evidence of his apparent change in attitude towards resistance activity. Lambert's intentions were well carried out by the
three. In a secret report describing their ten-day stay in Paris, they elaborated upon their discussions with UGIF-N. They saw three purposes to their
visit:[19] 1) to study the north's welfare system; 2) to verify the economic
situation of the organization and determine the level of assistance it required
from the south; and 3) to inquire into the nature of reorganization. During
their meetings with the leaders of UGIF-N, they strongly defended the
autonomous nature of the southern structure and proposed that the north
follow suit. The delegation further criticized the north for its intervention
in the south's affairs and for the disagreeable attitude of its members towards
immigrant Jews.[20] This indictment of UGIF-N reflected the point of view
of both the resistance organizations and UGIF-S;[21] both believed that de-
centralization was prerequisite to their proper functioning. With both councils holding firm to their divergent positions, the meetings failed to bring
about unification.

Nonetheless, UGIF-N persisted. The 11 May 1943 law on taxation of the
community and the deteriorating financial situation of the north prompted
Baur and Stora to make another journey to the south in June. They were
hoping not only to iron out these problems with the Consistory but also to
bring about reorganization, which they saw as their salvation.[22] Lambert
seemingly sensed the importance they attached to the meeting, and on the
eve of their arrival he canvassed his council to show a united stand.[23] Lambert
was not to be budged in his opposition to reorganization. He set down the
guidelines for the south's operation: the organization must remain independent, preserve the autonomous nature of its sections, and allow the north
the right of counsel but not of intervention. Once again, Lambert's position

prevailed, and in their joint meeting, UGIF-S council members made it clear to Baur that his interventions were not welcome.[24] They too saw the decentralized system as a blessing; it allowed greater mobility for the southern Jews and more room for illegal work. Baur's plan to restructure UGIF challenged these possibilities.

The Commissariat and German Interventions—Towards Reorganization

The federative nature of UGIF-S began to evoke greater opposition from the Commissariat in the spring of 1943. Although it opposed Baur's plan for reorganization, the Commissariat continued to look for ways to change UGIF-S, admonishing Lambert to alter its loose framework.[25] These threats of intervention by the authorities were not acted upon until a detailed report on UGIF's welfare services was submitted to Darquier in June 1943. The report revealed and strongly criticized the true nature of UGIF-S: the participating organizations maintained their former structure and budget, minimizing the unity of the overall organization and reducing completely the authority of the general administration. The administration could advise its participant services but had no way to impose a particular regulation. The report proposed that UGIF-S unify departments 1 and 5, establish more rigorous and uniform criteria for distributing welfare, and prepare a comprehensive list of its aid recipients.[26]

The Commissariat report served as the basis for Duquesnel's criticism of UGIF-S in his meeting with Georges Edinger on 22 June.[27] Duquesnel objected strongly to the dispersion of UGIF's operations and called upon the north to prevail upon the south in this regard. Edinger, in turn, received Duquesnel's support for appointing Baur as president of UGIF and may have asked for his intervention to impose reorganization on UGIF-S. That meeting seems to have broadened the understanding between Duquesnel and UGIF-N, and each apparently looked to the other to bring about a change in the state of UGIF. At any rate, the June report brought the Commissariat closer to UGIF-N's position and also served Antignac's intention of limiting Lambert's influence. Antignac warned Lambert that if UGIF did not conform to the Commissariat's demands in the areas of structure and welfare, those demands would be carried out "by the authorities."[28] Antignac intended this time to apply pressure on Lambert until he acted; however, at the same moment, the German authorities intervened in UGIF's affairs. The Commissariat had again shown itself to be incapable of imposing its orientation on UGIF.

The deep divisions between the two councils persisted even after Brunner's initial activity against the Jews of Paris. That was apparent from their response to the law of 11 May 1943. The councils had seemingly reached a decision to present a united stand, but in fact, each went his own way. UGIF-N adhered to the legal counsel to refrain from protesting, while the south unanimously decided to oppose the law.[29] Thus, only after Brunner's arrest of Baur did the first signs of reassessment appear. UGIF-S made intensive efforts on Baur's behalf, seeking to bring back his cousin and protesting before Laval, and showed sincere concern for the north.[30] But it was only after Lambert's arrest that the plans for reorganization took on a new direction. Lambert's removal allowed the north to assume leadership of UGIF and to try and implement the changes it desired, but no longer under its aegis alone; the German authorities would be constantly present.

At the end of August, Stora and Edinger met with the few remaining members of UGIF-S in the south and immediately took charge. Stora rejected Schah's proposal to send a joint delegation to the Commissariat to demand Lambert's release, since he intended to do so himself.[31] But the problem at hand was to find new individuals to bolster the southern council, and on their return to Paris, the northerners reported to the Commissariat that UGIF-S was in chaos.[32] They argued that only if the German authorities sincerely wanted UGIF to continue and were willing to guarantee their safety would they be able to recruit new leaders. However, such a guarantee would not be forthcoming; Stora himself was arrested the following day. Nevertheless, Edinger pushed ahead. On 3 September he reported to UGIF-N on the Commissariat's intention to disband the central organization of the south and relocate it in Paris; its representatives in the north would be required to make frequent visits. Although that demand was to be no easy task, the German authorities stood behind it, and Röthke himself gave serious attention to the project. In the following weeks, the correspondence between the councils increased, and Edinger obediently relayed the German orders to prepare for reorganization.[33] At last, at the "express demand of the German authorities,"[34] the south was invited to participate in a joint session on 25 October 1943 in Paris. The meeting took place immediately following Musnik's arrest, a further step by Brunner to curb the illegal children's work carried out by the scout movement. In general, the presence of Brunner and his threats to various UGIF leaders set the tone for the deliberations.

The meeting in Paris laid the foundation for restructuring UGIF by establishing closer contacts between the councils and moving UGIF-S headquarters out of Marseilles.[35] The new president of UGIF was granted supreme authority in relations with his French and German counterparts and was made responsible for deciding crucial questions relating to the administrative or general functioning of the organization. These new regulations, which necessitated transferring the presidency to Paris, extended his influence far beyond that of the previous presidents but seemed to fit the prerequisites Baur had demanded to revamp the organization. Now, ten months later, "complete harmony" could be achieved without opposition from the south.

However, even at this stage the French and German authorities were not overly enthusiastic, and they were in no hurry to bring about the new situation. The Commissariat had set January 1944 as the deadline for beginning the new operation, but Röthke envisioned that three months would elapse before unification could come into effect. Possibly both had come to realize that UGIF lacked the necessary influence over the Jewish community to carry out their schemes. The Commissariat and Röthke gave their complete approval to the decisions made at the meeting, but the Commissariat recognized that even after the implementation of these changes, real unity was still to come.[36] It foresaw greater efficiency and closer contact between the two councils but questioned whether the south would reach the same level of centralization that characterized the north. Darquier saw the solution in bringing in a strong, authoritarian leader. He proposed that Röthke release Baur from Drancy to head the new organization, for "of all the Jews with whom I was in contact, only André Baur would appear to me to be made of the right substance to try to succeed in this mission."[37] Röthke ignored the suggestion, turning to the technical problems facing the organization. Remaining cynical, he promised the UGIF leaders protection only if they strictly abided by the anti-Jewish laws.[38]

The German authorities related to UGIF at this stage in their characteristically contradictory fashion. On the one hand, during the negotiations in Paris, Brunner threatened retaliation for any UGIF efforts to hide children from the Germans.[39] Moreover, and again at Brunner's command, the German authorities in the south relentlessly pursued the leaders of UGIF, alarming those still in office. Consequently, UGIF-N was asked by its terrified colleagues in the south to intervene with the authorities to bring about a cessation of the arrests. Yet on the other hand, Röthke was not quite prepared to terminate UGIF's existence, and in late December 1943 he gathered the remnants of the two councils in Paris to finalize reorganization. Röthke again conditioned the continued existence of the southern operation upon its ending its "political activity"; his goals were similar to Brunner's but he went about them differently. For the councils, this seemingly two-faced enemy was bewildering. Although depleted and deprived of their forceful leaders, they fumbled on, unable to decide which enemy was more powerful—the threatening one or the mediating one. For the south, the problem was no longer how to maintain its rugged independent stand but rather how to man the council with new leaders and survive.[40] In the north, a new regime had come to power, one prone to follow the German directives and to yield to every German threat. In this predicament, the fate of the two councils became more intertwined than ever before.

At the beginning of 1944, after months of deliberations, reorganization became a reality. The central body of UGIF-S moved to Lyon, while the two departments under attack by the Commissariat merged into one administrative unit under Geissmann's supervision. The new regulations ostensibly terminated the autonomous nature of the organizations, granting the six regional representatives extensive authority in dealing with them, as well as with the French prefects and the German authorities in the area. These representatives were further authorized to close UGIF offices if necessary.[41] However, reorganization took place as UGIF-S was at a crossroads between dispersal and illegal activity and maintaining an official character.[42] Duquesnel, the Commissariat's official in charge of UGIF, was well aware of the prevalent mood in the councils. In his assessment, reunification was contrary to the intrinsic differences and orientations of the two councils, and although achieved, it was threatened by the continued arrests of the southern leadership. Duquesnel strongly advised the Commissariat to grant the UGIF leaders complete security if it wanted the organization to exist. For Duquesnel understood that whereas the northern leaders had become inclined to submit to the Germans, the southerners were more resilient and less prone to centralization.[43] Duquesnel's moderate approach to UGIF was not heeded by the German authorities, and the arrests continued in the south, encompassing UGIF personnel. The German raids compelled more and more UGIF workers to question the feasibility and logic of their open activity,[44] but they were encouraged by the council members to continue.[45]

Reorganization could not really take hold in the last months of the war in France. The abstract desires of the German and French authorities yielded to the concrete everyday situation: the councils seldom met together; the southern council rarely convened, nor did it rely on the "Solidarity Fund" or the community for support, and a joint account with the north was never created.[46] The official links held up by the authorities as signs of unification never materialized, although Geissmann and Edinger tended as the months progressed to consult with each other on critical issues. However, reorganization did have one significant effect. It created a new hierarchy between north and south, and in the dismal days of spring 1944, Geissmann was Edinger's subordinate. Thus, when Geissmann proposed that all local UGIF offices and regional representatives be closed and that the welfare services by maintained by messengers or post, he was forced to comply with Edinger's refusal. Geissmann's proposal was aimed at preventing further arrests of UGIF employees and aid recipients while avoiding deserting the needy.[47] Eventually many local offices in the south were closed, but only after further arrests were made on UGIF premises. Nevertheless, Geissmann traveled to Paris in early July to meet with the northern council and confer on possible dissolution. In the face of growing criticism from the community, native and immigrant, Geissmann and UGIF-S unanimously favored continued legal and illegal activity. On 13 July 1944, the northern council called on its workers to continue their functions. This apparent solidarity of the two councils at UGIF's end was probably the first instance in the organization's history of its leaders speaking in one voice.[48] It is not unlikely that their statements were occasioned by the vehement arguments in the community about UGIF's activity during the war.

So it appears that UGIF's structure and the level of intervention by the authorities prevented it from becoming the cohesive, centralized organization intended by Dannecker. Until mid-1943, the German authorities relied on the Commissariat and its anti-Semitic commissioner to bring UGIF into line, but this French creation lacked the authority and skill to do so. It did show interest in UGIF, especially as a way to expropriate Jewish property, but here, too, it failed to capitalize on all of its plans. The Commissariat accepted the northern model of UGIF and tried to duplicate it in the south, with little success. Thus, its efforts to revamp the organization were haphazard. When Brunner and Röthke entered the arena, pressed to increase their quota of Jews, they sidestepped the Commissariat but could not create a truly powerful Jewish organization. They went ahead with reorganization but at the same time depleted the leadership through continued arrests and deportations. In this atmosphere, UGIF could not become more influential than it had been before.

Within UGIF itself, no consensus existed. UGIF-N, tied to a legalistic approach, feared the response of the authorities and suspected that the independent policy of UGIF-S would bring disaster to all of French Jewry. Reorganization was proposed by Baur to prevent that eventuality and to strengthen UGIF-N's financial situation: UGIF-N believed in a centralized organization and "Jewish solidarity," and it may even have gone so far as to encourage the Commissariat to impose reorganization on the south, against its will. For some reason the Commissariat was reluctant for several months to accept this initiative, and when it finally did, German intervention was imminent. Throughout these negotiations, the south stood firm. Under Lambert's leadership, UGIF-S repeatedly rejected the schemes for unification, abiding by its commitment to autonomous activity. UGIF-S failed to come to the support of the north, pursued its own course, and allowed a certain amount of illegal activity to develop under its guise. Thus, the conflict between two councils continued until their primary spokesmen were arrested. The German intervention finally brought the councils together, creating a greater affinity between the northern zone and the "unoccupied zone." UGIF-S was forced to accept the new reality, preferring it to disbanding, and closed the gap with the north. But in effect, "UGIF" never really existed as a monolithic body until the last moments of its existence, when it faced the judgment of history.

Dismissal of the Immigrant Staff (1942–1943)

The problem of UGIF's immigrant staff first arose in August 1942, during the third wave of deportations from the south, which encompassed immigrant Jews in the cities. At that point, UGIF-S demanded that the French authorities place its workers on the same level as their northern colleagues. From that time on, the struggle to protect the immigrant staff members became a cause célèbre of UGIF's administration: success in this area would attest to its independent stature and prove to the immigrant community its efforts on their behalf. A close examination of this affair, from summer 1942 to spring 1943, reveals that the Commissariat initiated the dismissal of UGIF's immigrant workers without any pressure from the German administration.[49] Moreover, the Commissariat remained consistent in its demands, thereby leaving these workers unprotected and vulnerable to German deportation. UGIF's attempts to counter this order met with limited success and revealed again the inability of the councils to coordinate their strategies.

The immigrant Jews had lost French protection in 1940, but by 1941 they had become a liability to that society. For those who managed to receive employment in UGIF, a French public institution, a new guardian had seemingly been found. UGIF struggled to play that role effectively. As the deportations in the south decreased in early September 1942, Lambert gave special attention to this issue. At first the French minister of interior promised him the safety of all of his employees; however, the Marseilles police department tried to limit that protection to section heads alone. Lambert realized that the internal squabbles within Vichy worked against a blanket coverage for his staff, although he was led to believe that none of them would be deported. However, already in October the Commissariat was demanding restrictions on the immigrant staff, including a freeze on hiring, curtailment of freedom of movement, and replacement by French Jews, especially in the general administration of the organization. Furthermore, UGIF-S was asked to submit a list of all its foreign employees with their respective nationalities until mid-November. All of these actions were taken before the German occupation of the south, and they paved the way for the general order of dismissal.[50]

The German occupation further aggravated the tense relations between certain Commissariat officials and UGIF. On 9 December 1942 Antignac ordered Lambert to dismiss his immigrant employees to prevent the deportation of his entire staff. Lambert informed his council of the new crisis and his demand for six months' probation. But Lambert and his council were aware that the present Commissariat was not inclined to make compromises, and in their discussions on 22 December they laid the groundwork for the impending dismissal.[51] Lambert nonetheless continued to maintain his usual optimism, believing in his capability to salvage something through negotiation.[52]

On 1 December 1942, the Commissariat asked UGIF-N to submit a list of its foreign employees. Prior to responding, Baur and Lambert exchanged letters in which they discussed the *original German* demand to staff their offices with 50 percent immigrant Jews.[53] Although no mention of Antignac's order was made, Baur seems to have been informed of the Commissariat's intention and in typical fashion almost warned the Commissariat that "if the Commissioner deems it opportune to reduce this percentage [35 percent immigrant Jews], it appears desirable to assure prior consent of the occupying authorities."[54] Baur again adhered tightly to the legalistic approach, and before making any move he wanted to set the record straight. But it was not until 28 January 1943 that Darquier officially ordered him to dismiss all but 1 percent of his foreign staff, effective 31 March. This date was soon to become the deadline for the south, as well, unifying the fate of UGIF's immigrant staff.

The tragic week in Marseilles in January 1943 placed the entire Jewish community in the south in danger of deportation; several UGIF workers were also deported. The UGIF-S council immediately intervened with Pétain and Vichy officials to secure protection of their staff. Simultaneously, the council dealt with the dismissal of the foreign Jews. They approached it relativistically, requesting department heads to submit a list of indispensable foreign workers in case some could be retained.[55] Interestingly enough, the northern council took a much more radical stand. Following Darquier's letter, the council met on 2 February in a most somber atmosphere. Stora expressed the feelings of the council when he declared his solidarity with the immigrant workers and his goal to reverse the decision. A protest to the Commissariat in the spirit of his remarks was proposed.[56] On the following day, Baur met with Antignac and Röthke, and on 4 February 1943 he informed Duquesnel of his intervention with Röthke and the council's position: "my colleagues and I would prefer to resign rather than designate ourselves a part of our personnel, thereby exposing them to measures which certain precedents make us anticipate."[57]

For the first time, UGIF-N put itself on the line, threatening to resign if the Commissariat would not back down. It spoke openly and frankly of its anxieties: dismissal meant deportation. Moreover, it tried several different approaches simultaneously. Baur went to Röthke seemingly to ask for consideration. The Germans had originally demanded 50 percent immigrant representation, and he wanted to be sure that Röthke knew what was happening. Then he tried to play Duquesnel against Antignac. Baur was wary of Antignac and appreciated Duquesnel's more lenient attitude towards UGIF. He informed Duquesnel of Röthke's consent to leave from 1 to 15 percent of the foreign staff and hoped that that would give him the leverage to soften up Antignac's rigid position.[58] Several days later Baur wrote Antignac that Röthke had agreed to postpone the decision until his return from the south.[59] Antignac was provoked. He dashed off a sharp letter to Röthke in Darquier's name, demanding a clarification of Röthke's attitude.[60] Antignac would not be undermined by this French Jew. In Baur's absence, Antignac ordered the UGIF council immediately to present the list Darquier had requested two weeks earlier.[61] To overcome their uncertainty, Antignac added that this request was being made with the full consent of the German authorities. UGIF-N did not respond. In the south, Baur relayed the news of Röthke's dispensation, introducing a mood of optimism into the deliberations.[62]

On 22 February 1943, prior to Baur's return to Paris, Röthke ordered Israelowicz to submit the required list. Röthke's sudden action occasioned either by Darquier's inquiry or by his own decision to reaffirm control of the affair, took the council by surprise.[63] In response, it decided to impress upon the Commissariat the serious implications of dismissal for UGIF and its constituents. The council implored Darquier to consider the special efforts it had made to train many immigrant Jews for certain positions, in compliance with the German demand to employ 50 percent immigrant Jews. Once again UGIF presented its predicament logically, hoping to convince by exhibiting its model behavior. Stora and Edinger met with Antignac on the twenty-third and gave him this communication.[64] Although the council preferred not to submit a list of indispensable workers, it authorized Stora and Edinger to do so if necessary, "desirous to avoid creating an irrevocable situation and cutting off all possibilities of discussion."[65] The list was not requested. Antignac also agreed to postpone the council's decision until Baur's return, adding that it was UGIF's prerogative either to submit or to reject a priority list. As for the dismissed, their protection was in force until 31 March, and Antignac promised to intervene with Röthke to guarantee their safety beyond that date.[66] UGIF-N knew as well as Antignac did that these Jews would be pounced upon by the Germans the moment they were freed from their guardian.

On Baur's return, UGIF-N reached its decision, consistent with the moral attitude it had presented three weeks earlier: it was not within its bounds to submit a priority list.[67] The Commissariat's response was immediate and harsh. Because of its refusal, UGIF-N must dismiss all of its foreign employees by 31 March and return all of their *Ausweis*.[68] Darquier also rushed an impassioned letter to Röthke, condemning Baur's behavior and demanding an end to the north and south's delaying tactics "at the risk of immediate retaliation against the present leadership of UGIF."[69] In order to show that he meant business, Darquier sent Antignac to Vichy to meet Lambert and put him in his place and suggested to Röthke that he do the same with Baur.[70]

Darquier's answer did not frustrate UGIF-N's efforts completely. Undaunted, the council prepared for a confrontation with Röthke. The preliminary deliberations showed its reluctance to take a firm stand: the council agreed to demand a postponement of the order and the right to maintain 15 percent of the immigrant personnel, but in both areas it was willing to compromise. Moreover, it reviewed its principled decision to resign if no solution was available, replacing the absolute morality with a relative one. The protocol of the meeting stated succinctly: "If it is impossible to reach a common ground, the Administrative Council will ask to be removed from its functions. If it is possible to compromise, the members of the Council grant complete authority to Baur, Stora and Katz."[71]

The outcome of UGIF-N's 3 March meeting with Röthke is clouded with ambiguities. It is unclear whether Röthke allowed the council to choose thirty indispensable immigrant Jews, 10 percent of the entire immigrant staff, or whether the intervention failed. Baur seemed utterly dejected. The threats against the entire UGIF staff and fear of further raids against French Jews convinced him and the council to withdraw the decision to resign. Nothing was apparently achieved for the southern organization.[72] However, Lambert was informed otherwise by the Commissariat: 1 percent, or twelve individuals, could be retained.[73] Was that what Baur had meant when he spoke of failure? But Baur, unlike Lambert, continued to negotiate to "increase the percentage of foreign personnel to a proportion which will allow us to maintain all the organization's activities."[74] Indeed, his persistence paid off. The following week he reported that fifty workers, almost 20 percent of the foreign staff, were retained.[75] Although no conclusive evidence exists as to which authority granted UGIF-N this concession, it would appear that Röthke was responsible.[76] Baur was convinced that had Lambert been cooperative, the results for the south would have been similar. His opinion was shared by Schah, who attacked Lambert's partisan behavior and repeatedly demanded that he return to the Commissariat to reach the same agreement achieved by the north.[77] For Schah, Lambert's attitude was a further indication of UGIF-S's malfunctioning: "The initial cause is the ridiculous composition of the UGIF council in the free zone, a composition which is due to the incomprehensible refusal of the representatives of French Judaism to do their duty."[78] But Lambert had already surrendered: he notified the UGIF-S council at the end of March of his results—twelve immigrant workers were left on the roster, chosen by the department heads and by Lambert himself.[79] The council adopted Schah's criticism, and Lambert was asked to intervene once again with the Commissariat, which he did unsuccessfully in April.[80]

The fate of the workers not included in the special lists was predictable and sealed: arrest and deportation. Cognizant of what lay ahead, elements within UGIF-N attempted to conceal the identity of those workers and hide them; unfortunately, they were partially duped by the authorities. Disregarding his "promise" to UGIF-N that the workers would remain secure at their posts until 31 March, Röthke ordered their arrest on 15 March; the order referred only to the north. The raid took place on the night of 17 March and netted some sixty to eighty Jews, far below Röthke's expectations.[81] A much larger number were forewarned and hidden, while others escaped by means of the inexact lists. However, the falsification of the lists was not complete. Those Jews whose addresses appeared correctly were sacrificed. UGIF-N had aided some but had let others fall into the hands of the German authorities.[82] Although the council did not take Röthke's "promise" at face value, it could not completely cross over the lines and disperse all the possible victims. For the German and French authorities, even that deviation was cause for concern and a further sign of UGIF's illegal activity. Antignac reported to Röthke on the investigation and suggested ways to trap those Jews who escaped arrest and continued to receive their salaries while in hiding.[83]

As for the south, the outcome seems to have been far less traumatic. There is no indication that a mass raid on the southern council's dismissed employees followed, either in March or in the ensuing months. The discrepancy between the situations in the north and the south is puzzling. Was it a result of the effectiveness of the dispersal of southern agencies or a result of Nazi inconsistency? For although Nazi policy was guided by a global conception, it often deviated from the deterministic framework for local exigencies; this situation seems to be one of those cases, and a clear-cut explanation is wanting.

The efforts of the UGIF councils to protect their immigrant employees offer an interesting insight into the differences between them and their leaders. The decision-making process characteristic of UGIF-N was seldom duplicated in the south. UGIF-N appears to have been united, working as a council whose decisions were taken after open discussion at the council level. Independent, partisan machinations such as those of Lambert were rarely found in the north. UGIF-N convened to work out its approach and to make decisions, unlike UGIF-S, which often endorsed without question Lambert's interventions and actions already taken.

The immigrant employees were regarded as an integral part of UGIF, and in no way was their predicament taken lightly by their leaders. On the contrary, UGIF-N reacted with unusual forcefulness and appraised the French measure as a serious challenge to its existence. The decision to resign was not artificial; it was an expression of a higher moral code: however, UGIF-N gradually descended from that moral plateau, reaching a solution that epitomized its ambivalence. The alternative it chose was born of a constant fear that open rebellion would bring total destruction of the community. UGIF-N retreated to a less provocative stance, but not out of deliberate renunciation of the immigrant Jews' plight. Such was not the case in the south. From the outset, Lambert appeared resigned to the outcome, and his efforts to reverse the decision lacked his usual stamina. Moreover, for the first time, the council chastized Lambert for his timid negotiations. Was that a sign of Lambert's disinterest in the plight of the immigrant employees or a result of fatigue from the trying weeks of deportations from Marseilles and Lyon, or possibly mere acceptance of the Commissariat's assertive attitude in this affair?[84] No definite answer is available, but it would appear that each of these factors partially explains his uncommon behavior. However, the authorities also handled the affair erratically. UGIF South emerged scathed, but by no means as severely as the north: the former was allowed to hold only 1 percent of its immigrant staff, while the latter retained 20 percent, but the north was the target of a mass roundup, while the south was not. Finally, the dismissal and deportation of part of the immigrant staff were a further sign to elements within UGIF and outside it that legal activity was no longer feasible.

VII.

THE STRUGGLE OVER COMMUNITY LEADERSHIP, 1942–1944
THE CENTRAL CONSISTORY AND UGIF

The Period of Polemics

Established by Napoleon in 1808 to organize the religious affairs of the Jewish community, the Central Consistory (Consistoire Central des Israélites de France) actively pursued the goal of integrating Jews into French society. In the Consistory's conception, France was the promised land to be ardently served, and Judaism a religion to be observed in an organized and conservative fashion. The Consistory abided by the Napoleonic charter, abstaining from political involvement, both in its capacity as a government-supported institution (until 1905) and in accordance with its strictly religious definition of French Jewry. Through the years it became the recognized representative of French Jewry, but it failed to find support among the large immigrant community that flocked to France in the interwar years. Immigrant Jews rejected its conception of French Judaism and created alternate organizational frameworks. But this challenge to the Consistory was overshadowed by the more serious threats posed by the Vichy period. First came the *Statut des Juifs*, which rejected the Consistory's definition of French Jewry, and then came the establishment of the UGIF along racial lines. The Consistory found itself faced with a French government that repressed the basic civil rights of Jews, and with native Jews who agreed to join UGIF against the Consistory's counsel. Repudiated and dislodged from its historical place in French Jewish society, the Consistory was forced to grapple with the most fundamental attack on its existence.

After the war, the Consistory boasted of its intransigent attitude towards UGIF. It claimed to have condemned the organization from its constitution until the end of the war.[1] Indeed, we have seen with what antagonism and vigilance the Consistory led the campaign against the UGIF law in the second half of 1941, but the question remains whether it was actually in conflict with UGIF throughout the tragic historical events from January 1942 to July 1944.

From the outset, the efforts of the Consistory were directed essentially against UGIF-S, where the law of Vichy was the only existent one—and even if it ran contrary to the spirit of the French Revolution, there was still room for the Jews to continue to negotiate with Vichy. Such was not the case in the north. The Consistory never judged the members of UGIF-N in the same light. They believed that the special conditions of the occupation in Paris left them no alternative other than to assume their responsibility towards the council. Thus, from the outset, the Consistory's stance towards UGIF was not totally immovable but contained the seeds of a possible reconcilement. The UGIF councils earnestly sought the Consistory's moral support and backing, for they shared a common outlook with the Consistory executive and never denied its special place in French Jewry: furthermore, UGIF members recognized that the support of certain Jewish circles in France depended upon the Consistory's attitude. UGIF leaders were not motivated to replace the Consistory, but in any event they presented, especially in the south, a challenge to the Consistory by deciding to join UGIF without the Consistory's blessing and consent.

On 18 January 1942, the permanent representation of the Consistory convened in Lyon and unanimously resolved to condemn individuals who had joined the council, singling out in particular members associated with the Consistory (Lévy and Gamzon). The resolution was directed at UGIF-S: officials in the free zone "could not represent French nationals of the Jewish faith either individually or collectively."[2] The "unauthorized" talks in which Lambert had participated were criticized;[3] conversely, those who had abstained from joining the council and "by their dignity and firm attitude saved the honor of French Jewry"[4] were specially commended. The prevailing mood was one of intense displeasure with UGIF, and some of the Consistory members endeavored to isolate UGIF-S and force the Consistory into open confrontation with it.[5]

The moralistic attitude of the Consistory did not go unheeded by Albert Lévy, the target of these condemnations. He responded from a different moral stance. If the Consistory, he asked, was indeed true to its decision, was it prepared to have the UGIF members resign and to replace their functions? For him the presidency was no honor but a responsibility that could not be relinquished to "Aryan commissars" in the most tragic hour that Jews had experienced in France since the Revolution. Moreover, he hoped that the precarious nature of the period would allow for mutual respect and reconciliation between UGIF and the Consistory. However, the clash between these two moral perspectives only intensified as UGIF became a factor to contend with.[6]

The Consistory's position received further encouragement from UGIF-N. When Marcel Stora came on his secret mission to the south in March 1942, he held talks with the Consistory to bring about a change in UGIF leadership—specifically, the ousting of Lambert and Lévy from their strategic positions. Stora's grave charges against the two strongly impressed the Consistory, reinforcing its decision to withhold support of the southern council; at the same time, the Consistory resolved to transfer money illegally to UGIF-N ("a black fund"),[7] an indication of its positive attitude towards the latter.

The controversy between the UGIF and the Consistory was waged on different levels. The possibility that a Jewish leadership might be secular in character disturbed the Consistory, as it did the French rabbinate. Evidence of this anxiety can be found in Rabbi Maurice Liber's speech at a meeting on 2 March 1942, where he was the chief speaker on the theme "The Religious Tasks of the Central Consistory." He stressed that the religious associations must uphold their right to represent French Jewry and constitute a center of identification for every Jew who had ties with historical or traditional Judaism. Liber, who years earlier had stressed the need for the rabbinate's involvement in immigration issues, had befriended Lévy and Lambert when they worked together in CAR during the thirties.[8] Having actively pursued conciliation since December 1941, he now expressed his personal desire to mediate between the rival parties.[9]

However, reconciliation with UGIF was not to be achieved at the expense of the chief aim of the religious associations—with the Consistory at their head— i.e., defense of the principles of Judaism and recognition of the synagogue as the spiritual center for prayer and charity. Liber recognized the difficulties inherent in this definition, in view of the hypothesis that Jewish existence could assume another basis (racial, ethnic, political), but he feared that enforced membership in UGIF would lead to a further increase in the number of Jews indifferent or even opposed to religion. He therefore proposed a program for inducing contact with French Jewry only after examining the waves of internal Jewish migration and the ties with Consistory institutions. But on the organizational level, he struck a new chord. While strongly critical of the Consistory for being insufficiently concerned with preserving Jewish interests in the affairs of the community, he did not charge a single UGIF member with the responsibility for establishing the organization.

Liber's attitude was extremely significant, since it indicated a basically negative approach to UGIF without excluding the possibility of cooperation.

His message followed Helbronner's hostile speech before the plenum on 1 March 1942, when the Consistory president explained his attitude towards UGIF as a result of the attempt to turn the Jewish community into an "isolated community within the national community." Helbronner advocated a continuous battle against this tendency, consistent with his general design to preserve the civil rights of French Jewry. Therefore, he refused to have anything to do with UGIF.[10] Liber, however, was untiring during the following weeks in his effort to overcome the friction and reunify the community. Yet even his unselfish and authentic efforts went unrewarded: Lévy resigned from the Consistory, and Chief Rabbi Schwartz refused to retract his inflexible attitude.[11]

The interest of UGIF leaders in promoting communication with the Consistory stemmed from their desire to obtain official internal recognition. In the southern council's inaugural meeting on 4 May 1942, Lévy delivered a programmatic speech—written in part by Lambert—in which he set forth UGIF's social dogma and described the scope of its concern. Lévy was firm, asserting that the controversy within the community would deter neither him nor his colleagues from working as their consciences dictated, in the spirit of true social aid.[12] Accordingly, a special secret resolution was passed upholding the fruitful negotiations with the French authorities that enabled the various Jewish organizations to maintain a measure of economic and technical independence. The resolution also appealed to the Consistory to recognize the importance of close ties between the organizations at a time when the fate of French Jewry hung in the balance. This sincere call for unity was proof of UGIF's intention to operate on behalf of French Jewry, solely in the sphere of social work.[13] The council also authorized one of its members, André Lazard, to contact the members of the Consistory to coordinate a policy for joint action. These deliberations showed UGIF's sincere desire to terminate the rivalry and achieve real communication. Various members of the Consistory adopted a similar stance, but in mid-May the Consistory officially decided not to extend any help to UGIF-S and to refrain from meeting with its leaders. This fundamental resolution echoed Leon Meiss's statement in February 1942 that the Consistory would have no dealings of any kind with UGIF.[14]

Interestingly enough, the French authorities tried to intervene in the community's affairs and bring about a practical compromise between the two organizations. Whether the effort was connected with the future deportations and stemmed from the French estimation that the Jewish community was insufficiently cohesive or from some other motive, the fact remains that at the end of June, Maurice Couturier, the French official who was appointed chief accountant of UGIF, attempted to mediate between the organizations.

Couturier met Helbronner on the eve of a Consistory meeting. He tried to convince Helbronner to end the conflict within French Jewry and to hand over to UGIF the "Chief Rabbi's Fund" and other contributions received by the Consistory. Couturier claimed that if the institutions continued to be economically independent, the authorities would not be forced to levy a general tax on the Jewish community in the free zone.[15] However, the Consistory had as yet no inkling of the financial distress it was to suffer in 1943, and it was still far from making such a gesture of compromise. Consequently, implementation of Couturier's proposal was not considered at the Consistory's meeting; rather, the dismissal of Lambert and Lévy was discussed as a way of facilitating negotiations with UGIF. In response, the two now proposed as a sign of good will changes in Lambert's responsibilities. But again no compromise was in sight. Their replacement was clearly regarded by the Consistory as a precondition for the reinstatement of the Consistory's former standing in the community. Couturier was invested with no particular authority, and he, too, failed to bring an end to the controversy, which degenerated on more than one occasion into a personal vendetta that could not be easily overcome.[16]

The Consistory and the UGIF might have continued with their polemical relations had it not been for the intensification of anti-Jewish policy in the summer of 1942. The mass arrests in Paris in mid-July left no room for passivity. Both UGIF-S and the Consistory members were profoundly disturbed. In response, the Consistory dispatched a sharp protest to the Vichy government, maintaining that the cruel measures achieved "a degree of barbarity rarely found in history."[17] UGIF, for its part, considered ways of utilizing the visit planned for the end of July by Joseph Schwartz of the Joint, and of having him convey to America a protest to Germany. One school of thought held that in dealing with Germany, the Americans must be more forceful and warn Germany against violating international agreements on prisoners of war and against continuing the deportations, while threatening reprisals against German property in the United States. There was also some discussion of approaching the Vatican through the apostolic representation. On the community level, a UGIF official maintained that all interventions must be coordinated with the Consistory, whose leaders must detach themselves from any internal arguments in order to represent French Jewry: "The catastrophe which has now struck the Jews in the occupied area is so grave that the representation of French Jewry should, in spite of internal differences, concentrate all efforts on bringing it to an end or at least preventing its deterioration."[18] Since Schwartz's visit coincided with the deportations from the south, nothing concrete apparently came of these suggestions. Nevertheless, the attitude towards the Consistory guided the UGIF leaders during the deportations from the south in August 1942.

On learning of the French intentions to hand over 10,000 Jewish refugees from the free zone to the Gestapo, Lambert turned to Helbronner.[19] On 30 July he handed Helbronner the report that he had received and appealed to him to intervene with the French authorities together with Pierre Seligman. According to Lambert, Helbronner preferred to delay his answer for a few days. In the meanwhile, Lambert met Laval by chance and told him plainly that he preferred to see his secretary, Jacques Guérard, since UGIF was unauthorized to approach the prime minister. Lambert saw UGIF's role as a technical one and regarded the Consistory as the authentic representative of the community. He explained this division to Guérard, emphasizing that if Laval wished to meet with Jewish representatives, "I will send him the president of the Consistory and the president of UGIF."[20] Lambert saw Helbronner again on 2 August 1942 in the presence of both UGIF and Consistory members, and again he urged the formation of a joint delegation to protest the impending deportations. Helbronner refused. He added that should the Consistory decide to intervene in the matter, it would do so without the UGIF leaders. Thus it evolved that during the series of deportations in August and September, no joint intervention with UGIF took place, and the Consistory made no official protest until the end of August.[21]

Since the Consistory had protested profusely to the French authorities in the past about infringements of basic rights of the community, its procrastination in responding until the deportations were well under way was seriously condemned. The UGIF leadership interpreted the hesitance to act as a sign of indifference to the sufferings of the immigrant Jews, and as born of an illusion that the deportation of foreign Jews would enhance the security of native French Jews.[22] This accurate assessment of Helbronner's attitude and that of other members of the Consistory still fails to explain the entire development. The Consistory leaders had little hope that their plea to the French authorities would be more effective if it was sponsored jointly by the organization set up by Vichy, and they finally submitted a vehement protest condemning Vichy for surrendering thousands of foreign Jews to the Germans, while being fully aware of their fate. The protest even alluded to a systematic program of "extermination" that Germany was carrying out in the occupied countries. But the Consistory was careful not to overemphasize France's responsibility and returned to a less absolute demand. It reiterated its request that foreign Jews be placed in the same category as other foreigners, noting that if Vichy did not have the power to prevent further deportations, it should at least try to prevent the deportation of certain preferred groups.[23]

Tardy but impassioned, the Consistory's protest was made when it realized the full extent of the deportations, and it was probably occasioned by members dissatisfied with their leaders' attitudes. A certain split in the Consistory ranks seems to have developed, which also led to a changing attitude towards UGIF, distinguishable in the Consistory's meetings in late August. Some of the members were moved by the heavy burden that had befallen UGIF during the deportations, and their meetings (in Helbronner's absence) were marked by a conciliatory atmosphere. The chairman of the finance committee, Georges Wormser, suggested that two members of UGIF join the committee of the "Chief Rabbi's Fund," while William Oualid went against one of the Consistory's principles by proposing that the fund distribute money both to UGIF and to various welfare institutions. Wormser's suggestion was actually accepted, and although a final agreement concerning the joint fund was not reached for some time, these meetings constituted a step forward in the attitude towards UGIF's activities of distinguished members of the Consistory's permanent representation. General recognition of UGIF'S work and the contacts maintained by members of the organizations during the deportations had reduced the tension to the extent that Wormser even withdrew his objection to having Lévy and Lambert remain at their posts.[24] Consistory members had been shaken by the deportations, and although certain leaders maintained their anti-immigrant feelings, others began to reappraise the organization's commitment to all of French Jewry and its contact with UGIF. Nonetheless, the fundamental opposition to UGIF remained.

The impression that the Consistory and UGIF had taken an important step towards reconciliation was shared by a number of people. Joseph Schwartz, who had himself contributed to increased understanding between the organizations and had encouraged them to negotiate, reported that "peace talks" had begun. Though he viewed UGIF's existence as undesirable, even to its members, Schwartz considered the organization to be indispensable, since it had continued the welfare work and maintained thousands of needy.[25] UGIF hastened to take advantage of the change in atmosphere and announced rather prematurely that peace had been made with the Consistory. There was even talk of setting up a liaison committee to deal with future problems. Lévy, who had been particularly offended by the Consistory's criticisms, requested that Consistory member Roger Olchanski intervene with the permanent representation in order to speed up the process. "In this painful period which we are enduring," he wrote, "it is important that all those who are working for Jewry, in whatever role, coordinate their efforts and consult jointly before taking action."[26] However, the relative calm that returned to the south from mid-September dispelled the urgency for reaching complete agreement, and the proposed "peace" did not materialize.[27]

Toward Cooperation, 1942–1944

Although definite moves were made, the Consistory was in no hurry to end its conflict with UGIF. The matter was temporarily shelved in discussions held by the two councils. However, the threat presented by the German occupation of the south in November 1942 and the Consistory's severe financial situation were instrumental in bringing them closer together at the end of 1942.[28] At the end of December,[29] representatives of the two councils met to discuss their financial problems and the establishment of a united fund to further their various activities, to be supported by the entire Jewish community.[30] On the Consistory's side, those members who already in August had recognized the financial necessity of consolidating the ranks of French Jewry now tipped the scales in favor of this new approach. UGIF leaders, and Lambert in particular, regarded the Consistory's gesture as evidence that "the sincerity of our efforts and the usefulness of our activities are being acknowledged."[31] The conciliation, encouraged predominantly by economic considerations, took place on the eve of the deportations from Marseilles and Lyon, the strongholds of native French Jewry. These events strengthened the ties between the organizations and for the first time led to frequent consultations and even joint appeals by the leaders.

As will be recalled, the Germans initiated mass deportations of Marseilles's Jews to Drancy on 22 January 1943. Among their efforts to prevent the deportations, Lambert and chief rabbis Salzer and Hirschler wired the Consistory to intervene promptly with the Vichy government "in order to ensure the welfare and liberty of the members of our families who will soon be in danger."[32] This time the Consistory did not ignore their plight and reacted without delay. Helbronner wrote Laval, requesting the release of the deportees in order to preserve France's reputation in the eyes of its allies.[33] His appeal went unanswered and had no effect, except upon internal relations with UGIF. After the events in Marseilles, Lambert submitted to the Consistory a detailed, secret report on his attempts to intercede during the last week of January. Helbronner thanked Lambert for his devoted and invaluable work and granted him access to the Consistory.[34] Helbronner's response marks the turning point in his attitude towards Lambert and the beginning of a new era in the relations between the Consistory and UGIF.[35] Helbronner had seemingly reached the conclusion that the real enemy of the Consistory was neither Lambert nor UGIF but the German Gestapo and its French collaborators.

The Consistory's reappraisal of the Jewish predicament was affirmed in the Lyon raids that followed the deportations from Marseilles. Shocked by the German penetration into UGIF offices, members of the Consistory immediately endeavored to have the offices reopened and the deportees, including UGIF workers, released. The Consistory appealed to the Commissariat, and Chief Rabbi Schwartz pleaded with senior officials in the Vichy government. When the UGIF offices were reopened to the general public, the Consistory sanctioned their social work and unanimously passed a resolution stating that "the Central Consistory expresses its recognition of UGIF's charitable and social assistance, carried out with understanding and devotion for the sake of our unhappy coreligionists."[36] This affirmative approach amounted to outright recognition by the Consistory of the special role that UGIF was obliged to fulfill. The arrests of native French Jews and public officials had finally pushed aside the lingering antagonism.

The deteriorating status of French Jewry in the south reinforced the mutual recognition of these two bodies.[37] For example, cooperation was achieved when in May 1943 immigrant and native Jews were arrested in public premises in Marseilles. Lambert reported to Helbronner on his various interventions with German and French authorities to stop the arrests, which negated the armistice agreement. Since the Consistory was French Jewry's representative body, and UGIF limited itself to technical matters, Lambert asked Helbronner to intercede with Vichy.[38] Lambert's request did not go unanswered. On 12 May 1943, Helbronner sharply protested to Pétain about the continuous and indiscriminate arrests, which had even turned the public offices of UGIF into a focal point for the roundup of innocent Jews. Helbronner continued to belabor the legal aspects. Stating that the Consistory had thought it futile to protest, Helbronner eventually decided to intervene, since matters had gone beyond the mere restriction of rights. He reiterated the legal claim that the action violated the agreement with Germany, and he pleaded with France to condemn this infringement of its sovereign rights.[39]

During the period of rapprochement between the two organizations in the south, the Consistory maintained constant contact with UGIF-N and continued to send it money. UGIF-N regarded the Consistory as the authentic representative of French Jewry and requested legal and ethical opinions on problems that arose within UGIF's sphere of activity. The Consistory condoned the north's use of the "Solidarity Fund" and in May 1943 approved its utilization of the capital of defunct Jewish organizations, arguing that the funds were originally earmarked for alleviating the community's financial distress.[40] However, the Consistory apparently refrained from intervening in the controversy between the two UGIF councils on the question of reorganization, preferring a neutral position. In this new atmosphere of mutual concern and respect, the leading Jewish figures of these bodies faced the radicalization of German policy at the beginning of July 1943.[41] The ambitious designs of Brunner and Röthke to round up as many Jews as possible were acutely felt throughout France. To counteract this new German drive, the Jewish community leaders in the north and south appealed and protested to the French. As we have seen, Baur's mid-July request for a meeting with Laval boomeranged, and he was arrested in the first major step by the Germans to undermine the UGIF councils. The Central Consistory followed suit and in the middle of July turned to the Vichy government and condemned Brunner's new measures in Drancy.[42]

Baur's arrest, the change of regime in the camps, and the continued deportations influenced Joseph Fischer, the Consistory's representative in Nice, to make an uncommon move. Fischer urged Léon Meiss to coordinate with UGIF a joint delegation to the French authorities in order to obtain German concessions.[43] At the same time, Lambert made a similar suggestion to Meiss. The proliferation of anti-Semitic decrees seriously hampered UGIF's activities and diminished its effectiveness, and Lambert saw no other alternative.[44] The Consistory rejected both entreaties, and instead of sending a delegation to Vichy it protested once again to Laval, censuring Baur's arrest, Brunner's appointment, and the deportations of foreign-born Jews.[45] Fischer was insistent. He repeated his request, claiming that only by intervention and direct confrontation with the government leaders could French Jewry prevent its bitter fate.[46] Nevertheless, the Consistory members contented themselves with the written protest.[47]

Lambert, who believed in the efficacy of direct confrontation, was not willing to pass up the opportunity to present French Jewry's case before Laval. He was determined to go. On his way to Vichy on 13 August, he stopped off in Lyon, hoping to convince Meiss to reconsider and lend the Consistory's authority to the intervention. His attempt was to no avail; the tables had turned. Two years before, Lambert had been ostracized by the same Consistory leaders for his partisan negotiations at Vichy. Now he asked to be accompanied but was turned down. The following day, Lambert traveled alone to Vichy, where he met with Laval and Guérard. After the meeting he related to Meiss his feeling of despair: "Situation extremely tense, the atmosphere was deceitful; indifference regarding the problems which concern us while the demands are becoming more severe for all."[48] Lambert's mood reflected the reality. His arrest, the disastrous outcome of the intervention, chilled the French Jewish establishment. The leaders of the Consistory hastened to express to UGIF their sincere desire for his speedy return.[49]

In view of the reconciliation that it had reached with UGIF, the Consistory's refusal to participate in a joint delegation is puzzling. The Consistory had already become deeply concerned with the plight of French Jewry, and recognized the sincere efforts of UGIF leaders. But these deviations in its policy had seemingly failed to alter its basic viewpoint, which opposed fulfilling UGIF's role. This attitude was in accordance with the way in which the Consistory perceived itself—as the supreme authority of French Jewry, which advised and directed other organizations but refrained from active participation in their affairs. This dual position allowed the Consistory to maintain a fundamental a priori opposition to UGIF's existence while affirming and supporting its continued activity.[50] The Consistory's self-perception stood the test of time. That was particularly noticeable at the time of the arrests of Baur and Lambert.

Following the arrest of the UGIF leaders, a number of the remaining members gathered to discuss the crucial question—whether to persevere in their activities or abandon them. Both councils were faced with the same dilemma. The arrests had aroused fear and anxiety among the remaining UGIF leaders, and a number of them fled while it was still possible. The southern council was considerably reduced. However, after consulting with the Consistory and receiving its blessing and encouragement, the councils decided to continue their work.[51]

In this tense atmosphere, two UGIF representatives, Gamzon and Geissmann, met with the leaders of the Consistory to discuss the UGIF's future. Gamzon, in the name of the council, was on the eve of crucial talks with the Commissariat in Paris, and he sought the full backing of the Consistory. The dramatic meeting, in the presence of the Chief Rabbi of France, took place on 6 October 1943 in Lyon and recalls the Consistory's discussions concerning UGIF in December 1941. The same moral issues were raised: whether to resign or persist; the composition of the council; the "Solidarity Fund"; and the Consistory's support for UGIF. The protocol of the meeting reveals the total disarray within the UGIF council. Gamzon and other remaining members of the council were completely uninformed about the scope of Geissmann's contact with the Consistory. Geissmann had been appointed in early 1943 as liaison between the two organizations, and he frequently was invited to participate in Consistory meetings. The cordial relationship that he had established with the Consistory had contributed significantly to the reconciliation between the organizations.[52] Geissmann thus participated at this meeting in a dual capacity, both as an official of UGIF and as an ex-officio Consistory representative. Gamzon also had a dual role: he was still a member of the council while being actively involved in resistance activity. The confusion as to the roles of the participants influenced the deliberations.

Gamzon presented his demand: the Consistory should consent to establish a broad-based Jewish organization with UGIF to represent French Jewry with greater force and actively to oppose the German policy of liquidation. Although Gamzon's position was not upheld, the meeting, unlike those of December 1941, was marked by unity and an awareness of the common destiny. The atmosphere was gloomy as the participants anticipated further misery, both for themselves and for their coreligionists. Gamzon's remarks at the beginning of the session gave expression to that sentiment: "We have no illusions: one day we shall all be arrested, but before they take us away we want to achieve the maximum."[53] In this spirit, these leaders reached a common point of view: UGIF's existence was vital to the thousands in need of its services, while the continued internment of Lambert and Baur constituted a severe blow to UGIF and a threat to French Jewry's existence. The Consistory concurred with the prognosis of the UGIF council, that if the leaders were not released, no substitutes could be found.

The Consistory now viewed UGIF's existence as indispensable, but it again vetoed any open collaboration with the council and refused to accept responsibility for its actions. To Gamzon's request that the Consistory play an active role in choosing members of the council and openly support the utilization of the "Solidarity Fund," the Consistory leaders replied smugly. The Consistory was prepared to offer aid and encouragement, but it would not recruit members for UGIF and would only encourage suitable candidates to join. The final decision rested with UGIF, as in the case of the "Solidarity Fund." Helbronner would not sanction it or morally approve the utilization of the funds, but he left room for UGIF to ignore the Consistory's consent. In practical terms, the Consistory agreed to act as the supreme authority, to whom the UGIF could address specific problems and queries. The Consistory refused to renounce its fundamental position; as Léon Meiss, the vice-president of the Consistory stated: "We cannot participate in the administration of the UGIF, deputize for you or accept your responsibility."

Thus, even at this difficult moment, when it regarded the release of its leaders as an urgent necessity, the Consistory did not accede to the UGIF's request for a homogeneous Jewish policy. Even at a time when the murderous intentions were clear to all, the basic moral considerations that had divided the organizations in 1941 persisted, and they now obstructed the establishment of an umbrella organization for the whole of French Jewry.

The Lyon meeting took place some two weeks before Helbronner's arrest, and approximately three weeks before the meetings in Paris laid the foundation for the reorganization of UGIF. Coming as they did at the same time as the seizure of the La Rose children's home, these events changed the course of French Jewry. For it was only after Helbronner's arrest that the Consistory, led by Meiss, took a revolutionary step and urged discussions with representatives of various Jewish underground organizations. Together they finally created the underground umbrella organization CRIF (Conseil Représentatif des Juifs de France), which encompassed all sectors of the Jewish community.[54] Yet, the Consistory's decision to support underground work did not contradict its positive attitude towards UGIF's activity within a legal framework. CRIF did not call upon UGIF to disband, and in its agenda, consolidated in 1944, mention was even made of UGIF's important contribution in the field of social aid. Considering the diverse elements in CRIF, its moderate attitude towards UGIF could be explained only by the Consistory's influence.[55]

In the ensuing period, ties between the Consistory and UGIF-S grew tighter. Geissmann became head of UGIF-S, and at the beginning of 1944 its headquarters moved to Lyon, to the Consistory's satisfaction. The Consistory was continuously briefed on events inside UGIF, and all the organization's crucial problems were aired in mutual consultations. Moreover, the leaders agreed that several of their members could play an active role in both organizations.[56] The time had passed for quibbling about petty differences.

During the first half of 1944, native French Jews carried out their activities in a spirit of real unity. However, no sources exist that describe these activities or reveal whether, or to what extent, the UGIF leadership worked together with the Consistory leadership in underground affairs. Only one thing is known: constant contact existed between Meiss and Geissmann until the end of the war. Herein lies the key to understanding Meiss's moderate stand in the controversy among various Jewish organizations concerning UGIF's dissolution in the summer of 1944. Meiss showed greater empathy and tolerance towards the UGIF's activities than did the others, and he praised Geissmann and his colleagues for their devoted work to relieve Jewish suffering.[57] If Meiss nevertheless assented to the request to close the UGIF offices, it was because of the basic moral principle that guided the Consistory to reject working openly with UGIF throughout its entire existence, and not because he felt that UGIF's activities amounted to collaboration.

We have seen how the Consistory endeavored to pit its moral strength against the compulsory Jewish organization, which stood in opposition to the hallowed historic principles of French Jewry. The Consistory did not go so far as to boycott UGIF completely, and from the outset it justified the existence of UGIF-N and sympathized with the predicament of its leaders. In contrast, the Consistory sharply criticized UGIF-S and its leaders, but in the wake of the deportations from the south and the growing financial distress of French Jewry, it even acknowledged the importance of that council's relief work and the essential role played by its leaders. In 1943–1944, criticism gave way to recognition of the indispensable nature of UGIF-S, paving the way for widespread cooperation. Nevertheless, this reconciliation did not eliminate the Consistory's moral opposition to UGIF's existence, an attitude that it maintained throughout the war.

CONCLUSION

In the war years, the Jewish leadership in France functioned under severe conditions; the Vichy regime had nullified the emancipation that Jews had cherished since the French Revolution, and the Nazi conqueror had issued their death sentence. Entering the war as a heterogeneous group, a result of several large waves of immigration during the twentieth century, the French Jewish community was far from united. The native Jewish population felt secure in French society, lulled by the positive experience of previous generations and their profound identification with French culture in all its aspects. The immigrant Jews from Eastern Europe encountered a different France—a country that was retreating from its liberal tradition, that was gradually rescinding its lenient immigrant alien laws, and that set up internment camps for the refugees crowded into its borders. The Eastern European Jews had not severed their psychological, political, and sociocultural ties with the old country, and their attempt to revive former values in France was a source of constant friction between them and the established Jewish community.

The outbreak of World War II created a momentary focus for common experience; each community gave itself unstintingly to the war effort, clearly aware that the struggle against fascism was a sacred battle to protect both democratic principles and the Jews. The two communities were united in their belief that the Jews could not remain indifferent to the outcome of the war. As recent generations of Jews in Western and Central Europe had entered the military service as an expression of their deep attachment to their native countries, so during the first year of the war the Jews in France took pride in the tremendous sacrifices they made for France. However, the willingness of Jews to serve France with their lives did not sustain them in a time of crisis, and with the debacle, French Jewry found itself retreating to the prewar tumult. The dissolution of the Third Republic was a continuation of France's deep-seated antagonism towards liberal democracy and bore out the earlier fears of the Eastern European Jews. Accepting the division of France into two zones, Vichy ended the common fate of the Jewish community. For even though Vichy's racist laws ostensibly placed all Jews in an inferior status to other French citizens, they affected, first and foremost, the foreign Jews residing in the occupied zone.

The division of France had great import for the manner in which French Jewry dealt with the events of the war years. It changed the significance of the ties between the Jews and France and meant that the "French experience" was no longer the same even for all the native Jews. Occupation of the north led to a massive flight in the summer of 1940 to the southern part of France, which included the leaders of the community. Those who remained in the south lived through a different war from that experienced by those who returned to or remained under the German occupation. Although the former were deeply shaken by the Vichy laws of October 1940, they responded with a certain equanimity, preferring to explain these laws in terms of German influence. They continued to believe in France's tradition of equality and expected her to shield the Jews. Their composure was evident in the voluntary roof organization that they created, which lacked real content and preserved the individualistic spirit of the nineteenth century. In the north, the rupture with France was profound. Racial laws and the Aryanization of the economy drove thousands of Jewish families to bankruptcy, impelling the community's leaders to assent to organize a quasi-compulsory framework.

In both the north and the south, some Eastern European Jews sought a united community and encouraged joint action, but they were rebuffed by native Jews who were caught up in the xenophobic atmosphere. As time passed and German pressure increased, the situation reversed itself: native Jews tried to further cooperation, but the immigrant leaders turned their back on unity and left the task of representation to the native French Jews. Moving into underground activity, immigrant leaders strongly criticized those who maintained the status quo and frowned upon their legalistic thinking. The native leaders, on their part, had not alerted the community to an emergency situation, expecting a quick reversal. After they became aware of the more permanent nature of the cataclysm, they prevented the community's disintegration. However, they could not gain the support of the immigrant Jews, who continued to regard them as unreliable and indifferent to the sufferings of the Eastern European community.

In concentrating on the activities and goals of the Jewish councils in France, established after an SD order of August 1941, we have seen the internal vicissitudes of the established Jewish leadership. The creation of UGIF projected the unique aspect of each of the participant elements. For about three months, the Jewish leaders had the opportunity to weigh the aspects of the legislation and its implications for the Jewish community. These enlightening discussions, particularly in the south, acknowledged

French Jews' perception of their past history in France and showed how prominently that perception figured in their appraisal of the new situation, often more than their existential reality. In addition to being a most accurate monitor of the difficulty native Jews had in relinquishing their "French experience," these deliberations also reveal their denial of a common fate with other Jewish communities under the New Order. The tendency of native Jews to regard themselves as fully integrated citizens was replicated in other Jewish communities during the Holocaust, attesting to the singular attachment of Jews to their mother countries, a bond often more meaningful than their identification with the common fate of the Jewish people.

The French authorities revived the main trends of anti-Semitism of the 1930s, but not without internal conflict. One school of thought instituted laws circumscribing Jewish activities in France while disdaining cooperation with Germany; another viewed Germany as the standard-bearer of modern anti-Semitism and sought to emulate it in France. During the discussions on the establishment of UGIF, Vallat emerged as an exponent of the first orientation, and there is room for a certain reevaluation of his role as commissioner for Jewish affairs. Endangering his position to help protect French Jews, Vallat attempted to convince Jewish leaders in the north and south to join the roof organization, permitted them to participate in the formulation of the legislation, and revised clauses unacceptable to them. He also preferred to appoint moral and responsible leaders to the council for the benefit of the French Jews. A clear dialectic appears, common to the unprecedented days of the Holocaust: the same Vallat who actively initiated isolating Jews from French society and economic life and removing them from certain professions, was moderate in his dealings with the native Jews, to the extent that some even considered him a "philo-Semite." This attitude towards native Jews was intertwined with his anti-German stance, as is evidenced by his proposal to expand UGIF's responsibility to the south in order to block German control over that region and preserve French sovereignty. Other members of the Commissariat worked in a similar fashion throughout the war years and eased the Jewish tragedy to some small extent, but with the removal of Vallat, their impact diminished considerably. During the Darquier period, relations between UGIF and the Commissariat were constantly strained. Darquier and his entourage characterized the second school of thought within French anti-Semitism, and they went much further in both theory and practice in their cooperation with Nazi Germany. This circle associated France's entry into the New Order with the total denunciation of its Jews.

Analysis of relevant material indicates that the German authorities in France were rather patient with the formation of UGIF and were prepared to leave the negotiations to Vallat. German documents show that at this stage of the "Final Solution" in a Western European country, the Germans held out little hope for an authoritarian Jewish council and saw it mainly as a tool to intensify the isolation of the Jews from the rest of society, similar to Heydrich's order to the heads of the Einsatzgruppen during the invasion of Poland in September 1939. Thus, the SD did not alter the original limited goals of the Jewish council, even though by late 1941 the physical extermination of the Jews had become Nazi policy. This development contradicts the accepted image of the Jewish council extant in historiography. That conclusion is also borne out by study of the entire complex of UGIF activities in the north and south of France.

UGIF-N began to operate during trying times. Its leaders in Paris bowed to the existing reality, taking the view that the time was not right to abandon community activities. Initially, the organization sought to limit itself to social issues; however, it was soon forced to abandon that principle and began to meet the SD demands, as well as the needs of the deportees. UGIF-N relied upon Vallat, but when he was replaced it had to grapple with increasing animosity toward Jews without any help from the French authorities. Nevertheless, through summer 1942, the UGIF leaders hardly grasped the consequences of France's abandonment of the Jews, nor could they conceive the extent of France's active collaboration in the plans to deport them. Clearly, the UGIF-N leaders were not made privy to the discussions preceding the deportations and were assigned only limited social functions in the internment process. But certain information filtered through to them prior to the deportations, which UGIF hardly utilized to alert the community of the impending disaster. With all that was happening, UGIF continued within a legalistic framework, not abandoning its faith in the French and their legal system.

The events of the summer established the parameters of UGIF's activities for the duration of the war: thousands of Jews turned to it for aid, and hundreds of children remained under its care. As a roof organization, the council made few far-reaching decisions; both legal and underground work were carried out in its various sections, and the council as a unified body neither urged illegal activity nor proposed its abandonment. Its cautious response to the events was to carry on daily assistance and to deal with the factors that taxed the life of the Jews of Paris and the northern region. The beleaguered heads of UGIF remained convinced of their utility to the community in providing for the needy; they struggled to find ways to continue their services, yet their steadfastness placed hundreds of Jews in a precarious position. Responsibility, legalism, and concern could not yield to the more daring and uncertain road of the underground.

Established in a calmer atmosphere, UGIF-S was preceded by several months of intensive community discussions. These left their mark on the eventual formation of a federative organization that allowed for the extensive autonomy of affiliated societies. However, before the southern council was able to develop its social program, it was overwhelmed by the deportations from the south.

Vichy's acquiescence to the German demand to deport foreign Jews from the unoccupied zone evoked a vehement protest from UGIF-S and the international welfare organizations. UGIF-S tried to coordinate its position with the Consistory, but the latter's rejection of the southern council nullified these overtures and made a joint delegation to Vichy throughout the month of deportations an impossibility. Notwithstanding, that was not an act of disappropriating the immigrant Jews; during the internments, UGIF-S treated them with exceptional concern, doing its utmost to alleviate their plight.

The deportations marked a turning point for UGIF-S. For some of its affiliate organizations, the deportations to Drancy prompted the beginning of illegal activity alongside the official work. The UGIF-S leaders were aware of the duality and did not oppose it. Having voluntarily stripped itself of potential authority and influence over these organizations, UGIF-S rarely intervened in their affairs and seldom set down policies that circumscribed their activities. The ostensible attachment of the affiliates to UGIF shielded their autonomous policy, making it difficult to identify their activity with the leadership. In this fashion, the UGIF leadership continued to operate in the spirit of Jewish organizations established during the heyday of emancipation.

The January 1943 roundups in Marseilles, the heart of French Jewry in the south, were a landmark in the history of French Jewry during the Holocaust, in that they disclosed the fragile nature of all of French Jewry. Following the internments, the Central Consistory abandoned its opposition to UGIF in favor of support for the organization's activities for the defense of French Jewry. Moreover, it would appear that after the deportations from Marseilles, Lambert began to assist the underground activities, and key figures in the leadership tended towards a dual approach—supporting certain underground activity while safeguarding the continuity of the legal framework. This growing duality helps to explain the stubborn opposition of Lambert and the council to the reorganization plan suggested by André Baur.

Several important attributes of the councils' nature and interrelationship emerge from a study of the reorganization scheme. First, the idea of uniting the sections originated in the north, partly as a solution to its economic problems. Viewing the proposal as dangerous to its federative format, UGIF-S resisted it. Second, UGIF-S took advantage of the official missions to the north to help expand the underground network. Third, owing to UGIF's lack of influence in the community, its centralization seemed superfluous and unnecessary to the authorities. The SD showed interest only in September 1943, while the Commissariat actually opposed the proposition until summer 1943. Finally, the attempt at reorganization reveals the internal workings of the councils and their outlook. UGIF-N was not an authoritarian body but, in essence, was more cohesive and geared to a unified decision-making process; UGIF-S had sanctified the autonomous existence of its societies and left the council little room for formulating their policies.

A significant shift in UGIF activities occurred in the summer of 1943, when German measures intensified and the Italian sector came under German control. Disappointed with the number of deportees to Auschwitz, which was far below the quota assigned to France, the SD took new steps against the UGIF councils. But these German tactics were thwarted. The UGIF leaders maintained their moral integrity: with their councils' support, Baur refused to deal with police affairs, and Lambert forcefully protested against the radicalization of German policy. Their opposition led to their arrest and deportation.

With the new decrees and internments, the turmoil of French Jewry rose to a new peak. That was most visible in the south, where the Nazis continued their mad pursuit of more Jews. The affiliate organizations of UGIF-S, which had previously operated on both official and illegal levels, disbanded their official presence and moved almost exclusively into the sphere of underground activity. Disoriented and leaderless, the UGIF-S council could no longer withstand the process of reorganization, now supported by Röthke. Nonetheless, as in all bureaucratic administrations, inertia prevailed, and the organization endured.

UGIF-N assumed the responsibility for the upkeep of Drancy in the summer of 1943, and that became its central concern during the following year. Thousands remained in its care, and hundreds of children were still cared for in its homes. Rejecting repeated appeals from the Jewish underground to abandon their activities and disperse the homes, the councils stood firm in their conviction that their contribution to the welfare of the Jewish community was essential. Tragically and paradoxically, hundreds were eventually deported by the German police as they were being cared for by UGIF workers.

The dissolution of any administration is an intricate process, and it seeks to survive even when its basic purpose cannot be realized. Such was the case with UGIF. It continued to operate after the extensive deportations and the attacks on its institutions, including the children's homes. It took an internal community trial to dissolve its institutions.

Within the community, UGIF was a source of great friction. Condemned and maligned by immigrant and resistance organizations, it had few allies. We have seen that much had to happen before the historical leadership of the native Jews, the Consistory, began to respect UGIF's efforts, but it never granted the councils a blanket seal of approval. The leaders of the Consistory maintained their moral viewpoint until the war's end, an indication of the resilience of historical traditions even in the face of the Holocaust. The leaders of the Consistory, like many native French Jews, grappled with their past history and tried to explain their contemporary reality within its focus. By trying to find appropriate historical parallels to their predicament, they often blighted their own understanding.

Study of the manifold activities of UGIF in both the north and south of France has indicated that the monolithic image of the organization common in historiography should be reassessed. By tracing the development of the UGIF from 1941 on, and analyzing the aims and viewpoints of its leaders in chronological sequence, their strong emotional attachment to the French experience and to French culture looms large, as does their major effort to maintain Jewish welfare services. Severed from the French community by the Vichy laws and condemned by contrasting Jewish elements of society, the UGIF leadership assumed the burden of responsibility for the fate of the Jews and the needs of the community. Throughout UGIF's existence, its leaders accepted a limited and modest stand, struggling to save the relief services. Despite their efforts and often owing to their lack of foresight, hundreds of Jews fell victim to the Nazi mission, joining the more than 75,000 Jews deported from France to Auschwitz. Yet, the two councils, irrespective of their contrasting directions, had failed those Jews by being overly loyal to the humane goal of serving the needy.

LIST OF ABBREVIATIONS

AFSC	Archives of the American Friends Service Committee, Philadelphia
AJDC	Archives of the American Jewish Joint Distribution Committee, New York
AN	Archives Nationales, Paris
CAHJP	Central Archives for the History of the Jewish People, Jerusalem
CARNET	Lambert, Raymond-Raoul, *Carnet d'un témoin, 1940–1943*. Ed. Richard Cohen. Paris, 1985
CDJC	Centre de Documentation Juive Contemporaine, Paris
JTS	Archives of the Jewish Theological Seminary, New York
SMA	Saly Mayer Archive, American Jewish Joint Distribution Committee, New York
USC	Archives of Unitarian Service Committee, Harvard Divinity School, Cambridge, Massachusetts
WJC	Archives of World Jewish Congress, New York
WRB	Archives of the War Refugee Board, Roosevelt Archives, Hyde Park, New York
YIVO:RG	Archives of the YIVO Institute for Jewish Research, New York (Record Group)
YVA	Archives of the Yad Vashem Institute, Jerusalem

NOTES

I. French Jewry on the Eve of World War II

1. Phyllis Cohen Albert, *The Modernization of French Jewry: Consistory and Community in the Nineteenth Century.*
2. Michael Graetz, *From Periphery to Center: Chapters in Nineteenth Century History of French Jewry* (Hebrew; Jerusalem, 1982); Michel Abitol, "The Encounter between French Jewry and the Jews of North Africa: Analysis of a Discourse (1830–1914)," in *The Jews in Modern France*, ed. Frances Malino and Bernard Wasserstein, p. 38.
3. Robert F. Byrnes, *Anti-Semitism in Modern France.*
4. The above discussion is based on Zeev Sternhell, *Maurice Barrès et le nationalisme français* (Paris, 1972); idem, *La droite révolutionnaire, 1885–1914: les origines françaises du fascisme* (Paris, 1978); idem, "The Roots of Popular Anti-Semitism in the Third Republic," in *The Jews in Modern France*, ed. Frances Malino and Bernard Wasserstein, pp. 103–134.
5. Michael R. Marrus, *The Politics of Assimilation.*
6. Yerachmiel Cohen, "Parshat Dreyfus Vehayehudim," in *Sinat Yisrael Ledoroteha*, ed. Shmuel Almog, pp. 291–308.
7. Paula Hyman, *From Dreyfus to Vichy*, pp. 26–30.
8. Ibid., p. 81.
9. Ibid., pp.49–59.
10. Ibid., pp. 33–62.
11. Timothy Maga, "Closing the Door: The French Government and Refugee Policy, 1933–1939," *French Historical Studies* 12 (1982): 424–42.
12. H. S. Hughes, *The Obstructed Path: French Social Thought in the Years of Desperation, 1930–1960* (New York, 1966), pp. 65–102.
13. Lazare Landau, *De l'aversion à l'estime: Juifs et Catholiques en France de 1919 à 1939.*
14. Michael R. Marrus and Robert O. Paxton, *Vichy France and the Jews*, p. 36.
15. Maga, "Closing the Door," pp. 424–30; Marrus and Paxton, *Vichy France*, pp. 54–58.
16. Maga, "Closing the Door," pp. 434–38; Stephen A. Schuker, "Origins of the 'Jewish Problem' in the Third Republic," in *The Jews in Modern France*, ed. Frances Malino and Bernard Wasserstein, pp. 154–65.
17. Marrus and Paxton, *Vichy France*, p. 49.
18. Maga, "Closing the Door," pp. 438–42; Vicki Caron, "Prelude to Vichy: France and the Jewish Refugees in the Era of Appeasement," *Journal of Contemporary History* 20 (1985): 157–76.
19. Marrus and Paxton, *Vichy France*, p. 57.
20. David H. Weinberg, *A Community on Trial*, chap. 1.
21. Ibid., pp. 76, 95–96; cf. Schuker, "Origins," p. 173.
22. Reactions to anti-Semitism are discussed in depth in Weinberg, *Community*, chaps. 5, 6; see also Hyman, *From Dreyfus*, pp. 199–230.
23. Ruth Fabian and Corinna Coulmas, *Die deutsche Emigration in Frankreich nach 1933*; Rita Thalmann, "L'émigration du IIIᵉ Reich dans la France de 1933 à 1939," *Le Monde Juif*, n.s. 96 (October-December 1979): 127–39; Yehuda Bauer, *My Brother's Keeper*, pp. 138–39.

24. Fabian and Coulmas, *Die deutsche*, p. 65; Weinberg, *Community*, passim; Hyman, *From Dreyfus*, p. 265.

25. Hyman, *From Dreyfus*, p. 221; Bauer, *My Brother's*, p. 265.

26. Fabian and Coulmas, *Die deutsche*, passim.

27. Bauer, *My Brother's*, pp. 239, 265.

28. Ibid., pp. 237–39, 264–65.

29. Weinberg, *Community*, p. 187.

30. *L'Univers israélite*, 14 April 1939; Carnet, pp. 23–24.

II. The Fall of France: German Occupation and French Jewry, 1940–1942

1. Alfred A. Cobban, *A History of Modern France*, vol. 3, pp. 169–75.

2. David H. Weinberg, *A Community on Trial: The Jews of Paris in the 1930s*, pp. 171–205; Paula E. Hyman, *From Dreyfus to Vichy*, pp. 229–32; Vicki Caron, "Prelude to Vichy: France and the Jewish Refugees in the Era of Appeasement," *Journal of Contemporary History* 20 (1985): 168.

3. *L'Univers israélite*, 1 September 1939. On the celebrations of the anniversary during 1939, see Weinberg, *Community*, pp. 196–200.

4. *L'Univers israélite*, passim, 1939-May 1940; *Paix et Droit*, vols. 9, 10, passim, particularly articles by Alfred Berl.

5. *L'Univers israélite*, 3–10 November 1939, 17–24 November 1939; Pierre Geismar, ibid., 9–16 February 1940; *Le Judaïsme Sepharadi*, December 1939. See declaration of Sephardic leadership, ibid., 5 September 1939.

6. *L'Univers israélite*, 22, 29 September 1939; descriptions of immigrant activity, ibid., 15 September 1939, 20–27 October 1939, 12–19 January 1940, etc. See CAR's French and German leaflet "What Every Refugee Must Know," August 1939 (AJDC: general and emergency, France, 1939 [12–43]). Biélinky Diary, 12 October 1940; *Parizer Haint*, 29 September 1939.

7. Weinberg, *Community*, pp. 200–201.

8. Zosa Szajkowski, *Jews and the French Foreign Legion*, pp. 60–67.

9. *Parizer Haint*, 2, 3 September 1939; see also paper's special heading during most of September.

10. Weinberg, *Community*, pp. 203–205; cf. Szajkowski, *Foreign Legion*, p. 60; see Jacques Biélinky, "La Guerre totale contre la sauvagerie hitlerienne" (n.d.) (YIVO: Biélinky archive); Joseph Ratz, *La France que je cherchais: Les impressions d'un Russe engagé volontaire en France*; A. Rayski, ed., *Das Vort fun Vidershtant un Zieg*.

11. Yehuda Bauer, *American Jewry and the Holocaust: The American Jewish Joint Distribution Committee (1939–1945)*, pp. 154–55; Michael R. Marrus and Robert O. Paxton, *Vichy France and the Jews*, p. 65.

12. *L'Univers israélite*, 20–27 October 1939; report of 29 October 1939 (AJDC: general and emergency, France, 1939 [12–43]). The Joint's grant for November 1939 was $9,200.

13. Jarblum to World Jewish Congress, 19 April 1940 (JTS: Box 13; 21); also *L'Univers israélite*, 29 September, 6 October 1939; 10–17 May 1940.

14. Marrus and Paxton, *Vichy France*, p. 66; articles by Sijes and Avni in Yisrael Gutman and Efraim Zuroff, eds., *Rescue Attempts during the Holocaust* (Jerusalem: Yad-Vashem, 1977), pp. 537–62.

15. Jacques Biélinky, "Invasion de la France et le sort d'Israel," 3 June 1940 (YIVO: Biélinky archive). Cf. editorials in *Parizer Haint*, May 1940; letters of the Jewish Communist Eli Wallach, 1 March and 12 May 1940 (YVA: P7/27).

16. Pierre Geismar's speech before the Central Consistory, 7 April 1940, *L'Univers israélite*, 5–12 April 1940; Rabbi Hirschler's pronouncement "Aux armées" (CAHJP: F-359).

17. Jean Vidalenc, *L'exode de mai-juin 1940* (Paris, 1957); Bauer, *American Jewry*, p. 155; French official estimate, 23 July 1940 (AFSC: general files, 1940, foreign service); H. Sinder, "Lights and Shades of Jewish Life in France, 1940–1942," *Jewish Social Studies* 5 (1943): 367–82; Tcherikower Diary (YIVO: Tcherikower collection).

18. Robert O. Paxton, *Vichy France: Old Guard and New Order, 1940–1944*, pp. 3–50; Richard Cobb, *French and Germans, Germans and French: A Personal Interpretation of France under Two Occupations, 1914–1918/1940–1944*, pp. 90–91.

19. Léon Poliakov, *L'auberge des musiciens*, p. 78.

20. YIVO:RG 116, 56; Sinder, "Lights and Shades," passim. According to the October 1940 census ordered by the German authorities, CDJC: LXXIXa–10.

21. Bauer, *American Jewry*, pp. 43–45; Haim Avni, *Spain, the Jews, and Franco*, chap. 3.

22. Katzki report, 23 July 1940 (AJDC: general and emergency, January-August 1940 [12–43]; J. Schwartz report, 9 August 1940; Schwartz to N.Y. office, ibid., 19 September 1940; J. Kaplan, "French Jewry under the Occupation," *The American Jewish Yearbook 5706*, pp. 73–74; Raul Hilberg, *The Destruction of the European Jews*, vol. 2, pp. 614–15; YIVO:RG 245.5, II, France, 67; Bauer, *American Jewry*, p. 158.

23. Cobb, *French and Germans*, p. 91.

24. Carnet, 15 July 1940, p. 72.

25. Protocol of rabbinic convention, 3–4 September 1940 (YVA: 09/28–2).

26. EIF report, 10 August 1940 (JTS: Box 10); S. Hamel to J. Weill, 1 September 1940 (Hamel collection); interviews with D. Gamzon, 20 September 1979, and S. Hamel, 10 September 1979; A. Michel, *Les éclaireurs israélites de France pendant la seconde guerre mondiale*, pp. 83–85.

27. YVA: M25 (12); also *Massada: Discours des camps de concentration* (n.p., n.d. [1942]).

28. Report on Parisian Jewry, mid-1941 (AJDC: reports, 1940–1941 [3–14], p. 16); Rabi (W. Rabinovitch), *Anatomie du judaïsme français*; Marrus and Paxton, *Vichy France*, pp. 310–15. Correspondence between K. Cohen and G. Montandon, September 1941 (CDJC: XCV-136).

29. H. R. Kedward, *Resistance in Vichy France: A Study of Ideas and Motivation in the Southern Zone, 1940–1942*, chap. 1.

30. Marrus and Paxton, *Vichy France*, p. 13. The *statut* was published on 18 October 1940.

31. Biélinky Diary, 6 November 1940 (YIVO: Biélinky archive).

32. Carnet, 19 October 1940, p. 85.

33. War veterans to Pétain, 5 October 1940 (YIVO:RG 116, 33); Julien Weill to Pétain, 23 October 1940, ibid.; André Boris to Pétain, 10 November 1940, and Pierre Masse to Pétain, 20 October 1940, in Adam Rutkowski, ed., *La lutte des Juifs en France a l'époque de l'occupation (1940–1944)*, pp. 44–46; sermons and speeches in J. Kaplan, *Les temps d'épreuve*; idem, *Justice pour la foi juive: Pierre Pierrard interroge le grand rabbin Kaplan*.

34. Schwartz to Pétain, 22 October 1940, in E. Tcherikower, ed., *Yidn in Frankraykh*, vol. 2, pp. 295–97; on background, see Schwartz's report, JTS: Box 13; Schwartz to Pétain, 10 October 1940 (CAHJP: F-350). See protest of decorated World War I veterans to Pétain, 8 January 1941 (CDJC: CXCIII-4); Rutkowski, *La lutte*, pp. 49–50.

35. Paraphrase from Carnet, 6 November 1940, p. 85.

36. Tcherikower Diary, p. 35 (YIVO: Tcherikower collection).

37. Paxton, *Vichy France*, p. 40.

38. Rayski, *Das Vort*, p. 13; David Diamant, *Les Juifs dans la résistance française, 1940–1944: (Avec armes ou sans armes)*; Jacques Ravine, *La résistance organisée des Juifs en France (1940–1944)*.

39. Cf. Kedward, *Resistance*, chap. 3; *Unzer Vort*, passim; Alfred Grant, *Paris a Schot fun front*; Biélinky Diary, September 1940 (YIVO: Biélinky archive).

40. Weinberg, *Community*, pp. 191–93.

41. David Knout, *Contribution à l'histoire de la résistance juive en France 1940–1944*, pp. 139–45, 147ff; Jacques Lazarus, *Juifs au combat: Témoignage sur l'activité d'un mouvement de résistance*, pp. 28ff; Anny Latour, *The Jewish Resistance in France (1940–1944)*, pp. 24–25, 94; Claude Vigée, *La lune d'hiver*, pp. 52–72.

42. J. Jakoubowicz, *Rue Amelot: Hilf un Vidershtant*, pp. 7–8; report of 30 August 1945 (YIVO:RG 343, 159); AJDC: France, general and emergency (12–43); Hyman, *From Dreyfus*, p. 87.

43. YIVO: Tcherikower archive, 1237; RG 343, 6–9; Katzki report, 23 July 1940, and Tabatchnik report, 10 August 1940 (AJDC: France, general and emergency [12–43]); Y. Jakoubowicz, *Rue Amelot*, p. 12.

44. Biélinky Diary, 28 August 1940 (YIVO: Biélinky archive); YIVO:RG 343, 7, 12; Katzki report, 31 December 1940 (AJDC: France, reports 1940–1941 [3–14]).

45. Rapoport's remarks in meeting with UGIF leaders, 28 January 1942 (YVA: P7/8), quoted in Y. Cohen, "Towards the Establishment of UGIF-N (An Unknown Document from 1942)," *Yalkut Moreshet* 30 (1980): 139–56 (Hebrew); *L'Un des trente-six*, p. 28.

46. Katzki report, 31 December 1940 (AJDC: France, reports 1940–1941, [3–14]).

47. YIVO:RG 343, 1–17; ADJC report "situation morale" (AJDC: France, reports 1940–1941 [3–14]); H. Kershner to Quaker office in Philadelphia, 13 November 1940 (AFSC: France, refugees, 1940). Bauer, *American Jewry*, p. 172.

48. Biélinky Diary, 3 September 1940 (YIVO: Biélinky archive); Hyman, *From Dreyfus*, pp. 64, 120–24, 130–32.

49. Marrus and Paxton, *Vichy France*, pp. 77–81, 373; Serge Klarsfeld, ed., *Die Endlösung der Judenfrage in Frankreich: Deutsche Dokumente, 1941–1944*, p. 233.

50. YIVO: Tcherikower archive, 1650: "La rue Amelot et le Comité de Coordination de (?)"; YIVO:RG 343, 3 "Note concernant . . . d'Occupation"; report "situation morale" (AJDC: France, reports, 1940–1941 [3–14]), pp. 26–27. Jacques Adler, *Face à la persécution: Les organisations juives à Paris de 1940 à 1944*, pp. 37–45.

51. "La rue Amelot," n. 50.

52. Ibid., "Note concernant," n. 50; YVA: 09/11–1.

53. "Situation morale," n. 50.

54. "La rue Amelot," n. 50; "Note concernant," n. 50.

55. Ibid.

56. Sachs to invitees, 30 November 1940 (YIVO:RG 343, 3); Reichman's list, ibid.; Jakoubowicz, *Rue Amelot*, pp. 27–28; Biélinky Diary, 16 December 1940 (YIVO: Biélinky archive); Adler; *Face persécution*, p. 46.

57. Jakoubowicz, *Rue Amelot*, pp. 27–28.

58. Meetings of social workers, YVA: 09/11–13; YIVO: Tcherikower archive, 1650. Only 335,000 francs were contributed during the first five months of the appeal (YIVO:RG 343, 3). According to Dannecker's order, part of the money was earmarked for the preparation of a copy of the Jewish population register in the Seine for Jewish relief agencies (CDJC: CCXVII-4); cf. Zosa Szajkowski, *Analytical Franco-Jewish Gazetteer, 1939–1945*, p. 42.

59. Sachs to Jakoubowicz, 20 January 1941 (YIVO:RG 343, 8); in Jakoubowicz, *Rue Amelot*, p. 29.

60. Ibid., p. 30; *L'Un des trente-six*, p. 31; AJDC report, n. 47.

61. On meeting of 30 January 1941 and orientation of Comité, see YIVO:RG 343, 8; also YIVO:RG 210, I-9; Szajkowski, *Gazetteer*, p. 40.

62. Dannecker's report, 21 January 1941 (CDJC: V-59); Joseph Billig, *Le commissariat général aux questions juives (1941–1944)*, vol. 1, pp. 46–47.

63. Jakoubowicz, *Rue Amelot*, pp. 24–42; Szajkowski, *Gazetteer*, pp. 42–43; AJDC report, n. 50, pp. 26–27.

64. Grant, *Paris*, pp. 50–51; Szajkowski, *Gazetteer*, p. 40; Adler, *Face persécution*, pp. 161–68.

65. Based on weekly reports to German authorities, February and March 1941 (CDJC: CCXVII-4).

66. YIVO:RG 343, 15–17; report of Dobershütz-Sachs meeting, 7 March 1941 (CDJC: CCXVII-4); response of Jews in the south, report of 10–11 June 1941 (YIVO:RG 245.5, II, France, 67).

67. Meeting of 25 March 1941 (YIVO:RG 210, I-7).

68. Marrus and Paxton, *Vichy France*, pp. 81–83.

69. Various reports of the meeting: (YIVO:RG 210, I-3; RG 343, 8; CDJC: CCXVII-4); Jakoubowicz, *Rue Amelot*, p. 34; AJDC report, n. 50, p. 29; Adler, *Face persécution*, pp. 51–52.

70. Protocol of Comité's meeting, 31 March 1941 (CDJC: CCXVII-4); report submitted to Dannecker, YIVO:RG 210, I-3, report on Sachs-Dannecker meeting, 1 April 1941 (ibid.); Szajkowski, *Gazetteer*, p. 41; statutes in YIVO:RG 343, 8.

71. Conflicting evidence exists as to whether the Comité was informed in advance. "Informations Juives," 19 April 1941; Jakoubowicz, *Rue Amelot*, p. 36. Meetings of 3 and 17 (20?) April 1941 (CDJC: CCXVII-4); AJDC report, n. 50, pp. 28–29. Maurice Rajsfus, *Des Juifs dans la collaboration: L'UGIF 1941–1944*, pp. 285–91; Adler, *Face persécution*, pp. 53–55.

72. YIVO:RG 210, XC-10; Biélinky Diary, 26 April 1941; Szajkowski, *Gazetteer*, p. 41.

73. AJDC report, n. 50, p. 29.

74. *L'Activité des organisations juives en France sous l'occupation*, p. 191; Jakoubowicz, *Rue Amelot*, pp. 36–39.

75. AJDC report, n. 50, pp. 31–32; Marrus and Paxton, *Vichy France*, p. 89.

76. May and June meetings (CDJC: CCXVII-4).

77. David Diamant, *Le billet vert*; minutes of Comité meeting, 20 May 1941 (CDJC: CCXVII-4); Biélinky Diary, 13 and 14 May 1941.

78. Biélinky Diary, 16 May 1941; Diamant, *Le billet vert*, pp. 42–46; YIVO:RG 343, 15.

79. Biélinky Diary, 16 May 1941.

80. Minutes of 20, 21 May 1941 (CDJC: CCXVII-4); "Informations Juives" first appeared in Yiddish in early June. See report on synagogue lectures, ibid., 6 June 1941.

81. YIVO:RG 210, I-19.

82. YIVO: Tcherikower archive, 1605; Raymond Lindon, *Hommage à André Baur*; minutes of 21 May 1941 (CDJC: CCXVII-4).

83. Biélinky Diary, 22 May 1941.

84. Minutes of 6 June 1941 (CDJC: CCXVII-4).

85. Minutes of 9 June 1941 (CDJC: CCXVII-4); cf. minutes of 16 June 1941 (ibid.), 17 June 1941 (CDJC: CCCLXXXIX-33).

86. Remarks of Minkowski and Jakoubowicz, 6 June 1941 (CDJC: CCXVII-4); Jakoubowicz, *Rue Amelot*, pp. 40–41. Lisbon report to Joint N.Y., 16 July 1941 (AJDC: France, reports [1940–1941] [3–14]); Grinberg report, October 1941 (ibid.); YIVO: Tcherikower archive, 1650; Biélinky Diary, 1 August 1941.

87. Born in Pithiviers in 1906, Stora was little known among the immigrant leaders. Their appraisal appears in YIVO: Tcherikower archive, 1650; RG 210, I-20; Comité to Dannecker, 30 June 1941 (ibid., I-9); Szajkowski, *Gazetteer*, p. 41; Krouker's letter, 3 July 1941 (YIVO:RG 343, 2). Stora was not Laval's personal secretary, as mentioned in Adler, *Face persécution*, p. 83.

88. Szajkowski, *Gazetteer*, pp. 140–42; Rutkowski, *La lutte*, pp. 63–64; Adler, *Face persécution*, p. 173.

89. Marrus and Paxton, *Vichy France*, pp. 83–100.

90. YIVO:RG 210, 1–20, 32.

91. 27 June 1941 (YVA: 09/9–3); cf. Rajsfus, *La collaboration*, pp. 209–211.

92. Georges Bloch, "The Jews and Agriculture," July 1940 (YIVO:RG 210, XLIV-1); similarly Baur to Minister of Labor, 15 July 1941 (ibid.).

93. Jacques Ditte (Commissariat) to Comité, 10 July 1941 (ibid.); Labor secretary to Comité, 18 July 1941 (ibid.).

94. Biélinky Diary, 26 August 1941.

95. From text of appeal, YIVO:RG 210, 1–32.

96. Jakoubowicz was invited personally by Dannecker. Protocol of meeting, 18 August 1941 (YIVO:RG 343, 8); *Activité*, pp. 191ff; Rajsfus, *La collaboration*, p. 210; Jakoubowicz, *Rue Amelot*, p. 43; Adler, *Face persécution*, p. 62.

97. YIVO:RG 210, I-9; Jakoubowicz (?) report, YIVO: Tcherikower archive, 1650.

98. Ibid.

99. Biélinky Diary, late August 1941; Marrus and Paxton, *Vichy France*, pp. 223–24, 243.

100. E.g., 19 August 1941, "Informations Juives"; Jakoubowicz (?) report, YIVO: Tcherikower archive, 1650; Comité report, 19 September 1941 (YIVO:RG 210, I-9); Comité correspondence, 10, 13 October 1941 (ibid.); Stora's remarks, 28 January 1942 (YVA: P7/8).

101. Comité's organizational arrangement, CDJC: CCXVII-4; cf. Dannecker report, 1 July 1941 in H. Monneray, ed., *La persécution des Juifs en France et dans les autres pays de l'ouest présentée par la France à Nuremberg*, p. 97. No protocols of Comité meetings are extant from September 1941. See Juliette Stern's remarks, 28 January 1942 (YVA: P7/8), Cohen, "Towards the Establishment," p. 149.

102. Reports of 19 September and 23 December 1941 (YIVO:RG 210, I-9); YIVO:RG 210, I-29, 32; see also letter of Borstat (?), 3 December 1941 (AJDC: Paris [14–36]); Rapoport to south, 7 December 1941 (CDJC: CCXIII-138).

103. Report of 23 December 1941 (YIVO:RG 210, I-9); "Situation morale," n. 50, pp. 34–35.

104. "Situation morale," n.50, pp. 34–35; AJDC: France, general, 1940–1941 (3–14); Grinberg report, Comité report, 19 September 1941 (YIVO:RG 210, I-9).

105. Hyman to Morris Taylor, 18 September 1940 (AJDC: France, general [12–42]); Jarblum to Minister of Interior (Marquet) and Labor Minister Bélin, 21 July 1940 (CDJC: CCXIII-46).

106. Robert Aron, *Histoire de Vichy*, pp. 218–25; Paxton, *Vichy France*, pp. 168ff.

107. G. Picard to M. Troper, 3 August 1940 (AJDC: France, general [12–42]); September 1940 report to Joint (ibid.); Katzki report, 23 July 1940 (AJDC: France, general and emergency [12–43]).

108. YVA: 09/29–2.

109. Jarblum to Silberschein, 9 September 1940 (WJC: 186A); I. Jefroykin's (?) report (AJDC: [13–31]); Katzki report, 23 July 1940 (AJDC: France, general and emergency [12–43]).

110. J. Schwartz's wires to Joint, 30 July 1940, 2 and 7 August 1940 (AJDC: France, general and emergency [12–43]); Jarblum to Silberschein, 9 September 1940 (WJC: 186A); Cf. Szajkowski, *Gazetteer*, pp. 44–45.

111. YVA: 09/29–2; 09/28–2; J. Schwartz to Joint-N.Y., 30 September 1940 (AJDC: France, general [12–42]).

112. I. Schwartz's report, undated, JTS: Box 13.

113. I. Schwartz's letter, 16 October 1940 (YIVO:RG 245.5, II).

114. Katzki report, 6 November 1940 (AJDC: France, general [12–42]); discussions in Marseilles, YIVO:RG 245.5, II, 69.

115. Hirschler report, 30 October 1940 (YVA: 09/30–1). Earlier controversy with I. Schwartz, 7 May 1940 (CAHJP: F-355).

116. Conference report, YIVO:RG 245.5, II, 69; for subcommittees and participant organizations, see Szajkowski, *Gazetteer*, p. 45.

117. Albert Lévy's report, 13 January 1941 (CDJC: XXXI-22); I. Schwartz's telegram to Joint, 4 November 1940 (AJDC: France, general [12–42]). Bauer, *American Jewry*, pp. 161–72.

118. CCOJA minutes, 12 December 1940 (YIVO:RG 245.5, II, France-70); discussion of 15 January 1941 (YIVO:RG 245.5, II, France-67).

119. Jarblum to Marquet, 3 June 1940 (CDJC: CCXIII-46).

120. H. Katzki to J. Schwartz, 8 May 1941 (AJDC: France, general [12–42]); B. Kahn to M. Troper, 3 July 1941 (ibid.).

121. Jarblum to J. Helbronner, 22 May 1941 (AJDC: France, general [12–42], 1941).

122. CCOJA minutes, 10–11 June 1941 (YIVO:RG 245.5, II, France-67).

123. Cf. Helbronner's remarks, 14 December 1941 (YVA: P7/10).

124. Joint reports (AJDC: France, general, 1941 [12–41]); FSJF report to Troper, July 1941 (ibid.); A. Lévy to Katzki, 17 June 1941 (ibid.); Bauer, *American Jewry*, pp. 161–64, 170–71.

125. HICEM report, October 1941 (YIVO:RG 245.4, XII, France, A-17); Schah report, Leo Baeck Archive, AR-C (1584/3987), 1; YIVO:RG 245.4, II, France, A-33; Henry L. Feingold, *The Politics of Rescue*, p. 154.

126. Protocol of 10–11 June 1941 (YIVO:RG 245.5, II, France-67).

127. Ibid.

128. Hirschler, July 1941 report (Szajkowski collection). Also see CDJC: XXXI-138.

129. CCOJA's financial report, 3 February 1942 (CDJC: CCXIII-79).

130. CCOJA meeting, 16 September and 16 October 1941 (CDJC: CCXIII-71, 72).

III. The Establishment of UGIF

1. Joseph Billig, *Le commissariat général aux questions juives (1941–44)*, vol. 1, pp. 206–210; Eberhard Jäckel, *La France dans l'Europe de Hitler*; Geoffrey Warner, *Pierre Laval and the Eclipse of France, 1931–1945*, p. 354; Michael R. Marrus and Robert O. Paxton, *Vichy France and the Jews*, pp. 223–24.

2. CDJC: XXVIIIa-29; Billig, *Le commissariat*, vol. 1, pp. 210–11; Maurice Rajsfus, *Des Juifs dans la collaboration: L'U.G.I.F. (1941–1944)*, pp. 74–75.

3. Cf. Zosa Szajkowski, *Analytical Franco-Jewish Gazetteer, 1939–1945*, p. 46; CDJC: LXXIV-9, and Institut Hoover, *La Vie de la France sous l'occupation (1940–1944)*, vol. 2, pp. 668–69. There has often been confusion about what was expected by September 25. The German original clears it up: "Ich ersuche mich bis zu 25 September 1941 uber die von Ihnen geplanten Massnahmen zu unterrichten."

4. CDJC: LXXVI-16; Billig, *Le commissariat*, vol. 1, p. 211.

5. On different occasions Vallat mentioned two different German officials. See Institut Hoover, *La Vie de la France*, vol. 2, p. 668. Cf. Xavier Vallat, *Le nez de Cléopâtre: souvenirs d'un homme de droite (1919–1944)*, p. 254.

6. Ibid.

7. Cf. Billig, *Le commissariat*, vol. 1, p. 212; Szajkowski, *Gazetteer*, p. 46. Both rely on Vallat, *Le Nez*, p. 254. See Vallat's explanation for extending the council to the south, ibid. pp. 255–56.

8. Robert O. Paxton, *Vichy France: Old Guard and New Order, 1940–1944*, pp. 178–80; Marrus and Paxton, *Vichy France*, pp. 98–112.

9. Vallat to Lambert, 23 September 1941 (Maurice Brener collection, Paris).

10. Storz to Vallat, 25 September 1941 (CDJC: XXVIIa-1a), in Billig, *Le commissariat*, vol. 1, pp. 212–13; also Rajsfus, *La collaboration*, pp. 76–77.

11. CDJC: XXVIII-3.

12. CDJC: XXVIII-2.

13. Interviews with Lucienne Scheid-Levilion, 19 October 1977, and with Baur's brother-in-law Raymond Lindon, 23 October 1977, Paris. See Rajsfus, *La collaboration*, pp. 345–49.

14. Vallat reiterated this claim several times. See his trial, CDJC: LXXIV-9; Institut Hoover, *La vie de la France*, vol. 2; Vallat, *Le Nez*, pp. 252ff.; cf. Rajsfus, *La collaboration*, pp. 85–86.

15. Scheid-Haas's testimony at Vallat's trial, YVA: P7/31 p. 5 (5 December 1947), and in above interview. Vallat's testimony on the formation of UGIF seems logical, even if one rejects his commentary. See Rajsfus, *La collaboration*, pp. 85ff.

16. Lambert surmised whether Vallat linked all the Jewish organizations together. Carnet, 11 December 1941, p. 136.

17. Michael R. Marrus, *The Politics of Assimilation: A Study of the French Jewish Community at the Time of the Dreyfus Affair*, pt. 1.

18. Arnold Mandel, "Raymond-Raoul Lambert," *La Terre Retrouvée*, 25 August 1945, p. 6.

19. Ibid.

20. Drafts of several unpublished short stories were in Brener's collection. Lambert reviewed books in the thirties for *Revue Juive de Génève* (RJG), *Illustration Juive*, and many other periodicals.

21. *L'Univers israélite*, 6 and 13 January 1939.

22. Paxton, *Vichy France*, pp. 3, 20, 45.

23. Carnet, 12 July 1940, p. 67.

24. Ibid., 15 July 1940, pp. 69–73. Cf. Paxton, *Vichy France*, pp. 22–24, 132ff.

25. Some of the guidelines suggested by Lambert are worth noting: (a) military defeat never overwhelmed France (e.g., 1815, 1871); (b) the independent nature of the spiritual mission of France, unencumbered by historical developments (e.g., after 1870 France witnessed the vast colonial expansion); (c) victory weakens nations, while defeat "regenerates" (e.g., Germany, 1918); (d) the great French public servants rose in the darkest moments of France's history (e.g., Thiers, Clemenceau, Pétain).

26. Compare Gide's remarks entered in his journal on 17 July 1940 and quoted in Paxton, *Vichy France*, p. 34: "Yes, long before the war, France stank of defeat. She was already falling to pieces to such a degree that perhaps the only thing that could save her was, is perhaps, this very disaster in which to retemper her energies. Is it fanciful to hope that she will issue from this nightmare strengthened?"

27. Carnet, 20 December 1940, p. 87.

28. Ibid., 24 and 25 February 1941, pp. 92–94.

29. Ibid., 28 July 1941, p. 120.

30. Ibid., 4, 15, 22 June and 8 July 1941, pp. 102–111, 115.

31. Robert O. Paxton, *Parades and Politics at Vichy: The French Officer Corps under Marshal Pétain*, pp. 63–93.

32. Carnet, 8 March 1941, pp. 97–99.

33. Ibid., 16 May 1941, p. 102.

34. Many moving expressions of his personal identification could be brought to show Lambert's feelings during this period and throughout his wartime diary. Ibid., 2 October 1940, 6 November 1940, pp. 83, 85–86.

35. Ibid., 10, 16 May 1941, pp. 100–102.

36. Cable from Edouard Oungre to Max Gottschalk, 17 May 1941 (YIVO:RG 245.4, 4, XII, France, C-4). According to Oungre, Lambert's "anti-Nazi activity" as editor of *L'Univers israélite* and his involvement with political refugees led to the ransacking of his house by the Nazis in 1940 and made his visa request urgent. See also 23 May 1941 (YIVO:RG 245.4, XII).

37. Carnet, 4 June 1941, p. 103.

38. Ibid., 3 October 1941, p. 130. Lambert left two short accounts of this meeting: one in his diary and the other in a report presented to Lévy, detailing his interventions at Vichy from 20 September 1941(?) to 9 January 1942 (YIVO:RG 210, II-1, quoted

in part in Szajkowski, *Gazetteer*, pp. 125–27). See also Lévy's prepared speech, 2 March 1942 (YVA: P7/10).

39. CDJC: XXXI-144, 27 September 1941. The others represented native French welfare projects, and all but one were native Frenchmen: Edmond Israel, Albert Lévy, Professor David Olmer, Maurice Leven, William Oualid. Oualid was Algerian by birth. The absence of Marc Jarblum and the FSJF is significant.

40. Their meeting took place on either 4 or 6 October. In recalling his trip to Vichy, Helbronner expressed no regrets, since Vallat had positively responded to his requests. Helbronner's remarks at Consistory sessions 7 and 14 December 1941 (YVA: P7/10).

41. Helbronner had been deeply attached to Pétain since World War I and named his son Philippe in Pétain's honour. The Consistory continued to turn to Pétain until mid-1943. See a list of Consistory protests, YIVO:RG 116, 33; Szajkowski, *Gazetteer*, p. 50.

42. YIVO:RG 245.5, 2.

43. René Mayer to Lambert, 23 October 1941 (YVA: P7/11, Szajkowski, *Gazetteer*, p. 54; Rajsfus, *La collaboration*, pp. 89–90).

44. David H. Weinberg, *A Community on Trial: The Jews of Paris in the 1930s*, chap. 5; Paula E. Hyman, *From Dreyfus to Vichy: The Remaking of French Jewry, 1906–1939*, chap. 8.

45. 22 October 1941 (CDJC: CCXIII-72). At the previous meeting of CCOJA, no discussion took place on the law. See also YVA: P7/8.

46. CDJC: CCXIII-73. For example, one of the leaders of the scout movement: "It is both undignified and useless to negotiate with the Commissariat. Often it was said during the morning that the conference had a historic value. Let us not respond by finesse when it is required to be dignified and firm. To discuss with the Commissariat is useless. At least, let us not be ashamed before our children."

47. CDJC: CCXIII-73; Zosa Szajkowski, *Jews and the French Foreign Legion*, pp. 62–63; Weinberg, *Community*, pp. 236–46; Elisabeth Young-Bruehl, *Hannah Arendt: For Love of the World* (New Haven and London, 1982), pp. 146–48.

48. YVA: P7/13, anonymous author of report "Contribution à l'histoire de l'UGIF." According to Lambert, the report was prepared by David Olmer and William Oualid and was full of "errors and lies" (Lambert's notes on copy in Brener collection).

49. CDJC: CCXIII-74.

50. Correspondence of Ilya Dijour and George Bernstein (HICEM representatives in Lisbon), and W. Schah (Marseilles) to New York, early November (YIVO:RG 245.5, XII, Portugal, B-29). Correspondence between French OSE and head office New York (YIVO:RG 210, XCVII). Dijour and Bernstein encouraged several leading representatives to meet in Marseilles to negotiate with the French authorities.

51. Lambert's report (YIVO:RG 210, II-2). Lévy later enunciated his view: "contact with the government was necessary if we wanted if not to save, at least to protect our activity as long as possible and to gain time." Lévy's prepared speech, 2 March 1942 (YVA: P7/10).

52. Lambert's secret report on meeting (CDJC: CCXIII-17G, quoted in Rajsfus, *La collaboration*, p. 108).

53. Lambert shared these thoughts with René Mayer of HICEM, and together they sought ways to exclude HICEM from the law. In a report he prepared for the Commissariat, Mayer emphasized the mutual goal of the government and HICEM to decrease the foreign population in France. In order for HICEM to achieve that goal, it needed complete autonomy. See Lambert report, appendix 3, 17 November 1941; Carnet, 30 November 1941, p. 133.

54. CDJC: CCXIII-73.

55. 12 November 1941 (Szajkowski collection).

56. Helbronner's remark, 13 November 1941 (YVA: P7/10).

57. YIVO:RG 245.5, France, II, 68, p. 16. Cf. Lambert's position at the CCOJA conference, 24 October 1941 (CDJC: CCXIII-73).

58. Szajkowski, *Gazetteer*, pp. 130, 47. Pétain's office replied on 24 November 1941 that it would do all in its power to change the law, but that offer was insincere. There is no evidence of Pétain's intervention, but his name appears on the law.

59. CDJC: XXVIIIa-3, 4, 5.

60. Commissariat to Justice Department, 14 November 1941 (CDJC: XXVIIIa-7).

61. Lambert report (YIVO:RG 210:II-1). Carnet, 30 November 1941, p. 133. Henri Franck (1888–1912) was the French Jewish poet who published his noted poem "La Danse devant d'Arche" in 1912. Lambert's mention of him together with the arch-nationalist writer Maurice Barrès was a further reaffirmation of his nonconflicting duality.

62. Lambert report (YIVO:RG 210, II-1).

63. CDJC: CCXIII-77; YVA: P7/8. Szajkowski, *Gazetteer*, p. 47 is misleading. See also ibid., pp. 128–30, and YVA: P7/13. Helbronner to Lambert, 20 November 1941 (Brener collection).

64. The law was signed by Pétain, Darlan, Pucheu, Bouthillier, and Barthélemy; it was reprinted in various places, see L. Czertok and A. Kerlin, eds., *Les Juifs sous l'occupation: Recueil des textes français et allemands, 1940–1944*, pp. 102–103.

65. For a rare contrary view, see "Notes sur les rapports du Consistoire Central et la Commission Centrale des Oeuvres," 11 November 1941 (anonymous). The most striking claim was the need for politicization of the Consistory: "nous ne pouvons pas . . . nous dissimuler aujourd'hui que la cause des malheurs du Judaisme Français en 1941 est essentiellement une cause politique et que ces malheurs sont *voulus* par ceux-là même qui nous demandent de prendre en charge les conséquences de leur action. Il s'ensuit que la cause qui mettait au premier plan l'action des oeuvres est une cause politique et que séparer la politique de Judaisme Française de son action sociale par nous ne savons quel scrupule légaliste est l'équivalent d'un suicide." YVA: 09/30–3, see also Szajkowski, *Gazetteer*, pp. 53–54.

66. Carnet, 2 December 1941, pp. 134–35; Lambert report (YIVO:RG 210, II-1).

67. Olmer to Vallat, 3 December 1941 (CDJC: CCXIII-78).

68. YVA: P7/8.

69. Carnet, 11 December 1941, pp. 135–37; cf. Szajkowski, *Gazetteer*, pp. 128–29.

70. Lambert report, appendix 6 (YIVO:RG 210, II-1); YVA: P7/8, 09/30–2. Carnet, 11 December 1941, pp. 135–37.

71. Szajkowski, *Gazetteer*, p. 129.

72. For further attitudes towards this meeting, see Lambert report (YIVO:RG 210, II-1). Helbronner's letters to Pétain ("Père de la Patrie") 8 December 1941 (YVA: 09/30), also Szajkowski, *Gazetteer*, pp. 49–50. Helbronner still counted on Pétain for reversing the French decision. Rabbi Maurice Liber to Lambert, 11 December 1941 (CDJC: CCCLXVI-48). Liber tried to bring about a reconciliation between Rabbi Schwartz and Lambert. Lambert to Liber, ibid.

73. Zosa Szajkowski, "The French Central Jewish Consistory during the Second World War," *Yad Vashem Studies* 3 (Jerusalem, 1959): 190–91. See CDJC: CDXX-12; Szajkowski, *Gazetteer*, pp. 55, 57; Rajsfus, *La collaboration*, pp 90–91. Seven rabbis participated in the session.

74. Szajkowski, *Gazetteer*, p. 48; Rajsfus, *La collaboration*, p. 93. Lambert report (YIVO:RG 210, II-1, YVA: P7/13). Detailed report in protocol of Consistory meeting of 14 December 1941 (YVA: P7/10, also P7/1).

75. Lambert report (YIVO:RG 210, II-1). Lambert to Oualid, 13 December 1941 (CDJC: CDX-88), in Szajkowski, *Gazetteer*, p. 209, and Rajsfus, *La collaboration*, p. 93. For Lambert's personal reflections, Carnet, 28 December 1941, pp. 138–41. Rabbi Liber held Lambert responsible for initiating the list of nominees and including

his closest colleagues. Liber to Lambert, 7 December 1941 (CDJC: CCCLXVI-48). Vallat informed them of Robert Gamzon's consent to participate in the council.

76. 14 December 1941 (YVA: P7/10). Among the non-Consistory participants were Jarblum, Gamzon, and Rabbi Hirschler. Lambert was not present.

77. Ibid. Moral problems, such as the "Solidarity Fund" and salaries of the council members, were a source of much discussion.

78. 23, 24 December 1941. Sources for the above discussion: Lambert report; Lévy report (YVA: P7/10); Carnet, 28 December 1941, pp. 138–41; Consistory report on formation of UGIF, YVA: P7/13; AJDC: France, general and emergency—Katzki report. Lambert sent Vallat a cover letter informing him of the collective refusal.

79. CDJC: CCXIII-83, 138.

80. *La Terre Retrouveé*, 15 January 1965, quoted from YVA: P7/1.

81. Carnet, 8 January 1942, pp. 145–49.

82. René Mayer asked to be replaced by W. Schah, another HICEM official, who accepted to avoid the organization's falling into incompetent hands. Schah to Bernstein, 15 January 1942 (YIVO:RG 245.4, XII, France 19-B, 20). See also YVA: P7/13, P7/10. Szajkowski, *Gazetteer*, p. 51, notes 219, 221–24.

83. Carnet, 8 January 1942, p. 149. They were Raphaël Spanien (HICEM), Laura Weill (Alsatian Jewish Welfare Society), and André Lazard. Spanien's motives for joining were spelled out in a letter to Dijour, 2 April 1942 (YIVO:RG 245.4, XII, Portugal, 47-B), including his connections with the United States and his influence with Lambert, which "could contribute to calming his impetuosity."

84. Millner to Lambert, 25 January 1942; Lambert to Millner, 28 January 1942 (YIVO:RG 210, XCVIII-9). For a list of council members, see Czertok and Kerlin, *Recueil des textes*, p. 133: see also AJDC: France, general, 1941–1942.

85. Carnet, 8 January 1942, pp. 148–49.

86. Raul Hilberg, *The Destruction of the European Jews*, vol. 2, p. 629; Marrus and Paxton, *Vichy France*, pp. 225–27, 243.

87. Comments of Albert Manuel, Baur's uncle, at Central Consistory meeting, 14 December 1941 (YVA: P7/10). (Georges Edinger?) report, "La vérité sur l'UGIF. Enfin!" (CDJC: CDXXX-41). Cf. Rajsfus, *La collaboration*, pp. 307–320. On the fine, see Czertok and Kerlin, *Recueil des text*, pp. 107–108.

88. YVA: 09/6–1; CDJC: XCXI-16, quoted in Adam Rutkowski, ed., *La lutte des Juifs en France à l'époque de l'occupation, 1940–1944*, p. 77, and in Rajsfus, *La collaboration*, p. 121. The former presents the protest within the framework of resistance, the latter as "naiveté, resignation, and adhesion to the New Order." See also Weill-Hallé to Vallat, January 1942 (CDJC: CCXIII-128, quoted in ibid, pp. 101–102). Also Marcel Stora's remarks at secret meeting of Consistory, 11 March 1942 (Szajkowski collection).

IV. UGIF North under the Anvil of German Occupation, 1942–1944

1. See Raul Hilberg, ed., *Documents of Destruction* (Chicago, 1971), pp. 89–99.

2. Ibid., p. 92. Nazi officials estimated that 165,000 Jews were living in the occupied zone, and 700,000 in the unoccupied zone.

3. YVA: P7/8.

4. Y. Jakoubowicz, *Rue Amelot: Hilf un Vidershtant*, pp. 46–48.

5. A. Baur to L. Cabany, 16 January 1942. CDJC: CVIII-8. On Cabany, see Joseph Billig, *Le commissariat général aux questions juives (1941–1944)*, vol. 1, pp. 93–96. For UGIF's monthly budget, prepared in early 1942, see YIVO:RG 210, XX-29.

6. Pierre Arnoult, *Les finances de la France et l'occupation allemande (1940–*

1944), pp. 391–94. An extensive correspondence between UGIF and French banks concerning the fine is in YIVO:RG 210, V-1.

7. Jarblum to A. Silberschein, 30 March 1942 (YVA: M20/85).

8. YVA: 09/9–2; YIVO:RG 210-X.

9. Report of conversation between Dannecker and Baur, 13 January 1942 (YVA: 09/9–1).

10. Dissatisfaction with Vallat was not limited to Dannecker. Other German authorities expressed similar views. See Billig, *Le commissariat*, vol. 1, pp. 214–28; vol. 3, pp. 176–80; Serge Klarsfeld, ed., *Die Endlösung der Judenfrage in Frankreich: Deutsche Dokumente*, p. 37, pp. 40–43. Michael R. Marrus and Robert O. Paxton, *Vichy France and the Jews*, pp. 115–18. By January 1942, the German authorities had pretty much decided to dismiss Vallat and replace him with someone more amenable to the Reich's goals.

11. Baur's remarks on 28 January 1942 (YVA: P7/8).

12. Marrus and Paxton, *Vichy France*, p. 118.

13. Report of Stora's (Mr. X) meeting with the Central Consistory, 11 March 1942 (Szajkowski collection). See Zosa Szajkowski, *Analytical Franco-Jewish Gazetteer, 1939–1945*, pp. 49–50, 57. See *Le procès de Xavier Vallat présenté par ses amis*, pp. 146, 267, 272, 474–75. Stora summarized the UGIF's orientation: "Basically, Vallat tried to arrange a kind of complicity between himself and us." Szajkowski, *Gazetteer*, p. 58.

14. Dannecker to UGIF-N, 12 (13?) March 1942 (CDJC: XXVIII-89).

15. On the SD's plans, see Lucien Steinberg, *Les autorités allemands en France occupée*, pp. 266–71; G. Wellers, *L'étoile jaune à l'heure de Vichy*, pp. 361–68.

16. Baur to Vallat (CDJC: XXVIII-20). Billig, *Le commissariat*, vol. 1, p. 94. De Jarnieu was subsequently removed from office. See Dannecker to German embassy, 1 April 1942 (CDJC: LXXV-196). Jacques Adler, *Face à la persécution*, pp. 107–108.

17. See telegrams between Dannecker and Hoess, commandant of Auschwitz, and telegrams between Dannecker and Baur (CDJC: XXVb-24, 25, 25a). Wellers, *L'étoile*, p. 368.

18. Protocol of UGIF council meetings, 31 March 1942 (YIVO: IV-3); 5 May 1942 (YVA: 09/1-Szajkowski); 26 May 1942, (YVA: P7/12, 09/8–4).

19. Marrus and Paxton, *Vichy France*, pp. 227–28.

20. Baur to Red Cross, 29 May 1942 (YIVO:RG 210, IV-21). Auschwitz was rarely mentioned in UGIF correspondence. Cf. CDJC: CDXXIX (7 August 1942); YIVO:RG 210, XLIV-8 (1 October 1942). Wellers, *L'étoile*, p. 228, claimed that even in the summer of 1943, while in Drancy, Baur had no inkling of the meaning of deportations to the "East."

21. Jean Laloum, *La France antisémite de Darquier de Pellepoix*; Marrus and Paxton, *Vichy France*, pp. 286–93.

22. Ibid., p. 288.

23. UGIF's letters to French ministries for blankets, shoes, work clothes, etc.: AN: F_{12} 10204, file 4; AN F_{12} 10192, file 2. The latter file contains a rejection of a large order made by UGIF, later reversed after ministerial intervention.

24. UGIF council meeting, 9 June 1942 (YVA: 09/8–4). Galien and Baur even discussed possible changes in the council's formation. On 16 June Baur informed Galien that the special liaison service was already established (YVA: 09/1–Szajkowski).

25. 29 June 1942 (YIVO:RG 210, CVIII-9). On 18 July Galien sent the same letter to Albert Lévy (CDJC: XXVIII-109), and see XXVIII-110. On Galien's plans for an organized budget, see 26 May 1942 (YVA: 09/8–4); YIVO:RG 210, CVIII-8. UGIF's finance committee sensed that Galien's intentions were less than pure, but they expressed their fears in couched language: "We are certain that the government could not endeavor to reduce purely and simply hundreds of thousands of individuals to poverty, hoping that the limited resources of UGIF could maintain them, even miserably, for a long period of time."

26. Galien to Puech, 4 July 1942 (CDJC: XXVIII-111); 10 July 1942 (CDJC: XXVIII-115).

27. Galien to Baur, 1 July 1942 (YIVO:RG 210, CVIII-9). On other Commissariat proposals to solidify the interrelationship between the UGIF and the Jewish community in the north, see CDJC: XXVIII-32, 7 July 1942; Adler, *Face persécution*, p. 110.

28. Baur to Commissariat, 8 July 1942 (YVA: 09/6–1). Copy in YVA dated 6 July and presumably prepared by Stora; see Billig, *Le commissariat*, vol. 3, p. 317; Adler, *Face persécution*, p. 110.

29. Adler, *Face persécution*, p. 110. It appears that UGIF was unsuccessful in fulfilling the demand. See Duquesnel to Baur, 11 August 1942 (YVA: 09/6–1); CDJC: XXVIII-145.

30. CDJC: XXVb-55, in Klarsfeld, *Endlösung*, p. 84.

31. CDJC: XXVIII-36, see Billig, *Le commissariat*, vol. 3, p. 317.

32. CDJC: XXVb-58, in Klarsfeld, *Endlösung*, p. 87.

33. Ibid., p. 89 (CDJC: XXVb-60). Cf. a request from Röthke for materials via the UGIF, CDJC: XXVb-6.

34. Galien to Baur, 9 July 1942 (CDJC: XXVIII-113).

35. Galien to Baur, 15 July 1942 (CDJC: XXVIII-37). See Billig, *Le commissariat*, vol 3, p. 317; Maurice Rajsfus, *Des Juifs dans la collaboration. L'UGIF 1941–1944*, p. 139.

36. Jakoubowicz, *Rue Amelot*, p. 95.

37. See Claude Lévy and Paul Tillard, *La grande rafle du Vel d'Hiv (16 juillet 1942)*, pp. 14–15, 77–78, 137–38; *Le procès de Xavier Vallat*, pp. 336–71; *Le vrai procès de Xavier Vallat*, pp. 11–12.

38. Serge Klarsfeld, *Vichy-Auschwitz: Le rôle de Vichy dans la solution finale de la question juive en France. 1942*, pp. 121ff.

39. Lévy and Tillard, *Vel d'Hiv*, pp. 112–15, 78, 241; also CDJC: CDXXX-41, p. 65.

40. Baur's testimony in Wellers, *L'étoile*, pp. 395-96. The organization of the youth may be connected to a Commissariat proposal. See Commissariat to UGIF, 9 July 1942 (CDJC: XXVIII-23); Röthke's summary of the roundups, 18 July 1942 (CDJC: XLIX-67) in Klarsfeld, *Endlösung*, pp. 91–93; cf. Billig, *Le commissariat*, vol. 3, pp. 318–19.

41. Lévy and Tillard, *Vel d'Hiv*, pp. 110–11, is the only source for this protest; no archival source or date is mentioned. Probably sent to the Vichy government a few days after the deportations. Cf. Consistory's protest to Vichy, 28 July 1942, in Adam Rutkowski, ed., *La lutte des Juifs en France à l'époque de l'occupation (1940–1944)*, pp. 101–102.

42. 21 August 1942 (YVA: P7/12).

43. According to Scheid-Haas (interview 19 October 1977, private communication 18 November 1979), several individuals (namely, Jacques Ditte of the Commissariat and Permilleux, the prefect of police) provided UGIF with more accurate details, which were filtered through to the community. The same claim is made by the anonymous author (Edinger?) of an unpublished manuscript written after the war (CDJC: CDXXX-41). No confirmation of these claims exists.

44. Marrus and Paxton, *Vichy France*, pp. 270–79; Klarsfeld, *Vichy-Auschwitz*, pp. 161–81; Adler, *Face persécution*, chap. 7.

45. Duquesnel to Baur, 22 July 1942 (YVA: 09/6–1); ibid., 10 and 11 August 1942 (YVA: 09/6–1); Galien to Baur, 22 August 1942 (CDJC: XXVIII-121). Cf. Darquier to Röthke, 24 July 1942 (CDJC: XXVIII-180).

46. Baur to Galien, 13 August 1942 (CDJC: XXVIII-153).

47. Galien to Baur, 14 August 1942 (YVA: 09/6–1). He included the desired text with the "bonus" of offering a receipt to all who would participate. See CDJC: XXVIII, passim.

48. Galien to Baur, 9 September 1942 (CDJC: XXVIII-65); Galien to Röthke, 3 September 1942 (CDJC: XXVIII-61).

49. Baur to Darquier, 15 September 1942 (CDJC: CVIII-11). No report of the meeting exists.

50. Galien to Baur, 1 August 1942 (CDJC: XXVIII-138), in L. Czertok and A. Kerlin, eds., *Les Juifs sous l'occupation: Recueil des textes français et allemands, 1940–1944*, p. 163. See also CDJC: XXVIII-181, and Arnoult, *Les finances*, p. 393.

51. 7 August 1942 (YIVO:RG 210, V-1), and Baur to Galien, 11 August 1942 (YVA: 09/6–1). Members of the UGIF council (Baur, Musnik, Stora, Weill) were the dominant figures in the finance committee.

52. Undated confidential letter, sent between 18 August and 1 September 1942 (YIVO:RG 210, V-1).

53. Darquier to Baur (YVA: 09/6–2), in Czertok and Kerlin, *Les Juifs*, pp. 173–74.

54. Duquesnel to UGIF, 18 November 1943, in CDJC: CDXXX-41, p. 15.

55. The Commissariat's inability to receive cooperation from the prefects also contributed to this outcome. E.g., Commissariat to Prefect of Seine, 4 March 1943 (CDJC: XVIII-137).

56. Duquesnel to Baur, 4 and 19 August 1942 (CDJC: XXVIII-47, 165); Duquesnel's report, 23 September 1942 (CDJC: XXVIII-226).

57. In Czertok and Kerlin, *Les Juifs*, p. 166; see also Joseph Lubetzki, *La condition des Juifs en France sous l'occupation allemande (1940–1944): La législation raciale*, p. 107.

58. Carnet, 11 October 1942, p. 187. P. Seligman to Helbronner, 9 October 1942 (YVA: 09/30–2). The meeting took place on either 26 or 27 August. Cf. Szajkowski, *Gazetteer*, p. 97.

59. Seligman to Helbronner, 9 October 1942 (YVA: 09/30–2).

60. Galien to Baur, 23 September 1942 (CDJC: XXVIII-228); Adler, *Face persécution*, pp. 134–41.

61. Finance committee report, 14 September 1942 (YIVO:RG 210, XXIII-1); also Baur to Darquier, late August 1942 (YIVO:RG 210, V-1).

62. Baur to Darquier, 18 September 1942 (CDJC: CDXXIII-25); first draft of the letter, 16 September 1942 (YIVO:RG 210, CVIII-15).

63. Undated financial report (October-December [?] 1942) prepared by UGIF council for an unidentified Jewish organization (YVA: 09/25).

64. Szajkowski, *Gazetteer*, p. 63, and below nn. 70, 71.

65. Between 1 March 1942 and 1 October 1942, UGIF spent approximately 3.85 million francs monthly, reaching a total of 27 million francs. The "Solidarity Fund" was the major source. Financial report, late 1942 (YVA: 09/25).

66. Budget proposal, 28 December 1942 (YIVO:RG XX-18); finance committee report, 7 December 1942 (YVA: 09/1-Szajkowski).

67. Revised budget (YIVO:RG 210, XX-22); Duquesnel to Baur, 8 and 11 January 1943 (CDJC: XXVIII-147); Duquesnel to Huguenin, 14 January 1943 (CDJC: XXVIIIa-334); Billig, *Le commissariat*, vol. 1, p. 277. The Commissariat reduced the number of sections in the budget from 700 to 215 in order to keep a closer watch on UGIF's handling of funds.

68. CDJC: XXVIII-28ff., early 1943; also CDJC: DXLVI-37, 29 March 1943 (CDJC: XXVIII-146). Duquesnel's remarks (YIVO:RG 210, CVIII-4).

69. YVA: 09/25; if our reading is correct that *RR* refers to Lambert and *16* to Darquier, it follows that the suggestion was raised during their discussion in late August. See YVA: 09/31–2.

70. Finance report in YVA: 09/25.

71. YVA: 09/8–2.

72. UGIF to Commissariat, 21 October 1942 (YIVO:RG 210, XX-27). Protocol of finance committee's meeting, 19 November 1942 (YVA: 09/1-Szajkowski).

73. Minutes of UGIF's finance committee, 5, 7, 16, and 23 December 1942 (YVA: 09/1-Szajkowski), (YVA: 09/8–4).

74. Boué to Duquesnel, 20 January 1943 (CDJC: XXVIII-127). See Billig, *Le commissariat*, vol. 1, pp. 127–29, 309–12; ibid., vol. 3, pp. 180–82, 298–300. Boué was Darquier's subordinate.

75. Darquier to Baur, 23 January 1943 (YIVO:RG 210, XXIII-2) in Czertok and Kerlin, *Les Juifs*, p. 173; see also Billig, *Le commissariat*, vol. 3, p. 145; Duquesnel to Boué, 25 January 1943 (CDJC: XXVIII-122).

76. Finance committee minutes, 4 February 1943 (YVA: 09/8–4).

77. UGIF-N council meeting minutes, 3 March 1943 (YIVO:RG 210, CVIII-5); conference between Baur and the southern council, 15 February 1943 (YIVO:RG 210, XCII-12).

78. Finance committee minutes, 5 May 1943 (YVA: 09/8–4). On French and German conflict over the Jewish assets, see Billig, *Le commissariat*, vol. 3, pp. 147–49.

79. Baur's remarks in YVA: 09/8–4. See also 30 April 1943 (YIVO:RG 210, CVIII-3).

80. UGIF-N council meeting, 5 May 1943 (YVA: 09/8–4). See also minutes of 18 June 1943 (YVA: 09/8–4).

81. For the text of the law, see Czertok and Kerlin, *Les Juifs*, pp. 175–77.

82. The law ignored completely the issue of the blocked accounts. See Billig, *Le commissariat*, vol. 3, pp. 145–46.

83. Baur's report to finance committee, 9 July 1943 (YVA: 09/1-Szajkowski).

84. Roger de Segogne's report, 13 July 1943 (YIVO:RG 210, XXIII-2).

85. Baur held this position even prior to seeking legal counsel. Baur to Helbronner, 25 June 1943 (YVA: 09/9–1). See his remarks to UGIF-S representatives on 9 July 1942 (YIVO:RG 210, XXIII-1).

86. CDJC: XXVIII-222. This number compared with 1,452 Jews from the south. See report from September 1944 (!) summarizing 1943 (CDJC: XXVIII, a).

87. YIVO:RG 210, XXIII-1.

88. YIVO:RG 210, XXIII-1; 6 July 1943 (YVA: P7/12); CDJC: CDX-42. Finance committee report, 9 July 1943 (YVA: 09/1-Szajkowski).

89. Finance committee minutes, 9 August 1943 (YVA: 09/1-Szajkowski), YVA: 09/8–4.

90. Edinger to Baur, 9 August 1943 (!) (YIVO:RG 210, IV-17); also finance committee, 9 August 1943 (YVA: 09/8–4); Adler, *Face persécution*, pp. 138–41.

91. Marrus and Paxton, *Vichy France*, p. 307.

92. Ibid., pp. 321–29.

93. Ibid., p. 330.

94. On the Brunner period in Drancy, see Wellers, *L'étoile*, pp. 185–219; minutes of meeting taken by Israelowicz (YVA: 09/8–4; YIVO:RG 210, IV-4). See Szajkowski, *Gazetteer*, p. 62.

95. Wellers, *L'étoile*, pp. 191–93. Anonymous report on Drancy, mid-July 1943 (YVA: P7/37); Adler, *Face persécution*, pp. 141–44.

96. 30 June 1943 (YVA: 09/8–4).

97. Protocol of council meeting, 6 July 1943 (CDJC: CDX-42; YIVO:RG 210, IV-4, slightly different versions).

98. Baur to Duquesnel, 5 and 14 July 1943 (YIVO:RG 210, IV-4); Duquesnel to Baur, 19 July 1943 (YIVO:RG 210, CVIII-5). See CDJC: CDXXX-41, pp. 66–67; Brunner's remarks on 30 July 1943 (YVA: P7/37).

99. YIVO:RG 210, CVIII-5, also YVA: 09/1-Szajkowski. Baur asked to be received together with Scheid-Haas.

100. On Antignac, see Marrus and Paxton, *Vichy France*, pp. 288–89, 336-39; Billig, *Le commissariat*, vol. 1, pp. 291–94.

101. Meeting held on 13 July 1943 (CDJC: CDXXX-41, XCVI). Baur seems to

have had a previous clash with Antignac on the dismissal of foreign-born UGIF employees (YVA: 09/8–4), see chap. 6. Drancy report from 15 July 1943 (YVA: P7/37).

102. CDJC: CDXXX-41, p. 66.

103. Baur's brother-in-law and sister Mr. and Mrs. Raymond Lindon continued to hold to this version as late as 1977. (Private interview, Paris.)

104. Edinger to Central Consistory, 2 August 1943 (YVA: 09/8–2); Musnik to Lambert, no date (YVA: 09/9–3); Stora and Edinger to Lambert, 13 August 1943 (YIVO:RG 210, IV-11); Adler, *Face persécution*, p. 145.

105. Baur to Darquier, 2 August 1943 (CDJC: XXVIII-183). Darquier added that he had no jurisdiction to intervene with the Swiss authorities. See Rajsfus, *La collaboration*, p. 175. Duquesnel claimed that Baur was forced by the German authorities to make the request. The prison head replied that since Drancy was under German rule, the French could not intervene (YVA: JM/563). See Rajsfus, *La collaboration*, p. 176.

106. Antignac was the key link in this chain, and he provided Brunner with the necessary information. See Billig, *Le commissariat*, vol. 1, pp. 291–94.

107. Cf. Isaiah Trunk, *Judenrat*, pp. 317–31.

108. Antignac's report to Röthke, 22 April 1943, 18 May 1943 (CDJC: XXVIII-159), Rutkowski, *La lutte*, pp. 172–74. Edinger's remarks at Antignac's trial, 27 June 1946 (CDJC: XCVI), also Duquesnel's remarks. Edinger claimed that Brunner questioned him on 30 July 1943 on the inconsistencies between the list of welfare receivers and their addresses.

109. Duquesnel to Darquier, 30 July 1943 (CDJC: XXVIII-181), and his remarks at Antignac's trial, 27 June 1946 (CDJC: XCVI, p. 52).

110. YVA: P7/37, report of meeting with Brunner.

111. Report of section heads, 6 August 1943 (YVA: 09/8–4).

112. Unspecified instructions. However, during Brunner's first raid, several workers escaped, raising further suspicions about their activity. Possibly the instructions were given accordingly.

113. Minutes of 9 August 1943 (YVA: 09/8–4). Prior to the meeting, Edinger made a special declaration (YIVO:RG 210, IV-38). See Rajsfus, *La collaboration*, pp. 178–79; Adler, *Face persécution*, p. 146.

114. Minutes of 9 August 1943 (YVA: 09/8–4). "Emergency decisions" were made but not specified; it seems that Edinger and Stora were not granted absolute power. Cf. Rajsfus, *La collaboration*, p. 198.

115. 10 September 1943 (YIVO:RG 116, file 23). Among the deported were the heads of services 40, 42, and 10. Cf. Rajsfus, *La collaboration*, p. 179; Adler, *Face persécution*, pp. 146–48.

116. 10 September 1943 (YIVO:RG 116, file 23). Edinger and Duquesnel testimonies, CDJC: XCVI. The tendentious description in Rajsfus, *La collaboration*, p. 179, is untenable.

117. YVA: 09/8–2.

118. Ibid.

119. UGIF-N council meeting, 7 September 1943 (CDJC: CDX-52); special council meeting, 14 September 1943 (CDJC: CDX-54), at which Minkowski and section heads participated. See also 6 April 1943 (YIVO:RG 210, CVIII-2; CDJC: XXVIII-151). Cf. Rajsfus, *La collaboration*, p. 167.

120. 24 July 1942 (YVA: 09/2); repeated several times; cf. CDJC: CDXXVII-17.

121. Galien to prefect of Seine, 31 August and 23 September 1942 (CDJC: XXVIII-39; XXVIII-77); Galien's remarks, 2 November 1942 (CDJC: XXVIII-264) and Röthke's remarks October 1942 (ibid.); Israelowicz to Anonymous, 17 November 1942 (YVA: 09/8–3); Darquier-Röthke correspondence, March 1943 (CDJC: XXVIII-141).

122. CDJC: CDXXX-39; OSE report, November 1943 (YIVO:RG 245.4, XII, France, A-46).

123. Baur to OSE south, 28 June 1943 (CDJC: CDXXIV-40); A. Katz, 9 December 1943 (CDJC: CDXXVI-10, in Rajsfus, *La collaboration*, p. 239). On releases, see CDJC: CDXXVI-44.

124. UGIF report, YVA: 09/1- Szajkowski; CDJC: CDXXX-39, 41; on Rue Amelot, report of 16 October 1943 (YIVO:RG 343, 5, 12); Szajkowski, *Gazetteer*, pp. 90–93; Adler, *Face persécution*, p. 198.

125. Antignac report, in Rajsfus, *La collaboration*, pp. 259, 327–33; Alain Michel, *Les éclaireurs israélites de France pendant la seconde guerre mondiale*, pp. 136–50; CDJC: CDXXX-39, 41. L. Scheid-Haas to author, 18 November 1979; Adler, *Face persécution*, pp. 148–51.

126. Rajsfus, *La collaboration*, p. 338; Leá Raich, "Le service clandestin de sauvetage d'adultes," *La Terre Retrouvée*, 1 February 1945; cf. Szajkowski, *Gazetteer*, p. 70.

127. Schendel to UGIF headquarters, 25 April 1943 (CDJC: CDXXIV-7), in Rajsfus, *La collaboration*, p. 247.

128. Minutes UGIF-N council meetings, 25 April, 11 and 18 July 1944 (YVA: 09/8–4; 09/1-Szajkowski).

129. Rajsfus, *La collaboration*, pp. 258–60.

130. Schendel report, 31 August 1944 (YVA: 09/9–3), ibid., pp. 321–26; Beate Klarsfeld, *Wherever They May Be!*, pp. 231–33; Rutkowski, *La lutte*, pp. 276–79; Edinger to Commissariat, 24 and 27 July 1944, recorded 288 names; see also Serge Klarsfeld, *Le mémorial de la déportation des Juifs de France*, convoy 77; cf. Szajkowski, *Gazetteer*, p. 74; Wellers, *L'étoile*, p. 218.

131. UGIF-S council meeting, 25 July 1944 (YVA: 09/1-Szajkowski); also CDJC: CDXXX-41, p. 51; Jewish Communist condemnation, 29 August 1944 (Widener Library, Hebrew Division); Adler, *Face persécution*, p. 28.

132. Baur to Dannecker, 20 February 1942 (YIVO:RG 210, XI-1); Wellers, *L'étoile*, pp. 57, 120, 128–29, 164–65; YVA: 09/28–1; YIVO:RG 210, XI-13.

133. CDJC: CDXXX-41, p. 67; Billig, *Le commissariat*, vol. 2, pp. 226–32; L. Scheid-Haas to author, 18 November 1979; François Ditte, a Commissariat official, is often cited for his assistance in these matters, which eventually aroused Dannecker's opposition. He was removed from office in March 1943.

134. Among others, Rajsfus, *La collaboration*, pp. 265–83; Cynthia J. Haft, *The Bargain and the Bridle: The General Union of the Israelites of France, 1941–1944*, pp. 92–99.

135. Israelowicz's report, 31 December 1942 (YIVO:RG 210, XI-13); CDJC: CDXXIV-40; YVA: 09/5, 7, 27.

136. UGIF council to Israelowicz, 29 October 1942 (YIVO:RG 210, XI-10).

137. Rajsfus, *La collaboration*, pp. 265–83; Haft, *The Bargain*, pp. 93–94.

138. YVA: 09/8–4; YIVO:RG 210, IV-4.

139. Meeting of UGIF directors, 27 September 1943 (YVA: 09/8–4).

140. YVA: 09/14–16; CDJC: CDXXX-41, pp. 20ff; Wellers, *L'étoile*, pp. 185ff.

141. UGIF's 1944 budget proposal with Duquesnel's remarks, 27 November 1943 (CDJC: XXVIII-243); UGIF's finance committee meeting, 13 December 1943 (YIVO:RG 210, XXIII-1), YVA: 09/8–4; Czertok and Kerlin, *Les Juifs*, p. 18; Duquesnel to Röthke, 2 December 1943 (CDJC: XXVIII-235); Duquesnel to Laval, 23 November and 2 December 1943 (ibid.); Duquesnel to Minister of Finance, 10 January 1944 (YVA: 09/9–1); Edinger to Minister of Finance, 16 May 1944 (YIVO:RG 210, III-2); Billig, *Le commissariat*, vol. 1, p. 242.

142. CDJC: CDXXX-40; Wellers, *L'étoile*, pp. 218–19.

143. CDJC: CCXVII-26.

144. Tcherikower Archives, 1656; Z.S. (Zosa Szajkowski), "Das yiddishe gesellschaftliche leben in Paris zum jahr 1939," *Yidn in Frankraykh*, vol. 2, pp. 207ff.

145. YVA: 09/1-Szajkowski; YIVO:RG 343, 5; RG 210, XX-29; Jakoubowicz, *Rue Amelot*, pp. 63–66.

146. A similar number of meals were provided to orphanages and ORT institutions until summer 1944: see YVA: 09/27; YIVO:RG 343, #12; RG 210, XX-18, XX-22; CDJC: CDXXX-41, p. 51; cf. Szajkowski, *Gazetteer*, p. 67. Approximately 1.2 million meals were distributed from 1943 to 1944 in all UGIF institutions.

147. Baur to Commissariat, 2, 3 March 1943 (YVA: 09/28–4, 09/6–2). Also 7 April 1942 (YIVO:RG 210, XXXIII-2); YIVO:RG 210, CVIII-4.

148. Duquesnel to Baur, 23 September 1942 and 31 May 1943 (YIVO:RG 210, XX-15; RG 210, CVIII-4). Commissariat to Edinger, 2 February 1944 (YVA: 09/8–3); Commissariat report, 27 December 1943 (YVA: JM540).

149. Antignac to Röthke, 11 May 1943 (CDJC: XXVIIIb-72a); Duquesnel to Darquier, 11 November 1943 (CDJC: XXVIII-221).

150. Brener's(?) report, May 1944 (YVA: P7/37); CDJC: CDXXX-41; YVA: 09/27.

151. Szajkowski, *Gazetteer*, pp. 69–71.

152. UGIF-N council meetings, 4 July 1944-1 August 1944 (YVA: 09/1-Szajkowski); interview with Scheid-Haas, 19 October 1977; cf. Rajsfus, *La collaboration*, p. 188.

153. JTS: Box 15; CDJC: CDXXX-38; Szajkowski, *Gazetteer*, pp. 64, 134–40.

154. "Einheit" appeal to Joint, 8 September 1944 (AJDC: France, general and emergency); cf. G. de Rothschild to R. de Rothschild, October or November 1944 (ibid.).

155. Edinger to Nordon, 19 February 1943 (CDJC: CXXVII-17); in a similar vein, see Baur to Musnik, 3 June 1943 (YIVO:RG 210, XLIII-14); Israelowicz to Stora, 2 December 1942 (CDJC: CDXXIV-3).

V. UGIF in Southern France, 1942–1944

1. Carnet, 11 February 1942, pp. 150–51.

2. Lischka to Vallat, 7 February 1942, in Joseph Billig, *Le commissariat général aux questions juives (1941–1944)*, vol. 1, pp. 221–23, 225.

3. Carnet, 18 February 1942, pp. 154–55.

4. Ibid., 2 March 1942, p. 156.

5. Zosa Szajkowski, "Glimpses on the History of Jews in Occupied France," *Yad Vashem Studies* 2 (1958): 133–57; idem, *Analytical Franco-Jewish Gazetteer, 1939–1945*, pp. 142–46; Carnet, 27 March 1942, pp. 161–62.

6. 26 February 1942 (CDJC: XXVIII-15); Vallat to Lischka, 2 and 7 March 1942 (CDJC: XXVIII-7, 9, 14, 15).

7. Carnet, 27 March 1942, pp. 161–62.

8. YIVO:RG 210, XXIX-1; L. Czertok and A. Kerlin, eds., *Les Juifs sous l'occupation: Recueil des textes français et allemands, 1940–1944*, pp. 147–48.

9. Lambert's remarks, April 1942 (CDJC: XXVIII-71); also YVA: P7/8, 9, 12; CDJC: CCXIII-48, 54, 56, 57, 61; YIVO:RG 245.4, France, XII-22, 21.

10. Report of 17 January 1942 (CDJC: CCXIII-49). Member of FSJF to D. Rapoport, 10 February 1942 (CDJC: CCXIII-49).

11. Summary of Fédération meeting, 17 January 1942 (CDJC: CCXIII-49).

12. Protocol of meeting, 26 February 1942 (CDJC: CCXIII-49).

13. Jarblum's remarks, 26 February 1942 (CDJC: CCXIII-49). See his caustic letters to A. Silberschein on UGIF's leaders, 30 March 1942 and April (May?) 1942 (YVA: M20/85).

14. 26 February 1942 (CDJC: CCXIII-49).

15. Szajkowski, *Gazetteer*, p. 56. David H. Weinberg, *A Community on Trial: The Jews of Paris in the 1930s*, pp. 124ff.; Paula E. Hyman, *From Dreyfus to Vichy: The Remaking of French Jewry, 1906–1939*, pp. 207–208, 230–31.

16. CDJC: CCXIII-49. Jefroykin denied making this statement in an interview, on 18 October 1977, and attributed it to his father. The protocol explicitly referred

to "Mr. J. (son)." See his remarks at a Zionist youth conference in Montpellier, 10 May 1942.

17. Jarblum-Lambert meeting, 25 April 1942 (YVA: P7/2). Also YVA: P7/12, CDJC: CCXIII-54, 57, 61.

18. CDJC: CCXIII-57. Fédération Central Committee meeting, 27 June 1942 (CDJC: CCXIII-61).

19. Syngalowski to Lambert, 14 February 1942 (YIVO:RG 210, XCVII-4); Syngalowski to Minister of Interior, 14 February 1942 (YVA: 09/19); cf. Szajkowski, *Gazetteer*, p. 56.

20. YIVO:RG 245.4, France, XXI, A-26; RG 245.4, XII, B-20. R. Mayer to Lambert, 14 March 1942 (YIVO:RG 210, CIV-4). Spanien's comments, 2 April 1942 (YIVO:RG 245.4, Portugal, B).

21. J Rudnansky to Lambert, 25 March 1942 (YIVO:RG 210, XCVIII-9). Rudnansky to Alliance offices, YVA: 09/11–2.

22. Michael R. Marrus and Robert O. Paxton, *Vichy France and the Jews*, pp. 228–41; H. R. Kedward, *Resistance in Vichy France: A Study of Ideas and Motivation in the Southern Zone, 1940–1942*, chap. 9; Geoffrey Warner, *Pierre Laval and the Eclipse of France, 1931–1945*, chap. 9.

23. Seligman to Lambert, 6 May 1942 (CDJC: CDX-86).

24. Carnet, 25 May 1942, p. 169.

25. Marrus and Paxton, *Vichy France*, pp. 255–62; Serge Klarsfeld, *Vichy-Auschwitz: Le rôle de Vichy dans la solution finale de la question juive en France, 1942*, pp. 135–50; idem, ed., *Die Endlösung der Judenfrage in Frankreich: Deutsche Dokumente (1941–1944)*, pp. 75–103.

26. Schwartz to N.Y. office, 11 August 1942 (AJDC: general and emergency); Carnet, 6 September 1942, p. 177.

27. Lowrie report to T. Strong, 10 August 1942 (AFSC: Switzerland, refugees, 1942); Szajkowski, *Gazetteer*, pp. 139–41; Yehuda Bauer, *American Jewry and the Holocaust: The American Jewish Joint Distribution Committee, 1939–1945*, pp. 174–77.

28. Carnet, 6 September 1942, p. 177–78.

29. Meeting of Nîmes Committee, 9 September 1942 (Leo Baeck Archive: AR-C1584/3987, file 1); AFSC: Switzerland, refugees, 1942; AFSC: France, refugees, 1943. Lowrie to Strong, 22 August 1942 (AFSC: Switzerland, refugees): "every effort was made to save at least some special cases from deportation."

30. Spanien's(?) HICEM report for summer 1942 echoed this dilemma: "UGIF was obliged to restrain its humane protests to special categories since the general measure could not be annulled" (YIVO:RG 116, 42).

31. AFSC: France, 1942.

32. Among the various societies were Secours Suisse, Amitié Chrétienne, and CIMADE (Comité Inter-Mouvements auprès des Evacués). On the latter see Kedward, *Resistance*, pp. 34–35, 181–82. On the Unitarian Service Committee and its colorful leader, see Varian Fry, *Surrender on Demand*. See also Joseph Weill, *Contribution à l'histoire des camps d'internement dans l'anti-France*, p. 92.

33. HICEM report for August 1942 (YIVO:RG 116, 42, pp. 9–14); WJC, Rescue Department, drawer 264; Lowrie to Strong, 22 August 1942 (AFSC: refugees, Switzerland, 1942); Mrs. R. McClelland to James Vale, 24 August 1942 (ibid.).

34. Szajkowski, *Gazetteer*, pp. 115–16; CDJC: CCXIX-7, 8; Carnet, 11 October 1942, pp. 184–89. Spanien report, 25 September 1942 (YIVO:RG 245.4, XII, France A-29).

35. Schah to Ungre, August 1942 (YIVO:RG 245.4, XII, France, B-11).

36. Lambert to Laval, 26 August 1942 (YIVO:RG 116, 42: 4 letters); Lambert to Secretary General of National Police, 24 August 1942 (YVA: 09/19). Lambert to Millner, 27 August 1942 (CDJC: CDXIX-12). Spanien report, 25 September 1942

(YIVO:RG 245.4, XII, France, A-29). Carnet, 11 October 1942, pp. 188–89. Minutes UGIF-S council meeting, 15 October 1942 (YVA: 09/8–4; YIVO:RG 210, XCII-10).

37. Hirschler to Interior Minister Pucheu, 1 September 1942 (YVA: 09/28–2); Consistory protest, 25 August 1942, in A. Rutkowski, ed., *La lutte des Juifs en France a l'époque de l'occupation (1940–1944)*, pp. 116–17.

38. Lowrie to Strong, 22 August 1942 (AFSC: refugees, Switzerland, 1942). Lowrie report to Nîmes Committee, 19 September 1942 (Leo Baeck Archive, AR-C [1584/3987], no. 8).

39. R. McClelland report, 6 September 1942 (AFSC: refugees, Switzerland, 1942 3Bi). McClelland interpreted the cessation of special consideration for visa holders as a German order and added: "the measures had been announced to us by Monsieur Laval himself in Vichy as calculated to rid France of all foreign Jews, so it should not have made a great deal of difference to the French where these people went. *This more or less confirmed the generally accepted theory that the measure is one of extermination on the part of the Germans*" (my emphasis).

40. Lambert to National Policy, 13 September 1942 (CDJC: CDXVI-139); Lambert to inspector of foreign laborers, 11 September 1942 (ibid.); Lambert to Guérard, 4 September 1942 (YIVO:RG 210, XCII-10): Lévy to Pétain, 4 September 1942 (ibid.); Pétain to Lévy, 8 September 1942 (ibid.); Lowrie to Strong, 17 September 1942 (AFSC: refugees, Switzerland, 1942); Carnet, 11 October 1942, pp. 188–89.

41. For a list of the deportations, see Klarsfeld, *Vichy-Auschwitz*, pp. 158–59; idem, *Endlösung*, pp. 131–46.

42. *L'OSE sous l'occupation allemande en France*; Hillel Kieval, "Legality and Resistance in Vichy France: The Rescue of Jewish Children," *Proceedings of the American Philosophical Society* 124 (1980): 339–66. Donald Lowrie, *The Hunted Children*; Georges Garel, "La sort des enfants juifs pendant la guerre," *Le Monde Juif* 38 n.s. 89 (1978): 20–25. Nili Keren, "The Rescue of Jewish Children in France," *Yalkut Moreshet* 36 (1983): 101–150 (Hebrew).

43. Hirschler's remarks at Nîmes Committee conference, 9 September 1942; Szajkowski, *Gazetteer*, pp. 121–22; Lowrie's confidential report (Leo Baeck Archives, AR-C [1584/3987], no. 8).

44. SEC's September report on UGIF activity, CDJC: LXXXIX-39.

45. AFSC: Switzerland, refugees, 1942; France, refugees, 1943; general, refugees, Switzerland, 1942. AJHS: S. S. Wise Papers, Box 65, section 10; YIVO:RG 210, CIV-5; Lehman Papers (19–521), Columbia University; Leo Baeck Archives (Ar-C [1584/3987], no.7); CDJC: CCXVII-20 (1–4); Szajkowski, *Gazetteer*, pp. 119–25. Michael R. Marrus, "Vichy et les enfants juifs," *L'Histoire*, no. 22 (1980): 6–15; Marrus and Paxton, *Vichy France*, pp. 266–69. Bauer, *American Jewry*, pp. 259–63.

46. Ibid., p. 269.

47. See below.

48. Marrus and Paxton, *Vichy France*, pp. 294–307, 315–21; YIVO:RG 210, XCII-57.

49. Lambert to prefects, 28 October 1942 (YVA: 09/19); Lambert's confidential report, 9 December 1942 (ibid.); minutes of UGIF-S council, 22 December 1942 (CDJC: CDX-10), 15 February 1943 (YVA: 09/12–1). Head of Section 1, department 1 to Lambert, 1 December 1942 (CDJC: CDXV-64); UGIF to Darquier, 10 January 1943 (CDJC: CDXVI-209).

50. Report of 1 June 1943–30 July 1943 (YIVO:RG 210, XCVI-2). See also CDJC: CDXVII-62, CDXXVIII. R. Kahn to Lambert, 12 August 1943 (YIVO:RG 210, CI-18). Lambert and Wormser's intervention in Vichy, 20 May 1943 (CDJC: CDX-14).

51. Protocol of UGIF councils' joint session, 26 January 1944 (CDJC: CDX-20); Geissmann to Director of Refugees, 21 June 1944 (YVA: 09/1-Szajkowski).

52. Carnet, 13 February 1943, p. 216, relating to meeting with Antignac.

53. Darquier to Lambert, 4 and 5 January 1943 (YIVO:RG 210, XCII-97).

54. Carnet, 13 February 1943, p. 216. Lambert to Seligman, 8 and 30 January 1943 (CDJC: CDX-102, 103); Fleg to Pétain, 31 January 1943 (CDJC: LVIII-4), in Rutkowski, *La lutte*, pp. 139–40; Pétain to Fleg, 23 April 1943 (CDJC: CDX-103). See also Alain Michel, *Les éclaireurs israélites de France pendant la seconde guerre mondiale*, pp. 128–32.

55. Darquier to Lambert, 18 January 1943 (CDJC: XXVIII-20); Billig, *Le commissariat*, vol. 1, p. 287. Gamzon to scouts, 28 January 1943 (CDJC: CDXIX-287). See also Maurice Rajsfus, *Des Juifs dans la collaboration: L'UGIF, 1941–1944*, p. 157.

56. André Sauvageot, *Marseille dans la tourmente, 1939–1944*; Eberhard Jäckel, *La France dans l'Europe de Hitler*, pp. 387–88; Marrus and Paxton, *Vichy France*, p. 307.

57. Carnet, 1 February 1943; Lambert and Hirschler reports to Consistory (YIVO:RG 116, 25).

58. CDJC: CCXVI-154, p. 2; *L'OSE*, p. 47; Szajkowski, *Gazetteer*, p. 253 refers to 100 arrests; Pétain protested against the violation of French sovereignty and the indiscriminate arrests of native French Jews, 2 March 1943 (CDJC: XXVIIIb-31); de Brinon's response, ibid.

59. Minutes UGIF-S council, 15 February 1943 (YVA: 09/12–1, CDJC: CDXI-157). Lambert to department 1, 27 February and 1 March 1943 (CDJC: CDXII-57). Report on regional representatives, YIVO:RG 210, XCIII-109. Lambert to Baur, 12 March 1943 (CDJC: CDXII-32). Brener's testimony, 19 June 1946 (CDJC: XCVI, p. 27). Bauer, *American Jewry*, pp. 241–43, 262–63.

60. Schah to Lambert, 13 April 1943 (YIVO:RG 210, CIV-8); Lambert to Schah, 16 April 1943 (unavailable).

61. Klarsfeld, *Endlösung*, pp. 195–98; Marrus and Paxton, *Vichy France*, p. 308; Carnet, 18 May 1943, pp. 222–29.

62. Carnet, 18 May 1943, pp. 222–29; Lambert to Helbronner, 7 May 1943 (CDJC: CCCLXIII-89); cf. Rajsfus, *La collaboration*, p. 172; minutes UGIF-S council meeting, 20 May 1943 (YVA: 09/12–1).

63. Lowrie report, 29 July 1943 (USC).

64. Lambert to Commissariat, 28 May 1943 (CDJC: CDX-113), and to André Lazard, 9 June 1943 (CDJC: CDX-87).

65. Robert Lévy to Lambert, 11 June 1943 (CDJC: CDXXVIII); Lambert to council members, 26 June 1943, 7 and 8 July 1943 (YIVO:RG 210, XCII-132, 61); Couturier to UGIF, 30 June 1943 (YIVO:RG 210, CVI-9). Seligman to Lambert, 9 and 17 July 1943 (CDJC: CDX-91); Schah to Lambert, 15 July 1943 (CDJC: CDX-89); UGIF-S council meetings, 16 June 1943 and 27 July 1943 (YVA: 09/12–1). Lambert to Darquier, 31 July 1943 (YIVO:RG 210, XCII-100), in Billig, *Le commissariat*, vol. 1, p. 281.

66. Klarsfeld, *Endlösung*, pp. 210–13. Various sources laid the responsibility for Lambert's arrest on Antignac; see CDJC: X-92, XCVI, p. 27; Léon Poliakov, "Jewish Resistance in France," *YIVO Annual of Jewish Social Science* 8 (1953): 257.

67. Antignac to Lambert, 16 August 1943 (CDJC: XXVIII-190); Darquier to Laval, 16 August 1943 (CDJC: XXVIII-191); Billig, *Le commissariat*, vol. 1, pp. 281–83.

68. CDJC: CDX-3; YIVO:RG 210, IV-4; 18 May 1943 (CDJC: XXVIII-159), in Rutkowski, *La lutte*, pp. 172–74; Carnet, 16 May 1943, pp. 220–21, 286–88. Isaac Schneersohn, "Naissance du CDJC," *Le Monde Juif* 7 (1953): 4–5; Henri Hertz, "Le drame juif et le drame de la France," ibid. 18 (1963): 34–37; Gaston Lévy, *Souvenirs d'un medecin d'enfants à l'OSE en France occupée et en Suisse 1940–1945* (Paris and Jerusalem, n.d.), pp. 42–43.

69. Warner, *Pierre Laval*, pp. 374–76; Marrus and Paxton, *Vichy France*, pp. 321–29; Klarsfeld, *Endlösung*, pp. 210–13; Jean Laloum, *La France antisémite de Darquier de Pellepoix*, pp. 45–48.

70. Léon Poliakov and Jacques Sabille, *Jews under the Italian Occupation*, pp.

39–44; Meir Michaelis, *Mussolini and the Jews: German-Italian Relations and the Jewish Question in Italy 1922–1945*, pp. 305–311; Klarsfeld, *Endlösung*, pp. 217–20; Zanvel Diamant, "Jewish Refugees on the French Riviéra," *YIVO Annual of Jewish Social Science* 8 (1953): 264–80; reports from Nice to Jarblum (AJDC: SMA, 32, 33).

71. 27 August 1943 (CDJC: CDX-16); 2 September 1943 (CDJC: XXVIII-198).

72. Sessions of UGIF-S, 7 and 28 September 1943 (YVA: 09/12–1); Herbert Katzki's report, 17 September 1943 (AJDC: France, general, 1942–1944). Laure Weill's resignation, 11 October 1943 (CDJC: CDX-100).

73. 6 October 1943. See Yerachmiel Cohen, "French Jewry's Dilemma on the Orientation of Its Leadership: From Polemics to Conciliation, 1942–1944," *Yad Vashem Studies* 14 (1981): 196–204.

74. Szajkowski, *Gazetteer*, p. 168; interviews with Brener, 24 October and 2 November 1977, and with Jefroykin, 18 October 1977. Alice Salomon wrote Brener from Drancy: "Gaston has yet to realize that he must scuttle in order to avoid further casualties" (Brener Collection, n.d.). See also *Notre Voix*, September 1944.

75. Lambert to Brener, 26 October 1943; Carnet, p. 244.

76. OSE report, 3 January 1944 (YIVO:RG 494, 20); also *L'OSE*.

77. OSE report, 3 January 1944 (YIVO:RG 494, 20); 16 December 1943 (YVA: JM 540, reel 4); Bauer, *American Jewry*, pp. 238, 247, 250.

78. Szajkowski, *Gazetteer*, p. 59; minutes of meeting, 6 October 1943; Cohen, "French Jewry," pp. 196–204; interview with Geissmann, October 1977, Paris.

79. Carcassonne to Edinger, 15 February 1944 (YVA: 09/9–2); Carcassonne to Geissmann, 29 February 1944 (YVA: 09/27).

80. Schah to Guggenheim, 18 February 1944 (ADJC: SMA, 35A).

81. Klarsfeld, *Endlösung*, pp. 224–29; OSE report, May 1944 (WRB: Box 59).

82. Geissmann to Edinger, 7 April 1944 (CDJC: CDX-59); cf. Rajsfus, *La collaboration*, p. 185. A. Schah to Geissmann, 6 April 1944 (YIVO:RG 210, CIV-12), Geissmann to A. Schah, 7 April 1944 (YIVO:RG 210, CIV-12). Kurt Schendel to Geissmann, 14 April 1944 (YIVO:RG 210, XCII-99).

83. Edinger to Geissmann, 14 April 1944 (CDJC: CDXXIII-28[2]); Geissmann to Edinger, 5 May 1944 (CDJC: CDX-59).

84. Geissmann to UGIF branches, 26 May 1944 (CDJC: CDX-59); Geissmann to Edinger, 30 May 1944 (YIVO:RG 210, III-4); *Notre Voix*, June 1944, p. 4.

85. Hémardinquer to Geissmann, 4 and 5 August 1944 (YVA: 09/27).

86. Minutes of July-August 1944 discussion in Szajkowski, *Gazetteer*, pp. 134–35.

87. Ibid.

88. Minutes UGIF-S council meeting, 15 October 1942 (YIVO:RG 210, XCII-10).

89. Joseph Ariel, "Jewish Self-Defence and Resistance in France during World War II," *Yad Vashem Studies* 6 (1967): 226. Budget for 1943, 165 million francs (YIVO:RG 210, XCII-10), and for 1944, 120 million. The latter was the source of an interesting discussion among the Commissariat officials; see 26 December 1943 (CDJC: XXVIII-244); Darquier to Geissmann, 29 January 1944 (CDJC: CDXXIII-29); Geissmann to Commissariat, 22 December 1943 (YVA: 09/12–2). See also Darquier to Laval, 13 July 1943 (CDJC: DXLIV-39).

90. YIVO:RG 210, XCIII contains extensive material on the organizations' workings.

91. Among others, 25 June 1942 (YIVO:RG 210, XCIV-80), 31 July 1942 (YVA: 09/12–3). Report of Toulouse bureau, 27 September 1942 (YVA: 09/12–2). General report of 1942, 18 February 1943 (YIVO:RG 210, XCIII-4).

92. Geissmann to R. Kahn, 9 July 1942; Duquesnel to Darquier, 21 June 1943 (CDJC: XXVIII-169); S. Lowrie to Lyon office, 9 November 1943 (YVA: 09/19); minutes UGIF-S council, 9 March 1944.

93. Lyon bureau's report, September 1943 (YIVO:RG 210, XCIII).

94. In September 1942, 2,232 Jews received approximately 300 francs each; in March 1944, 5,200 Jews received a 225 franc stipend each. R. Kahn's report, 18 November 1943 (YIVO:RG 210, XCIV-89). See also CDJC: CDXV-17.

95. Kieval, "Legality," pp. 341–42; *L'OSE*; Bauer, *American Jewry*, pp. 153–54.

96. For a monthly account of the OSE's activity, see YIVO:RG 210, XCVIII.

97. Schwartz to Joint-New York, 26 October 1942 (WRB: Box 2).

98. Kieval, "Legality," passim; *L'OSE*, passim; Bauer, *American Jewry*, pp. 247–51.

99. Lowrie to Katzki, 8 September 1943 (AJDC: France, emergency and general). S. Mayer to Schwartz, 17 October 1943 (AJDC: SMA, 32); report of conversation between Mayer and Schwartz, 14 February 1944 (AJDC: SMA, 35A). Undated report on the fate of Jewish children in France (YIVO:RG 245.4, XII, France A-46).

100. Undated report on the fate of Jewish children in France (YIVO:RG 254.4, XII, France A-46).

101. Ibid. See Jarblum's report to Mayer, 18 November 1943 (AJDC: SMA, 32). On Alain Mossé, see CDJC: CCXVI-154.

102. Joseph Weill to Saly Mayer, 14 January 1944 (AJDC: SMA, 35A); L. Gurvic to OSE-New York, 6 January 1944 (YIVO:RG 494, 20).

103. Statistics vary and are inconclusive. Cf. Kieval, "Legality," p. 366; Bauer, *American Jewry*, pp. 248, 250.

104. May 1944 report (WRB: file 59). OSE had a 4 million franc monthly budget for the first half of 1944; Klarsfeld, *Endlösung*, p. 223.

105. Here, too, statistics are inconclusive. According to some reports, approximately 570 children reached Switzerland between January and June 1944. See World Jewish Congress report, 28 April 1944 (WRB: Box 62); varia (WRB: Box 59). Also Haim Avni, "The Zionist Underground in Holland and France and the Escape to Spain," in Yisrael Gutman and Efraim Zuroff, eds., *Rescue Attempts during the Holocaust: Proceedings of the Second Yad Vashem International Historical Conference* (Jerusalem: Yad Vashem, 1977) pp. 555–90.

106. 5 April 1944 (YIVO:RG 254.4, XII, France A-46).

107. AJDC: general, 1941 [12–41]; April 1942 (CDJC: CCXIII-53); Jarblum to Switzerland, April(?) 1942 (YVA: P7/13).

108. YVA: 09/19; YIVO:RG 210, C; CIII-4, XCII-103; CDJC: CDXVII-18.

109. Report from beginning of 1943 (YVA: 09/27).

110. 21 June 1943 (CDJC: XXVIII-169); Antignac to Lambert, 30 June 1943 (CDJC: XXVIII-172); also CDJC: XXVIII-255, 259, 262, 265.

111. May 1944 confidential report (WRB: Box 59).

112. CDJC: CCXIII-68, CCXIII-56; YIVO:RG 210, C-1; YVA: P7/4.

113. Lambert to Lewin (confidential), 3 July 1942 (YVA: P7/9).

114. YVA: P7/1; ADJC: France, general 1941–1943.

115. May 1943 report (YIVO:RG 210, C-1); CDJC: CDX-30; Lambert to Lewin, 4 and 5 March 1943 (YVA: P7/9).

116. AJDC: SMA, 32–35A; Bauer, *American Jewry*, p. 257.

117. Avni, "Zionist Underground," p. 588.

118. Jarblum to Katzki, 23 July 1943 (AJDC: SMA, 32).

119. Jefroykin's Barcelona report, August 1944 (AJDC: SMA, France, reports 1944–1945, pp. 13–19).

120. HICEM 1942 report (YIVO:RG 254.4, XII, France, A-33).

121. Carl Ludwig, *La politique pratiquée par la Suisse à l'égard des réfugiés au cours des années 1933 à 1955*, p. 194; Alfred A. Häsler, *The Lifeboat Is Full*, pp. 82, 181; Bauer, *American Jewry*, pp. 226–32; cf. Spanien and Bernstein report, 20 October 1942 (YIVO:RG 245.4, XII, Portugal, B-54).

122. Mrs. R. McClelland to J. Vail, 11 October 1942 (AFSC: France, refugees, 5Ai, 1942). Gerhart Riegner to Rabbi Stephen Wise, 24 September 1942 (WJC: drawer 184): "Only a wide action of the Americans especially of the U.S. can induce

the Authorities here to adopt a more liberal attitude. A fortnight ago we cabled you accordingly and we hope that the United States Authorities will not refuse to give assurance to the Swiss Government that a considerable number of visas will be granted for the newly arriving refugees."

123. HICEM 1942 report (YIVO:RG 245.4, XII, France A-33); Fernande Leboucher, *The Incredible Mission of Father Benoît*; Haim Avni, *Spain, The Jews, and Franco*, pp. 98–99, 102–103; cf. Bernstein report, 4 December 1942 (YIVO:RG 245.4, II-26), and Spanien and Bernstein, 20 October 1942 (YIVO:RG 245.4, XII, Portugal, B-54).

124. HICEM 1942 report (YIVO:RG 245.4, XII, France A-33, pp. 18–19); AJDC: SMA, 35; Avni, *Spain*, pp. 102–103.

125. Schah to Spanien, 23 December 1943 (YIVO:RG 245.4, XII, France B-27).

126. Spanien to HIAS New York, 22 January 1943 (YIVO: RG 245.4, XII, France B-34); Szajkowski, *Gazetteer*, p. 92; HICEM 1943 report.

127. Dijour report, late 1943 (YIVO:RG 245.4, II-37).

128. Bernstein to HIAS New York, 21 March 1943 (YIVO:RG 245.4, II-27); 27 October 1942 (CDJC: XXXIII-24); early 1943 (CDJC: CXII-8, 9); 22 February, 2 and 8 April 1943 (CDJC: LXXII-34).

129. Bernstein, May 1945 report (YIVO:RG 245.4, XII, France, A-21).

130. Avni, *Spain*, p. 198, holds true for Switzerland, as well. According to one estimate, 1,300 Jews were brought to Switzerland by "organized Jewry"; see Jarblum-Riegner to Kubowitzki, 28 August 1944 (WRB: 63).

131. Michel, *Les éclaireurs*, pp. 83–88, 103–108; Robert Gamzon, *Les eaux claires*.

132. Michel, *Les éclaireurs*, passim; S. R. Kapel, *Jewish Combat in Occupied France* (Jerusalem, 1981), pp. 108–114 (Hebrew); CDJC: CCXVII-8-12; Brandeis University, special collections; JTS: Box 15; AJDC: SMA, 35A; interviews with S. Hamel, 10 September 1979, and with Denise Gamzon, 20 October 1979; see also Anny Latour, *La résistance juive en France, 1940–1944*, passim.

VI. Conflicting Strategies: UGIF North and South, 1942–1944

1. Carnet, 8 January 1942, p. 147; Vallat repeatedly made this claim in his trial, see *Le procès de Xavier Vallat présenté par ses amis*; Jacques Adler, *Face à la persécution*, pp. 128–29.

2. Minutes of meeting with Central Consistory, 11 March 1942 (Szajkowski collection); see Zosa Szajkowski, *Analytical Franco-Jewish Gazetteer, 1939–1945*, p. 57.

3. Carnet, 27 March 1942, p. 162.

4. Commissariat to Lévy, 14 October 1942 (CDJC: XXVIII-84); Baur to Commissariat, 21 October 1942 (YIVO:RG 210, CVIII-11); Commissariat to Baur, 13 November 1942 (YIVO:RG 210, CVIII-12); Lambert to Lévy, 30 October 1942 (CDJC: CDX-100); Commissariat to Röthke, 23 October 1942 (CDJC: XXVIII-90); Duquesnel to Röthke, 17 November 1942 (CDJC: XXVIII-112). Protocol of UGIF-S council meeting, 22 and 23 December 1942 (YIVO:RG 210: XCII-10); cf. Szajkowski, *Gazetteer*, p. 63.

5. YIVO:RG 210, IV-4, n.d. Baur and Katz remained until 25 February 1943. Carnet, 13 February and 21 March 1943, pp. 216–17. On 4 March Baur notified Lambert that on the basis of their conversations he had submitted the proposal to the French and Röthke (YIVO:RG 210, III-14).

6. YIVO:RG 210, IV-4; Adler, *Face persécution*, p. 131.

7. Lambert to Baur, 12 March 1943 (YVA: 09/1-Szajkowski). In Baur's letter to Lambert, 4 March 1943 (YIVO:RG 210, III-14), he made one remark that must surely have angered Lambert: "It appears to me that the occupying powers are critical of

UGIF-S for their involvement in political questions instead of purely social activity. I informed them that this notion does not correspond to the reality, but nonetheless I advise you to watch carefully that the activities in your centers do not lend themselves to similar suppositions."

8. CDJC: CDX-1, 2.

9. Duquesnel's memorandum, 4 March 1943 (CDJC: XXVIII-136). We have not found a German response to the proposal, or a correspondence between Röthke and the Commissariat on this issue. See Maurice Rajsfus, *Des Juifs dans la collaboration: L'UGIF, 1941–1944*, p. 163.

10. "Lévy's" speech (CDJC: CDX-9). Carnet, 26 March 1943, p. 218.

11. YIVO:RG 210, IV-4.

12. Lambert to Gamzon, 5 March 1943 (CDJC: CDX-72); also 20 March 1943 (CDJC: CDX-94). Antignac's opposition to Baur in YIVO:RG 210, XCII-12; see Rajsfus, *La collaboration*, p. 162.

13. For a list of these regional representatives, see Szajkowski, *Gazetteer*, p. 141.

14. Council meeting (YIVO:RG 210, XCII-12; YVA:09/12–1, and see YVA: 09/8–4); Adler, *Face persécution*, pp. 131–32.

15. Report of UGIF-N council meeting, 13 April 1943 (YIVO:RG 210, IV-4).

16. Commissariat to UGIF-S, 30 April 1943 (YIVO:RG 210, CVIII-3). Baur, who was informed of the Commissariat's criticism, responded that he would impress upon the south the issue's importance. 5 May 1943 (YIVO:RG 210, CVIII-4). Cf. above n. 7.

17. Duquesnel to Huguenin, 21 April 1943 (CDJC: DXLIV-43). Correspondence between Commissariat and UGIF-S, 5 and 15 May 1943, Lambert to Commissariat, 28 May 1943 (CDJC: CDX-113). See also YVA: 09/9–1.

18. According to both Jefroykin (18 October 1977, Paris) and Brener (24 October 1977, Paris), the delegation was only to carry out resistance activity. See CDJC: CDX-3, 41; cf. Rajsfus, *La collaboration*, pp. 168–70; Adler, *Face persécution*, pp. 132–33.

19. The secret memorandum was not submitted to the Commissariat. See CDJC: CDX-3; YIVO:RG 210, IV-4. Minutes UGIF-S council meeting, 20 May 1943 (YVA: 09/12–1), which contradicts testimony of Brener and Jefroykin. On their resistance activity while in Paris, see Antignac to Röthke, 18 May 1943 (CDJC: XXVIII-159), in A. Rutkowski, ed., *La lutte des Juifs en France à l'époque de l'occupation (1940–1944)*, pp. 172–74; cf. Rajsfus, *La collaboration*, p. 332.

20. CDJC: CDX-3, p. 6; cf. Szajkowski, *Gazetteer*, p. 61.

21. See Jefroykin's remarks, CDJC: CDX-3, p. 5.

22. Couturier's remarks to UGIF-N's finance committee, 18 June 1943 (YVA: 09/1-Szajkowski); Rajsfus, *La collaboration*, p. 165.

23. Lambert to council members and leading figures in UGIF-S, 9 June 1943 (CDJC: CDX-2).

24. Minutes of 16 June 1943 (CDJC: CDX-13); also UGIF-N council meeting, 29 June 1943 (YIVO:RG 210, IV-4). Lambert to UGIF-S council, 7 and 8 July 1943 (YIVO:RG 210, XCII-137, 161), and Schah to Lambert, 15 July 1943 (CDJC: CDX-89).

25. Duquesnel to Commissariat southern zone, 30 April 1943 (CDJC: XXVIIIb-54), in Joseph Billig, *Le commissariat général aux questions juives (1941–1944)*, vol. 1, p. 287.

26. Internal Commissariat report, 21 June 1943 (CDJC: XXVIII-169).

27. Two versions of this meeting exist; see YIVO:RG 210, IV-4.

28. Antignac to Lambert, 30 June 1943 (CDJC: XXVIII-172), in Billig, *Le commissariat*, vol. 1, p. 288; cf. Duquesnel to Commissariat southern zone, 30 April 1943 (CDJC: XXVIIIb-54); also Antignac to Lambert, 16 July 1943 (CDJC: XXVIII-190), in Billig, *Le commissariat*, vol. 1, pp. 281–82. For Lambert's response, see Carnet, 2 July 1943, p. 233.

29. Minutes UGIF-S council meeting, 27 July 1943 (YVA: 09/12–1); Schah to Lam-

bert, 15 July 1943 (CDJC: CDX-89); Lambert to Antignac, 31 July 1943 (YIVO:RG 210, XCII-100), in Billig, *Le commissariat*, vol. 1, p. 281.

30. Correspondence between Musnik and Lambert (YVA: 09/9–3); Musnik was in the south in August to coordinate the UGIF's tactics for Baur's release. See protocol UGIF-N, 10 August 1943 (YIVO:RG 210). Carnet, 18 August 1943, p. 237.

31. CDJC: CDX-16. See UGIF-S council members (?) to Commissariat on Lambert, 30 September 1943 (YVA: 09/6–2). The letter called upon France to fulfill its commitment to a public institution, as established by French law. Lambert had expected his council to resign in protest. Lambert to Brener, 10 October 1943, Carnet, p. 241.

32. Meeting with Commissariat, 2 September 1943 (CDJC: XXVIII-198).

33. On Röthke's activity, see CDJC: CDX-51, 56; YVA: 09/9–2. Edinger to Gaston Kahn, 28 September 1943 (YVA: 09/9–2).

34. Edinger to Kahn, 6 October 1943 (YVA: 09/1–2). See Rajsfus, *La collaboration*, pp. 165–66.

35. Protocol of 25 October 1943 meeting (YVA: 09/8–4).

36. Commissariat to UGIF-N, 16 November 1943 (CDJC: XXVIII-225).

37. Darquier to Röthke, 9 November 1943 (CDJC: XXVIII-219). Rajsfus, *La collaboration*, p. 166–67, tendentiously brings up only part of the letter. Commissariat to UGIF-N to Röthke, CDJC: CDX-18.

38. Röthke to Darquier, 11 November 1943 (CDJC: XXVIII-200); Commissariat to UGIF-N, 17 November 1943 (CDJC: XXVIII-125). Cf. Rajsfus, *La collaboration*, p. 167. German report entitled "Union Allgemeines" (YVA: 09/8–3).

39. Schendel to Edinger, 11 November 1943 (YVA: 09/9–2).

40. A similar view was expressed by a Commissariat official to Duquesnel, 19 November 1943 (CDJC: XXVIII-229).

41. YIVO:RG 210, XCII-6; for changes in the councils, see L. Czertok and A. Kerlin, eds., *Les Juifs sous l'occupation: Recueil des textes français et allemands, 1940–1944*, p. 180.

42. Billig, *Le commissariat*, vol. 1, p. 290.

43. Duquesnel to Darquier, 28 December 1943, ibid., pp. 142–43, 288–89.

44. E.g., Geissmann to Edinger, 9 February 1944 (YVA: 09/1-Szajkowski), after the arrests in the UGIF offices in Chambéry; Hémardinquer to Edinger, 26 February 1944; 4 March 1944, Hémardinquer to Geissmann, 29 February 1944 (YVA: 09/1-Szajkowski).

45. Schah to Guggenheim, 18 February 1944 (AJDC: SMA, France 35); Edinger to UGIF official in Bordeaux, 19 December 1943 (YIVO:RG 210, XXXI-15).

46. 26 January 1944 (CDJC: XXVIII-262); Antignac to Edinger, 2 February 1944 (CDJC: XXVII-256). On the cooperation of the councils, see Edinger's report, 9 January 1944, and Edinger to Schendel, 10 March 1944 (YVA: 09/1-Szajkowski).

47. Jefroykin report, August 1944 (AJDC: France, reports, 1944–1945), p. 15.

48. YVA: 09/1-Szajkowski; resolution of 13 July 1944 (JTS: Box 15); Rajsfus, *La collaboration*, pp. 382–83; Szajkowski, *Gazetteer*, p. 64.

49. Cf. Billig, *Le commissariat*, vol. 1, p. 292; Adler, *Face persécution*, pp. 123–28.

50. YIVO:RG 210, CIV-5; RG 245.5, II, France, 71; CDJC: CDXVII-11; YVA: 09/6–1. On 22 October 1942, the Commissariat presented to Lévy the series of regulations; cf. Carnet, 3 November 1942, p. 194.

51. Carnet, 18 December 1942, p. 201. Minutes UGIF-S council, 22 and 23 December 1942 (YIVO:RG 210, XCII-10; CDJC: XXVIII-116). Lambert's remarks on 7 January 1943 (YIVO:RG 210, XCII-74).

52. Carnet, 13 February 1943, p. 216. Lambert to Schah, 17 January 1943 (YIVO:RG 210, CIV-8). HICEM to Lambert, 22 January 1943 (YIVO:RG 245.4, XII, France B-32). Schah was critical of Lambert's handling of the affair and involved HICEM headquarters in New York.

53. YVA: 09/9–1.

54. Baur to Commissariat, 24 December 1942 (CDJC: XXVIII-284). See also CDJC: XXVIII-124; YIVO:RG 210, IV-4; Billig, *Le commissariat*, vol. 1, p. 292; Szajkowski, *Gazetteer*, p. 81.

55. Correspondence between department heads and Lambert, YIVO:RG 210, CVII-14; XCII-74; CIV-8.

56. 2 February 1943 (YIVO:RG 343, no.131). Stora to Rabbi E. Bloch, Poitier (YIVO:RG 210, XXXI-24): "We have no intention of yielding on this point, but if we are not satisfied, it is evident that a large majority of our employees will be endangered." The council distributed a letter of solidarity among its employees; Adler, *Face persécution*, pp. 125–26.

57. Baur to Duquesnel, 4 February 1943 (YVA: 09/6–2). See German translation of the letter, 8 February 1943 (YVA: 09/8–4).

58. Baur met Antignac on 3 February 1943. A heated conversation ensued, in which Baur presented the council's decision to resign. Baur received Antignac's permission to meet Röthke, which he did that same evening. Baur was convinced that Röthke showed more flexibility than Antignac. See detailed report, 22 June 1943(!), prepared by Israelowicz (YVA: 09/8–4). See Rajsfus, *La collaboration*, p. 158.

59. Billig, *Le commissariat*, vol. 1, p. 292.

60. Ibid.

61. Antignac to UGIF-N, 15 February 1943 (CDJC: XXVIIIb-188).

62. Billig, *Le commissariat*, vol. 1, p. 293.

63. YIVO:RG 210, IV-4, pp. 31–33; Darquier to Röthke, 22 February 1943 (CDJC: XXVIII-130). Cf. Szajkowski, *Gazetteer*, p. 81, and Rajsfus, *La collaboration*, p. 158.

64. YIVO:RG 210, IV-4. Extensive quotes from Baur's letter to the Commissariat, 24 December 1942 (CDJC: XXVIII-284), were included. Another version of the letter, with slight discrepancies, dated 9 February, was apparently authored by Baur but not sent. YVA: 09/6–2. Cf. Rajsfus, *La collaboration*, pp. 204–205.

65. Report of special sessions, 22 and 23 February 1943 (YIVO:RG 210, IV-4), p. 32.

66. Ibid.; Rajsfus, *La collaboration*, p. 159; Adler, *Face persécution*, pp. 126–27.

67. Baur, Edinger, and Stora to Commissariat, 26 February 1943 (YVA: 09/6–2). Adler, *Face persécution*, p. 127.

68. Darquier to UGIF council, 26 February 1943 (YVA: 09/6–2).

69. Darquier to Röthke, 26 February 1943, in Billig, *Le commissariat*, vol. 1, p. 285.

70. Lambert to Schah, 27 February 1943 (YIVO:RG 210, CIV-8).

71. UGIF-N deliberations, 2 March 1943 (YIVO:RG 210, IV-4), also in Rajsfus, *La collaboration*, p. 160; Adler, *Face persécution*, p. 127.

72. Baur to Darquier, 7 March 1943 (YVA: 09/6–2). UGIF-N council meeting, 9 March 1943 (YIVO:RG 210, IV-4). Baur to Helbronner, 7 March 1943 (YIVO:RG 210, IV-29): "The authorities were intransigent and led us to believe that the failure to implement their injunction will lead to very grave consequences not only for the foreign personnel but for our entire organization. . . . All the possibilities of conciliation have been exhausted today, the Administrative Council sees itself in the very painful obligation to dismiss the non-French personnel." See also YIVO:RG 210, III-14. Cf. Szajkowski, *Gazetteer*, p. 81.

73. CDJC: CDX-90. Report of Lambert's meeting with Antignac in Vichy on 1–3(?) March 1943, Carnet, 26 March 1943, p. 218.

74. Baur to Schah, 10 March 1943 (YIVO:RG 210, CVII-14). See also YVA: 09/9–1.

75. UGIF-N council meetings, 9 and 16 March 1943 (YIVO:RG 210, IV-4). Baur to Lambert, 21 May 1943 (YIVO:RG 210, III-4), noted that 53 remained in UGIF's employment. That was seemingly the final count. See also Stora's remarks at joint council session, 29 March 1943 (YVA: 09/12–1). Cf. Rajsfus, *La collaboration*, p. 160.

76. CDJC: DXLIV-43.

77. Lambert's remarks on Baur's letter to Schah, 10 March 1943 (YIVO:RG 210, CVII-14). Also at UGIF-N council, 29 March 1943 (YIVO:RG 210, XCII): "How I pleaded to obtain this small concession—while Paris received nothing"(!). See Millner to Lambert, 18 April 1943 (YIVO:RG 210, XCVIII-10); Schah to Lambert, 18 March 1943 (YIVO:RG 210, XCVIII-10). Lambert's comments, CDJC: CDX-90. Schah sent Spanien (23 March 1943 [YIVO:RG 245.4, XII, France B-34]) the entire correspondence, including a "most violent" letter that Baur wrote to him concerning Lambert's behavior (unavailable).

78. Schah to Spanien (23 March 1943 [YIVO:RG 245.4, XIII, France B-34]).

79. Lambert's remarks, 29 March 1943 (YIVO:RG 210, XCII-11). Lambert's remarks on Baur's letter to Schah (CDJC: CDX-90). Lambert to Baur, 12 March 1943 (YVA: 09/1-Szajkowski).

80. Minutes joint session, 29 March 1943 (YVA: 09/12–1). UGIF-N council members pushed in that direction. Lambert to Schah, 28 April 1943 (YIVO:RG 210, CIV-8). Carnet, 16 April 1943, p. 219. Also YVA: 09/6–2 (Commissariat letter) and CDJC: CDX-173.

81. In Billig, *Le commissariat*, vol. 1, pp. 384–85; ibid., pp. 292–93. Cf. Rajsfus, *La collaboration*, p. 161.

82. Cf. Rajsfus, *La collaboration*, pp 160–61.

83. Antignac to Röthke, 11 May 1943 (CDJC: XXVIIIb-72a), one of three documents submitted to him on UGIF's illegal work. Ibid., pp. 321–29.

84. Duquesnel to Huguenin, 21 April 1943 (CDJC: DXLIV-43).

VII. The Struggle over Community Leadership, 1942–1944

1. Anonymous report, CDJC: CCCLXVI-36, p. 6.

2. YVA: P7/10. Cf. Central Consistory discussion of 14 December 1941, ibid.

3. YVA: P7/10. Cf. Carnet, 11 February 1942, p. 151.

4. YVA: P7/10.

5. Szajkowski collection.

6. Lévy report, YVA: P7/10, includes correspondence between Helbronner and Lévy. On 28 February Lévy presented his side before a small circle of Consistory members, but his detailed report prepared for presentation at a general meeting was canceled by Helbronner.

7. Protocol 11 March 1942, Szajkowski collection. See Zosa Szajkowski, *Analytical Franco-Jewish Gazetteer, 1940–1944*, p. 63.

8. Paula E. Hyman, *From Dreyfus to Vichy: The Remaking of French Jewry, 1906–1939*, pp. 123–24.

9. YVA: 09/30–2; cf. Szajkowski, *Gazetteer*, p. 55; Zosa Szajkowski, "Secular versus Religious Life in France," in Jacob Katz, ed., *The Role of Religion in Modern Jewish History* (New York, 1975), pp. 125–27. See Liber to Lambert, 9 March 1942 (CDJC: CCCLXVI-48).

10. Minutes of Consistory plenum, 1 March 1942 (YVA: 09/30–1).

11. Lambert to Liber, 21 March 1942; Liber to Lambert, 27 March 1942 (CDJC: CCCLXVI-48): "Is my desire for truth, clarity, and openness so unique that it cannot be satisfied either in Lyon [the Consistory] or in Marseilles [UGIF]?" Carnet, 5 May 1942, pp. 167–68. Lévy to Liber, 5 May 1942 (CDJC: CCCLXVI-48).

12. YVA: P7/10, Szajkowski, *Gazetteer*, p. 133. Cf. Lévy's speech at a meeting of the southern council, 10 July 1942 (YVA: 09/12–1).

13. YVA: 09/27, in Szajkowski, *Gazetteer*, pp. 133–34. This decision was passed on to certain Jewish leaders, including Rabbi Liber. See Lévy to Liber, 1 May 1942 (CDJC: CCCLXVI-48).

14. Geissmann to Lambert, 19 May 1942 (YIVO:RG 210, XCII-70); also Carnet, 17 June 1942, p. 170.

15. According to CDJC: CCXIII-57, 61 (27 June 1942), Couturier traveled to Lyon at the request of the Consistory.

16. Carnet, 17 June 1942, p. 170. The same conclusion was reached by Joseph Schwartz. Schwartz report, 17 June 1942 (AJDC: France, 1942, Lisbon, 1253).

17. Adam Rutkowski, ed., *La lutte des Juifs en France a l'époque de l'occupation (1940–1944)*, pp. 101–102.

18. YVA: 09/8–3.

19. Schwartz to New York office, 11 August 1942 (AJDC: Lisbon, 1286); Carnet, 6 September 1942, p. 178. See also Helbronner's reaction to the news, which reached Rabbi Hirschler, Szajkowski, *Gazetteer*, pp. 116–17.

20. Carnet, 6 September 1942, p. 180. Meeting of UGIF council, 15 October 1942 (YIVO:RG 210, XCII-10).

21. The permanent representation of the Consistory decided to send a delegation to Laval, but it appears that that never happened. Yet it appears that Léon Meiss, the Consistory's vice-president, protested before Vichy officials prior to the official protest. See Consistory meetings of 23, 24 August 1942 (YVA: 09/30–1).

22. See Schah's letter from August 1942 (YIVO:RG 245.4, XII, France, B-11). Schah contended that even the Christian churches were shocked at the silence of Jewish representatives during the deportations. Substantiation of this claim has been provided by Father Glasberg's strong criticism of Helbronner's indifference to the distress of the foreign Jews. See *Colloque sur les églises et les chrétiens dans la IIe guerre mondiale. La région Rhône-Alpes*, p. 203; Carnet, 6 September 1942, pp. 179–80. Also Jarblum's acrimonious letter to Helbronner, 18 September 1942 (YVA: P7/25).

23. 25 August 1942, in Rutkowski, *La lutte*, pp. 115–17. The protest probably replaced a personal intervention with French authorities; the Consistory also distributed copies of the protest among prominent individuals in France.

24. 23–24 August 1942 (YVA: 09/30–1).

25. Schwartz was impressed with UGIF's professional work and considered it worthy of financial support. 25 August 1942 (AJDC: France, general, 1942–1944, Lisbon, 1309; France, October 1941–1943 [14–2] reports, Lisbon 1293). Olmer to Seligman, 28 July 1942, ibid. Also James Bernstein (HICEM-Lisbon) to New York office, 3 August 1942 (YIVO:RG 245, 4, XII, A-28).

26. 28 September 1942, YIVO:RG 210, XCII-50. Lévy to Lazard, 4 September 1942 (YVA: 09/8–1; CDJC: CDX-82).

27. On 2 October 1942, Lambert wrote to Olchanski that he was pleased with the proposal to establish a committee and suggested 19 October 1942 for the first meeting. At the Consistory meeting of that day, however, mention was made of a future meeting between Olmer and Lévy, which Helbronner had said must be "definitely limited" in purpose (YVA: 09/30–1). The coordinating committee did not last long, judging from Lambert's telegram to Lévy of 30 October 1942 (YIVO:RG 210, CDX-100). The telegram also hinted at Helbronner's intention to resign. Cf. Szajkowski, *Gazetteer*, p. 59.

28. Consistory session, 30 November 1942 (YVA: 09/30–1); see also report of Central Consistory meeting of 10 January 1943, 8 February 1943 (JTS: Box 4).

29. UGIF executive discussion, YIVO:RG 210, CDX-10, XCII-12.

30. It seems that months passed before the fund was set up, if it ever was. See Geissmann's report, 21 July 1943, 28 July 1943 (YVA: 09/2–2). Notwithstanding, the Consistory, through the "Chief Rabbi's Fund," allocated funds to UGIF's direction1, which aided French Jews. Report of Consistory's Committee for Social Aid, 18 October 1942 (JTS: Box 14).

31. Lambert to Seligman, 8 January 1943 (CDJC: CDX-103); see YVA: 09/30–1; Carnet, 3 January 1943, p. 206.

32. Carnet, 1 February 1943, p. 215; Lambert and Hirschler report (YIVO:RG 116, file 25).

33. Helbronner to Laval, 27 January 1943 (JTS: Box 13); cf. appeals to law of October 1940.

34. Helbronner to Lambert, 1 February 1943 (Brener collection). See also Helbronner's speech to the Consistory plenum on 28 February 1943 (YVA: 09/30–1), and Hirschler's remarks (CDJC: CCXIX-12).

35. See Helbronner's remarks on 6 October 1943, in Yerachmiel Cohen, "French Jewry's Dilemma on the Orientation of its Leadership," *Yad Vashem Studies* 14 (1981): 197.

36. Late February 1943 (YVA: 09/30–1).

37. Many examples can be cited that indicate this change; see CDJC: CDXI-75, CCCLXVI-44; YIVO:RG 210, XCII-100, 129, 139; XCIV-84.

38. Lambert to Helbronner, 7 May 1943, CDJC: CCCLXIII-189, in Maurice Rajsfus, *Des Juifs dans la collaboration. L'UGIF (1941–1944)*, p. 206.

39. YVA: 09/30–2; YIVO:RG 116, file 33, in part, *L'Activité des organisations Juives en France sous l'occupation*, pp. 28–29.

40. Baur to Helbronner, 21 May 1943 (YIVO:RG 210, IV-29); Helbronner's agreement, YVA: 09/8–4; Baur to Albert Manuel, March 1943 (YVA: 09/8–2); concerning transfer of funds to UGIF-N, YVA: 09/25. See also YIVO:RG 210, XXVIII-1, XCII-96.

41. Seligman to Lambert, 18 May 1943 (CDJC: CDX-92); Lambert to Lazard, 9 June 1943 (CDJC: CDX-87).

42. 13 July 1943 (YVA: 09/30–2).

43. On 1 August 1943, Fischer criticized the Consistory for allowing Meiss and a UGIF representative to go separately to Vichy (YVA: P7/10). Cf. Zosa Szajkowski, "The French Central Jewish Consistory during the Second World War," *Yad Vashem Studies* 3 (1959): 193–94. See below, n. 47.

44. Lambert to Meiss, 2 August 1943 (YIVO:RG 210, XCII-26). On 4 August, Lambert wrote to a member of his council that "in agreement with the Consistory" he had sought an audience with Laval.

45. 2 August 1943 (YIVO:RG 116, file 31, in part Szajkowski, *Gazetteer*, p. 50, and in part Rutkowski, *La lutte*, pp. 185–86).

46. Fischer to Meiss, 5 August 1943 (YVA: P7/10).

47. The Consistory seemingly refrained from sending a delegation in both July and August; instead it sent two written protests, on 13 July 1943 and 2 August 1943. Apart from Fischer's first letter, there is no mention of a UGIF delegation in July; apparently, between his two letters Fischer learned that Meiss had not gone to Vichy. Consequently, on 5 August he again urged him to go.

48. Lambert to Meiss, 14 August 1943 (AJDC: SMA, France, general, 1941–1943). Carnet, 18 August 1943, pp. 236–37, 283. Consistory meeting, 11 August 1943 (YVA: P7/10). Also YIVO:RG 210, XCII-26.

49. Consistory meeting, 25 August 1943 (YVA: P7/10), Meiss to Geissmann, YIVO:RG 210, XCII-11; see also Rabbi Hirschler to Robert Sommer, 6, 7, 12 September 1943 (YIVO:RG 221, files 11, 14).

50. Hence our rejection of Szajkowski's conclusion that the Consistory's refusal to join the delegation was linked to its attitude towards foreign Jews.

51. Meeting of UGIF-S with representatives from the north, 27 August 1943 (YIVO:RG 210, CDX-16). Meetings of 7 and 28 September 1943 (YVA: 09/12–1). Georges Edinger to Albert Manuel, 5 August 1943 (YIVO:RG 210, IV-29). See also CDJC: XXVIII-198.

52. Interview with Geissmann, 17 October 1977, Paris. See Helbronner's remarks in Cohen, "French Jewry," p. 197.

53. Cohen, "French Jewry," p. 196.

54. See Annie Kriegel, "Résistants communistes et Juifs persécutés," *L'Histoire* 3 (1979): 93–123.

55. Abraham Rayski, "Une grande heure dans l'histoire de la résistance juive: la fondation du Conseil Représentatif des Juifs de France," *La Revue du Centre de Documentation Juive Contemporaine* 24, no. 51 (1968): 32–37; see Chief Rabbi Kaplan's letter 7 September 1964, *Un grand Juif: Léon Meiss* (Paris, 1967).

56. YIVO:RG 210, III-3; ibid., XCII-41 (22 May 1944); RG 221, file 9; CDJC, CDXII-50.

57. Szajkowski, *Gazetteer*, pp. 139–40.

BIBLIOGRAPHY

Archival Material

Archives of American Friends Service Committee, Philadelphia
Files on refugees—France, Switzerland
Files on AFSC overseas policy—France, Philadelphia
Files on France during World War II

Archives of American Jewish Historical Society, Waltham
Rabbi Stephen S. Wise Collection

Archives of the American Jewish Joint Distribution Committee, New York
France Collection—reports; general and emergency; economic reports
Saly Mayer Archive—French files

Archives Nationales, Paris
Folders relating to UGIF purchases of goods

Leo Baeck Archives, New York
Folders on French internment camps; activity of Nîmes committee

Brandeis University—Special Collections
Random collection of underground newspapers, resistance leaflets, material on
scout movements

Maurice Brener Collection, Paris
Lambert Diary; material concerning Lambert

Centre de Documentation Juive Contemporaine, Paris
Extensive material on the Commissariat Général aux Questions Juives; relations
with UGIF and German authorities
Large collection on the UGIF, the FSJF and other Jewish organizations
Some twenty files on the operation of Section d'Enquête et Contrôl

Varian Fry Papers, Columbia University Library, New York
Folders on Fry's activity in France, 1940–1941

Archives of the Jewish Theological Seminary, New York
France, Boxes 10–15 Uncatalogued; rich documentation on the Central Consistory

Governor H. Lehmann Papers, Columbia University, New York
Papers relating to his activity as a member of the American Joint Distribution
Committee

Léon Meiss Papers, Paris
Random collection of papers relating to Meiss

Archives of Maurice Moch, Paris
Material on the Central Consistory

Roosevelt Presidential Archives, Hyde Park, New York
Files of War Refugee Board on France; files of the Presidential Council on
Refugees

Zosa Szajkowski Collection, New York
Random collection on various aspects of the war period

Unitarian Service Committee, Harvard Divinity School, Cambridge, Massachusetts
  Several files on organization's activity in France during World War II

Archives of the World Jewish Congress, New York
  Several drawers on rescue activity in France

Archives of the Yad Vashem Institute, Jerusalem
  Several important collections:
  09 French Collection
  P7 Jarblum Archive
  03 Testimony Collection—testimonies on France
  M20 Relico Collection—folders relating to France
  M25 Papers of Mouvement National Hébreu

Archives of the YIVO Institute for Jewish Research, New York
  Major collection for Jews in France during World War II
    Record Groups (RG)
      RG 116   Jews in France during World War II
      RG 210   Union Générale des Israélites de France Collection
      RG 221   Aumônerie Générale Collection
      RG 245.4   HIAS-HICEM Collection, Series I
      RG 245.5   HIAS-HICEM Collection, Series II
      RG 335.5   AJDC in Lisbon Collection
      RG 340   Kehillat Haredim Collection
      RG 343   Records of Rue Amelot
      RG 494   OSE in America Collection
Files from Tcherikower Archive; Tcherikower Diary (1940)
Biélinky Archive; Biélinky Diary

Printed Primary Sources and Secondary Literature

Abetz, Otto. *Das Öffene Problem: Ein Rückblick auf zwei Jahrzehnte Deutscher Frankreichpolitik.* Cologne: Greven Verlag, 1951.

L'Activité des organisations juives en France sous l'occupation. Paris: Éditions du Centre, 1947.

Adler, Jacques. *Face à la persécution: Les organisations juives à Paris de 1940 à 1944.* Translated by André Charpentier. Paris: Calmann-Lévy, 1985.

Agar, Herbert. *The Saving Remnant: An Account of Jewish Survival since 1914.* London: Rupert Hart-Davis, 1960.

Akten zur Deutschen Auswärtigen Politik, 1918–1945. Series E, vol. 1. Gottingen: Vandenhoeck und Ruprecht, 1969–79.

Albert, Phyllis Cohen. *The Modernization of French Jewry: Consistory and Community in the Nineteenth Century.* Hanover and London: University Press of New England, 1977.

Arad, Yitzhak; Gutman, Yisrael; and Margaliot, Abraham, eds. *Documents on the Holocaust: Selected Sources on the Destruction of the Jews of Germany and Austria, Poland, and the Soviet Union.* Jerusalem: Yad Vashem, 1981.

Arendt, Hannah. *Eichmann in Jerusalem: A Report on the Banality of Evil.* Revised and enlarged edition. New York: Viking Press, 1965.

Ariel, Joseph. "Jewish Self-Defence and Resistance in France during World War Two." *Yad Vashem Studies* 6 (1967): 221–50.

Arnoult, Pierre. *Les finances de la France et l'occupation allemande (1940–1944).* Paris: Presses Universitaires de France, 1951.

Aron, Robert. *Histoire de Vichy.* Paris: Fayard, 1954.

Atchildi, Asaf. "Rescue of Jews of Bukharan, Iranian, and Afghan Origin in Occupied France (1940–1944)." *Yad Vashem Studies* 6 (1967): 257–81.

Avni, Haim. *Spain, the Jews, and Franco.* Translated by E. Shimoni. Philadelphia: Jewish Publication Society of America, 1982.

———. "The Zionist Underground in Holland and France and the Escape to Spain." In *Rescue Attempts during the Holocaust,* ed. Yisrael Gutman and Efraim Zuroff, pp. 555–90. Jerusalem: Yad Vashem, 1977.

Baudot, Marcel. *L'opinion publique sous l'occupation.* Paris: Presses Universitaires de France, 1960.

Bauer Yehuda. *American Jewry and the Holocaust.* Detroit: Wayne State University Press, 1981.

———. *My Brother's Keeper: A History of the American Jewish Joint Distribution Committee, 1929–1939.* Philadelphia: Jewish Publication Society of America, 1974.

———. *The Holocaust in Historical Perspective.* Seattle: University of Washington Press, 1978.

———. "Tguvotehah shel Hamanhigut Hayehudit Lemediniut Hanazim." *Yalkut Moreshet* 20 (1975): 109–125.

Delperrié de Bayac, Jacques. *Histoire de la milice, 1918–1945.* Paris: Fayard, 1970.

Berg, Roger. "Le souvenir d'André Baur et Raymond-Raoul Lambert." *Le Monde Juif* 4, n.s. 26 (1949): 13–14.

Billig, Joseph. *La solution finale de la question juive.* Paris: Serge et Beate Klarsfeld et C.D.J.C., 1977.

———. *Le commissariat général aux questions juives (1941–1944).* 3 volumes. Paris: Éditions du Centre. 1955–1960.

Blumenthal, N., ed. *Documents from the Lublin Ghetto: Judenrat without Direction.* Jerusalem: Yad Vashem, 1967.

Bolle, P. "Les protestants français et leurs églises pendant la seconde guerre mondiale." *Revue d'histoire moderne et contemporaine* 27 (1979): 286–97.

Bosseler, N., and Steichen, R. *Livre d'or de la résistance luxembourgeoise de 1940–1945.* Esch-sur-Alzette, 1952.

Browning, Christopher. *Fateful Months: Essays on the Emergence of the Final Solution.* New York: Holmes and Meier, 1985.

Bulawko, Henry. "Comment on devient résistant." *Les Nouveaux Cahiers* 37 (1974): 25–32.

Byrnes, Robert F. *Anti-Semitism in Modern France.* New Brunswick, N.J.: Rutgers University Press, 1950.

Cahiers et courriers clandestins du Témoignage Chrétien, 1941–1944. 2 volumes. Paris, 1980.

Cairns, John C., ed. *Contemporary France: Illusion, Conflict, and Regeneration.* New York: New Viewpoints, 1978.

Caron, Vicki. "Prelude to Vichy: France and the Jewish Refugees in the Era of Appeasement." *Journal of Contemporary History* 20 (1985): 157–76.

———. "The UGIF: The Failure of the Nazis to Establish a Judenrat on the Eastern European Model." Center for Israel and Jewish Studies/Working Papers, no. 1, Columbia University, 1977.

Cobb, Richard. *French and Germans, Germans and French: A Personal Interpretation of France under Two Occupations, 1914–1918/1940–1944.* Hanover (N.H.): University Press of New England, 1983.

Cobban, Alfred. *A History of Modern France.* Vol. 3. Harmondsworth: Penguin Books, 1965.

Cohen, Joseph. *Journal d'un Rabbin: Extraits.* Paris: Impr. Mazarine, 1967.

Cohen, Kadmi. *L'état d'Israel.* Paris: Éditions Kra., 1930.

Cohen, Yerachmiel (Richard). "A Jewish Leader in Vichy France, 1940–1943: The Diary of Raymond-Raoul Lambert." *Jewish Social Studies* 43 (1981): 291–310.

————. "French Jewry's Dilemma on the Orientation of Its Leadership (From Polemics to Conciliation: 1942–1944)." *Yad Vashem Studies* 14 (1981): 167–204.

————. *Leshe'elat Ahrayutam shel Hayehudim Betahalih Hashmadatam alyadey Hanazim kefi Shehy Mitbatet Bektaveyhem shel Bruno Bettelheim, Raul Hilberg, veHanna Arendt ubapulmus Sevivam.* Master's thesis, Hebrew University of Jerusalem, 1972.

————. "Letoldot Hakamat HaUGIF Bezfon Zarfat (Te'udah Bilti Yedu'ah Mishnat 1942)." *Yalkut Moreshet* 30 (1980): 139–56.

————. "Parshat Dreyfus Vehayehudim." In *Sinat Yisrael Ledoroteha,* ed. Shmuel Almog, pp. 291–308. Jerusalem: Zalman Shazar Center, 1980.

————. "The Jewish Community of France in the Face of Vichy-German Persecution: 1940–1944." In *The Jews in Modern France,* ed. Frances Malino and Bernard Wasserstein, pp. 181–204. Hanover and London: University Press of New England, 1985.

————. "Vichy Vehayehudim—Bikoret al M.R. Marrus ve R.O. Paxton, Vichy France and the Jews, New York, 1981." *Zion* 47 (1982): 347–65.

Colloque sur les églises et les chrétiens dans la IIᵉ guerre mondiale. La région Rhône-Alpes. Lyon: Presses Universitaires de Lyon, 1978.

Le combattant volontaire juif, 1939–1945. Paris: Impr. Abexpress, 1971.

Conseil représentatif des Juifs de France: C.R.I.F. Vingt-cinq années d'activités, 1944–1969. Paris: C.R.I.F., 1970.

Czertok, L., and Kerlin, A., eds. *Les Juifs sous l'occupation: Recueil des textes français et allemands 1940–1944.* Paris: C.D.J.C., 1945.

Dank, Milton. *The French against the French.* Philadelphia: J.B. Lippincott, 1974.

Darville, Jacques, and Wichené, Simon. *Drancy la juive ou la deuxième inquisition.* Cachan (Seine): A. Breger, 1945.

Dejonghe, Etienne. "Le nord isolé: occupation et opinion (mai 40 - mai 42)." *Revue d'histoire moderne et contemporaine* 26 (1979): 48–98.

La délégation française auprès de la commission allemande d'armistice: Recueil des documents publié par le gouvernement français. 5 volumes. Paris: A. Costes, 1947–1959.

Diamant, David. *Héros juifs de la résistance française.* Paris: Éditions Renouveau, 1962.

————. *Le billet vert.* Paris: Éditions Renouveau, 1977.

————. *Les Juifs dans la résistance française, 1940–1944.* Paris: Le Pavillon, 1971.

Diamant, Zanvel. "Jewish Refugees on the French Riviéra." *YIVO Annual of Jewish Social Studies* 8 (1953): 264–80.

Du temps de l'étoile jaune. Paris, n.d.

Eligulashvilli, Levi. "How the Jews of Gruziya in Occupied France Were Saved." *Yad Vashem Studies* 6 (1967): 251–55.

Fabian, Ruth, and Coulmas, Corinna. *Die deutsche Emigration in Frankreich nach 1933.* Munich: Saur, 1978.

Fall of France: Causes. Monographs on Europe, no. 2. Center for European Studies, Harvard University. Cambridge, 1980.

Fall of France: Results. Monographs on Europe, no. 5. Center for European Studies, Harvard University. Cambridge, 1982.

Feingold, Henry L. *The Politics of Rescue: The Roosevelt Administration and the Holocaust, 1938–1945.* New Brunswick: Rutgers University Press, 1970.

————. "Who Shall Bear Guilt for the Holocaust: The Human Dilemma." *American Jewish History* 68 (1979): 261–82.

Friedländer, Saul. *When Memory Comes.* Translated by Helen R. Lane. New York: Farrar, Straus Giroux, 1979.

Friedman, Saul S. *No Haven for the Oppressed: United States Policy toward Jewish Refugees, 1938–1945.* Detroit: Wayne State University Press, 1973.

Fry, Varian. *Surrender on Demand.* New York: Random House, 1945.

Gamzon, Robert. *Les eaux claires: journal, 1940–1944*. Paris: Éclaireurs Israélites de France, 1981.
Garel, Georges. "La sort des enfants juifs pendant la guerre." *Le Monde Juif* 38, n.s. 89 (1978): 20–25.
George, Pierre. *France: A Geographical Study*. New York: Harper and Row, 1974.
Gordon, Bertram M. *Collaboration in France during the Second World War*. Ithaca: Cornell University Press, 1980.
Gourfinkel, Nina. *L'autre patrie*. Paris: Éditions du Seuil, 1953.
Le gouvernement de Vichy, 1940–1942: Institutions et politiques. Paris: A. Colin, 1972.
Un grand Juif: Léon Meiss. Paris, 1967.
Grant, Alfred. *Paris a Schot fun Front*. Paris: Oifsnei Farlag, 1958.
Green, Warren. "The Fate of the Oriental Jews in Vichy France." *Wiener Library Bulletin* 32 (1979): 40–51.
Gutman, Yisrael, and Haft, Cynthia J., eds. *Patterns of Jewish Leadership in Nazi Europe, 1933–1945*. Jerusalem: Yad Vashem, 1979.
Gygès, *Les Israélites dans la société française: Témoignages et documents*. Paris: La Librairie Française, 1956.
Haft, Cynthia J. *The Bargain and the Bridle: The General Union of the Israelites of France, 1941–1944*. Chicago: Dialog Press, 1983.
Hammel, Frédéric Chimon. *Souviens-toi d'Amalek: Témoignage sur la lutte des Juifs en France, 1938–1944*. N.p., 1982.
Häsler, A. A. *The Lifeboat Is Full: Switzerland and the Refugees, 1933–1945*. Translated by C. L. Markham. New York: Funk and Wagnalls, 1969.
Hilberg, Raul. "Hageto Kezurat Memshal (Nituah shel "Hayudenrat" leYishayahu Trunk)." *Yalkut Moreshet* 20 (1975): 89–108.
———. *The Destruction of the European Jews*. 3 vols. 2d rev. and definitive ed. New York and London: Holmes and Meier, 1985.
Hoffmann, Stanley. *Essais sur la France*. Paris: Éditions du Seuil, 1974.
Hommage à des victimes de la barbarie nazie. Paris: Synagogue de L'Union Libérale Israélite, 1946.
Hyman, Paula E. "Challenge to Assimilation: French Jewish Youth Movements between the Wars." *Jewish Journal of Sociology* 18 (1976): 105–114.
———. *From Dreyfus to Vichy: The Remaking of French Jewry, 1906–1939*. New York: Columbia University Press, 1979.
———. "From Paternalism to Cooptation: The French Jewish Consistory and the Immigrants, 1906–1939." *YIVO Annual of Jewish Social Science* 17 (1978): 217–37.
Imposed Jewish Governing Bodies under Nazi Rule. YIVO Colloquium (Yiddish). New York: YIVO, 1972.
Institut Hoover. *La vie de la France sous l'occupation (1940–1944)*. 3 vols. Paris: Plon, 1957.
Jäckel, Eberhard. *La France dans l'Europe de Hitler*. Translated by D. Meunier. Paris: Fayard, 1968.
Jakoubowicz, Y. *Rue Amelot: Hilf un Vidershtant*. Paris: Colonie Scolaire, 1948.
Jarblum, Marc. "La dissolution de la fédération des sociétés juives de France par l'UGIF." *Quand Même* (1947).
Jefroykin, Jules, "L'organisation juive de combat." *Les Nouveaux Cahiers* 37 (1974): 18–24.
Kapel, Shmuel René. "J'etais l'aumônier des camps du mid-ouest de la France (août 1940 - décembre 1942)." *Le Monde Juif* 33, n.s. 87 (1977): 93–116; 33, n.s. 88 (1977): 154–82.
———. *Ma'avak Yehudi Bezarfat Hakvushah*. Jerusalem: Yad Vashem, 1981.
Kaplan, Jacob. "French Jewry under the Occupation." *American Jewish Yearbook* 47 (1945): 71–118.

———. *Les temps d'épreuve: Sermons et allocutions*. Paris: Les Éditions de Minuit, 1952.

———. *Pierre Pierrard interroge le grand rabbin Kaplan: Justice pour la foi juive*. Vendôme: Centurion, 1977.

Kedward, Harry Roderick. *Resistance in Vichy France: A Study of Ideas and Motivation in the Southern Zone, 1940–1942*. Oxford: Oxford University Press, 1978.

Keren-Patkin, Nilly. "Hatzalat Hayeladim Hayehudim Bezarfat." *Yalkut Moreshet* 36 (1983): 101–150.

Kieval, Hillel J. "Legality and Resistance in Vichy France: The Rescue of Jewish Children." *Proceedings of the American Philosophical Society* 124 (1980): 339–66.

Klarsfeld, Beate. *Wherever They May Be!* Translated by M. Stearns and N. Gerardi. New York: Vanguard Press, 1975.

Klarsfeld, Serge. *Additif au mémorial de la déportation des Juifs de France*. Paris: Beate et Serge Klarsfeld, 1980.

———. *Le livre des otages*. Paris: Les Éditeurs Français Réunis, 1979.

———. *Le mémorial de la déportation des Juifs de France*. Paris: Beate et Serge Klarsfeld, 1978.

———. *Vichy-Auschwitz: le rôle de Vichy dans la solution finale de la question juive en France, 1942*. Paris: Fayard, 1983.

Klarsfeld, Serge, ed. *Die Endlösung der Judenfrage in Frankreich: Deutsche Dokumente, 1941–1944*. Paris: Beate et Serge Klarsfeld, 1977.

———. *Recueil de documents des dossiers des autorités allemandes concernant la persécution de la population juive en France (1940–1944)*. 8 volumes. Paris, n.d.

Knout, David. *Contribution à l'histoire de la résistance juive en France, 1940–1944* Paris: C.D.J.C., 1947.

Kriegel, Annie. "Historical Truth and Political Lies." *Forum* 39 (1980): 1–13.

———. "Résistants Communistes et Juifs persécutés." *Histoire* 3 (1979): 93–123.

Kulka, Otto Dov. " 'Haba'ayah Hayehudit' Bereyh Hashlishi: Mekomah Kegorem Be'Ideologia Ubamidini'ut Hanazional Sozialistit Umashma'utah Lekviya'at Ma'amadam Upe'ilutam shel Hayehudim." Ph.D. dissertation, Hebrew University of Jerusalem, 1975.

———. *Hamegamot Be "Pitaron Haba'ayah Hayehudit" Bereyh Hashlishi: Mivhar Mekorot*. Jerusalem: Akademon, 1969.

———. "Lebeyrur Hamediniyut Hayehudit shel Ha-SD Be'artzot Hakevushot Harishonot." *Yalkut Moreshet* 18 (1974): 163–84.

Laloum, Jean. *La France antisémite de Darquier de Pellepoix*. Paris: Syros, 1979.

Lambert, Raymond-Raoul. *Carnet d'un témoin, 1940–1943*. Edited by Richard Cohen. Paris: Fayard, 1985.

———. "La propagande antisémite en France depuis la guerre." *Le Monde Juif* 25, n.s. 55 (1969): 7–10.

Landau, Lazare. *De l'aversion à l'estime: Juifs et catholiques en France de 1919 à 1939*. Paris: Centurion, 1980.

Latour, Anny. *The Jewish Resistance in France (1940–1944)*. Translated by Irene R. Ilton. New York: Holocaust Library, 1981.

Lazarus, Jacques. *Juifs au combat*. Paris: Éditions du Centre, 1947.

Leahy, William D. *I Was There*. London: V. Gollancz, 1950.

Leboucher, Fernande. *The Incredible Mission of Father Benoît*. London: Doubleday, 1970.

Lehrmann, C. *La communauté juive du Luxembourg dans le passé et dans le présent*. Esch-sur-Alzette: Imprimerie coopérative luxembourgeoise, 1953.

Lévy, Claude, and Tillard, Paul. *La grande rafle du vel' d'hiv (16 juillet 1942)*. Paris: Robert Laffont, 1969.

Lindon, Raymond. *Hommage à André Baur*. N.p., n.d.

Livre de Maison du Docteur André Bernheim. N.p., n.d.
Lowrie, Donald Alexander. *The Hunted Children.* New York: W. W. Norton, 1963.
Lubetzki, Joseph. *La condition des Juifs en France sous l'occupation allemande (1940–1944): La legislation raciale.* Paris: C.D.J.C., 1945.
Ludwig, Carl. *La politique pratiquée par la Suisse à l'égard des réfugiés au cours des années 1933 à 1955.* N.p., n.d.
Luirard, Monique. "Les Juifs dans la Loire pendant la seconde guerre mondiale." *Cahiers d'histoire* 16 (1971): 181–215.
Maga, Timothy P. "Closing the Door: The French Government and Refugee Policy, 1933–1939." *French Historical Studies* 12 (1982): 424–42.
Malino, Frances, and Wasserstein, Bernard, eds. *The Jews in Modern France.* Hanover and London: University Press of New England, 1985.
Margaliot, Abraham. "She'elat Hahasavah Hamikzoiot Vehaproductivizaziya kemoked di'un bekerev Yehuday Germania bethilat Harayh Hashlishi." *Yalkut Moreshet* 29 (1980): 99–120.
———. "The Reaction of the Jewish Public in Germany to the Nuremberg Laws." *Yad Vashem Studies* 12 (1977): 75–108.
Marrus, Michael R. *The Politics of Assimilation.* New York: Oxford University Press, 1971.
———. "Vichy avant Vichy." *Histoire* 3 (1979): 77–92.
———. "Vichy et les enfants juifs." *L'Histoire* 22 (1980): 6–15.
Marrus, Michael R., and Paxton, Robert O. *Vichy France and the Jews.* New York: Basic Books, 1981.
Massada: Discours des camps de concentration. N.p., n.d.
Mazor, Michel. "L'influence nazi sur le sort des Juifs dans la zone non-occupée de France." *Le Monde Juif* 28, n.s. 66 (1972): 27–38.
Mehlman, Jeffrey, *Legacies of Anti-Semitism in France.* Minneapolis: University of Minnesota Press, 1983.
Michaelis, Meir. *Mussolini and the Jews: German-Italian Relations and the Jewish Question in Italy, 1922–1945.* Oxford: Clarendon Press, 1978.
Michel, Alain. *Les éclaireurs israélites de France pendant la seconde guerre mondiale.* Paris: Édition des E.I.F., 1984.
Michel, Henri. *La drôle de guerre.* Paris: Hachette, 1971.
———. *Vichy: Année 40.* Paris: Robert Laffont, 1966.
Milward, Allan Steele. *The New Order and the French Economy.* Oxford: Clarendon Press, 1970.
Monneray, Henry, ed. *La persécution des Juifs en France et dans les autres pays de l'ouest présentée par la France à Nuremberg.* Paris: Éditions du Centre, 1947.
Mosse, George Lachmann. *Toward the Final Solution: A History of European Racism.* New York: Howard Fertig, 1978.
L'OSE sous l'occupation allemande en France. Geneva: Union OSE, 1947.
Paxton, Robert O. *Parades and Politics at Vichy: The French Officer Corps under Marshall Pétain.* Princeton: Princeton University Press, 1966.
———. *Vichy France: Old Guard and New Order, 1940–1944.* New York: A. A. Knopf, 1972. New York: Columbia University Press, 1982.
Pierrard, Pierre. *Juifs et catholiques français de Drumont à Jules Isaac (1886–1945).* Paris: Fayard, 1970.
Poliakov, Léon. "An Opinion Poll on Anti-Jewish Measures in Vichy France." *Jewish Social Studies* 15 (1953): 135–50.
———. "Jewish Resistance in France." *YIVO Annual of Jewish Social Science* 8 (1953): 252–63.
———. *La condition des Juifs en France sous l'occupation italienne.* Paris: Éditions du Centre, 1946.
———. *L'auberge des musiciens: Mémoirs.* Paris, 1981.

————. *L'étoile jaune*. Paris: Éditions du Centre, 1949.

Poliakov, Léon, and Sabille, Jacques. *Jews under the Italian Occupation*. Paris: C.D.J.C., 1955.

Le procès de Xavier Vallat. Paris, 1948.

Le procès de Xavier Vallat présenté par ses amis. Paris: Éditions du Conquistador, 1948.

Pougatch, Isaac. *Robert Gamzon*. Paris: Service Technique pour l'Education, 1972.

Poznansky, Renée. "La résistance juive en France." *Revue d'histoire de la deuxième guerre mondiale* 137 (1985): 3–32.

Rabi (Rabinovitch, Wladimir). *Anatomie du judaisme français*. Paris: Éditions du Minuit, 1962.

————. "L'église catholique sous l'Occupation." *Le Monde Juif* 33, n.s. 85 (1977): 39–40.

Raich, Leá. "La WIZO sous l'Occupation." *La Terre Retrouvée*, 1 February 1945.

Rajsfus, Maurice. *Des Juifs dans la collaboration: L'U.G.I.F. (1941–1944)*. Paris: E.D.I., 1980.

Ratz, Joseph. *La France que je cherchais: Les impressions d'un Russe engagé volontaire en France*. Limoges, 1945.

Ravine, Jacques. *La résistance organisée des Juifs en France (1940–1944)*. Paris: Julliard, 1973.

Rayski, Abraham. "Une grande heure dans l'histoire de la résistance juive: la fondation du conseil répresentatif des Juifs de France." *Le Monde Juif* 24, n.s. 51 (1968): 32–37.

————. "Les immigrés dans la résistance." *Les Nouveaux Cahiers* 37 (1974): 10–17.

Rayski, Abraham, ed. *Das Vort fun Vidershtant un Zieg*. Paris: Centre de Documentation du l'Union des Juifs pour la Résistance et l'Entraide, 1949.

Reitlinger, Gerald. *The Final Solution: The Attempt to Exterminate the Jews of Europe, 1939–1945*. 2d ed. London: Valentine Mitchell, 1968.

Roblin, Michel. *Les Juifs de Paris*. Paris: Éditions A. et J. Picard, 1952.

Rutkowski, Adam. "Directives allemandes concernant les arrestations et les déportations des Juifs de France en avril-août 1944." *Le Monde Juif* 32, n.s. 82 (1976): 53–65.

————. "Le camp d'internement de Gurs." *Le Monde Juif* 36, n.s. 100 (1980): 128–47.

————. ed. *La lutte des Juifs en France à l'époque de l'occupation (1940–1944)*. Paris: C.D.J.C., 1975.

Sauvageot, André. *Marseilles dans la tourmente, 1939–1944*. Paris: Ozanne, 1949.

Schrager, Faivel. *Oifn rund fun tzwei tkoufes*. Paris, 1976.

Schramm, Hanna. *Menschen in Gurs: Erinnerungen an ein Französisches Interierungslager, 1940–1941*. Worms: G. Heintz, 1977.

Sinder, Henri. "Lights and Shades of Jewish Life in France, 1940–1942." *Jewish Social Studies* 5 (1943): 367–82.

Spiegel, Renato. "Ha'antishemiy'ut Bezarfat ben Shtei Milhamot-Haolam." *Yalkut Moreshet* 24 (1977): 51–86.

Steinberg, Lucien. *La comité de défence des Juifs en Belgique, 1942–1944*. Brussels: Édition de l'université de Bruxelle, 1973.

————. *Les autorités allemandes en France occupée: inventaire commenté de la collection de documents conservés au C.D.J.C.* Paris: C.D.J.C., 1966.

————. *The Jews against Hitler (Not as a Lamb)*. Translated by Marion Bunter. London: Gordon and Cremonesi, 1978.

Sternhell, Zeev. *Ni droite ni gauche. L'idéologie fasciste en France*. Paris: Éditions du Seuil, 1983.

Szajkowski, Zosa. *Analytical Franco-Jewish Gazetteer, 1939–1945*. New York: S. Frydman, 1966.

————. "Glimpses on the History of Jews in Occupied France." *Yad Vashem Studies* 2 (1958): 133–58.

————. "Incident at Compiègne." *Conservative Judaism* 21 (1967): 27–33.

————. *Jews and the French Foreign Legion.* New York: Ktav Publishing House, 1975.

————. "Jews in the Foreign Legion." *Conservative Judaism* 21 (1967): 22–34.

————. "Secular versus Religious Life in France." In *The Role of Religion in Modern Jewish History*, ed. Jacob Katz, pp. 107–127. New York: Association for Jewish Studies, 1975.

————. "The French Central Jewish Consistory during the Second World War." *Yad Vashem Studies* 3 (1959): 187–202.

————. "The Growth of the Jewish Population of France." *Jewish Social Studies* 8 (1946): 179–96.

————. "The Organisation of the 'UGIF' in Nazi-Occupied France." *Jewish Social Studies* 9 (1947): 239–56.

————. "Vi azoy dos opteiln di kirch fun der mulukha in 1905 hot bavirkt di yiddishe kehilles in Frankraykh." *Davka* 5 (1954): 382–91.

Tcherikower, Elias, ed. *Yidn in Frankraykh.* 2 vols. New York: YIVO, 1942.

Tchoubinsky, Baruch. *Léo Glazer.* Paris: Comité général de défense des Juifs, 1947.

Thalman, Rita. "L'émigration du IIIᵉ reich dans la France de 1933 à 1939." *Le Monde Juif* 35, n.s. 96 (1979): 127–39.

Trunk, Isaiah. *Judenrat: The Jewish Councils in Eastern Europe under the Nazi Occupation.* New York: Macmillan Co., 1972.

Umbreit, Hans. *Der Militärbefehlshaber in Frankreich, 1940–1944.* Boppard a.R.: H. Boldt, 1968.

L'un des trente-six. Paris: Éditions Kyoum, 1946.

Vallat, Xavier. *La croix, les lys et la peine des hommes.* Paris: Les Quatre fils Aymon, 1960.

————. *Le nez de Cléopâtre: Souvenirs d'un homme de droite (1919–1945).* Paris: Les Quatre fils Aymon, 1957.

Vanino, Maurice. *Le temps de la honte; de Rethondes à l'Ile d'Yeu.* Paris: Edit. Créator, 1952.

Vigée, Claude. *La lune d'hiver.* Paris: Flammarion, 1970.

Le vrai procès de Xavier Vallat. Paris, n.d.

Warner, Geoffrey. *Pierre Laval and the Eclipse of France, 1931–1945.* London: Eyre and Spottiswoode, 1968.

Weill, Joseph. *Contribution à l'histoire des camps d'internement dans l'anti-France.* Paris: Éditions du Centre, 1946.

Weinberg, David H. *A Community on Trial: The Jews of Paris in the 1930s.* Chicago: University of Chicago Press, 1977.

————. *Les Juifs à Paris de 1933 à 1939.* Translated by M. Pouteau. Paris: Calmann-Lévy, 1974.

Wellers, Georges. "Déportation des Juifs en France sous l'Occupation: Légendes et réalités." *Le Monde Juif* 36, n.s. 99 (1980): 75–108.

————. *L'étoile jaune à l'heure de Vichy: De Drancy à Auschwitz.* Paris: Fayard, 1973.

————. "Vichy et les Juifs: A propos d'un article de M. Claude Gounelle." *Le Monde Juif* 32, n.s. 81 (1976): 1–28.

Wellers, Georges; Kaspi, André; and Klarsfeld, Serge, eds. *La France et la question juive, 1940–1944.* Paris: Éditions Sylvie Messinger, 1981.

Wischnitzer, Mark. *Visas to Freedom: The History of HIAS.* Cleveland: World Publishing Co., 1956.

Wyman, David. *Paper Walls: America and the Refugee Crisis, 1938–1941.* Amherst: University of Massachusetts Press, 1968.

Yahil, Leni. "The Jewish Leadership in France." In *Patterns of Jewish Leadership in Nazi Europe*, ed. Yisrael Gutman and Cynthia J. Haft, pp.317–34. Jerusalem: Yad Vashem, 1979.

Interviews

Roger Berg, Central Consistory official, Paris, September 1977.

Maurice Brener, former Joint liaison, Paris, October-November 1977.

Frédéric Empaytaz, former prefect, St. Germaine-en-Laye, April 1984.

Dr. Denise Gamzon, professor of French literature, Tel-Aviv, October 1979.

Raymond Geissmann, lawyer and former UGIF leader, Paris, October 1977.

Toni Green, former resistance activist, Tel-Aviv, 1980.

Rabbi Abraham Deutsch, formerly from Limoges, Jerusalem, 1979.

Dr. Shimeon Hamel, former activist in scout movement Kibbutz Ein-Hanatsiv, October 1979.

Jules Jefroykin, former Joint liaison, Paris, October 1977.

Rabbi Shmuel René Kapel, Jerusalem, 1979.

Yvonne Lambert, Paris, April 1984.

Raymond Lindon, Paris, October 1977.

Maurice Moch, former CRIF secretary, Paris, October 1977.

Professor André Neher and Dr. René Bernheim Neher, Jerusalem, 1979.

Andrée Salomon, OSE activist, Jerusalem, 1979.

Lucienne Scheid-Haas Levilion, former UGIF-N council member, Paris, October 1977.

INDEX

THE LIBRARY
ST. MARY'S COLLEGE OF MARYLAND
ST. MARY'S CITY, MARYLAND   20686